D0146517

HENRY D. THOREAU

Journal

VOLUME 1: 1837-1844

JOHN C. BRODERICK, *GENERAL EDITOR*

EDITED BY
ELIZABETH HALL WITHERELL
WILLIAM L. HOWARTH
ROBERT SATTELMEYER
THOMAS BLANDING

PRINCETON, NEW JERSEY
PRINCETON UNIVERSITY PRESS
MCMLXXXI

CENTER FOR EDITIONS OF
AMERICAN AUTHORS
AN APPROVED TEXT
MODERN LANGUAGE
ASSOCIATION OF AMERICA
®

*The Committee emblem means that one of a panel of textual
experts serving the Committee has reviewed the text and
textual apparatus of the original volume by thorough and
scrupulous sampling, and has approved them for sound
and consistent editorial principles employed and
maximum accuracy attained. The accuracy of the text
has been guarded by careful and repeated proofreading
of printer's copy according to standards set by the Committee.*

*The editorial preparation of this volume, and costs
associated with its publication, were supported by
grants from the Editing and Publication Programs of the
National Endowment for the Humanities, an independent
federal agency. During the early stages of editing, support
was provided through the Center for Editions of American
Authors of the Modern Language Association.*

Editorial Board

The Writings

Walden, J. Lyndon Shanley (1971)
The Maine Woods, Joseph J. Moldenhauer (1972)
Reform Papers, Wendell Glick (1973)
Early Essays and Miscellanies,
    Joseph J. Moldenhauer et al. (1975)
A Week on the Concord and Merrimack Rivers,
    Carl F. Hovde et al. (1980)
Excursions
Translations
Correspondence
Poems
Cape Cod
Nature Essays
Journal

Contents

·1·

October 22, 1837–December 2, 1839

TRANSCRIBED 1841

Henry D. Thoreau.

Gleanings—
Or What Time
Has not Reaped
Of My
Journal.

4

"By all means use sometimes to be alone,
Salute thyself. See what thy soul doth wear.
Dare to look in thy chest; for 'tis thy own:
And tumble up and down what thou find'st there.
    Who cannot rest till he good fellows find,
        He breaks up house, turns out of doors his mind."
                                    The Church Porch.
                                        Herbert.

"Friends and companions, get you gone!
'Tis my desire to be alone;
Ne'er well, but when my thoughts and I
Do domineer in privacy."
                            Burton (Anat. Mel.)

"Two Paradises are in one,
To live in Paradise alone."
                            Marvell's "Garden"

Oct 22nd 1837.

"What are you doing now?" he asked, "Do you keep a journal?"— So I make my first entry to-day.

Solitude—

To be alone I find it necessary to escape the present–I avoid myself. How could I be alone in the Roman emperor's chamber of mirrors? I seek a garret. The spiders must not be disturbed, nor the floor swept, nor the lumber arranged. – –

– – The Germans say – – Es ist alles wahr wodurch du besser wirst. – –

{*One-fourth page blank*}

Oct. 24th 1837.

The Mould our Deeds Leave.

Every part of nature teaches that the passing away of one life is the making room for another. The oak dies down to the ground, leaving within its rind a rich virgin mould, which will impart a vigorous life to an infant forest – – The pine leaves a sandy and sterile soil–the harder woods a strong and fruitful mould. – –
So this constant abrasion and decay makes the soil of my future growth. As I live now so shall I reap. If I grow pines and birches, my virgin mould will not sustain the oak, but pines and birches, or, perchance, weeds and brambles, will constitute my second growth. – –

{*One-fifth page blank*}

Oct 25th 1837.

Spring

She appears and we are once more children; we commence again our course with the new year. Let the maiden no more return, and men will become poets for very grief. No sooner has winter left us time to regret her smiles, than we yield to the advances of poetic frenzy. "The flowers look kindly at us from the beds with their child eyes—and in the horizon, the snow of the far mountains dissolves into light vapor." Goethe. Torq. Tasso. — —

The Poet.
"He seems to avoid—even to flee from us,
To seek something which we know not,—
And perhaps he himself after all knows not."

Ibid

{*One-fifth page blank*}

Oct 26th 1837.

"His eye hardly rests upon the earth;
His ear hears the one-clang of nature;
What history records—what life gives,
Directly and gladly his genius takes it up:
His mind collects the widely dispersed,
And his feeling animates the inanimate.
Often he ennobles what appeared to us common,
And the prized is as nothing to him.
In his own magic circle wanders
The wonderful man, and draws us
With him to wander, and take part in it:
He seems to draw near to us, and remains afar from us:
He seems to be looking at us, and spirits forsooth,
Appear to him strangely in our places."

Ibid.

How Man Grows.

"A noble man has not to thank a private circle for his culture. Fatherland and world must work upon him. Fame and infamy must he learn to endure. He will be constrained to know himself and others. Solitude shall no more lull him with her flattery. The foe *will* not–the friend *dares* not spare him. Then striving the youth puts forth his strength, feels what he is, and feels himself soon a man."

"A talent is builded in solitude,
A character in the stream of the world."

"He only fears man who knows him not, and he who avoids him will soonest misapprehend him."   Ibid.

Ariosto—

"As nature decks her inward rich breast in a green variegated dress, so clothes he all that can make men honorable in the blooming garb of the fable.—
The well of superfluity bubbles near, and lets us see variegated wonder-fishes. The air is filled with rare birds, the meads and copses with strange herds, wit lurks half concealed in the verdure, and wisdom from time to time lets sound from a golden cloud sustained words, while frenzy wildly seems to sweep the well-toned lute, yet holds itself measured in perfect time"

Beauty

"That beauty is transitory which alone you seem to honor."

                              Goethe. Torq. Tasso.

Oct 27th 1837.

The Fog. – –
The prospect is limited to Nobscot and Anursnack–.
The trees stand with boughs downcast like pilgrims
beaten by a storm, and the whole landscape wears a
sombre aspect.

So when thick vapors cloud the soul, it strives in vain
to escape from its humble working day valley, and
pierce the dense fog which shuts out from view the
blue peaks in its horizon, but must be content to scan its
near and homely hills. – –

Ducks At Goose-Pond.

Oct 29th 1837.
– – Two ducks, of the summer or wood species,
which were merrily dabbling in their favorite basin,
struck up a retreat on my approach, and seemed
disposed to take French leave, paddling off with swan-like
majesty. They are first rate swimmers beating me at a
round pace, and, what was to me a new trait in the
duck character, dove every other moment and swam
three or four feet under water, in order to escape my
attention. Just previous to immersion they seemed to
give each other a significant nod, and then, as if by
common consent, 'twas heels up and head down in the
shaking of a duck wing; and when they reappeared,
it was amusing to observe with what a self satisfied,
darn-it-how-he-nicks-'em air they paddled off to repeat
the experiment.

The Arrowhead.
A curious incident happened some four or six weeks
ago which I think it worth the while to record. John
and I had been searching for Indian relics, and been

successful enough to find two arrowheads and a pestle, when, of a Sunday evening, with our heads full of the past and its remains, we strolled to the mouth of Swamp-bridge brook. As we neared the brow of the hill forming the bank of the river, inspired by my theme, I broke forth into an extravagant eulogy on those savage times, using most violent gesticulations by way of illustration.

"There on Nawshawtuct," said I, "was their lodge, the rendezvous of the tribe, and yonder, on Clamshell hill their feasting ground. This was no doubt a favorite haunt; here on this brow was an eligible look-out post. How often have they stood on this very spot, at this very hour, when the sun was sinking behind yonder woods, and gilding with his last rays the waters of the Musketaquid, and pondered the days success and the morrow's prospects, or communed with the spirits of their fathers gone before them, to the land of shades! — — "Here," I exclaimed, "stood Tahatawan; and there, (to complete the period,) is Tahatawan's arrowhead"

We instantly proceeded to sit down on the spot I had pointed to, and I, to carry out the joke, to lay bare an ordinary stone, which my whim had selected, when lo! the first I laid hands on, the grubbing stone that was to be, proved a most perfect arrowhead, as sharp as if just from the hands of the Indian fabricator!!!

{*One-fifth page blank*}

Oct 30th 1837.

Sunrise

First we have the grey twilight of the poets, with dark and barry clouds diverging to the zenith. Then glows the intruding cloud in the east, as if it bore a precious jewel in its bosom; a deep round gulf of golden grey

indenting its upper edge, while slender rules of fleecy
vapor–radiating from the common centre–like
light-armed troops fall regularly into their places.

Nov. 3d 1837.
Sailing with and against the Stream.
If one would reflect let him embark on some placid
stream, and float with the current. He cannot resist the
Muse. As we ascend the stream, plying the paddle with
might and main, snatched and impetuous thoughts
course through the brain. We dream of conflict
–power–and grandeur. But turn the prow downstream,
and rock, tree, kine, knoll, assuming new and varying
positions, as wind and water shift the scene–favor
the liquid lapse of thought–far-reaching and sublime,
but ever calm and gently undulating.

Nov. 5th 1837.
Truth.
Truth strikes us from behind, and in the dark, as
well as from before and in broad day-light.

Nov. 9th 1837.
Still streams run deepest.
It is the rill whose "siluer sands and pebbles sing
eternall ditties with the spring"– The early frosts bridge
its narrow channel, and its querrulous note is
hushed– Only the flickering sunlight on its sandy bottom
attracts the beholder. But there are souls whose depths
are never fathomed–on whose bottom the sun never
shines. We get a distant view from the precipitous
banks, but never a draught from their mid-channels.
Only a sunken rock or fallen oak, can provoke a
murmur– And their surface is a stranger to the icy
fetters which bind fast a thousand contributory rills.

Nov. 12th 1837.

Discipline.

I yet lack discernment to distinguish the whole lesson
of to-day; but it is not lost–it will come to me at last.
My desire is to know *what* I have lived, that I may
know *how* to live henceforth.

Nov. 13th 1837.

Sin destroys the Perception of the Beautiful.

This shall be the test of innocence– If I can hear a
taunt, and look out on this friendly moon, pacing the
heavens in queen-like majesty, with the accustomed
yearning.

Truth—

Truth is ever returning into herself. I glimpse one
feature to-day–another to-morrow–and the next day
they are blended.

Nov. 15th 1837.

Goethe.

"And now that it is evening, a few clouds in the mild
atmosphere rest upon the mountains, more stand still
than move in the heavens, and immediately after sunset
the chirping of crickets begins to increase,–then feels
one once more at home in the world, and not as an
alien–an exile. I am contented as though I had been born
and brought up here, and now returned from a Greenland
or whaling voyage. Even the dust of my Fatherland, as
it is whirled about the wagon, which for so long a time
I had not seen, is welcome. The clock and bell-jingling
of the crickets is very agreeable–penetrating–and not
without a meaning. Pleasant is it when roguish boys
whistle in emulation of a field of such songstresses. One
imagines that they really enhance each other. The
evening is perfectly mild as the day. Should an

inhabitant of the south, coming from the south–hear of my rapture, he would deem me very childish. Alas! what I here express have I long felt under an unpropitious heaven. And now is this joy to me an exception–which I am henceforth to enjoy–a necessity of my nature." "Ital. Reise."

Nov. 16th 1837.
Ponkawtassett.
There goes the river, or rather is, "in serpent error wandering"–the jugular vein of Musketaquid. Who knows how much of the proverbial moderation of the inhabitants was caught from its dull circulation.

The snow gives the landscape a washing day appearance–here a streak of white, there a streak of dark–it is spread like a napkin over the hills and meadows. This must be a rare drying day; to judge from the vapor that floats over the 'vast clothes' yard.

A hundred guns are firing and a flag flying in the village in celebration of the whig victory. Now a short dull report–the mere disk of a sound shorn of its beams–and then a puff of smoke rises in the horizon to join its misty relatives in the skies.

Goethe.
He gives such a glowing description of the old tower, that they who had been born and brought up in the neighborhood, must needs look over their shoulders, "that they might behold with their eyes, what I had praised to their ears"–"and I added nothing, not even the ivy which for centuries had decorated the walls" "Ital. Reise."

Nov. 17th 1837.

Sunrise.

Now the king of day plays at bo-peep round the world's corner and every cottage window smiles a golden smile—a very picture of glee— I see the water glistening in the eye. The smothered breathings of awakening day strike the ear with an undulatory motion—over hill and dale, pasture and woodland, come they to me, and I am at home in the world.

The Sky.

If there is nothing new on earth, still there is something new in the heavens. We have always a resource in the skies. They are constantly turning a new page to view. The wind sets the types in this blue ground, and the inquiring may always read a new truth.

Virgil

Nov. 18th 1837.

—"Pulsae referunt ad sidera valles—" is such a line as would save an epic; and how finely he concludes his "agrestem musam", now that Silenus has done, and the stars have heard his story—

> Cogere donec oves stabulis, numerumque referre
> Jussit, et invito processit Vesper Olympo.

Harmony

Nature makes no noise. The howling storm—the rustling leaf—the pattering rain—are no disturbance, There is an essential and unexplored harmony in them. Why is it that thought flows with so deep and sparkling a current when the sound of distant music strikes the ear. When I would muse I complain not of a rattling tune on the piano—a Battle of Prague even—if it be harmony—but an irregular—discordant drumming is intolerable.

Shadows.

When a shadow flits across the landscape of the
Soul—where is the substance? Has it always its origin
in sin? And is that sin within or without me?

Nov. 20th 1837.

Virgil.

I would read Virgil, if only that I might be reminded
of the identity of human nature in all ages. I take
satisfaction in "jam laeto turgent in palmite gemmae,"
or "Strata jacent passim sua quaeque sub arbore poma."
It was the same world, and the same men inhabited it.

{*One-fifth page blank*}

Nov. 21st 1837.

Nawshawtuct.

One must needs climb a hill to know what a world he
inhabits. In the midst of this Indian summer I am
perched on the topmost rock of Nawshawtuct—a velvet
wind blowing from the south west— I seem to feel the
atoms as they strike my cheek. Hills, mountains,
steeples stand out in bold relief in the horizon—while
I am resting on the rounded boss of an enormous
shield—the river like a vein of silver encircling its
edge—and thence the shield gradually rises to its rim
the horizon. Not a cloud is to be seen, but villages—villas
—forests—mountains—one above another, till they are
swallowed up in the heavens. The atmosphere is such
that as I look abroad upon the length and breadth of the
land—it recedes from my eye, and I seem to be looking
for the threads of the velvet.

Thus I admire the grandeur of my emerald
carriage—with its border of blue—in which I am rolling
through space.

Nov. 26th 1837.

Thoughts

I look around for thoughts when I am overflowing myself. While I live on, thought is still in embryo—it stirs not within me. Anon it begins to assume shape and comeliness, and I deliver it, and clothe it in its garment of language. But alas! how often when thoughts choke me do I resort to a spat on the back—or swallow a crust—or do anything but expectorate them.

Nov. 28th 1837.

Hoar Frost & Green River.

Every tree fence and spire of grass—that could raise its head above the snow, was this morning covered with a dense hoar frost. The trees looked like airy creatures of darkness caught napping— On this side they were huddled together, their grey hairs streaming, in a secluded valley, which the sun had not yet penetrated—and on that they went hurrying off in Indian file by hedge-rows and watercourses—while the shrubs and grasses—like elves and fairies of the night, sought to hide their diminished heads in the snow.

The branches and taller grasses were covered with a wonderful ice-foliage—answering leaf for leaf to their summer dress. The centre—diverging—and even more minute fibres—were perfectly distinct—and the edges regularly indented.

These leaves were on the side of the twig or stubble opposite to the sun, (when it was not bent toward the east) meeting it for the most part at right angles, and there were others standing out at all possible angles upon these, and upon one another.

It struck me that these ghost leaves and the green ones whose forms they assume, were the creatures of the same law. It could not be in obedience to two several laws, that the vegetable juices swelled gradually into the perfect leaf on the one hand, and the crystalline particles trooped to their standard in the same admirable order on the other.

The river viewed from the bank above appeared of a yellowish green color, but on a nearer approach this phenomenon vanished—and yet the landscape was covered with snow.

Dec 5th 1837.

Ice-Harp.

My friend tells me he has discovered a new note in nature which he calls the Ice-harp. Chancing to throw a handful of pebbles upon the pond where there was an air chamber under the ice—it discoursed a pleasant music to him.

Herein resides a tenth muse—and as he was the man to discover it—probably the extra melody is in him.

Dec 8th 1837.

Goethe.

He is generally satisfied with giving an exact description of objects as they appear to him, and his genius is exhibited in the points he seizes upon and illustrates. His description of Venice and her environs as seen from the Marcusthurm, is that of an unconcerned spectator, whose object is faithfully to describe what he sees, and that too, for the most part, in the order in which he saw it. It is this trait which is chiefly to be prized in the book—even the reflections of the author do not interfere with his descriptions.

It would thus be possible for inferior minds to produce invaluable books.

Dec 10th 1837.

Measure.

Not the carpenter alone carries his rule in his
pocket— Space is quite subdued to us. The meanest
peasant finds in a hair of his head, or the white crescent
upon his nail, the unit of measure for the distance of
the fixed stars. His middle finger measures how many
digits into space—he extends a few times his thumb and
finger, and the ocean is *spanned*—he stretches out his
arms, and the sea is *fathomed*.

Dec 12th 1837.

Thought.

There are times when thought elbows her way
through the underwood of words to the clear blue
beyond;

> "O'er bog, or steep, through strait, rough, dense, or rare,
> With head, hands, wings, or feet, pursues *her* way,
> And swims, or sinks, or wades, or creeps, or flies;"—

But let her don her cumbersome working day garment,
and each sparkling dewdrop will seem a "slough of
despond."

Peculiarity.

When we speak of a peculiarity in a man or a
nation—we think to describe only one part—a mere
mathematical point—but it is not so. It pervades all.
Some parts may be further removed than others from
this centre, but not a particle so remote as not to be
either shined on or shaded by it.

Thorns

No faculty in man was created with a useless or
sinister intent—in no respect can he be wholly bad, but

the worst passions have their root in the best—as
anger—for instance, may be only a perverted sense of
wrong—which yet retains some traces of its origin. So a
spine is proved to be only an abortive branch, "which,
notwithstanding, even as a spine, bears leaves, and, in
Euphorbia heptagona, sometimes flowers and fruit."

Dec 15th 1837.
Jack-Frost
As further confirmation of the fact that vegetation
is a kind of crystallization, I observe that upon the edge
of the melting frost on the windows, Jack is playing
singular freaks; now bundling together his needle-shaped
leaves so as to resemble fields waving with grain, or
shocks of wheat rising here and there from the stubble.
On one side the vegetation of the torrid zone is
presented you—high-towering palms, and wide spread
bannians, such as we see in pictures of oriental
scenerey— On the other are arctic pines, stiff-frozen,
with branches downcast, like the arms of tender men
in frosty weather. In some instances the panes are
covered with little feathery flocks, where the particles
radiate from a common centre—the number of radii
varying from three to seven or eight. The crystalline
particles are partial to the creases and flaws in the glass,
and when these extend from sash to sash—form complete
hedge-rows, or miniature watercourses, where dense
masses of crystal foliage—"high over-arched imbower".

Dec 16th 1837.
Frozen Mist.
The woods were this morning covered with thin bars
of vapor—the evaporation of the leaves according to
Sprengel, which seemed to have been suddenly stiffened
by the cold. In some places it was spread out like gauze

over the tops of the trees, forming extended lawns,
where elves and fairies held high tournament;

> "before each van
> Prick forth the aery knights, and couch their spears,
> Till thickest legions close."

The east was glowing with a narrow, but ill-defined
crescent of light, the blue of the zenith mingling in all
possible proportions with the salmon color of the
horizon— And now the neighboring hilltops telegraph
to us poor crawlers of the plain the Monarch's golden
ensign in the east—and anon his "long-levelled rules"
fall sector-wise, and humblest cottage windows greet
their Lord.

Facts.

How indispensable to a correct study of nature is a
perception of her true meaning— The fact will one day
flower out into a truth. The season will mature and
fructify what the understanding had cultivated. Mere
accumulators of facts—collectors of materials for the
master-workmen, are like those plants growing in dark
forests, which "put forth only leaves instead of
blossoms."

                                    Dec 17th 1837.

Druids

In all ages and nations we observe a leaning towards
a right state of things. This may especially be seen in
the history of the priest—whose life approaches most
nearly to that of the ideal man— The druids paid no
taxes, and "were allowed exemption from warfare and
all other things." The clergy are even now a priveleged
class.

In the last stage of civilization—Poetry—Religion and
Philosophy will be one—and this truth is glimpsed in the

first– The druidical order was divided into
Druids–Bards–and Ouates. "The Bards were the poets
and musicians, of whom some were satyrists, and some
encomiasts. The Ouates sacrificed, divined, and
contemplated the nature of things. The Druids
cultivated physiology and moral philosophy; or, as
Diodorus says, were their philosophers and theologians."

Dec. 18th 1837.

Göthe

He required that his heroine, Iphigenia, should say
nothing which might not be uttered by the holy Agathe,
whose picture he contemplated.

Immortality Post

The nations assert an immortality *post* as well as
ante. The Athenians wore a golden grasshopper as an
emblem that they sprang from the earth, and the
Arcadians pretended that they were προσεληνου, or before
the moon–

The Platos do not seem to have considered this back
reaching tendency of the human mind.

What's in a Name.

Men are pleased to be called the sons of their
fathers–so little truth suffices them–and whoever
addresses them by this or a similar title, is termed a
poet. The orator appeals to the sons of Greece–of
Britania–of France–or of Poland; and our fathers'
homely name acquires some interest from the fact that
Sakai-suna means sons-of-the-Sakai.

Dec 19th 1837.

Hell.

Hell itself may be contained within the compass
of a spark.

Saxons

The fact seems at first an anomalous one, that the less a people have to contend for the more tenacious they are of their rights. The Saxons of Ditmarsia contended for a principle, not for their sterile sands and uncultivated marshes.

We are on the whole the same saxons that our fathers were, when it was said of them—"They are emulous in hospitality, because to plunder and to lavish is the glory of an Holsatian; not to be versed in the science of depredation is, in his opinion, to be stupid and base."

The French are the same Franks, of whom it is written. "Francis familiare est ridendo fidem frangere"— "Gens Francorum infidelis est. Si perjeret Francus quid novi faciet, qui perjuriam ipsam sermonis genus putat esse non criminis."

Crystals

I observed this morning that the ice at swamp-bridge was checquered with a kind of mosaic work of white creases or channels—and when I examined the under side, I found it to be covered with a mass of crystallizations from three to five inches deep—standing, or rather depending, at right angles to the true ice, which was about an eigth of an inch thick— There was a yet older ice six or eight inches below this.

The crystals were for the most part triangular prisms—with the lower end open—though, in some cases, they had run into each other so as to form four or five sided prisms. When the ice was laid upon its smooth side, they resembled the roofs and steeples of a Gothic city, or the vessels of a crowded haven under a press of canvass.

I noticed also that where the ice in the road had melted and left the mud bare, the latter, as if

crystallized, discovered countless rectilinear fissures,
an inch or more in length–a continuation, as it were,
of the checquered ice.

Dec 22nd 1837.

About a year ago, having set aside a bowl which had
contained some rhubarb grated in water, without
wiping it, I was astonished to find a few days afterward,
that the rhubarb had crystallized, covering the bottom
of the bowl with perfect cubes, of the color and
consistency of glue, and a tenth of an inch in diameter.

Dec 23d 1837.

Crystals

Crossed the river today on the ice– Though the
weather is raw and wintry–and the ground covered
with snow–I noticed a solitary robin–who looked as if
he needed to have his services to the Babes in the
Woods speedily requieted.

In the side of the high bank by the leaning hemlock,
there were some curious crystallizations. Wherever
the water, or other causes, had formed a hole in the
bank–its throat and outer edge–like the entrance to a
citadel of the olden time, bristled with a glistening ice
armor In one place you might see minute ostrich
feathers, which seemed the waving plumes of the
warriors filing into the fortress, in another the glancing
fan-shaped banners of the Liliputian host–and in
another the needle-shaped particles collected into
bundles resembling the plumes of the pine, might pass
for a phalanx of spears.

The whole hill was like an immense quartz rock–with
minute crystals sparkling from innumerable crannies.

I tried to fancy that there was a disposition in these
crystallizations to take the forms of the contiguous
foliage

Dec 27th 1837.

Revolutions

Revolutions are never sudden. Not one man, nor many men, in a few years or generations, suffice to regulate events, and dispose mankind for the revolutionary movement. The hero is but the crowning stone of the pyramid–the keystone of the arch. Who was Romulus or Remus–Hengist or Horsa–that we should attribute to them Rome or England? They are famous or infamous because the progress of events has chosen to make them its stepping stones. But we would know where the avalanche commenced–or the hollow in the rock whence springs the Amazon.

The most important is apt to be some silent and unobtrusive fact in history. In 449 three Saxon cyules arrived on the British coast– "Three scipen gode comen mid than flode, three hundred cnihten"– The pirate of the British coast was no more the founder of a state, than the scourge of the German shore.

Heroes

The real heroes of minstrelsy have been ideal, even when the names of actual heroes have been perpetuated. The real Arthur, who "not only excelled the experienced past, but also the possible future", of whom it was affirmed for many centuries that he was not dead, but "had withdrawn from the world into some magical region; from which at a future crisis he was to reappear, and lead the Cymri in triumph through the island"–whose character and actions were the theme of the bards of Bretagne, and the foundation of their interminable romances–was only an ideal impersonation.

Men claim for the ideal an actual existence also–but do not often expand the actual into the ideal. "If you do not believe me, go into Bretagne, and mention in the streets or villages, that Arthur is really dead like other men; you will not escape with impunity; you will be either hooted with the curses of your hearers, or stoned to death."

Homesickness

The most remarkable instance of homesickness–is that of the colony of Franks transplanted by the Romans from the German Ocean to the Euxine, who at length resolving to a man to abandon the country–seized the vessels which carried them out, and reached at last their native shores, after innumerable difficulties and dangers–upon the mediterranean and Atlantic.

The interesting Facts in History.

How cheering is it after toiling through the darker pages of history–the heartless and fluctuating crust of human rest and unrest–to alight on the solid earth where the sun shines–or rest in the checquered shade. The fact that Edwin of Northumbria "caused stakes to be fixed in the highways where he had seen a clear spring"; and that "brazen dishes were chained to them, to refresh the weary sojourner, whose fatigues Edwin had himself experienced"–is worth all Arthur's twelve battles. The sun again shines along the high way–the landscape presents us sunny glades and occasional cultivated patches–as well as dark primeval forests–and it is *merry* England after all.

{*One and one-fifth pages blank*}

Dec. 31st 1837

As the least drop of wine colors the whole goblet, so the least particle of truth colors our whole life. It is never isolated, or simply added as dollars to our stock. When any real progress is made, we unlearn and learn anew, what we thought we knew before. We go picking

up and laying side by side the *disjecta membra* of truth,
as he who picked up one by one a row of a hundred
stones, and returned with each separately to his basket.

{*One-third page blank*}

                                              Jan 6th 1838
                    Heaven on Earth.
As a child looks forward to the coming of the
summer—so could we contemplate with quiet joy the
circle of the seasons returning without fail eternally.
As the Spring came round during so many years of the
gods, we could go out to admire and adorn anew our
Eden, and yet never tire.

                                              Jan 15th 1838.
                    Saxons
After all that has been said in praise of the Saxon
race—we must allow that our blue eyed and fair haired
ancestors were originally an ungodly and reckless crew.

                                              Jan 16th 1838.
                We make our own Fortune.
Man is like a cork which no tempest can sink, but it
will float securely to its haven at last. The world is never
the less beautiful though viewed through a chink or
knot hole.

                                              Jan 21st 1838
Man is the artificer of his own happiness. Let him
beware how he complains of the disposition of
circumstances for it is his own disposition he blames.
If this is sour, or that rough, or the other steep—let him
think if it be not his work. If his look curdles all hearts,
let him not complain of a sour reception—if he hobble in
his gait, let him not grumble at the roughness of the

way–if he is weak in the knees–let him not call the hill
steep. This was the pith of the inscription on the wall of
the Swedish inn–"You will find at Trolhate excellent
bread, meat and wine, provided you bring them with
you!"

Hoar Frost

Every leaf and twig was this morning covered with a
sparkling ice armor, even the grasses in exposed fields
were hung with innumerable diamond pendents, which
jingled merrily when brushed by the foot of the
traveller. It was literally the wreck of jewels and the
crash of gems– It was as though some superincumbent
stratum of the earth had been removed in the
night–exposing to light a bed of untarnished crystals.
The scene changed at every step–or as the head was
inclined to the right or the left– There were the
opal–and sapphire–and emerald–and jasper–and
beryl–and topaz–and ruby.

Such is beauty ever–neither here nor there, now nor
then–neither in Rome nor in Athens–but wherever
there is a soul to admire. If I seek her elsewhere because
I do not find her at home, my search will prove a
fruitless one.

Feb. 7th 1838.

Zeno

Zeno the stoic stood in precisely the same relation to
the world that I do now. He is forsooth bred a merchant,
as how many still–and can trade and barter, and
perchance higgle–and moreover can he be shipwrecked
and cast ashore at the Piraeus–like one of your Johns
or Thomases.

He strolls into a shop and is charmed by a book–by
Xenophon.– and straightway a philosopher. The sun

of a new *lebens-tag* rises to him–serene–unclouded–which looks over στοα.– And still the fleshly Zeno sails on, shipwrecked, buffetted, tempest-tossed–but the true Zeno sails ever a placid sea. Play high, play low–rain–sleet–or snow–it's all the same with the stoic. This rising and falling of the springs–now this side then that–serves to preserve the balance of the coach. "Propriety and decorum". were his Palinurus–not the base progeny of fashion–but the ready suggestions of a delicate taste.

And when evening comes he sits down unwearied to the review of his day–what's done that's to be undone–what not done at all still to be done. Himself Truth's unconcerned help-mate. Truly another system of book-keeping this, than that the Cyprian trader to Phoenicia practised–

This was he who said to a certain garrulous young man–"On this account have we two ears and but one mouth, that we may hear more, and speak less."

The five senses are but so many modified ears. That he had talked concerned not our philosopher, but his audience–and herein we may see how it is more noble to hear than to speak. The wisest may apologize that he only said so to hear himself talk–for if he *heard* not, as well for him had he never spoken. What is all this gabble to the gabbler? only the silent reap the profit of it.

Feb. 9th 1838
Society
It is wholesome advice–"to be a man amongst folks"– Go into society if you will, or if you are unwilling; and take a human interest in its affairs. If you mistake these Messieurs and Mesdames for so many men and women, it is but erring on the safe

side—or rather it is their error and not yours. Armed with a manly sincerity, you shall not be trifled with—but drive this business of life.— It matters not how many men are to be addressed—rebuked—provided one man rebuke them.

Small Talk

To manage the small talk of a party, is to make an effort to do what was at first done, admirably because naturally, at your fireside.

Feb. 13th 1838.

Influence

It is hard to subject ourselves to an influence. It must steal upon us when we expect it not—and its work be all done ere we are aware of it. If we make advances it is shy—if, when we feel its presence, we presume to pry into its free-masonry—it vanishes and leaves us alone in our folly—brimful but stagnant—a full channel, it may be, but no inclination.

Fear

All fear of the world or consequences is swallowed up in a manly anxiety to do Truth justice.

Feb 15th 1838.

Old Books.

The true student will cleave ever to the good—recognizing no no Past—no Present; but wherever he emerges from the bosom of time, his course is not with the sun—eastward or westward, but ever towards the seashore. Day and night pursues he his devious way—lingering by how many a Pierian spring—how many an Academus grove—how many a sculptured portico!— all which—spring—grove—and

portico–lie not so wide, but he may take them
conveniently in his way.

Feb. 16th 1838.

Greece.

In imagination I hie me to Greece as to enchanted
ground. No storms vex her coasts–no clouds encircle
her Helicon or Olympus–no tempests sweep the
peaceful Tempe–or ruffle the bosom of the placid
Aegean; but always the beams of the summer's sun
gleam along the entablature of the Acropolis–or are
reflected through the mellow atmosphere from a
thousand consecrated groves and fountains. Always her
sea-girt isles are dallying with their zephyr guests–and
the low of kine is heard along the meads–and the
landscape sleeps–valley–and hill–and woodland–a
dreamy sleep. Each of her sons–created a new heaven
and a new earth for Greece.

Feb. 18th 1838.

Sunday

Rightly named Suna-day or day of the sun– One is
satisfied in some angle by woodhouse and garden
fence–to bask in his beams–to exist barely–the livelong
day.

Spring

I had not been out long to-day when it seemed that
a new Spring was already born–not quite weaned it is
true, but verily entered upon existence. Nature struck
up "the same old song in the grass", despite eighteen
inches of snow, and I contrived to smuggle away a grin
of satisfaction by a smothered–"pshaw–and is that
all?"

{Two leaves missing}

Feb. 27th 1838
Goethe.

He jogs along at a snails pace, but ever mindful that
the earth is beneath and the heavens above him— His
Italy is not merely the fatherland of lazzaroni and
macaroni, but a solid turf-clad soil—daily illumined by
a genial sun—and nightly gleaming in the still
moonshine—to say nothing of the frequent showers
which are so faithfully recorded.— That sail to Palermo
was literally a ploughing through of the waves from
Naples to Trinacria—the sky over head; and the sea with
its isles on either hand.

His hearty good will to all men is most amiable; not
one cross word has he spoken, but on one occasion, the
post boy *snivelling* "Signor perdonate! questa è la mia
patria," he confesses "to me poor northerner came
something tear-like into the eyes."

Feb 19th 1838

Each summer sound
Is a summer round.

March 1st 1838
Spring.

March fans it—April christens it—and May puts on its
jacket and trowsers. It never grows up, but
Alexandrian-like "drags its slow length along"—ever
springing, bud following close upon leaf—and when
winter comes it is not annihilated, but creeps on
mole-like under the snow, showing its face nevertheless
occasionally by fuming springs and watercourses.

So let it be with man—let his manhood be a more
advanced and still advancing youth—bud following hard
upon leaf— By the side of the ripening corn—let's have

a second or third crop of peas and turnips–decking the
fields in a new green– So amid clumps of *sere* herds
grass flower the violet and buttercup spring-born.

March 3d 1838
Homer.
Three thousand years and the world so little
changed!– The Iliad seems like a natural sound which
has reverberated to our days. Whatever in it is still
freshest in the memories of men–was most childlike
in the poet. It is the problem of old age a second
childhood exhibited in the life of the world.– Phoebus
Apollo went like night

–ὁ δ' ἤϊε νυκτὶ ἐοικώς.

This either refers to the gross atmosphere of the
plague–darkening the sun–or to the crescent of
night–rising solemn and stately in the east–while the
sun is setting in the west.

Then Agamemnon darkly lowers on Calchas, prophet
of evil–ὄσσε δέ οἱ πυρὶ λαμπετόωντι ἐΐκτην.– Such a fire-eyed
Agamemnon as you may see at town-meetings–and
elections, as well here as in Troy neighborhood.

March 4th 1838
A Sunday Scene.
Here at my elbow sit five notable, or at least
noteworthy, representatives of this nineteenth century
–of the gender feminine. One a sedate–indefatigable
knitter, not spinster, of the old school–who had the
supreme felicity to be born in days that tried men's
souls–who can, and not unfrequently does, say with
Nestor, another of the old school–"But you are younger
than I. For time was when I conversed with greater men
than you. For not at any time have I seen such men, nor

shall see them, as Perithous and Dryas; and ποιμενα λαῶν—"
or in one word, sole "shepherd of the people" Washington.

And when Apollo has now six times rolled westward,
or seemed to roll, and now for the seventh time shows
his face in the east, eyes well nigh glazed, long glassed,
which have fluctuated only between lamb's wool and
worsted, explore ceaseless some good sermon book. For
six days shalt thou labor and do all thy knitting, but on
the seventh, forsooth—thy reading.

Opposite, across this stone hearth, sits one of no
school, but rather one who schools, a spinster who spins
not, with elbow resting on the book of books, but with
eyes turned towards the vain trumpery of that shelf
—trumpery of sere leaves—blossoms—and waxwork—built
on sand, that presumes to look quite as gay—smell quite
as earthy, as though this were not by good rights the
sun's day. I marked how she spurned that innocent every
day book, "Germany by De Stael", as though a viper had
stung her—better to rest the elbow on The Book—than the
eye on such a page.

Poor book! this is thy last chance

– –

Happy I who can bask in this warm spring sun which
illumines all creatures, as well when they rest as when
they toil, not without a feeling of gratitude! Whose life
is as blameless—how blameworthy soever it be, on the
Lord's mona-day as on his suna-day – – Thus much at
least a man may do; he may not impose on his
fellows—hardly on himself. Thus much *let* a man
do—confidently and heartily live up to his thought—for
its error if there be any will soonest appear in practice,
and if there be none, so much may he reckon as actual
progress in the way of living.

Homer

The poet does not leap—even in imagination, from
Asia to Greece through mid air, neglectful of the fair
sea and still fairer land beneath him, but jogs on
humanly observant over the intervening segment of a
sphere—

—ἐπεὶ ἦ μάλα πολλὰ μεταξύ
Ὄυρεά τε σκιόεντα, θάλασσα τε ἠχήεσσα.—

—for there are very many
Shady mountains, and resounding seas between—

March 5th 1838

How often, when Achilles like one—διάνδιχα
μερμήριξεν—whether to retaliate or suppress his wrath,
has his good Genius, like Pallas Athene, gliding down
from heaven, θυμῳ φιλέουσά τε κηδομένη τε,—stood behind
him, and whispered peace in his ear!

Men may dispute about the fact—whether a goddess
did actually come down from heaven, calling it a poet's
fancy, but was it not, considering the stuff that gods are
made of, a very truth?

The Age of Honey.

"And to them rose up the sweet-worded Nestor—the
   shrill orator of the Pylians,
And words *sweeter than honey* flowed from his tongue"

Een in old Homer's day was honey sweet—not yet is
sour—tickling the palate of the blind old man, forsooth,
with fresher sweet; then, as now, whene'er from leaky
jar, or drivelling lips, it daubed the festive board,
proving a baneful lure to swarms of parasites, Homers
cotemporaries, but alas! like Phithian hero, vulnerable
in heel.

What to do.

But what does all this scribbling amount
to? – – What is now scribbled in the heat of the

moment one can contemplate with somewhat of
satisfaction, but alas! to-morrow—aye to-night—it is stale,
flat—and unprofitable—in fine, is not, only its shell
remains—like some red parboiled lobster-shell—which
kicked aside never so often still stares at you in the
path. – – What may a man do and not be ashamed of
it? He may not do nothing surely, for straightway he
is dubbed Dolittle—aye! christen himself first—and
reasonably, for he was first to duck. But let him do
something, is he the less a Dolittle? Is it actually
something done—or not rather something undone— Or
if done, is it not badly done—or at most well done
comparatively?

Such is man—toiling—heaving, struggling, ant-like—to
shoulder some stray unappropriated crumb, and deposit
it in his granary; then runs out, complacent—gazes
heavenward, earthward (for even pismires can look down)
heaven and earth meanwhile looking downward-upward,
—there seen of men,—world-seen,—deed-delivered, vanishes
into all-grasping night.

And is he doomed ever to run the same course? Can he
not wriggling, screwing, self-exhorting,—self-constraining,
wriggle or screw out something that shall live—respected,
intact, intangible, not to be sneezed at? —Carlyleish—

March 6th 1838

– – How can a man sit down and quietly pare his
nails, while the earth goes gyrating ahead amid such a
din of sphere music, whirling him along about her axis
some twenty four thousand miles between sun and
sun? but mainly in a circle some two millions of miles
actual progress. And then such a hurly-burly on the
surface—wind always blowing—now a zephyr, now a
hurricane—tides never idle, ever fluctuating, no rest for
Niagara, but perpetual ran-tan on those limestone
rocks—and then that summer simmering which our ears
are used to—which would otherwise be christened

confusion worse confounded, but is now ironically
called "silence audible"–and above all the incessant
tinkering named hum of industry–the hurrying to and
fro and confused jabbering of men– Can man do less
than get up and shake himself?

March 7th 1838.

Composition

We should not endeavor coolly to analyze our
thoughts, but keeping the pen even and parallel with
the current, make an accurate transcript of
them – – Impulse is after all the best linguist, and
for his logic, if not conformable to Aristotle, it cannot
fail to be most convincing. – – The nearer we approach
to a complete but simple transcript of our thought–the
more tolerable will be the piece, for we can endure to
consider ourselves in a state of passivity–or in
involuntary action; but rarely our efforts, and least of
all our rare efforts.

Scraps from a Lecture on "Society" written March 14th
1838. delivered before our Lyceum April 11th.

Every proverb in the newspapers originally stood for
a truth. Thus the proverb that–Man was made for
society–so long as it was not allowed to conflict with
another important truth, deceived no one; but now that
the same words have come to stand for another thing,
it may be for a lie, we are obliged, in order to preserve
its significance, to write it anew, so that properly it will
read–Society was made for man.

Man is not at once born into society–hardly into the
world– The world that he is hides for a time the world
that he inhabits. – –

That which properly constitutes the life of every man is a profound secret. Yet this is what every one would give most to know—but is himself most backward to impart.

Hardly a rood of land but can show its fresh wound or indelible scar, in proof that earlier or later man has been there.

The mass never comes up to the standard of its best member, but on the contrary degrades itself to a level with the lowest— As the reformers say, it is a levelling down, not up— Hence the mass is only another name for the mob. The inhabitants of the earth assembled in one place, would constitute the greatest mob. – – The mob is spoken of as an insane and blinded animal; magistrates say it must be humored; they apprehend it may incline this way or that, as villagers dread an inundation, not knowing whose land may be flooded, nor how many bridges carried away.

One goes to a cattleshow expecting to find many men and women assembled, and beholds only working oxen and neat cattle. He goes to a commencement thinking that there at least he may find the men of the country, but such, if there were any, are completely merged in the day, and have become so many walking commencements—so that he is fain to take himself out of sight and hearing of the orator, lest he lose his own identity in the non-entities around him.

But you are getting all the while further and further from true society. Your silence was an approach to it, but your conversation is only a refuge from the encounter of men. As though men were to be satisfied with a meeting of heels, and not heads.

Nor is it better with private assemblies, or meetings
together with a sociable design of acquaintances so
called—that is to say of men and women who are
familiar with the lineaments of each other's
countenances—who eat, drink, sleep, and transact all
the business of living within the circuit of a mile. — —

With a beating heart he fares him forth, by the light
of the stars, to this meeting of gods. — — But the
illusion speedily vanishes; what at first seemed to him
nectar and ambrosia, is discovered to be plain bohea
and short ginger bread.

Then with what speed does he throw off his straight
jacket of a godship—and play the one eared,
two-mouthed mortal—thus proving his title to the
epithet applied to him of old by Homer—of $\mu\epsilon\rho o\psi\ \alpha\nu\theta\rho\omega\pi os$,
or that possesses an articulating voice. — — But
unfortunately we have as yet invented no rule by which
the stranger may know when he has culminated. We
read that among the Finlanders when one "has
succeeded in rendering himself agreeable, it is a custom
at an assemblage for all the women present to give him
on the back a sudden slap, when it is least expected;
and the compliment is in proportion to the weight of
the blow."

It is provoking when one sits waiting the assembling
together of his neighbors around his hearth, to behold
merely their clay houses, for the most part newly
shingled and clap-boarded, and not unfrequently with
a fresh coat of paint, trundled to his door. He has but
to knock slightly at the outer gate of one of these
shingle palaces, to be assured that the master or
mistress is not at home.

After all the field of battle possesses many advantages
over the drawing room. There at least is no room for
pretension or excessive ceremony, no shaking of hands

or rubbing of noses, which make one doubt your
sincerity, but hearty as well as hard handplay— It at
least exhibits one of the faces of humanity, the former
only a mask.

The utmost nearness to which men approach each
other amounts barely to a mechanical contact. As when
you rub two stones together, though they emit an
audible sound, yet do they not actually touch each other.

In obedience to an instinct of their nature men have
pitched their cabins, and planted corn and potatoes
within speaking distance of one another, and so formed
towns and villages, but they have not associated, they
have only assembled, and society has signified only a
convention of men.

When I think of a playhouse, it is as if we had
not time to appreciate the follies of the day in detail as
they occur, and so devoted an hour of our evening to
laughing or crying at them in the lump. – – Despairing
of a more perfect intercourse, or perhaps never
dreaming that such is desirable, or at least possible,
we are contented to act our part in what deserves to be
called the great farce, not drama, of life, like pitiful and
mercenary stock actors, whose business it is to keep up
the semblance of a stage.

Our least deed, like the young of the land crab, wends
its way to the sea of cause and effect as soon as born,
and makes a drop there to eternity.

Let ours be like the meeting of two planets, not
hastening to confound their jarring spheres, but drawn
together by the influence of a subtile attraction, soon to

roll diverse in their respective orbits, from this their perigee, or point of nearest approach.

If thy neighbor hail thee to inquire how goes the world—feel thyself put to thy trump to return a true and explicit answer. Plant the feet firmly, and will he nill he, dole out to him with strict and conscientious impartiality his modicum of a response.

Let not society be the element in which you swim, or are tossed about at the mercy of the waves, but be rather a strip of firm land running out into the sea, whose base is daily washed by the tide, but whose summit only the spring tide can reach.

But after all such a morsel of society as this will not satisfy a man. But like those women of Malamocco and Pelestrina, who when their husbands are fishing at sea, repair to the shore and sing their shrill songs at evening, till they hear the voices of their husbands in reply borne to them over the water—so go we about indefatigably; chanting our stanza of the lay, and awaiting the response of a kindred soul out of the distance.

{*One-fourth page blank*}

April 1st 1838.
The Indian Axe.
The Indian must have possessed no small share of vital energy—to have rubbed industriously stone upon stone for long months, till at length he had rubbed out an axe or pestle— As though he had said in the face of the constant flux of things—I at least will live an enduring life.

April 15th 1838.

Conversation.

Thomas Fuller relates that "In Merionethshire, in Wales, there are high mountains, whose hanging tops come so close together that shepherds on the tops of several hills may audibly talk together, yet will it be a day's journey for their bodies to meet, so vast is the hollowness of the valleys betwixt them." As much may be said in a moral sense of our intercourse in the plains, for though we may audibly converse together, yet is there so vast a gulf of hollowness between, that we are actually many days' journey from a veritable communication.

April 8th 1838

Friendship.

I think awhile of Love, and while I think,
    Love is to me a world,
    Sole meat and sweetest drink,
    And close connecting link
        Tween heaven and earth.

I only know it is, not how or why,
    My greatest happiness;
    However hard I try,
    Not if I were to die,
        Can I explain.

I fain would ask my friend how it can be,
    But when the time arrives,
    Then Love is more lovely
    Than anything to me,
        And so I'm dumb.

For if the truth were known, Love cannot speak,
    But only thinks and does;
    Though surely out 'twill leak
    Without the help of Greek,
        Or any tongue.

A man may love the truth and practise it,
 Beauty he may admire,
 And goodness not omit,
 As much as may befit
  To reverence.

But only when these three together meet,
 As they always incline,
 And make one soul the seat,
 And favorite retreat
  Of loveliness;

Where under kindred shape, like loves and hates
 And a kindred nature,
 Proclaim us to be mates,
 Exposed to equal fates
  Eternally;

And each may other help, and service do,
 Drawing Love's bands more tight,
 Service he ne'er shall rue
 While one and one make two,
  And two are one;

In such case only doth man fully prove
 Fully as man can do,
 What power there is in Love
 His inmost soul to move
  Resistlessly.

   – –

Two sturdy oaks I mean, which side by side,
 Withstand the winter's storm,
 And spite of wind and tide,
 Grow up the meadow's pride,
  For both are strong

Above they barely touch, but undermined
 Down to their deepest source,
 Admiring you shall find
 Their roots are intertwined
  Insep'rably.

{One-half page blank}

April 24th 1838.

Steam ships

—Men have been contriving new means and modes of motion— Steam ships have been westering during these late days and nights on the Atlantic waves—the fuglers of a new evolution to this generation — — Meanwhile plants spring silently by the brook sides—and the grim woods wave indifferent—the earth emits no howl—pot on fire simmers and seethes—and men go about their business. — —

{*One-half page blank*}

April 26th 1838.

The Bluebirds

In the midst of the poplar that stands by our door,
We planted a bluebird box,
And we hoped before the summer was o'er
A transient pair to coax.

One warm summer's day the bluebirds came
And lighted on our tree,
But at first the wand'rers were not so tame
But they were afraid of me.

They seemed to come from the distant south,
Just over the Walden wood,
And they skimmed it along with open mouth
Close by where the bellows stood.

Warbling they swept round the distant cliff,
And they warbled it over the lea,
And over the blacksmith's shop in a jiff
Did they come warbling to me.

They came and sat on the box's top
Without looking into the hole,
And only from this side to that did they hop,
As 'twere a common well-pole.

Methinks I had never seen them before,
Nor indeed had they seen me,
Till I chanced to stand by our back door,
And they came to the poplar tree.

In course of time they built their nest
And reared a happy brood,
And every morn they piped their best
As they flew away to the wood.

Thus wore the summer hours away
To the bluebirds and to me,
And every hour was a summer's day,
So pleasantly lived we.

They were a world within themselves,
And I a world in me,
Up in the tree—the little elves—
With their callow family.

One morn the wind blowed cold and strong,
And the leaves when whirling away;
The birds prepared for their journey long
That raw and gusty day.

Boreas came blust'ring down from the north,
And ruffled their azure smocks,
So they launched them forth, though somewhat loth,
By way of the old Cliff rocks.

Meanwhile the earth jogged steadily on
In her mantle of purest white,
And anon another spring was born
When winter was vanished quite.

And I wandered forth o'er the steamy earth,
And gazed at the mellow sky,
But never before from the hour of my birth
Had I wandered so thoughtfully.

For never before was the earth so still,
And never so mild was the sky,
The river, the fields, the woods, and the hill,
Seemed to heave an audible sigh.

I felt that the heavens were all around,
And the earth was all below,
As when in the ears there rushes a sound
Which thrills you from top to toe.

I dreamed that I was an waking thought–
A something I hardly knew–
Not a solid piece, nor an empty nought,
But a drop of morning dew.

'T'was the world and I at a game of bo-peep,
As a man would dodge his shadow,
An idea becalmed in eternity's deep–
'Tween Lima and Segraddo.

Anon a faintly warbled note
From out the azure deep,
Into my ears did gently float
As is the approach of sleep.

It thrilled but startled not my soul;
Across my mind strange mem'ries gleamed,
As often distant scenes unroll
When we have lately dreamed

The bluebird had come from the distant South
To his box in the poplar tree,
And he opened wide his slender mouth,
On purpose to sing to me.

Journey to Maine

May 3d-4th

Boston-to-Portland– What indeed is this earth to us
of New England but a field for Yankee speculation?
The nantucket whaler goes afishing round it–and so
knows it, what it is–how long–how broad–and that no
tortoise sustains it. – – He who has visited the confines

of his real estate, looking out on all sides into space—will feel a new inducement to *be* the Lord of creation — —

We must all pay a small tribute to Neptune—the chief engineer must once have been sea-sick.

Midnight—head over the boat's side—between sleeping and waking—with glimpses of one or more lights in the vicinity of Cape Ann. Bright moonlight— The effect heightened by seasickness.— Beyond that light yonder have my lines hitherto been cast, but now I know that there lies not the whole world, for I can say it is there and not here. — —

Portland May 4th — — There is a proper and only right way to enter a city, as well as to make advances to a strange person—neither will allow of the least forwardness nor bustle. — — A sensitive person can hardly elbow his way boldly—laughing and talking, into a strange town, without experiencing some twinges of conscience, as when he has treated a stranger with too much familiarity.

Portland to Bath—via Brunswick—Bath to Brunswick—May 5th. — —

Each one's world is but a clearing in the forest—so much open and inclosed ground. — — When the mail coach rumbles into one of these—the villagers gaze after you with a compassionate look, as much as to say "Where have you been all this time, that you make your dèbut in the world at this late hour? nevertheless, here we are, come and study us, that you may learn men and manners.

Brunswick to Augusta via Gardiner & Hollowwell.— May 6th — — May 7th. We occasionally meet an individual of a character and disposition so entirely the reverse of our own, that we wonder if he can indeed be another man like ourselves. — — We doubt if we ever could draw any nearer to him, and understand him. Such was the old English gentleman whom I met with to-day in H. Though I peered in at his eyes I could not discern myself reflected therein — — The chief wonder was how we could ever arrive at so fair-seeming an intercourse–upon so small ground of sympathy. — — He walked and fluttered like a strange bird at my side–prying into and making a handle of the least circumstance– The bustle and rapidity of our communication were astonishing–we skated in our conversation. All at once he would stop short in the path, and in an abstracted air, query whether the steamboat had reached Bath or Portland–addressing me from time to time as his familiar genius, who could understand what was passing in his mind without the necessity of uninterrupted oral communication. — —

Augusta to Bangor–via China–May 8th

Bangor to Oldtown May 10th — — The rail-road from Bangor to Oldtown is civilization shooting off in a tangent into the forest.– I had much conversation with an old Indian at the latter place, who sat dreaming upon a scow at the water side–and striking his deer-skin moccasins against the planks–while his arms hung listlessly by his side. He was the most communicative man I had met. — — Talked of hunting and fishing–old times and new times. Pointing up the Penobscot he observed–"Two or three miles up the river one beautiful country!" And then as if he would come as far to meet me as I had gone to meet him–he exclaimed–"Ugh! one very hard time!" But he had mistaken his man.

Bangor to Belfast via Saturday-Cove. May 11th
Belfast May 12th
To Castine by sail boat "Cinderilla". May 13th
Castine to Belfast by packet Cap. Skinner May 14th

Found the the Poems of Burns and an odd volume of
the Spectator in the cabin.

Belfast to Bath–via Thomaston May 15th
To Portland May 16th
To Boston and Concord May 17th 1838.

{*Two-thirds page blank*}

May 21st 1838.

So mild the air a pleasure 'twas to breathe,
For what seems heaven above was earth beneath.
The school boy loitered on his way to school,
Scorning to live so rare a day by rule.

— —

Soured neighbors chatted by the garden pale,
Nor quarrelled who should drive the needed nail—
The most unsocial made new friends that day,
As when the sunshines husbandmen make hay

— —

How long I slept I know not, but at last
I felt my consciousness returning fast,
For zephyr rustled past with leafy tread,
And heedlessly with one heel grazed my head.

— —

My eyelids opened on a field of blue,
For close above a nodding violet grew,
A part of heaven it seemed, which one could scent,
Its blue commingling with the firmament.

———— May Morning ————

Walden.   June 3d 1838.

— — True, our converse a stranger is to speech,
Only the practised ear can catch the surging words,
That break and die upon thy pebbled lips.
Thy flow of thought is noiseless as the lapse of thy own
     waters,
Wafted as is the morning mist up from thy surface,
So that the passive Soul doth breathe them in,
And is infected with the truth thou wouldst express.

— —

E'en the remotest stars have come in troops
And stooped low to catch the benediction
Of thy countenance. Oft as the day came round,
Impartial has the sun exhibited himself
Before thy narrow skylight– Nor has the moon
For cycles failed to roll this way
As oft as elsewhither, and tell thee of the night.
No cloud so rare but hitherward it stalked,
And in thy face looked doubly beautiful.
O! tell me what the winds have writ within these
    thousand years,
On the blue vault that spans thy flood–
Or sun transferred and delicately reprinted
For thy own private reading. Somewhat
Within these latter days I've read,
But surely there was much that would have thrilled the
    Soul,
Which human eye saw not
Much would I give to read the first bright page,
Wet from thy virgin press, when Eurus–Boreas–
And the host of airy quill-drivers
First dipped their pens in mist.

June 14th 1838

Truth–Goodness–Beauty–those celestial thrins,
Continually are born; e'en now the universe,
With thousand throats–and eke with greener smiles,
Its joy confesses at their recent birth.

Strange that so many fickle gods, as fickle as the weather,
Throughout Dame Natures provinces should always pull
    together.

June 16th 1838.

In the busy streets, domains of trade,
Man is a surly porter, or a vain and hectoring bully,
Who can claim no nearer kindredship with me
Than brotherhood by law.

July 8th 1838

Cliffs

The loudest sound that burdens here the breeze
Is the wood's whisper; 'tis when we choose to list
Audible sound, and when we list not,
It is calm profound. Tongues were provided
But to vex the ear with superficial thoughts.
When deeper thoughts upswell, the jarring discord
Of harsh speech is hushed, and senses seem
As little as may be to share the extacy.

July 13th 1838.

Heroism

What a hero one can be without moving a finger–the
world is not a field worthy of us, nor can we be satisfied
with the plains of Troy– A glorious strife seems waging
within us, yet so noiselessly that we but just catch the
sound of the clarion ringing of victory, borne to us on
the breeze. – – There are in each the seeds of a heroic
ardor, Seeds, there are seeds enough which need only
to be stirred in with the *soil where they lie*, by an
inspired voice or pen, to bear fruit of a divine flavor.

July 15th 1838.

Suspicion.

What though friends misinterpret your conduct, if it
is right in sight of God and Nature. The wrong, if there
be any, pertains only to the wrongdoer, nor is the
integrity of your relations to the universe affected–but
you may gather encouragement from their mistrust. If
the friend withhold his favor, yet does greater float
gratuitous on the zephyr.

August 4th 1838.

Truth.

Whatever of past or present wisdom has published
itself to the world, is palpable falsehood till it come and
utter itself by my side.

August 5th 1838.
Sphere music
Some sounds seem to reverberate along the plain, and
then settle to earth again like dust; such are Noise
–Discord–Jargon. But such only as spring heavenward,
and I may catch from steeples and hill tops in their
upward course, which are the more refined parts of the
former–are the true sphere music–pure, unmixed music
–in which no wail mingles.
Divine Service in the Academy-Hall.
In dark places and dungeons these words might
perhaps strike root and grow–but utter them in the day
light and their dusky hues are apparent. From this
window I can compare the written with the preached
word–within is weeping, and wailing, and gnashing of
teeth–without, grain fields and grasshoppers, which give
those the lie direct.

August 10th 1838
The Time of the Universe.
Nor can all the vanities that so vex the world alter one
whit the measure that night has chosen–but ever it must
be short particular metre. The human soul is a silent
harp in God's quire whose strings need only to be swept
by the divine breath, to chime in with the harmonies of
creation. Every pulse beat is in exact time with the
crickets chant, and the tickings of the deathwatch in the
wall. Alternate with these if you can.

August 13th 1838.
Consciousness
If with closed ears and eyes I consult consciousness
for a moment–immediately are all walls and barriers
dissipated–earth rolls from under me, and I float, by the
impetus derived from the earth and the system–a

subjective–heavily laden thought, in the midst of an unknown & infinite sea, or else heave and swell like a vast ocean of thought–without rock or headland. Where are all riddles solved, all straight lines making there their two ends to meet–eternity and space gambolling familiarly through my depths. I am from the beginning–knowing no end, no aim. No sun illumines me,–for I dissolve all lesser lights in my own intenser and steadier light— I am a restful kernel in the magazine of the universe.

Resource
Men are constantly dinging in my ears their fair theories and plausible solutions of the universe–but ever there is no help–and I return again to my shoreless –islandless ocean, and fathom unceasingly for a bottom that will hold an anchor, that it may not drag.

Aug. 19th 1838
Sabbath Bell.
The sound of the sabbath bell whose farthest waves are at this instant breaking on these cliffs–does not awaken pleasing associations alone.– Its muse is wonderfully condescending and philanthropic.– One involuntarily leans on his staff to humor the unusually meditative mood.– It is as the sound of many catechisms and religious books twanging a canting peal round the world–and seems to issue from some Egyptian temple, and echo along the shore of the Nile–right opposite to Pharaoh's palace and Moses in the bulrushes–startling a multitude of storks and aligators basking in the sun.

Not so these larks and pewees of Musketaquid. – – One is sick at heart of this pagoda worship–it is like the beating of gongs in a Hindoo subterranean temple.

Aug. 21st 1838
Holy War.
Passion and appetite are always an Unholy land in
which one may wage most holy war. Let him steadfastly
follow the banner of his faith till it is planted on the
enemy's citadel.– Nor shall he lack fields to display his
valor in, nor streights worthy of him. For when he has
blown his blast, and smote those within reach, invisible
enemies will not cease to torment him, who yet may be
starved out in the garrisons where they lie.

Aug. 22nd 1838.
Scripture.
How thrilling a noble sentiment in the oldest books–in
Homer The Zendavesta–or Confucius!– It is a strain of
music wafted down to us on the breeze of time, through
the aisles of innumerable ages. By its very nobleness it
is made near and audible to us.

Aug. 26th 1838.
Evening Sounds.
How strangely sounds of revelry strike the ear, from
over cultivated fields, by the wood side, while the sun is
declining in the west. It is a world we had not known
before. We listen and are capable of no mean act or
thought– We tread on Olympus and participate in the
councils of the gods – –

Homer
It does one's heart good if Homer but say the sun
sets.– or
"As when beautiful stars accompany the bright moon
through the serene heavens; and the woody hills and
cliffs are discerned through the mild light, and each star
is visible, and the shepherd rejoices in his heart."

Aug. 27th 1838.

The Loss of a Tooth.

Vérily I am the creature of circumstances. Here I have
swallowed an indispensable tooth, and so am no whole
man, but a lame and halting piece of manhood.– I am
conscious of no gap in my soul, but it would seem that
now the entrance to the oracle has been enlarged, the
more rare and commonplace the responses that issue
from it. – – I have felt cheap, and hardly dared hold
up my head among men, ever since this accident
happened. Nothing can I do as well and freely as
before–nothing do I undertake but I am hindered and
balked by this circumstance. What a great matter a little
spark kindleth– I believe if I were called at this moment
to rush into the thickest of the fight, I should halt for
lack of so insignificant a piece of armor as a tooth.
Virtue and Truth go undefended, and Falsehood and
Affectation are thrown in my teeth–though I am
toothless– One does not need that the earth quake for
the sake of excitement–when so slight a crack–proves
such an impassible moat. But let the lame man shake
his leg, and match himself with the fleetest in the race.
So shall.he do what is in him to do. If you are toothless,
and speak a lingo–open your mouth wide and gabble
never so resolutely.

Aug. 29th 1838.

Deformity.

Here on the top of Nawshawtuct, this mild August
afternoon, I can discern no deformed thing. The
prophane haymakers in yonder meadow–are yet the
haymakers of poetry–forsooth Faustus and Amyntas.
Yonder school-house of brick, than which near at hand
nothing can be more mote-like to my eye, serves even to
heighten the picturesqueness of the scene. Barns and

out-buildings, which in the nearness mar by their presence the loveliness of nature, are not only endurable, but observed where they lie by some waving field of grain, or patch of woodland, prove a very Cynosure to the pensive eye. Let man after infinite hammering and din of crows uprear a deformity in the plain, yet will nature have her revenge on the hilltop. Retire a stone's throw and she will have changed his base metal into gold.

Crickets

The crackling flight of grasshoppers is a luxury; and pleasant is it when summer has once more followed in the steps of winter–to hear scald cricket piping a Nibelungenlied in the grass.– It is the most infinite of singers. Wiselier had the Greeks chosen a golden cricket, and let the grasshopper eat grass. One opens both his ears to the invisible–incessant quire, and doubts if it be not earth herself chanting for all time.

Genii

In the vulgar daylight of our self conceit, good genii are still overlooking and conducting us–as the stars look down on us by day as by night–and we observe them not.

Sept. 2nd 1838

Sphere Music

The cocks chant a strain of which we never tire. Some there are who find pleasure in the melody of birds, and chirping of crickets–aye, even the peeping of frogs. Such faint sounds as these are for the most part heard above the weeping, and wailing, and gnashing of teeth, which so unhallow the sabbath among us. – – The moan the earth makes is after all a very faint sound, infinitely inferior in volume to its creakings of joy and gleeful

murmurs–so that we may expect the next balloonist will
rise above the utmost range of discordant sounds into
the region of pure melody. – – Never so loud was the
wail but it seemed to taper off into a piercing melody,
and note of joy–which lingered not amid the clods of the
valley.

Sept 3d 1838.
Creeds.
The only faith that men recognize is a creed– But the
true creed which we unconsciously live by, and which
rather adopts us than we it, is quite different from the
written or preached one. – – Men anxiously hold fast to
their creed, as to a straw, thinking this does them good
service because their sheet anchor does not drag.

Sept 5th 1838
Rivers.
For the first time it occurred to me this afternoon what
a piece of wonder a river is.– A huge volume of matter
ceaselessly rolling through the fields and meadows of
this substantial earth–making haste from the high
places, by stable dwellings of men and Egyptian
pyramids; to its restless reservoir– One would think
that, by a very natural impulse, the dwellers upon the
headwaters of the Mississippi and Amazon, would follow
in the trail of their waters to see the end of the matter.

Sept 7th 1838
Homer.
When Homer's messengers repair to the tent of
Achilles–we do not have to wonder how they get
there–but step by step accompany them along the shore
of the resounding sea

Sept. 16th 1838.
Flow of Spirits in Youth.

How unaccountable the flow of spirits in youth.– You
may throw sticks and dirt into the current, and it will
only rise the higher, Dam it up you may, but dry it up
you may not, for you cannot reach its source. If you stop
up this avenue or that, anon it will come gurgling out
where you least expected, and wash away all fixtures.
Youth grasps at happiness as an inalienable right. The
tear does no sooner gush than glisten– Who shall say
when the tear that sprung of sorrow–first sparkled with
joy?

Sept 20th 1838
Alma Natura

It is a luxury to muse by a wall-side in the sunshine
of a September afternoon–to cuddle down under a gray
stone, and hearken to the siren song of the cricket. Day
and night seem henceforth but accidents–and the time is
always a still even tide, and as the close of a happy
day.– Parched fields and mulleins gilded with the
slanting rays are my diet.– I know of no word so fit to
express this disposition of nature as–Alma-Natura.

Sept. 23d 1838
Compensation

If we will be quiet and ready enough, we shall find
compensation in every disappointment. If a shower
drives us for shelter to the maple grove–or the trailing
branches of the pine–yet in their recesses, with
microscopic eye, we discover some new wonder in the
bark, or the leaves, or the fungi at our feet. We are
interested by some new resource of insect economy–or
the chick-a-dee is more than usually familiar. We can
study Natures nooks and corners then.

Oct 21st 1838

Homer.

Hector hurrying from rank to rank is likened to the
moon wading in majesty from cloud to cloud— We are
reminded of the hour of the day by the fact that the wood
cutter spreads now his morning meal in the recesses of
the mountains, having already laid his axe at the root
of many lofty trees.

Oct. 23d 1838.

Nestor's simple repast—after the rescue of Machaon
—is a fit subject for poetry. The woodcutter may sit down
to his cold victuals—the hero to soldier's fare—and the
wild Arab—to his dried dates and figs—without offence
— But not so a modern gentleman to his dinner.

Nestor's account of the march of the Pylians against
the Epeians is extremely lifesome.— "A certain river,
Minyas by name, leaps seaward near to Athens, where
we Pylians wait the dawn, both horse and foot. Thence
with all haste we sped us on the morrow, ere the day
closed, accoutred for the fight, even to Alpheus' sacred
source" &c &c. – – We imagine we hear the subdued
murmuring of the Minyas, discharging its waters into
the main the livelong night, and the hollow sound of the
Aegean breaking on the shore, and are cheered at the
close of a toilsome march by the gurgling fountains of
Alpheus—and the oaks are waving a welcome to us.

Oct 24th 1838

It matters not whether these strains originate there in
the grass—or float thitherward like atoms of light from
the minstrel days of Greece.

"The snow flakes fall thick and fast on a winter's day.
The winds are lulled, and the snow falls incessant,
covering the tops of the mountains, and the hills, and

the plains where the lotus tree grows, and the cultivated
fields. And they are falling by the inlets and shores of
the foaming sea, but are silently dissolved by the waves."

{*Two-fifths page blank*}

Dec 7th 1838
Speculation
We may believe it, but never do we live a quite free
life, such as Adam's, but are enveloped in an invisible
network of speculations— Our progress is only from one
such speculation to another, and only at rare intervals
do we perceive that it is no progress. — — Could we for
a moment drop this by-play—and simply wonder—without
reference or inference!

Dec 8th 1838
Byron
Nothing in nature is sneaking or chop-fallen—as
somewhat maltreated and slighted—but each is satisfied
with its being, and so is as lavender and balm.— If
skunk cabbage is offensive to the nostrils of men, still
has it not drooped in consequence, but trustfully
unfolded its leaf of two hands' breadth. What was it to
Lord Byron whether England owned or disowned him,
whether he smelled sour, and was skunk cabbage to the

{*Two leaves missing*}

English nostril—or violet-like—the pride of the land,
and ornament of every lady's boudoir.— Let not the
oyster grieve that he has lost the race—he has gained as
an oyster.

{*Four-fifths page blank*}

Dec 15th 1838.

Fair-Haven
When winter fringes every bough
With his fantastic wreath,
And puts the seal of silence now
Upon the leaves beneath.

When every stream in its pent house
Goes gurgling on its way,
And in his gallery the mouse
Nibbleth the meadow hay.–

Methinks the summer still is nigh,
And lurketh there below,
As that same meadow mouse doth lie
Snug underneath the snow.

And if perchance the chic-a-dee
Lisp a faint note anon,
The snow is summer's canopy,
Which she herself put on.

Rare blossoms deck the cheerful trees,
And dazzling fruits depend,
The north wind sighs a summer breeze,
The nipping frosts to fend–

Bringing glad tidings unto me,
While that I stand all ear,
Of a serene eternity,
That need not winter fear.

Out on the silent pond straightway
The restless ice doth crack,
And pond sprites merry gambols play
Amid the deaf'ning rack.

Eager I press me to the vale
As I had heard brave news,
How nature held high festival,
Which it were hard to lose.

I crack me with my neighbor ice,
And sympathizing quake,
As each new rent darts in a trice
Across the gladsome lake.

One with the cricket in the ground,
And fuel on the hearth,
Resounds the rare domestic sound
Along the forest path.

Fair Haven is my huge tea-urn,
That seethes and sings to me,
And eke the crackling faggots burn—
A homebred minstrelsy.

Some scraps from an essay on "Sound and Silence" written in the latter half of this month. Dec. 1838.

As the truest Society approaches always nearer to Solitude—so the most excellent Speech finally falls into Silence. We go about to find Solitude and Silence, as though they dwelt only in distant glens, and the depths of the forest—venturing out from these fastnesses at midnight.— Silence *was*—say we—before even the world was, as if creation had displaced her—and were not her visible frame-work and foil. — — It is only favorite dells that she deigns to frequent, and we dream not that she is then imported into them, when we wend thither—As Selden's butcher busied himself with looking after his knife, when he had it in his mouth. For where man is, there is Silence.

Silence is the communing of a conscious soul with itself. — — If the soul attend for a moment to its own infinity, then and there is silence. She is audible to all

men–at all times–in all places–and if we will we may
always hearken to her admonitions.

Silence is ever less strange than noise – – lurking
amid the boughs of the hemlock or pine–just in
proportion as we find ourselves there. – – The
nuthatch, tapping the upright trunks by our side,–is
only a partial spokesman for the solemn stillness.

She is always at hand with her wisdom, by road sides
and street corners–lurking in belfries–the cannon's
mouth–and the wake of the earthquake–gathering up
and fondling their puny din in her ample bosom.

Those divine sounds which are uttered to our inward
ear–which are breathed in with the zephyr–or reflected
from the lake–come to us noiselessly bathing the temples
of the soul, as we stand motionless amid the rocks.

The halloo is the creature of walls and mason
work–the whisper is fittest in the depths of the wood–or
by the shore of the lake–but silence is best adapted to
the acoustics of space.

All sounds are her servants and purveyors
–proclaiming not only that their mistress is, but is a
rare mistress, and earnestly to be sought after. Behind
the most distinct and significant, hovers always a more
significant silence which floats it. The thunder is only
our signal gun, that we may know what communion
awaits us– Not its dull sound, but the infinite expansion
of our being which ensues we praise–and unanimously
name sublime.

All sound is nearly akin to Silence–it is a bubble on
her surface which straightway bursts–an emblem of the

strength and prolifickness of the undercurrent. – – It is a faint utterance of Silence–and then only agreeable to our auditory nerves–when it contrasts itself with the former. In proportion as it does this–and is a heightener and intensifier of the Silence–it is harmony and purest melody.

Every melodious sound is the ally of Silence–a help and not a hindrance to abstraction.

Certain sounds more than others have found favor with the poets only as foils to silence.

Anacreon's Ode to the Cicada.

We pronounce thee happy, cicada,
For on the tops of the trees,
  Sipping a little dew
Like any king thou singest.
For thine are they all,
Whatever thou seest in the fields,
And whatever the woods bear.
Thou art the friend of the husbandmen.
In no respect injuring any one;
And thou art honored among men,
Sweet prophet of summer.
The muses love thee,
And Phoebus himself loves thee,
And has given thee a shrill song;
Age does not wrack thee,
Thou skilful–earth-born–song-loving,
Unsuffering–bloodless one;
Almost thou art like the gods.

Silence is the universal refuge–the sequel of all dry discourses and all foolish acts–as balm to our every chagrin–as welcome after satiety as disappointment.

That back-ground which the painter may not daub, be he master or bungler, and which, however awkward a figure he may have made in the fore ground, remains ever our inviolable asylum.

With what equanimity does the silent consider how his world goes—settles the awards of virtue and justice—is slandered and buffetted never so much and views it all as a phenomenon— He is one with Truth—Goodness—Beauty.— no indignity can assail him—no personality disturb him. — —

The orator puts off his individuality, and is then most eloquent when most silent. He listens while he speaks—and is a hearer along with his audience.

Who has not hearkened to her infinite din? She is Truth's speaking trumpet—which every man carries slung over his shoulder, and when he will may apply to his ear. She is the sole oracle—the true Delphi and Dodona—which kings and courtiers would do well to consult—nor will they be balked by an ambiguous answer. Through her have all revelations been made. Just as far as men have consulted her oracle, they have obtained a clear insight, and their age been marked for an enlightened one. But as often as they have gone gadding abroad to a strange Delphi—and her mad priestess —they have been benighted—and their age Dark or Leaden.— These are garrulous and noisy eras—which no longer yield any sound—but the Grecian, or *silent* and melodious, Era, is ever sounding in the ears of men.

A good book is the plectrum with which our silent lyres are struck— In all epics, when, after breathless attention, we come to the significant words "he said"—then especially our inmost man is addressed. − − We not unfrequently refer the interest which belongs to our own unwritten sequel–to the written and comparatively lifeless page. Of all valuable books this same sequel makes an indispensable part– It is the author's aim to say, once and emphatically, "he said" This is the most the book maker can attain to. If he make his volume a foil whereon the waves of silence may break, it is well. It is not so much the sighing of the blast, as that pause, as Grey expresses it, "When the gust is recollecting itself," that thrills us, and is infinitely grander than the importunate howlings of the storm.

At evening, Silence sends many emissaries to me–some navigating the subsiding waves which the village murmur has agitated.

It were vain for me to interpret the Silence–she cannot be done into English– For six thousand years have men translated her, with what fidelity belonged to each, still is she little better than a sealed book. A man may run on confidently for a time, thinking he has her under his thumb, and shall one day exhaust her, but he too must at last be silent, and men remark only how brave a beginning he made. For when he at length dives into her, so vast is the disproportion of the told to the untold, that the former will seem but the bubble on the surface where he disappeared.

Never the less will we go on–like those Chinese cliff swallows, feathering our nests with the froth–so they may one day be bread of life to such as dwell by the sea shore.

{*One-half page blank*}

Anacreontics

Dec 23d 1838.

Return of Spring.

Behold, how spring appearing
The Graces send forth roses;
Behold, how the wave of the sea
Is made smooth by the calm;
Behold, how the duck dives;
Behold, how the crane travels;
And Titan shines constantly bright.
The shadows of the clouds are moving;
The works of man shine,
The earth puts forth fruits;
The fruit of the olive puts forth.
The cup of Bachus is crowned.
Along the leaves, along the branches,
The fruit, bending them down, flourishes.

Cupid Wounded.

Love, once among roses
    A sleeping bee
Did not see, but was stung.
And being wounded in the finger
Of his hand cried for pain.
Running as well as flying
To the beautiful Venus,
I am killed, Mother, said he,
I am killed, and I die.
A little serpent has stung me
Winged, which they call
A bee—the husbandmen.
And she said, If the sting
Of a bee afflicts you,
How, think you, are they afflicted,
Love, whom you smite?

Jan 11th 1839

The Thaw.
— —

I saw the civil sun drying earth's tears—
Her tears of joy that only faster flowed,

— —

Fain would I stretch me by the highway side,
To thaw and trickle with the melting snow,
That mingled soul and body with the tide,
I too may through the pores of nature flow.

— —

But I alas nor tinkle can nor fume,
One jot to forward the great work of Time,
'Tis mine to hearken while these ply the loom,
So shall my silence with their music chime.

Jan 20th 1839.

The Dream Valley.

The prospect of our river valley from Tahatawan
cliff—appeared to me again in my dreams.

Last night as I lay peering with shut eyes
Into the golden land of dreams,
Methought I gazed adown a quiet reach
Of land and water prospect,
Whose low beach
Was peopled with the now subsiding hum
Of happy industry—whose work is done.

'Twas *there* the world, whatever good or ill,
Nor needed thought, with rude officiousness.
Go plant another vale behind the hill.

And as I turned me on my pillow o'er,
I heard the lapse of waves upon the shore,
Distinct as it had been at broad noonday,
And still they lapse, and will lapse evermore.

Love.

We two that planets erst had been
Are now a double star,
And in the heavens may be seen,
Where that we fixed are.

Yet whirled with subtle power along,
Into new space we enter,
And evermore with spheral song
Revolve about one centre.

— —

The deeds of king and meanest hedger,
Stand side by side in heaven's ledger.

{*One-fifth page blank*}

'Twill soon appear if we but look
At evening into earth's day book,
Which way the great account doth stand
Between the heavens and the land.

The Evening Wind.
The eastern mail comes lumbering in
With outmost waves of Europe's din;
The western sighs adown the slope,
Or mid the rustling leaves doth grope,
Laden with news from Californ',
Whateer transpired hath since morn,
How wags The world by brier and brake,
From hence to Athabasca lake.

— —

{*One-third page blank*}

Feb. 8th 1839.
Poetizing.
When the poetic frenzy seizes us, we run and scratch
with our pen, delighting, like the cock, in the dust we
make, but do not detect where the jewel lies, which
perhaps we have in the meantime cast to a distance, or
quite covered up again.

Feb. 9th 1839
It takes a man to make a room silent.

Feb. 10th 1839
The Peal of the Bells.
When the world grows old by the chimney side,
Then forth to the youngling rocks I glide—
Where over the water, and over the land,
The bells are booming on either hand.

Now up they go ding, then down again dong,
And awhile they swing to the same old song,

{See Textual Note 68.3}

And the metal goes round 't a single bound,
A-lulling the fields with its measured sound—
Till the tired tongue falls with a lengthened boom,
As solemn and loud as the crack of doom.
  Then changed is their measure to tone upon tone,
And seldom it is that one sound comes alone,
For they ring out their peals in a mingled throng,
And the breezes waft the loud ding-dong along.

When the echo has reached me in this lone vale,
I am straightway a hero in coat of mail,
I tug at my belt and I march on my post,
And feel myself more than a match for a host.

I am on the alert for some wonderful Thing,
Wich somewhere's a taking place,
'Tis perchance the salute which our planet doth ring
When it meeteth another in space.

{One-third page blank}

Feb 25th 1839.

The Shrike
Hark—hark—from out the thickest fog
Warbles with might and main
The fearless shrike, as all agog
To find in fog his gain.

His steady sails he never furls
At any time o' year,
And perched now on winter's curls,
He whistles in his ear.

March 3d 1839
The Poet.

He must be something more than natural–even supernatural. Nature will not speak through but along with him. His voice will not proceed from her midst, but breathing on her, will make her the expression of his thought. He then poetizes, when he takes a fact out of nature into spirit – – He speaks without reference to time or place. His thought is one world, her's another. He is another nature–Nature's brother.

{*One leaf missing*}

Kindly offices do they perform for one another– Each publishes the other's truth.

April 4 1839
Morning

The atmosphere of morning gives a healthy hue to our prospects. – – Disease is a sluggard that overtakes–never encounters, us. We have the start each day, and may fairly distance him before the dew is off; but if we recline in the bowers of noon, come up with us he may after all. The morning dew breeds no cold. We enjoy a diurnal reprieve in the beginning of each day's creation. – – In the morning we do not believe in expediency–we will start afresh, and have no patching–no temporary fixtures. – – The after-noon man has an interest in the past, his eye is divided–and he sees indifferently well either way.

Drifting.

Drifting in a sultry day on the sluggish waters of the pond, I almost cease to live–and begin to be. A boat-man stretched on the deck of his craft, and dallying with the noon, would be as apt an emblem of eternity for me, as the serpent with his tail in his mouth. I am never so prone to lose my identity. I am dissolved in the haze.

Sunday April 7th 1839.
Disappointment
The tediousness and detail of execution never occcur to the genius projecting–it always ante-dates the completion of its work. It condescends to give time a few hours to do its bidding in.

Resolve.
Most have sufficient contempt for what is mean to resolve that they will abstain from it, and a few virtue enough to abide by their resolution, but not often does one attain to such lofty contempt as to require no resolution to be made.

April 8th 1839.
The Teamster.
There goes a six-horse team, and a man by its side.– He has rolled out of his cradle into a Tom-and-Jerry–and goes about his business, while nature goes about hers, without standing agape at his condition. – – As though sixty years were not enough for these things. What have death, and the cholera, and the immortal destiny of man, to do with the shipping interests? – – There is an unexplained bravery in this. What with bare astonishment one would think that man had his hands full for so short a term. But this is no draw back on the lace working and cap making interests. Some attain to such a degree of sang-froid and non chalance as to be weavers of toilet cushions, and manufacturers of pin-heads without once flinching, or the slightest affection of the nerves, for the period of a natural life.

April 9th 1839
Fat Pine for Spearing.

Fat roots of pine lying in rich veins as of gold or silver—even in old pastures, where you would least expect it, make you realize that you live in the youth of the world—and you begin to know the wealth of the planet. Human nature is still in its prime then. Bring axe—pick-axe, and shovel—and tap the earth here where there is most sap—the marrowy store gleams like some vigorous sinew—and you feel a new suppleness in your own limbs. – – These are the traits that conciliate man's moroseness, and make him civil to his fellows; every such pine root is a pledge of suavity. If he can discover absolute barrenness in any direction there will be some excuse for peevishness.

{*One-fifth page blank*}

April 14th 1839.
Society.

There is a terra firma in society as well as in geography—some whose ports you may make by dead reckoning in all weather—all the rest are but floating and fabulous Atlantides—which sometimes skirt the western horizon of our intercourse . . . They impose only on sea-sick mariners who have put into some Canary island, on the frontiers of society.

April 24th 1839
Circumstances.

Why should we concern ourselves with what has happened to us, and the unaccountable fickleness of events, and not rather how we have happened to the universe, and it has demeaned it self in consequence? – – Let us record in each case the judgment we have awarded to circumstances.

Acquaintance.

Cheap persons will stand upon ceremony, because there is no other ground but to the great of the earth we need no introduction—nor do they need any to us.

April 25th 1839

The Kingdoms of the Earth.

We see a reality hovering over things, not an actuality underneath and behind them. Take the earth and all the interests it has known—what are they beside one deep surmise that pierces and scatters them? The independent beggar disposes of all with one hearty significant curse by the road-side— 'Tis true they are not worth a "tinker's damn".

April 30th 1839

Picture.

Of some illuminated pictures which I saw last evening—one representing the plain of Babylon, with only a heap of brick dust in the centre, and an uninterrupted horizon bounding the desert, struck me most.

I would see painted a boundless expanse of desert, prairie, or sea—without other object than the horizon.

The heavens and the earth—the first and last painting—where is the artist who shall undertake it?

{*Three leaves missing*}

May 16th 1839

Vice & Virtue.

Virtue is the very heart and lungs of vice—it cannot stand up but it lean on Virtue. – –

Who has not admired the twelve labors? And yet nobody thinks if Hercules had sufficient motive for racking his bones to that degree. – – Men are not so much virtuous

as patrons of virtue, and every one knows that it is
easier to deal with the real possessor of a thing than the
temporary guardian of it.

May 17th −39

The Form of Strength.

We say justly that the weak person is flat, for like all
flat substances, he does not stand in the direction of his
strength, that is on his edge, but affords a convenient
surface to put upon. He slides all the way through life.
Most things are strong in one direction; a straw
longitudinally; a board in the direction of its edge; a
knee transversely to its grain; but the brave man is a
perfect sphere, which cannot fall on its flat side; and is
equally strong every way. The coward is wretchedly
spheroidal at best, too much educated or drawn out on
one side, and depressed on the other; or may be likened
to a hollow sphere, whose disposition of matter is best
when the greatest bulk is intended.

May 21st −39

Self-culture

Who knows how incessant a surveillance a strong man
may maintain over himself—how far subject passion and
appetite to reason, and lead the life his imagination
paints? Well has the poet said—　　"by manly mind
　　　　　　Not e'en in sleep is will resigned."
By a strong effort, may he not command even his brute
body in unconscious moments?

June 4th −39

My Attic.

I sit here this fourth of June—looking out on men and
nature from this that I call my perspective window
—through which all things are seen in their true relations.

This is my upper empire–bounded by four walls–viz.
three of boards yellow-washed, facing the north, west,
and south, respectively–and the fourth of
plaster–likewise yellow-washed, fronting the
sunrise– To say nothing of the purlieus, and out-lying
provinces, unexplored as yet but by rats.

The words of some men are thrown forcibly against
you–and adhere like burs.

Saturday June 22nd –39
Rencounter

I have within the last few days come into contact with
a pure uncompromising spirit, that is somewhere
wandering in the atmosphere, but settles not positively
anywhere. Some persons carry about them the air and
conviction of virtue, though they themselves are
unconscious of it–and are even backward to appreciate
it in others. Such it is impossible not to love–still is their
loveliness, as it were, independent of them, so that you
seem not to lose it when they are absent, for when they
are near it is like an invisible presence which attends
you.

That virtue we appreciate is as much ours as
another's. We see so much only as we possess.

July 4th –39.

The "Book of Gems"
–With cunning plates the polished leaves were decked,
Each one a window to the poet's world,
So rich a prospect that you might suspect
In that small space all paradise unfurled.
It was a right delightful road to go,
marching through pastures of such fair herbage,
O'er hill and dale it lead, and to and fro,
From bard to bard, making an easy stage.

And ever and anon you'd slake your thirst
By the way-side from out some poet's well,
Which from the teeming ground did bubbling burst,
And tinkling thence adown the page it fell.
Aye, after you had many paces ta'en,
Still through the leaves its music might you hear,
Until fresh murmurings had drowned that strain
And other Springs fell faintly on the ear.

July 11th –39

Anursnuck

–At length we leave the river and take to the road
which leads to the hill top, if by any means we may spy
out what manner of earth we inhabit. East–west–north
and south–it is farm and parish–this world of ours. One
may see how at convenient–eternal intervals men have
settled themselves–without thought for the
universe. – – How little matters it all they have built
and delved there in the valley–it is after all but a feature
in the landscape– Still the vast impulse of nature
breathes over all– The eternal winds sweep across the
interval *to-day*, bringing mist and haze to shut out their
works– Still the crow caws from Nawshawtuct to
Anursnuck–as no feeble tradesman nor smith may
do–and in all swamps the hum of moskitoes drowns this
modern hum of industry.

Every Man is a Roman Forum.

All things are up and down–east and west to *me*. In
me is the forum out of which go the Appian and Sacred
ways, and a thousand beside, to the ends of the world– If
I forget my centralness, and say a bean winds with or
against the *sun*, and not right or left, it will not be true
south of the equator.

{*Two-fifths page blank*}

June 24th –39

Sympathy

Lately alas I knew a gentle boy,
Whose features all were cast in Virtue's mould,
As one she had designed for Beauty's toy,
But after manned him for her own stronghold.

On every side he open was as day,
That you might see no lack of strength within,
For walls and ports do only serve alway
For a pretence to feebleness and sin.

Say not that Caesar was victorious,
With toil and strife who stormed the House of Fame
In other sense this youth was glorious,
Himself a kingdom whereso'eer he came.

No strength went out to get him victory,
When all was income of its own accord;
For where he went none other was to see,
But all were parcel of their noble lord.

He forayed like the subtle haze of summer,
That stilly shows fresh landscapes to our eyes,
And revolutions works without a murmur,
Or rustling of a leaf beneath the skies.

So was I taken unawares by this,
I quite forgot my homage to confess;
Yet now am forced to know, though hard it is,
I might have loved him, had I loved him less.

Each moment, as we nearer drew to each,
A stern respect withheld us farther yet,
So that we seemed beyond each other's reach,
And less acquainted than when first we met.

We two were one while we did sympathize,
So could we not the simplest bargain drive;
And what avails it now that we are wise,
If absence doth this doubleness contrive?

Eternity may not the chance repeat,
But I must tread my single way alone,
In sad remembrance that we once did meet,
And know that bliss irrevocably gone.

The spheres henceforth my elegy shall sing,
For elegy has other subject none;
Each strain of music in my ears shall ring
Knell of departure from that other one.

Make haste and celebrate my tragedy;
With fitting strain resound ye woods and fields;
Sorrow is dearer in such case to me
Than all the joys other occasion yields.

Is't then too late the damage to repair?
Distance, forsooth, from my weak grasp hath reft
The empty husk, and clutched the useless tare,
But in my hands the wheat and kernel left.

If I but love that virtue which he is,
Though it be scented in the morning air,
Still shall we be truest acquaintances,
Nor mortals know a sympathy more rare.

{*One-half page blank*}

July 18th −39

The Assabet.
Up this pleasant stream let's row
For the livelong summer's day,
Sprinkling foam where'er we go
In wreaths as white as driven snow—
Ply the oars, away! away!

Now we glide along the shore,
Chucking lillies as we go,
While the yellow-sanded floor
Doggedly resists the oar,
Like some turtle dull and slow.

Now we stem the middle tide
Ploughing through the deepest soil,
Ridges pile on either side,
While we through the furrow glide,
Reaping bubbles for our toil.

Dew before and drought behind,
Onward all doth seem to fly;
Nought contents the eager mind,
Only rapids now are kind,
Forward are the earth and sky.

Sudden music strikes the ear,
Leaking out from yonder bank,
Fit such voyagers to cheer—
Sure there must be naiads here,
Who have kindly played this prank.

There I know the cunning pack
Where yon self-sufficient rill
All its tell tale hath kept back,
Through the meadows held its clack,
And now babbleth its fill.

Silent flows the parent stream,
And if rocks do lie below
Smothers with her waves the din,
As it were a youthful sin,
Just as still and just as slow.

But this gleeful little rill,
Purling round its storied pebble,
Tinkles to the self same tune
From December until June,
Nor doth any drought enfeeble.

See the sun behind the willows,
Rising through the golden haze,
How he gleams along the billows—
Their white crests the easy pillows
Of his dew besprinkled rays.

Forward press we to the dawning,
For Aurora leads the way,
Sultry noon and twilight scorning,
In each dew drop of the morning
Lies the promise of a day.

Rivers from the sun do flow,
Springing with the dewy morn,
Voyageurs 'gainst time do row,
Idle noon nor sunset know,
Ever even with the dawn.

Since that first away! away!
Many a lengthy league we've rowed,
Still the sparrow on the spray,
Hastes to usher in the day
With her simple stanza'd ode.

July 20th −39.

The Breeze's Invitation.

Come let's roam the breezy pastures,
Where the freest zephyrs blow,
Batten on the oak tree's rustle,
And the pleasant insect bustle,
Dripping with the streamlet's flow.

What if I no wings do wear,
Thro' this solid seeming air
I can skim like any swallow
Whoso dareth let her follow,
And we'll be a jovial pair.

Like two careless swifts let's sail,
Zephyrus shall think for me−
Over hill and over dale,
Riding on the easy gale,
We will scan the earth and sea.

Yonder see that willow tree
Winnowing the buxom air,
You a gnat and I a bee,
With our merry minstrelsy
We will make a concert there.

One green leaf shall be our screen,
Till the sun doth go to bed,
I the king and you the queen
Of that peaceful little green,
Without any subject's aid.

To our music Time will linger,
And earth open wide her ear,
Nor shall any need to tarry
To immortal verse to marry
Such sweet music as he'll hear.

{*Three-fifths page blank*}

July 24th –39.

Nature doth have her dawn each day,
But mine are far between;
Content, I cry, for sooth to say,
Mine brightest are, I ween.

For when my sun doth deign to rise,
Though it be her noontide,
Her fairest field in shadow lies,
Nor can my light abide.

Sometimes I bask me in her day,
Conversing with my mate;
But if we interchange one ray,
Forthwith her heats abate.

Through his discourse I climb and see,
As from some eastern hill,
A brighter morrow rise to me
Than lieth in her skill.

As 'twere two summer days in one,
Two Sundays come together,
Our rays united make one Sun,
With fairest summer weather.

July 25th –39

There is no remedy for love but to love more.

Sept 17th –39

The Wise rest.

–Nature never makes haste; her systems revolve at an
even pace. The bud swells imperceptibly–without hurry
or confusion, as though the short spring days were an
eternity. All her operations seem separately for the time,
the single object for which all things tarry.– Why then
should man hasten as if any thing less than eternity
were allotted for the least deed? Let him consume never
so many aeons, so that he go about the meanest task
well–though it be but the paring of his nails. If the
setting sun seems to hurry him to improve the day while
it lasts, the chant of the crickets fails not to reassure
him–even-measured as of old–teaching him to take his
own time henceforth forever. –The wise man is
restful–never restless or impatient– He each moment
abides there where he is, as some walkers actually rest
the whole body at each step, while others never relax
the muscles of the leg till the accumulated fatigue
obliges them to stop short.

As the wise is not anxious that time wait for him,
neither does he wait for it.

Oct. 22nd –39.

– – Nature will bear the closest inspection. She
invites us to lay our eye level with her smallest leaf, and
take an insect view of its plain – –

Nov. 5th —39.

Aeschylus.

—There was one man lived his own healthy Attic life in those days. The words that have come down to us evidence that their speaker was a seer in his day and generation. At this day they owe nothing to their dramatic form, nothing to stage machinery, and the fact that they were spoken under these or those circumstances; All display of art for the gratification of a factitious taste, is silently passed by to come at the least particle of absolute and genuine thought they contain. The reader will be disappointed, however, who looks for traits of a rare wisdom or eloquence—and will have to solace himself, for the most part, with the poet's humanity—and what it was in him to say.— He will discover that, like every genius, he was a solitary liver and worker in his day.

— — We are accustomed to say that the common sense of this age belonged to the seer of the last—as if time gave him any vantage ground—But not so— I see not but Genius must ever take an equal start, and all the generations of men are virtually at a stand-still, for it to come and consider of them. — — Common sense is not so familiar with any truth but Genius will represent it in a strange light to it. Let the seer bring down his broad eye to the most stale and trivial fact—and he will make you believe it a new planet in the sky.

As to criticism, man has never to make allowance to man—there is naught to excuse—naught to bear in mind.

All the past is here present to be tried, let it approve itself if it can.

Prom. Desmo.

Kratos says in the commencement—

"We are come to the far-bounding plain of earth,
"To the Scythian way, to the unapproached solitude.

At the command of Kratos and Bia, Vulcan proceeds to rivet Prometheus to the rock, interspersing consolation like this—

> "—to you well pleased
> "The various robed night will conceal the light;
> "But the sun disperses again coolness & dawn.

When the work of chaining is done Prometheus breaks silence—

> "O divine ether, and ye swift-winged winds,
> "Fountains of rivers, and ye countless smilings
> "Of the ocean waves, thou earth mother of all,
> "And thou all-seeing orb of the sun—I call;
> "Behold me,—what, a God, I suffer at the hands of Gods.

In alternate dialogue with the chorus of ocean nymphs, Prometheus tells the story of his misfortunes, and how his wisdom was derived from the mother of the Gods. — —

> "How the future should be accomplished she foretold,
> "That not according to power, nor according to strength
> "Was the advantage, but those excelling in craft
>   Should prevail.

Accordingly taking with him his mother he sided with Jupiter.

Oceanus too comes with comfort and the promise of intercession with the father; and Prom. describes to the chorus the condition in which his philanthropy found mankind.

— —

> "At first indeed seeing they saw in vain,
> "And hearing they heard not; but like the forms
> "Of dreams, for that long time, vainly confounded
> "All, nor yet knew they dwellings
> "Made of tiles, exposed to the sun, nor wood-work;
> "But underground they dwelt, as puny
> "Ants, in sunless corners of caves.
> "And there was nothing to them, neither of winter
>   any sign,
> "Nor of flower giving spring, nor of fruitful
> "Summer, that was sure; but without knowledge

"They did all, till I taught them the risings
"Of the stars, and their goings down difficult to
    determine.
"And moreover numbers the chief of knowledges
"I invented for them, and the disposition of letters,
"And memory–muse-mother, doer of all things.
"And I first tamed wild animals and made them
"Obedient to the yoke, and that they might be
"Alternate workers with the bodies of men in the
"Severest toils, I harnessed the rein loving horses
"To the car–the ornament of over-wealthy luxury.
"And no other than I invented the sea wandering
"Flaxen-winged vehicles of sailors – –

Next follows the episode of Io–who in her wanderings comes this way. Having related her *past* adventures, she prepares to hear the future from Prom.

                        –"nor pitying
"Comfort me with false stories, for of ills I say
"That the worst is made up words.

In Prometheus' revelation occur some passages of lively narrative.

"And you will come to an insolent river, not falsely
    named;
"Which you may not pass, for it is not easy to ford,
"Till you come to Caucasus itself, highest of
"Mountains; where the river spurts out its tide
"From the very temples; and it is necessary, passing
"Over the star-neighbored summits, to go
"The southern way, where you will come to the
"Man-hating army of the Amazons; who shall one
"Day inhabit Themiscyra, by the Thermodon,
"Where is that rugged tooth of the sea Salmydesia,
"Inhospitable to sailors, stepmother of ships.

When Prom. has insulted Mercury the messenger of Zeus; and the earth begins to rock to the father's thunderbolts–the hero concludes the drama with–

"O revered mother, O ether revolving the
"Common light to all,
"You see me, how unjustly I suffer.

Growth.

We are not apt to remember that we grow. — — It is
curious to reflect how the maiden waiteth patiently,
confiding as the unripe houstonia of the meadow, for the
slow moving years to work their will with her—perfect
and ripen her. — — like it to be fanned by the
wind—watered by the rain—and receive her education at
the hands of nature. — —

These young buds of manhood in the streets
are like buttercups in the meadows—surrendered to
nature as they.

Nov 7th

I was not aware till to-day of a rising and risen
generation.— Children appear to me as raw as the fresh
fungi on a fence rail— By what degrees of consanguinity
is this succulent and rank-growing slip of manhood
related to me? — — What is it but another herb—ranging
all the kingdoms of nature, drawing in sustenance by a
thousand roots and fibres from all soils.

Nov. 8th —39

Laconicism

Prom.'s answer to Io's question who has bound him to
the rock—is a good instance.

Βούλουμα μὲν τὸ δῖον, 'Ηφαίστου δὲ χείρ.

The will indeed of Zeus, of Vulcan the hand.
also

Πταίσας δὲ τῷδε πρός κακῷ, μαθήσεται,

"Οσον τό, τ' ἄρχειν καὶ τὸ δουλούειν δίχα

Such naked speech is the standing aside of words to
make room for thoughts.

Nov. 13th —39

Regret

Make the most of your regrets—never smother your
sorrow but tend and cherish it till it come to have a
separate and integral interest. To regret deeply is to live

afresh. By so doing you will be astonished to find
yourself restored once more to all your emoluments.

Nov. 14th −39
Despondency.
There is nowhere any apology for despondency.
Always there is life—which, rightly lived, implies a divine
satisfaction. I am soothed by the rain drop on the door
sill—every globule that pitches thus confidently from the
eaves to the ground, is my life insurance— Disease and
a rain drop cannot coexist— The east wind is not itself
consumptive, but has enjoyed a rare health from of
old— If a fork or brand stand erect *good is* portended
by it— They are the warrant of universal innocence.

Nov. 19th −39
Farewell
—Light hearted, thoughtless, shall I take my way,
When I to thee this being have resigned,
Well knowing where upon a future day,
With us'rer's craft, more than myself to find.—

Nov. 22nd −39
Linnaeus.
Linnaeus setting out for Lapland, surveys his "comb"
and "spare shirt," "leather breeches," and gauze cap to
keep off gnats," with as much complacency as
Buonaparte would a park of artillery to be used in the
Russian Campaign— His eye is to take in fish, flower,
and bird, quadruped and biped— The quiet bravery of
the man is admirable. These facts have even a *novel*
interest.

Nov 29 −39
Many brave men have there been, thank Fortune, but
I shall never grow brave by comparison. When I
remember myself I shall forget them.

Dec 2nd –39
Bravery.
–A rare landscape immediately suggests a suitable
inhabitant–whose breath shall be its wind–whose moods
its seasons–and to whom it will always be fair. – – To
be chafed and worried, and not as serene as nature–does
not become one whose nature is as steadfast as she. – –
   We do all stand in the front ranks of the battle every
moment of our lives; where there is a brave man there
is the thickest of the fight–there the post of honor– Not
he who procures a substitute to go to Florida is exempt
from service–he gather his laurels in another field. – –
   Waterloo is not the only battle ground– As many and
fatal guns are pointed at my breast now as are contained
in the English arsenals.

{One and one-fourth pages blank}

May 11th 1839.
   "The farmer keeps pace with his crops, and the
revolutions of the seasons; but the merchant with the
fluctuations of trade–consider how they walk in the
streets."

1838.
   "Sometimes I hear the veery's silver clarion; or the
brazen note of the impatient jay–or in secluded woods
the chicadee doles out her scanty notes which sing the
praise of heroes, and set forth the loveliness of virtue
evermore." –Phe-be.

{One-third page blank}

Feb 19th 1838.
   Each summer sound
   Is a summer round.

My *Boots*

Oct 16th 1838

Anon with gaping fearlessness they quaff
The dewy nectar with a natural thirst,
Or wet their leathern lungs where cranberries lurk,
With sweeter wine than Chian, Lesbian, or
    Falernian far.
Theirs was the inward lustre that bespeaks
An open sole—unknowing to exclude
The cheerful day—a worthier glory far
Than that which gilds the outmost rind with
    darkness visible—
Virtues that fast abide through lapse of years,
Rather rubbed in than off.

Noon.

—Straightway dissolved,
Like to the morning mists—or rather like the
    subtler mists of noon—
Stretched I far up the neighboring mountains' sides,
Adown the valleys—through the nether air,
Bathing with fond expansiveness of soul,
The tiniest blade as the sublimest cloud.

— —

What time the bittern, solitary bird,
Hides now her head amid the whispering fern,
And not a paddock vexes all the shore—
Nor feather ruffles the incumbent air,
Save where the wagtail interrupts the noon.

{*Three-fifths page blank*}

{*Back endpaper*}

· 2 ·

Fall 1839–July 27, 1840

TRANSCRIBED 1841

From A Chapter on Bravery—Script. Dec. 1839

Bravery deals not so much in resolute action, as in healthy and assured rest. Its palmy state is a staying at home, and compelling alliance in all directions.

The brave man never heareth the din of war; he is trustful and unsuspecting; so observant of the least trait of good or beautiful, that if you turn toward him the dark side of anything—he will still see only the bright.

One moment of serene and confident life is more glorious than a whole campaign of daring. We should be ready for all issues; not daring to die, but daring to live.— To the brave even danger is an ally.

In their unconscious daily life all are braver than they know. Man slumbers and wakes in his twilight with the confidence of noon day—he is not palsied nor struck dumb by the inexplicable riddle of the universe. A mere surveyor's report or clause in a preemption bill, contains matter of quite extraneous interest, of a subdued but confident tone, evincing such a steadiness in the writer, as would have done wonders at Bunkers hill or Marathon. Where there is the collected eye, there will not fail the effective hand— χεὶρ δ' ὁρᾷ τὸ δράσιμον.—

Science is always brave, for to know is to know good; doubt and danger quail before her eye. What the coward overlooks in his hurry, she calmly scrutinizes, breaking ground like a pioneer for the array of arts in her train.— Cowardice is unscientific—for there cannot

be a science of ignorance– There may be a science of
war–for that advances–but a retreat is rarely well
conducted, if it is–then is it an orderly advance in the
face of circumstances.

If his fortune deserts him, the brave man in pity still
abides by her.

Samuel Johnson and his friend Savage, compelled by
poverty to pass the night in the streets, resolve that they
will stand by their country.

The state of complete manhood is virtue–and virtue
and bravery are one– This truth has long been in the
languages. All the relations of the subject are hinted
at in the derivation and analogies of the Latin words
vir and *virtus*; and the Greek $\alpha\gamma\alpha\theta o\varsigma$ and $\alpha\rho\iota\sigma\tau o\varsigma$. Language
in its settled form is the record of men's second thoughts;
a more faithful utterance than they can momentarily
give. What men say is so sifted and obliged to approve
itself as answering to a common want, that nothing
absolutely frivolous obtains currency in the language.
The analogies of words are never whimsical and
meaningless, but stand for real likenesses– Only the
ethics of mankind, and not of any particular man give
point and vigor to our speech.

The coward was born one day too late, for he has
never overtaken the present hour. He is the younger
son of creation, who now waiteth till the elder decease.
He does not dwell on the earth as though he had a
deed of the land in his pocket–not as another lump
of nature–as imperturbable an occupant as the stones
in the field. He has only rented a few acres of time and
space, and thinks that every accident portends the
expiration of his lease. He is a nonproprietor–a serf–in

his moral economy nomadic—having no fixed abode.
When danger appears he goes abroad and clings to
straws.

Bravery and Cowardice are kindred correlatives with
Knowledge and Ignorance Light and Darkness—Good
and Evil.

If you let a single ray of light through the shutter, it
will go on diffusing itself with out limit till it enlighten
the world, but the shadow that was never so wide at first
as rapidly contracts till it comes to naught. The shadow
of the moon when it passes nearest the sun, is lost in
space ere it can reach our earth to eclipse it. Always the
system shines with uninterrupted light, for as the Sun
is so much larger than any planet, no shadow can travel
far into space. We may bask always in the light of the
system, always may step back out of the shade. No
man's shadow is as large as his body, if the rays make a
right angle with the reflecting surface.— Let our lives be
passed under the equator, with the sun in the meridian.
There is no ill which may not be dissipated like the
dark, if you let in a stronger light upon it. Overcome
evil with good. Practise no such narrow economy as
they, whose bravery amounts to no more light than a
farthing candle, before which most objects cast a shadow
wider than themselves.

It was a conceit of Plutarch, accounting for the
preference given to signs observed on the left hand,
that men may have thought, "things terrestrial and
mortal directly over against heavenly and divine things,
and do conjecture that the things which to us are on the
left hand, the gods send down from their right hand."
If we are not blind, we shall see how a right hand is

stretched over all, as well the unlucky as lucky, and that the ordering soul is only right-handed, distributing with one palm all our fates.

Men have made war from a deeper instinct than peace. War is but the compelling of peace. – –

When the world is declared under martial law, every Esau retakes his birthright, and what there is in him does not fail to appear. He wipes off all old scores and commences a new account. The world is interested to know how any soul will demean itself in so novel a position. But when war too, like commerce and husbandry, gets to be a routine, and men go about it as indented apprentices, the hero degenerates into a marine, and the standing army into a standing jest.

No pains are spared to do honor to the brave soldier. All guilds and corporations are taxed to provide him with fit harness and equipment– His coat must be red as the sunset–or blue as the heavens. Gold or silver –pinchback or copper–solid or superficial–mark him for fortune's favorite. The skill of a city enchaces and tempers his sword blade–the Tyrian dye confounds him with emperors and kings. Wherever he goes, music precedes and prepares the way for him. His life is a holiday and the contagion of his example unhinges the universe. The world puts by work and comes out to stare. He is the one only man. He recognizes no time honored casts and conventions–no fixtures but transfixtures–no governments at length settled on a permanent basis. One tap of the drum sets the political and moral harmonies all ajar. His ethics may well bear comparison with the priest's. He may rally, charge, retreat in an orderly manner–but never flee nor flinch.

Each more melodious note I hear
Brings sad reproach to me,
That I alone afford the ear,
Who would the music be.

The brave man is the sole patron of music; he
recognizes it for his mother tongue; a more mellifluous
and articulate language than words, in comparison with
which speech is recent and temporary. It is his voice.
His language must have the same majestic movement
and cadence, that philosophy assigns to the heavenly
bodies. The steady flux of his thought constitutes time
in music. The universe falls in and keeps pace with it,
which before proceeded singly and discordant. Hence
are poetry and song. When Bravery first grew afraid
and went to war, it took music along with it. The soul
delighted still to hear the echo of its own voice. Especially
the soldier insists on agreement and harmony always.
Indeed, it is that friendship there is in war that makes
it chivalrous and heroic. It was the dim sentiment of a
noble friendship for the purest soul the world has seen,
that gave to Europe a crusading era.

The day of tilts and tournaments has gone by, but no
herald summons us to the tournament of love.

The brave warrior must have harmony if not melody
at any sacrifice. Consider what shifts he makes. There
are the bag-pipe–the gong–the trumpet–the drum–either
the primitive central African or Indian, or the brass
European. Ever since Jerico fell down before a blast of
ram's horns, the martial and musical have gone hand in
hand. – – If the soldier marches to the sack of a town,
he must be preceded by drum and trumpet, which shall
identify his cause with the accordant universe. All woods

and walls echo back his own spirit, and the hostile
territory is then preoccupied for him. He is no longer
insulated but infinitely related and familiar. The roll-call
musters for him all the forces of nature.

All sounds, and more than all silence, do fife and drum
for us. The least creaking doth whet all our senses, and
emit a tremulous light, like the Aurora Borealis, over
things. As polishing expresses the vein in marble and
the grain in wood, so music brings out what of heroic
lurks anywhere.

To the sensitive soul, The universe has its own fixed
measure, which is its measure also, and as a regular
pulse is inseparable from a healthy body, so is its
healthiness dependent on the regularity of its rythm.
In all sounds the soul recognizes its own rythm, and
seeks to express its sympathy by a correspondent
movement of the limbs. When the body marches to the
measure of the soul, then is true courage and invincible
strength.

The coward would reduce this thrilling sphere music
to a universal wail—this melodious chant to a nasal cant.
He thinks to conciliate all hostile influences by compelling
his neighborhood into a partial concord with himself,
but his music is no better than a jingle which is akin
to a jar—jars regularly recurring.

He blows a feeble blast of slender melody, because
nature can have no more sympathy with such a soul,
than it has of cheerful melody in itself. Hence hears he
no accordant note in the universe, and is a coward, or
consciously outcast and deserted man. But the brave
man, without drum or trumpet, compels concord every
where every where by the universality and tunefulness
of his soul.

"Take a metallic plate" says Coleridge, "and strew sand on it; sound a harmonic chord over the sand, and the grains will whirl about in circles, and other geometrical figures, all, as it were, depending on some point relatively at rest. Sound a discord, and every grain will whisk about without any order at all, in no figures, and with no points of rest."

The brave man is such a point of relative rest, over which the soul sounds ever a harmonic chord.

Music is either a sedative or a tonic to the soul. I read that "Plato thinks the gods never gave men music, the science of melody and harmony, for mere delectation or to tickle the ear; but that the discordant parts of the circulations, and beauteous fabric of the soul, and that of it that roves about the body, and many times for want of tune and air, breaks forth into many extravagances and excesses, might be sweetly recalled and artfully wound up to their former consent and agreement."

By dint of wind and stringed instruments the coward endeavours to put the best face on the matter–whistles to keep his courage up.

There are some brave traits related by Plutarch. viz. "Homer acquaints us how Ajax, being to engage in a single combat with Hector, bade the Grecians pray to the gods for him; and while they were at their devotions, he was putting on his armor."

On another occasion a storm arises–"Which as soon as the pilot sees, he falls to his prayers, and invokes his tutelar daemons, but neglects not in the mean time to hold to the rudder, and let down the main yard."

"Homer directs his husbandman, before he either plow or sow; to pray to the terrestrial Jove, and the venerable Ceres, but with his hand upon the plowtail."

Ἀρχὴ γὰρ ὄντως τοῦ νικᾶν τὸ θαρρεῖν.
Verily, to be brave is the beginning of victory.

The Romans "made Fortune sirname to Fortitude,"
for Fortitude is that alchemy that turns all things to good
fortune. The man of fortitude, whom the Latins called
fortis, is no other than that lucky person whom *fors*
favors, or *vir summae fortis*. If we will, every bark may
"carry Caesar and Caesar's fortune" For an impenetrable
shield, stand inside yourself; he was no artist but an
artisan, who first made shields of brass. For armor of
proof, *meâ virtute me involvo*, I wrap myself in my
virtue,

> Tumble me down, and I will sit
> Upon my ruins, smiling yet

{*One-fifth page blank*}

The bravest deed, which for the most part is left quite
out of history, which alone wants the staleness of a deed
done, and the uncertainty of a deed doing, is the life
of a great man. To perform exploits is to be temporarily
bold, as becomes a courage that ebbs and flows, the
soul quite vanquished by its own deed subsiding into
indifference and cowardice, but the exploit of a brave
life consists in its momentary completeness.

{*One-half page blank*}

Friendship– Fall of 1839.

Then first I conceive of a true friendship, when some
rare specimen of manhood presents itself.– It seems the

mission of such to commend virtue to mankind, not by
any imperfect preaching of her word, but by their own
carriage and conduct.– We may then worship moral
beauty without the formality of a religion.

They are some fresher wind that blows–some new
fragrance that breathes. They make the landscape and
the sky for us.

The rules of other intercourse have quite lost their
pertinence when applied to this.

We are one virtue–one truth–one beauty. All nature
is our satellite, whose light is dull and reflected– She is
subaltern to us–an episode to our poem–but we are
primary and radiate light and heat to the system.

I am only introduced once again to myself.
Conversation–contact–familiarity–are the steps to
it–and instruments of it, but it is most perfect when
these are done, and distance and time oppose no barrier.

I need not ask any man to be my friend, more than
the sun the earth to be attracted by him,–it is not his
to give, nor mine to receive. I cannot pardon my enemy
let him pardon himself.

Commonly we degrade Love and Friendship by
presenting them under the aspect of a trivial dualism.

What matter a few words more or less with my
friend–with all mankind–they will still be my friends
in spite of themselves. Let them stand aloof if they
can – – As though the most formidable distance could
rob me of any real sympathy or advantage. No–when
such interests are at stake–time, and distance, and
difference–fall into their own places.

But alas to be actually separated from that parcel of heaven—we call our friend—with the suspicion that we shall no more meet in nature—is source enough for all the elegies that ever were written. But the true remedy will be to recover our friend again piecemeal, wherever we can find a feature, as Aeetes gathered up the members of his son which Medea had strewn in her path.

The more complete our sympathy, the more our senses are struck dumb, and we are repressed by a delicate respect—so that to indifferent eyes we are least his friend, because no vulgar symbols pass between us.— On after thought perhaps we come to fear that we have been the losers by such seeming indifference—but in truth that which withholds us is the bond between us.

My friend will be as much better than my-self as my aspiration is beyond my attainment.

———————

This is most serene autumn weather— The chirp of crickets may be heard at noon over all the land— As in summer they are heard only at nightfall, so now by their incessant chirp they usher in the evening of the year.— The lively decay of autumn promises as infinite duration and freshness, as the green leaves of spring.

{*Two-thirds page blank*}

Jan. 10th 1840.

The Fisher's son.

I know the world where land and water meet,
By yonder hill abutting on the main,
One while I hear the waves incessant beat,
Then turning round survey the land again.

Within a humble cot that looks to sea
Daily I breathe this curious warm life,
Beneath a friendly havens sheltering lea
My noiseless day with myst'ry still is rife.

'Tis here, they say, my simple life began,
And easy credit to the tale I lend,
For well I know 'tis here I am a man,
But who will simply tell me of the end?

These eyes fresh opened spied the far off sea,
Which like a silent god father did stand,
Nor uttered one explaining word to me—
But introduced straight god mother Land.

And yonder still stretches that silent main,
With many glancing ships besprinkled oer,
And earnest still I gaze and gaze again
Upon the self same waves and friendly shore.

Till like a watery humor on the eye
It still appears whichever way I turn,
Its silent waste and mute oerarching sky
With close-shut eyes I clearly still discern.

And yet with lingering doubt I haste each morn
To see if ocean still my gaze will greet,
And with each day once more to life am born,
And tread once more the earth with infant feet.

—

My years are like a stroll upon the beach,
As near the ocean's edge as I can go;
My tardy steps its waves do oft o'erreach;
Sometimes I stay to let them over flow.

Infinite work my hands find there to do,
Gathering the relics which the waves up cast;
Each storm doth scour the deep for something new,
And every time the strangest is the last.

My sole employment 'tis and scrupulous care,
To place my gains beyond the reach of tides,
Each smoother pebble and each shell more rare,
Which ocean kindly to my hand confides.

I have no fellow laborer on the shore,
They scorn the strand who sail upon the sea,
Sometimes I think the ocean they've sailed o'er
Is deeper known upon the strand to me.

The middle sea can show no crimson dulse,
Its deeper waves cast up no pearles to view,
Along the shore my hand is on its pulse
Whose feeble beat is elsewhere felt by few.

My neighbors come sometimes with lumb'ring carts,
As it would seem, my pleasant toil to share,
But straightway take their loads to distant marts,
For only weeds and ballast are their care.

———

'Tis by some strange coincidence if I
Make common cause with ocean when he storms,
Who can so well support a separate sky,
And people it with multitude of forms.

Oft in the stillness of the night I hear
Some restless bird presage the coming din,
And distant murmurs faintly strike my ear
From some bold bluff projecting far within.

My stillest depths straightway do inly heave
More genially than rests the summer's calm,
The howling winds through my soul's cordage grieve,
Till every shelf and ledge gives the alarm.

Far from the shore the swelling billows rise,
And gathering strength come rolling to the land,
And as each waves retires, and murmur dies,
I straight pursue upon the streaming sand.

Till the returning surge with gathered strength
Compels once more the backward way to take,
And creeping up the beach a cable's length,
In many a thirsty hollow leaves a lake.

Oft as some ruling star my tide has swelled
The sea can scarcely brag more wrecks than I,
Ere other influence my waves has quelled
The staunchest bark that floats is high and dry.

{*One-fifth page blank*}

{*One leaf missing*}

Jan 19th 1840

By a strong liking we prevail
Against the stoutest fort,
At length the stoutest heart will quail,
And our alliance court

Jan. 26th 1840

Friends.

They are like air bubbles on water hastening to flow together.

History tells of Orestes and Pylades–Damon & Pythias–but why should not we put to shame those old reserved worthies by a community of such?

Constantly, as it were through a remote skylight, I have glimpses of a serene friendship-land–and know the better why brooks murmur and violets grow.

This conjunction of souls, like waves which meet and break, subsides also backward over things, and gives all a fresh aspect.

I would live henceforth with some gentle soul such a life as may be conceived–double for variety, single for harmony. Two only that we might admire at our

oneness—one because indivisible. Such community to be
a pledge of holy living— How could aught unworthy be
admitted into our society? To listen with one ear to each
summer sound—to behold with one eye each summer
scene—our visual rays so to meet and mingle at the
object as to be one bent and doubled— With two tongues
to be wearied, and thought to spring ceaselessly from a
double fountain.

Jan. —40
Poetry.
No definition of poetry is adequate unless it be poetry
itself. The most accurate analysis by the rarest wisdom
is yet insufficient—and the poet will instantly prove it
false, by setting aside its requisitions – – It is indeed
all that we do not know.

The poet does not need to see how meadows are
something else than earth—grass, and water, but how
they are thus much— He does not need discover that
potatoe blows are as beautiful as violets'—as the farmer
thinks—but only how they are so much as potatoe blows.

The poem is drawn out from under the feet of the
poet—his whole weight has rested on this ground.

It has a logic more severe than the logician's.

You might as well think to go in pursuit of the
rainbow, and embrace it on the next hill—as to embrace
the whole of poetry even in thought.
The best book is only an advertisment of it—such as
is sometimes sewed in with its cover.

Its eccentric and unexplored orbit embraces the
system.

Jan 27th –40

What a tame life we are living—how little heroic it is.
Let us devise never so perfect a system of living, and
straightway the soul leaves it to shuffle along its own
way alone. It is easy enough to establish a durable and
harmonious routine—immediately all parts of nature
consent to it. The sun dial points to the noon mark—and
the sun rises and sets to it. Our neighborhood is never
fatally obstinate when such a scheme is to be instituted;
but forthwith all men lend a hand—and ring the bell—and
find fuel and lights—put by work and don their best
garments—with an earnest conformity which matches
the operations of nature. There is always a present and
extant life which all combine to uphold—though its
insufficiency is manifest enough. Still the sing-song
goes on.

{*One-fifth page blank*}

{*Two leaves missing*}

Jan 29th –40

A friend in history looks like some premature soul.
– The nearest approach to a community of love in these
days is like the distant breaking of waves on the seashore.
An ocean there must be for it washes our beach.
This alone do all men sail for—trade for—plough
for—preach for—fight for.

Aeschylus.
The Greeks, as the Southerns generally, expressed
themselves with more facility than we in distinct and
lively images, and as to the grace and completeness with
which they treated the subjects suited to their genius
they must be allowed to retain their ancient supremacy.

But a rugged and uncouth array of thought, though
never so modern, may rout them at any moment. It
remains for other than Greeks to write the literature of
the next century.

Aeschylus had a clear eye for the commonest things.
His genius was only an enlarged common sense.

He adverts with chaste severity to all natural facts.
His sublimity is Greek sincerity and simpleness—naked
wonder which mythology had not helped to explain.

Tydeus' shield had for device

   "An artificial heaven blazing with stars;
   "A bright full moon in the midst of the shield,
   "Eldest of stars, eye of night, is prominent.

The Greeks were stern but simple children in their
literature. We have gained nothing by the few ages which
we have the start of them. This universal wondering at
those old men is as if a matured grown person should
discover that the aspirations of his youth argued a
diviner life than the contented wisdom of his manhood.

He is competent to express any of the common manly
feelings. If his hero is to make a boast, it does not lack
fullness—it is as boastful as could be desired—he has a
flexible mouth, and can fill it readily with strong round
words—so that you will say the man's speech wants
nothing—he has left nothing unsaid, but he has actually
wiped his lips of it.

Whatever the common eye sees at all and expresses as
best it may—he sees uncommonly and describes with
rare completeness— The multitudes that thronged the
theatre could no doubt go along with him to the end.
The Greeks had no transcendent geniuses like Milton
and Shakespear—whose merit only posterity could fully
appreciate

The social condition of genius is the same in all ages.
Aeschylus was undoubtedly alone and without sympathy
in his simple reverence for the mystery of the universe.

————————

Criticism on Aulus Persius Flaccus.

Feb. 10th 1840.

{*One-fifth page blank*}

Feb. 11th –40

"Truth" says Lord Bacon, "may perhaps come to
the price of a pearl, that sheweth best by day; but it will
not rise to the price of a diamond or carbuncle, which
sheweth best in varied lights." Like the pearl, truth
shines with a steady but pale light which invites to
introspection–it is intrinsically bright–not accidentally
as the diamond. We seem to behold its rear always–as
though it were not coming toward us but retiring from
us. Its light is not reflected this way, but we see the
sombre and wrong side of its rays. As the dust in his
beams makes known that the sun shines.

Falsehoods that glare and dazzle are sloped toward us,
reflecting full in our faces even the light of the sun–wait
till sunset or go round them, and the falsity will be
apparent.

It is never enough that our life is an easy one–we
must live on the stretch. Not be satisfied with a tame and

{*Two leaves missing*}

undisturbed round of weeks and days–but retire to our
rest like soldiers on the eve of a battle, looking forward
with ardor to the strenuous sortie of the morrow. "Sit not

down in the popular seats and common level of virtues,
but endeavor to make them heroical. Offer not only
peace offerings but holocausts unto God." To the brave
soldier the rust and leisure of peace are harder than the
fatigues of war. As our bodies court physical encounters,
and languish in the mild and even climate of the tropics,
so our souls thrive best on unrest and discontent.

He enjoys true leisure–who has time to improve
his soul's estate.

{Two-fifths page blank}

Feb. 12th –40
Opposition is so strong a likeness as to remind us
of the difference.

Truth has properly no opposite for nothing gets so far
up on the other side as to be opposite– She looks
broadcast over the field and sees no opponent.

The ring-leader of the mob will soonest be admitted
into the councils of state.

Knavery is more foolish than folly–for that half
knowing its own foolishness it still persists. The knave
has reduced folly to a system–is the prudent common
sense fool– The witling has the simplicity and directness
of genius–is the inspired fool. His incomprehensible
ravings become the creed of the dishonest of a succeeding
era.

{One-fifth page blank}

Feb. 13th –40
An act of integrity is to an act of duty what the
French verb *etre* is to *devoir*. Duty is *ce que devrait etre*

Duty belongs to the understanding–but Genius
is not dutiful–the highest talent is dutiful.– Goodness
results from the wisest use of talent.

The perfect man has both genius and talent–the one
is his head–the other his foot–by one he is–by the
other he lives.

The unconsciousness of man–is the consciousness of
God–the end of the world.

The very thrills of Genius are disorganizing The
body is never quite acclimated to *its* atmosphere–but
how often succumbs and goes into a decline!

{*One-fourth page blank*}

Feb. 14th –40

Beauty lives by rhymes. Double a deformity is a
beauty. Draw this blunt quill over the paper, and fold it
once transversely to the line–pressing it suddenly before
the ink dries–and a delicately shaded and regular
figure is the result, which art cannot surpass.

A very meagre natural history suffices to make me
a child–only their names and genealogy make me
love fishes. I would know even the number of their fin
rays–and how many scales compose the lateral line.
I fancy I am amphibious and swim in all the brooks and
pools in the neighborhood, with the perch and bream,
or doze under the pads of our river amid the winding
aisles and corridors formed by their stems, with the
stately pickerel.

I am the wiser in respect to all knowledges, and the
better qualified for all fortunes, for knowing that there is
a minnow in the brook– Methink I have need even
of his sympathy–and to be his fellow in a degree– I do
like him sometimes when he balances himself for an
hour over the yellow floor of his basin.

Feb. 15 –40

The good seem to inhale a more generous atmosphere
–and be bathed in a more precious light–than other men.
Accordingly Virgil describes the *Sedes beatas* thus–
    –Largior hic campos aether et lumine vestit
    Purpureo: Solemque suum, sua sidera nōrunt.

Feb. 16 –40

Divination is prospective memory.

There is a kindred principle at the bottom of all
affinities– The magnet cultivates a steady friendship
with the pole–all bodies with all others. The friendliness
of nature is that goddess Ceres–who presides over
every sowing and harvest, and we bless the same in sun
& rain. The seed in the ground tarries for a season
with its genial friends there–all the earths–and grasses
–and minerals are its hosts who entertain it hospitably
–and plenteous crops and teeming wagons are the result.

Feb. 18 –40

All romance is grounded on friendship– What is this
rural–this pastoral–this poetical life but its invention?
Does not the moon shine for Endymion? Smooth
pastures and mild airs are for some Coridon and Phyllis
– Paradise belongs to Adam and Eve. Platos republic
is governed by Platonic love.

Feb. 20th –40

The cowards' hope is suspicion–the hero's doubt–a
sort of hope. The gods neither hope nor doubt.

{*One-fifth page blank*}

Feb. 22nd 40

The river is unusually high owing to the melting of
the snow. Men go in boats over their gardens and potatoe
fields–and all the children in the village are on tiptoe
to see whose fence will be carried away next. Great
numbers of muskrats, which have been driven out of
their holes by the water, are killed by the sportsmen. – –

They are to us instead of the beaver. The wind from
over the meadows is laden with a strong scent of musk,
and by its racy freshness advertises us of an unexplored
wildness. Those back woods are not far off. I am
affected by the sight of their cabins of mud and grass
–raised four or five feet, along the river, as when I read
of the pyramids, or the barrows of Asia.

People step brisker in the street for this unusual
movement of the waters. You seem to hear the roar of a
water fall and the din of factories where the river
breaks over the road.

Who would have thought that a few feet might not
have been spared from the trunks of most trees?– such
as grow in the meadows and are now surrounded by
that depth of water have a dwarfish appearance. No
matter whether they are longer or shorter–they are now
equally out of proportion.

{*Three-fourths page blank*}

Feb. 24th –40

The Freshet.
– – A stir is on the Worc'ter hills,
And Nobscott too the valley fills–
Where scarce you'd fill an acorn cup
In summer when the sun was up,
No more you'll find a cup at all,
But in its place a waterfall.

Oh that the moon were in conjunction
To the dry land's extremest unction,
Till every dyke and pier were flooded,
And all the land with islands studded,
For once to teach all human kind,
Both those that plough and those that grind,
There is no fixture in the land,
But all unstable is as sand.

– –

The river swelleth more and more,
Like some sweet influence stealing o'er
The passive town; and for awhile
Each tussuck makes a tiny isle,
Where, on some friendly Ararat,
Resteth the weary water rat.

No ripple shows Musketaquid,
Her very current e'en is hid,
As deepest souls do calmest rest
When thoughts are swelling in the breast;
And she that in the summer's drought
Doth make a rippling and a rout,
Sleeps from Nawshawtuct to the cliff,
Unruffled by a single skiff;
So like a deep and placid mind
Whose currents underneath it wind–
For by a thousand distant hills
The louder roar a thousand rills,
And many a spring which now is dumb,
And many a stream with smothered hum,
Doth faster well and swifter glide
Though buried deep beneath the tide.

Our village shows a rural Venice,
Its broad lagunes where yonder fen is,
Far lovelier than the Bay of Naples
Yon placid cove amid the maples,
And in my neighbor's field of corn
I recognise the Golden Horn.

Here nature taught from year to year,
When only red men came to hear,
Methinks 'twas in this school of art
Venice and Naples learned their part,
But still their mistress, to my mind,
Her young disciples leaves behind.

{*Seven-eighths page blank*}

Feb. 26th –40

The most important events make no stir on their
first taking place–nor indeed in their effects directly.
They seem hedged about by secresy. It is concussion
–or the rushing together of air to fill a vacuum–which
makes a noise. The great events to which all things
consent, and for which they have prepared the way,
produce no explosion, for they are gradual, and create
no vacuum which requires to be suddenly filled. As a
birth takes place in silence, and is whispered about the
neighborhood; but an assassination which is at war with
the constitution of things creates a tumult immediately.

Corn grows in the night.

Feb. 27th –40

Some geniuses seem to hover in the horizon like
heat lightening–which is not accompanied with
fertilizing rain to us, but we are obliged to rest contented
with the belief that it is purifying the air somewhere.

Others make known their presence by their effects
–like that vivid lightening which is accompanied by
copious rain and thunder, and though it clears our
atmosphere, sometimes destroys our lives.

Others still impart a steady and harmless light at
once to large tracts–as the Aurora Borealis–and this

phenomenon is hardest to be accounted for–some thinking it to be a reflection of the polar splendor–others a subtle fluid which pervades all things, and tends always to the zenith.

All are agreed that these are equally electrical phenomena–as some clever persons have shown by drawing a spark with their knuckles. Modern philosophy thinks it has drawn down lightening from the clouds.

{*One-fourth page blank*}

Feb. 28th –40
On the death of a friend, we should consider that the fates through confidence have devolved on us the task of a double living–that we have henceforth to fulfil the promise of our friend's life also, in our own, to the world.

" 29 " –40
A friend advises by his whole behavior, and never condescends to particulars–another chides away a fault –he loves it away. While he sees the other's error, he is silently conscious of it, and only the more loves truth himself; and assists his friend in loving it–till the fault is expelled and gently extinguished.

March 2nd –40
Love is the burden of all natures odes–the song of the birds is an epithalamium–a hymeneal. The marriage of the flowers spots the meadows and fringes the hedges with pearls and diamonds. In the deep water, in the high air, in woods and pastures, and the bowels of the earth, this is the employment and condition of all things.

March 4th –40

I learned to-day that my ornithology had done me no
service– The birds I heard, which fortunately did not
come within the scope of my science–sung as freshly as
if it had been the first morning of creation, and had
for background to their song an untrodden wilderness
–stretching through many a Carolina and Mexico of
the soul.

March 6th –40

There is no delay in answering great questions–for
them all things have an answer ready– The Pythian
priestess gave her answers instantly, and ofttimes before
the questions were fairly propounded. Great topics
do not wait for past or future to be determined–but the
state of the crops or Brighton market no bird concerns
itself about.

March 8th 40

The wind shifts from northeast and east, to north-west
and south, and every icicle which has tinkled on the
meadow grass so long–trickles down its stem and seeks
its water level unerringly with a million comrades.
In the ponds the ice cracks with a busy and inspiriting
din–and down the larger streams is whirled, grating
hoarsely and crashing its way along–which was so
lately a firm field for the woodman's team and the
fox–sometimes with the tracks of the skaters still fresh
upon it–and the holes cut for pickerel. Town committees
inspect the bridges and causeways–as if by mere
eye-force to intercede with the ice, and save the treasury.

In the brooks the slight grating sound of small cakes
of ice floating with various speed, is full of content and
promise, and where the water gurgles under a natural

bridge you may hear these hasty rafts hold conversation
in an under tone.

Every rill is a channel for the juices of the meadow.
Last years grasses and flower stalks have been steeped
in rain and snow, and now the brooks flow with meadow
tea–thoroughwort mint, flagroot and pennyroyal, all
at one draught.

In the ponds the sun makes incroachments around
the edges first, as ice melts in a kettle on the fire–darting
his rays through this crevice; and preparing the deep
water to act simultaneously on the under side.

{*Three-fifths page blank*}

– 1840

Two years and twenty now have flown—
Their meanness time away has flung,
These limbs to man's estate have grown,
But cannot claim a manly tongue.

Amidst such boundless wealth without
I only still am poor within;
The birds have sung their summer out,
But still my spring does not begin.

In vain I see the morning rise,
In vain observe the western blaze,
Who idly look to other skies,
Expecting life by other ways.

The sparrow sings at earliest dawn
Building her nest without delay;
All things are ripe to hear her song,
And now arrives the perfect day.

– –

Shall I then wait the Autumn wind
Compelled to seek a milder ray,
And leave no empty nest behind,
No wood still echoing to my lay?

March 16 —40

The cabins of the settlers are the points whence
radiate these rays of green, and yellow and russet over
the landscape—out of these go the axes and spades with
which the landscape is painted. How much is the
Indian summer and the budding of spring related to
the cottage? Have not the flight of the crow and the
gyrations of the hawk a reference to that roof?

The ducks alight at this season on the windward
side of the river—in the smooth water—and swim about
by twos and threes, pluming themselves and diving
to peck at the root of the lily and the cranberries which
the frost has not loosened. It is impossible to approach
them within gunshot when they are accompanied by the
gull, which rises sooner and makes them restless— They
fly to windward first in order to get under weigh, and
are more easily reached by the shot if approached on
that side. When preparing to fly they swim about with
their heads erect, and then gliding along a few feet
with their bodies just touching the surface, rise heavily
with much splashing and fly low at first if not suddenly
aroused, but otherwise rise directly to survey the
danger. The cunning sportsman is not in haste to
desert his position, but waits to ascertain if having got
themselves into flying trim, they will not return over
the ground in their course to a new resting place.

March 20th —40

In society all the inspiration of my lonely hours
seems to flow back on me, and then first have expression.
Love never degrades its votaries—but lifts them up to

higher walks of being–they *over-look* one another– All
other charities are swallowed up in this–it is gift and
reward both.

We will have no vulgar Cupid for a go-between, to
make us the playthings of each-other–but rather
cultivate an irreconcilable hatred in stead of this

March 21st –40

The world is a fit theater to-day in which any part
may be acted– There is this moment proposed to me
each kind of life that men lead any where–or that
imagination can paint. By another spring I may be a
mail carrier in Peru–or a South African planter–or
a Siberian exile–or a Greenland whaler, or a settler on
the Columbia river–or a Canton merchant–or a soldier
in Florida–or a mackerel fisher off Cape Sable – – or a
Robinson Crusoe in the Pacific–or a silent navigator
of any sea– So wide is the choice of parts–what a pity if
the part of Hamlet be left out!

I am freer than any planet– No complaint reaches
round the world. I can move away from public opinion
–from government–from religion–from education–from
society. Shall I be reckoned a rateable poll in the
county of Middlesex–or be rated at one spear under the
palm trees of Guinea? Shall I raise corn and potatoes
in Massachusetts–or figs and olives in Asia Minor?
Sit out the day in my office in State Street–or ride it out
on the steppes of Tartary?

For my Brobdinag I may sail to Patagonia–for
my Lilliput to Lapland. In Arabia and Persia, my
day's adventures will surpass the Arabian-nights
entertainments. I may be a logger on the head waters
of the Penobscott, to be treated in fable hereafter as an
amphibious river god–and to have as sounding a name

as Triton— Carry firs from Nootka to China—and so
be more renowned than Jason and his golden fleece—or
go on a South Sea exploring expedition to be hereafter
recounted along with the periplus of Hanno. I may
be Marco Polo or Mandeville and find my Cathay beyond
the Great lakes.

These are but few of my chances.

Thank fortune we are not rooted to the soil and here
is not all the world. The buckeye does not grow in
New England—the mocking bird is rarely heard here.
Why not keep pace with the day and not allow of a
sunset—nor fall behind the summer and the migrations
of birds. Shall we not compete with the buffalo who
keeps pace with the seasons—cropping the pastures of
the Colorado till a greener and sweeter grass awaits him
by the Yellowstone. The wild goose is more a cosmopolite
than we—he breaks his fast in Canada—takes a luncheon
in the Susquehannah—and plumes himself for the night
in a Louisiana bayou. The pigeon carries an acorn in
his crop from the king of Holand's to Mason & Dixon's
line. Yet we think if rail fences are pulled down and
stone walls set up on our farms—bounds are henceforth
set to our lives and our fates decided. If you are chosen
town clerk forsooth you cant go to Terra del Fuego
this summer.

But what of all this, a man may gather his limbs
snugly within the shell of a mamoth squash; with
his back to the north eastern boundary; and not be
unusually straightened after all.

Our limbs indeed have room enough but it is our souls
that rust in a corner. Let us migrate interiorly without
intermission, and pitch our tent each day nearer the
western horizon— The really fertile soils and luxuriant

prairies lie on this side the Aleghanies— There has
been no Hanno of the Affections— Their domain is
untravelled ground to the Moguls' dominions.

March 22nd —40

While I bask in the sun on the shores of Walden
pond, by this heat and this rustle I am absolved from all
obligation to the past— The council of nations may
reconsider their votes—the grating of a pebble annuls
them.

" 27th —40

How many are now standing on the European coast
—whom another spring will find located on the Red
river—or Wisconsin— To-day we live an antediluvian
life on our quiet homesteads—and tomorrow are
transported to the turmoil and bustle of a crusading era.

Think how finite after all the known world is. Money
coined at Philadelphia is a legal tender over how much
of it— You may carry ship biscuit—beef and pork
—quite round to the place you set out from.— England
sends her felons to the other side for safe keeping and
convenience.

{*Three-fifths page blank*}

March 30th —40

Pray what things interest me at present?
A long soaking rain—the drops trickling down the
stubble—while I lay drenched on a last year's bed of wild
oats, by the side of some bare hill, ruminating. These
things are of moment— To watch this crystal globe just
sent from heaven to associate with me—while these
clouds and this sombre drizzling weather shut all in—we

two draw nearer and know one another. The gathering
in of the clouds with the last rush and dying breath
of the wind, and then the regular dripping of twigs and
leaves the country o'er—the impression of inward
comfort and sociableness—the drenched stubble and
trees that drop beads on you as you pass—their dim
outline seen through the rain on all sides drooping in
sympathy with yourself— These are my undisputed
territory. This is Nature's English comfort. The birds
draw closer and are more familiar under the thick
foliage—composing new pieces on their roosts for the
sunshine.

{*One leaf missing*}

April 4th –40
  We look to windward for fair weather.

April 8th –40
  How shall I help myself? By withdrawing into
the garret, and associating with spiders and mice
—determining to meet myself face to face sooner or later.
Completely silent and attentive I will be this hour, and
the next, and forever. – – The most positive life that
history notices has been a constant retiring out of
life—a wiping ones' hands of it—seeing how mean it is,
and having nothing to do with it.

" 9th –40
  I read in Cudworth how "Origen determines, that
the stars do not make but signify; and that the heavens
are a kind of Divine volume, in whose characters they
that are skilled may read or spell out human events."
Nothing can be truer, and yet Astrology is possible.
  Men seem to be just on the point of discerning a truth
when the imposition is greatest.

April 17th −40
Farewell etiquette! My neighbor inhabits a hollow
sycamore, and I a beech tree. What then becomes
of morning calls with cards—and deference paid to
door knockers and front entries—and presiding at one's
own table?

" 19th −40
The infinite bustle of nature of a summer's noon,
or her infinite silence of a summer's night—gives
utterance to no dogma. They do not say to us even with
a seer's assurance, that this or that law is immutable
—and so ever and only can the universe exist. But they
are the indifferent occasion for all things—and the
annulment of all laws.

{*One-fifth page blank*}

April 20th −40.
The universe will not wait to be explained. Whoever
seriously attempts a theory of it is already behind his
age. His yea has reserved no nay for the morrow
The wisest solution is no better than dissolution
— Already the seer *whispers* his *convictions* to bare
walls—no audience in the land can attend to them.

An early morning walk is a blessing for the whole day
— To my neighbors who have risen in mist and rain I
tell of that clear sunrise and the singing of birds as
some traditionary mythus. I look back to those fresh but
now remote hours as to the old dawn of time—when a
solid and blooming health reigned—and every deed
was simple and heroic.

{*One-third page blank*}

April 22nd –40

Thales was the first of the Greeks who taught that
souls are immortal–and it takes equal wisdom to discern
this old fact to-day. What the first philosopher taught
the last will have to repeat– The *world* makes no
progress.

I cannot turn on my heel in a carpeted room–what a
gap in the morning is a breakfast–a supper supersedes
the sunset.

Methinks I hear the Rance des Vaches and shall
soon be tempted to desert.

Will not one thick garment suffice for three thin
ones? Thus I shall be less compound, and can lay my
hand on myself in the dark.

{*One-third page blank*}

{*Two leaves missing*}

May 14th –40

A kind act or gift lays us under obligation not so
much to the giver as to Truth and Love. We must then
be truer and kinder ourselves– Just in proportion
to our sense of the kindness–and pleasure at it–is the
debt paid.– What is it to be *grateful* but to be *gratified*
–to be *pleased?*

The nobly poor will dissolve all obligations by nobly
accepting a kindness.

When we are not sensible of kindness we run in debt
–and are bankrupt. Not to be pleased by generous
deeds at any time, but to sit crabbedly silent in a corner
–is imprisonment for debt– It is to see the world
through a grating. Not to let the light of virtuous actions

shine on us at all times—through every crevice, is to
live in a dungeon.

War is the sympathy of concussion— We would fain
rub one against another—its rub may be friction merely
but it would rather be titillation. We discover in the
quietest scenes how faithfully war has copied the
moods of peace. Men do not peep into heaven but they
see embattled hosts there. Miltons' heaven was a camp.
When the sun bursts through the morning fog I seem
to hear the din of war louder than when his Chariot
thundered on the plains of Troy. Every man is a warrior
when he aspires. He marches on his post. The soldier
is the practical idealist—he has no sympathy with
matter, he revels in the annihilation of it. So do we all
at times. When a freshet destroys the works of man—or a
fire consumes them—or a Lisbon earthquake shakes
them down—our sympathy with persons is swallowed up
in a wider sympathy with the universe. A crash is apt
to grate agreeably on our ears.

Let not the faithful sorrow that he has no ear for
the more fickle harmonies of creation, if he is awake to
the slower measure of virtue and truth. If his pulse
does not beat in unison with the musician's quips and
turns, it accords with the pulse beat of the ages.

{*Four-fifths page blank*}

June 11th —40
We had appointed Saturday Aug. 31st 1839 for
the commencement of our White Mountain expedition
— We awake to a warm drizzling rain which threatens
delay to our plans, but at length the leaves and grass

are dried, and it comes out a mild afternoon, of such a
sober serenity and freshness that nature herself seems
maturing some greater scheme of her own. All things
wear the aspect of a fertile idleness– It is the eventide of
the soul. After this long dripping and oozing from
every pore–nature begins to respire again more healthily
than ever. So with a vigorous shove we launch our
boat from the bank, while the flags and bullrushes
curtsy a God-speed–and drop silently down the stream.–
As if we had launched our bark in the sluggish current
of our thoughts, and were bound nowhither.

Gradually the village murmur subsides–as when one
falls into a placid dream and on its Lethe tide is floated
from the past into the future.–   or as silently as
fresh thoughts awaken us to new morning or evening
light

Our boat was built like a fisherman's dory–with
thole pins for four oars. Below it was green with a
border of blue–as if out of courtesy the green sea and
the blue heavens. It was well calculated for service
–but of consequence difficult to be dragged over shoal
places or carried round falls.–

A boat should have a sort of life and independence of
its own– It is a sort of amphibious animal–a creature
of two elements–a fish to swim and a bird to fly–related
by one half of its structure to some swift and shapely
fish–and by the other to some strong winged and
graceful bird. The fins of the fish will tell where to set
the oars–and the tail give some hint for the form and
position of the rudder. And so may we learn where there
should be the greatest breadth of beam and depth in the
hold. The bird will show how to rig and trim the sails,
and what form to give to the prow that it may ballance
the boat, and divide the air and water best.

The boat took to the water–from of old there had
been a tacit league struck between these two–and now it
gladly availed itself of the old law that the heavier
shall float the lighter.

Two masts we had provided, one to serve for a tent
pole at night–and likewise other slender poles that we
might exchange the tedium of rowing for poling in
shallow reaches. At night we lay on a buffalo skin under
a tent of drilled cotton–eight feet high and as many
in diameter–which effectually defend from dampness
– So short a step is it from tiled roofs to drilled cotton
–from carpeted floors–to a buffalo skin.–

There were a few berries left still on the hills,
hanging with brave content by the slenderest threads.

As the night stole over such a freshness stole across
the meadow that every blade of cut grass seemed to
teem with life.

We stole noiselessly down the stream, occasionally
driving a pickerel from the covert of the pads–or a
bream from her nest–and the small green bittern would
now and then sail away on sluggish wings from some
recess of the Shore. With its patient study by rocks and
sandy capes, has it wrested the whole of her secret
from nature yet? It has looked out from its dull eye
for so long, standing on one leg–on moon and stars
sparkling through silence and dark–and now what a
rich experience is its– What says it of stagnant pools
–and reeds–and damp night fogs? It would be worth
while to look in the eye which has been open and
seeing at such hours and in such solitudes.

When I behold that dull yellowish green I wonder
if my own soul is not a bright invisible green. I would
fain lay my eye side by side with its–and learn of it.

End of my Journal of 546 ps

June 14th 1840

—Λόγος τοῦ ᾽έργου ᾽άνευ ὕλης.— Arist. Def. Art.

———

῾Ο χρή σε νοεῖν νόου ᾽άνθει. Chaldaic Oracles.

———

᾽Εγώ εἰμι πᾶν τὸ γεγονὸς, καὶ ᾽όν, καὶ ἐσόμενον, καὶ τὸν ἐμὸν πέπλον οὐδείς πω θνητὸς απεκάλυψεν.
Inscription upon the temple at Sais.

———

Plotinus aimed at—"ἐπαφὴν, and παρουσίαν ἐπιστήμης κρείττονα, and τὸ ἑαυτῶν κέντρον τῷ οἷον πάντων κέντρῳ συνάπτειν."

———

Μέλλει τὸ θεῖον δ᾽ ἐστὶ τοιοῦτον φύσει.
Eurip. in Orest. v. 420

———

"The right Reason is in part divine, in part human; the second can be expressed, but no language can translate the first."

Empedocles.

————————

June 14th 1840

—"in glory and in joy,
Behind his plough, upon the mountain side"!

I seemed to see the woods wave on a hundred mountains, as I read these lines, and the distant rustling of their leaves reached my ear.

June 15th 1840
I stood by the river today considering the forms of the elms reflected in the water. For every oak and

birch too, growing on the hill top, as well as for elms
and willows, there is a graceful etherial tree making
down from the roots—as it were the original idea of the
tree, and sometimes nature in high tides brings her
mirror to its foot and makes it visible— Anxious nature
sometimes reflects from pools and puddles the objects
which our grovelling senses may fail to see relieved
against the sky, with the pure ether for background.

It would be well if we saw ourselves as in perspective
always—impressed with distinct outline on the sky—side
by side with the shrubs on the river's brim. So let our
life stand to heaven as some fair sun lit tree against the
western horizon, and by sunrise be planted on some
eastern hill to glisten in the first rays of the dawn.

Why always insist that men incline to the moral side
of their being—? Our life is not all moral. Surely, its
actual phenomena deserve to be studied impartially. The
science of Human Nature has never been attempted,
as the science of nature has— The dry light has never
shone on it. Neither physics nor metaphysics have
touched it.
  We have not yet met with a sonnet, genial and
affectionate, to prophane swearing—breaking on the still
night air, perhaps, like the hoarse croak of some bird.
Noxious weeds and stagnant waters have their lovers,
—and the utterer of oaths must have honied lips, and be
another Attic bee after a fashion—for only prevalent
and essential harmony and beauty can employ the laws
of Sound and of light.

June 16th 1840

The river down which we glided for that long
afternoon was like a clear drop of dew with the heavens
and the landscape reflected in it. And as evening drew

on faint purple clouds began to be reflected in its water
—and the cow-bells tinkled louder and more incessantly
on the banks—and like shy water rats we stole along
near the shore, looking out for a place to pitch our camp.

It seems insensibly to grow lighter as night shuts in
—the farthest hamlet begins to be revealed, which
before lurked in the shade of the noon. It twinkles now
through the trees like some fair evening star—darting its
ray across valley and wood.

Would it not be a luxury to stand up to ones chin in
some retired swamp for a whole summer's day, scenting
the sweet fern and bilberry blows, and lulled by the
minstrelsy of gnats and mosquitoes? A day passed in
the society of those Greek sages, such as described in the
"Banquet" of Xenophon, would not be comparable with
the dry wit of decayed cranberry vines, and the fresh
Attic salt of the moss beds. Say twelve hours of genial
and familiar converse with the leopard frog. The sun to
rise behind alder and dogwood, and climb boyantly
to his meridian of three hands' breadth—and finally sink
to rest behind some bold western hummock. To hear
the evening chant of the mosquito from a thousand
green chapels—and the bittern begin to boom from his
concealed fort—like a sunset gun!

Surely, one may as profitably be soaked in the juices
of a marsh for one day, as pick his way dry shod over
sand. Cold and damp—are they not as rich experience as
warmth and dryness?

So is not Shade as good as sunshine—Night as day?
Why be eagles and thrushes always, and owls and
whip-poor-wills never.?

I am pleased to see the landscape through the bottom
of a tumbler— it is clothed in such a mild quiet light,

and the barns and fences checquer and partition it with
new regularity. These rough and uneven fields stretch
away with lawn-like smoothness to the horizon. The
clouds are finely distinct and picturesque—the light blue
sky contrasting with their feathery whiteness. They
are fit drapery to hang over Persia. The smith's shop
—resting in such a Grecian light is worthy to stand beside
the Parthenon. The potato and grain fields are such
gardens as he imagines who has schemes of ornamental
husbandry.

If I were to write of the dignity of the farmer's life
—I would behold his farms and crops through a tumbler
—all the occupations of men are ennobled so.

Our eyes too are convex lenses – — but we do not
learn with the eyes—they introduce us, and we learn after
by converse with things.

{*One-third page blank*}

June 17th 1840

Our lives will not attain to be spherical by lying on
one or the other side for ever, but only by resigning
ourselves to the law of gravity in us, will our axis
become coincident with the celestial axis, and by
revolving incessantly through all circles, shall we
acquire a perfect sphericity.

Men are inclined to lay the chief stress on likeness
and not on difference— We seek to know how a thing
is related to us and not if it is strange. We call those
bodies warm whose temperature is many degrees below
our own, and never those cold which are warmer than
we. There are many degrees of warmth below blood
heat, but none of cold above it.

Even the motto "business before friends" admits of
a high interpretation. No interval of time can avail to
defer friendship.– The concerns of time must be
attended to in time– I need not make haste to explore
the whole secret of a star–if it were vanished quite out
of the firmament,–so that no telescope could longer
discover it, I should not despair of knowing it entirely
one day.

We meet our friend with a certain awe, as if he had
just lighted on the earth, and yet as if we had some
title to be acquainted with him by our old familiarity
with sun and moon.

                                        June 18th 1840
I should be pleased to meet man in the woods– I
wish he were to be encountered like wild caribous and
moose.

I am startled when I consider how little I am *actually*
concerned about the things I write in my journal.

Think of the Universal History–and then tell me
–when did burdock and plantain sprout first?
A fair land, indeed, do books spread open to us,
from the Genesis down,–but alas! men do not take them
up kindly into their own being, and breathe into them
a fresh beauty–knowing that the grimmest of them
belongs to such warm sunshine and still moonlight as
the present.

Of what consequence whether I stand on London
bridge for the next century–or look into the depths of
this bubbling spring which I have laid open with
my hoe?

June 19th 1840

The other day I rowed in my boat a free—even lovely
young lady—and as I plied the oars she sat in the stern
—and there was nothing but she between me and the sky
So might all our lives be picturesque if they were free
enough—but mean relations and prejudices intervene to
shut out the sky, and we never see a man as simple
and distinct as the man-weathercock on a steeple,

The faint bugle notes which I hear in the west seem
to flash on the horizon like heat lightning. Cows low in
the street more friendly than ever—and the note of the
whip-poor-will born over the fields is the voice with
which the woods and moonlight woo me.

I shall not soon forget the sounds which lulled me
when falling asleep on the banks of the Merrimack.

Far into night I hear some tyro beating a drum
incessantly with a view to some country muster, and am
thrilled by an infinite sweetness as of a music which the
breeze drew from the sinews of war. I think of the line
    "When the drum beat at dead of night"
How I wish it would wake the whole world to march to
its melody—but still it drums on alone in the silence
and the dark — —

Cease not thou drummer of the night, thou too shalt
have thy reward. The stars and the firmament hear
thee, and their aisles shall echo thy beat till its call is
answered, and the forces are mustered. The universe is
attentive as a little child to thy sound, and trembles
as if each stroke bounded against an elastic vibrating
firmament. I should be contented if the night never
ended—for in the darkness heroism will not be deferred,
and I see fields where no hero has couched his lance.

June 20th 1840

Perfect sincerity and transparency make a great
part of beauty—as in dew drops—lakes, and diamonds. A
spring is a cynosure in the fields. All muscovy glitters
in the minute particles of mica on its bottom—and the
ripples cast their shadows flickeringly on the white
sand, as the clouds which flit across the landscape.

Something like the woodland sounds will be heard
to echo through the leaves of a good book.— Sometimes
I hear the fresh emphatic note of the ovenbird, and am
tempted to turn many pages.— sometimes the hurried
chuckling sound of the squirrel when he dives into
the wall.

If we only see clearly enough how mean our lives are
they will be splendid enough.

Let us remember not to strive upwards too long,
but sometimes drop plumb down the other way, and
wallow in meanness: From the deepest pit we may see
the stars, if not the sun. Let us have presence of mind
enough to sink when we cant swim—at any rate, a
carcass had better lie on the bottom than float an offence
to all nostrils. It will not be falling—for we shall ride
wide of the earth's gravity as a star, and always be
drawn upward still—(semper cadendo nunquam cadit)
—and so by yielding to universal gravity, at length
become fixed stars.

Praise begins when things are seen partially.

When the heavens are obscured to us, and nothing
noble or heroic appears, but we are oppressed by
imperfection and short-coming on all hands, we are apt
to suck our thumbs and decry our fates. As if nothing

were to be done in cloudy weather or if heaven were not
accessible by the upper road men would not find out
a lower. Sometimes I feel so cheap that I am inspired,
and could write a poem about it—but straightway I
cannot for I am no longer mean. Let me know that I am
ailing and I am well. We should not always beat off
the impression of trivialness, but make haste to welcome
and cherish it. Water the weed till it blossoms; with
cultivation it will bear fruit. There are two ways to
victory—to strive bravely—or to yield. How much pain the
last will save we have not yet learned.

June 21st 1840.

Copied from pencil.

"Aug. 31st 1839.— Made seven miles, and moored
our boat on the west side of a little rising ground which
in the spring forms an island in the river, the sun going
down on one hand, and our eminence contributing
its shadow to the night, on the other. In the twilight so
elastic is the air that the sky seems to tinkle over farm
house and wood — — Scrambling up the bank of our
terra incognita we fall on huckleberries which have
slowly ripened here, husbanding the juices which the
months have distilled, for our peculiar use this night. If
they had been rank poison, the entire simplicity and
confidence with which we plucked them would have
insured their wholesomeness. The devout attitude of the
hour asked a blessing on that repast— It was fit for
the setting sun to rest on."

"From our tent here on the hillside, through that
isosceles door, I see our lonely mast on the shore,
it may be as an eternity fixture, to be seen in landscapes
henceforth, or as the most temporary stand-still of
time—the boat just come to anchor, and the mast still
rocking to find its balance."

"No human life is in night—the woods—the boat—the
shore—yet is it life like. The warm pulse of a young life

beats steadily underneath all. This slight wind is where
one artery approaches the surface and is skin deep."

"While I write hear, I hear the foxes trotting about
me over the dead leaves, and now gently over the grass,
as if not to disturb the dew which is falling. Why
should we not cultivate neighborly relations with the
foxes?— As if to improve upon our seeming advances
comes one to greet us nose-wise under our tent curtain.
Nor do we rudely repulse him. Is man powder and
the fox flint and steel? Has not the time come when men
and foxes shall lie down together?"

"Hist! there, the musquash by the boat is taking
toll of potatoes and melons. Is not this the age of
a community of goods? His presumption kindles in
me a brotherly feeling.— Nevertheless, I get up to
reconnoitre, and tread stealthily along the shore to make
acquaintance with him. But on the river side I can see
only the stars reflected in the water—and now by some
ripple ruffling the disk of a star, I discover him."

"In the silence of the night the sound of a distant
alarm bell is borne to these woods. Even now men have
fires and extinguish them, and with distant horizon
blazings and barkings of dogs, enact the manifold drama
of life"

"We begin to have an interest in sun, moon, and stars.
What time riseth Orion—which side the pole gropeth
the bear? East—West—North—and South—where are
they? What clock shall tell the hours for us?" Billerica
—midnight.

Sunday Sept. 1st 1839

Under an oak on the bank of the canal in Chelmsford.
"From Ball's hill to Billerica meeting house the river
is a noble stream of water, flowing between gentle hills

and occasional cliffs—and well wooded all the way.
It can hardly be said to flow at all, but rests in the lap
of the hills like a quiet lake. The boatmen call it a dead
stream. For many long reaches you can see nothing
to indicate that men inhabit its banks. — — Nature
seems to hold a sabbath herself to-day—a still warm sun
on river and wood, and not breeze enough to ruffle the
water. Cattle stand up to their bellies in the river,
and you think Rembrandt should be here."

"camped under some oaks in Tyngsboro, on the east
bank of the Merrimack, just below the ferry."

"Sept. 2nd Camped in Merrimack, on the west bank,
          by a deep ravine."

"Sept 3d In Bedford, on the west bank, opposite a
          large rock, above Coos falls."

"Sept 4th Wednesday—Hooksett—east bank, two or
          three miles below the village, opposite Mr.
          Mitchels'."

"Sept 5th— Walked to Concord—10 miles."

"Sept 6th By stage to Plymouth—40 miles, and on foot
          to Tilton's inn, Thornton. The scenery
          commences on Sanbornton square, Whence
          the White Mountains are first visible. In
          Campton it is decidedly mountainous."

"Sept 7th Walked from Thornton through Peeling and
          Lincoln to Franconia. In Lincoln visited
          —"Stone Flume" and "Basin", and in
          Franconia the "Notch", and saw the "old
          man of the mountain"

Dimensions of the Flume.

Length of Cascade – –	616	feet
From Cascade to Flume – –	291	"
From the lower end of the Flume to the large rock – –	453	"
From the lower end of the Flume to the first waterfall	680	"
" " " to the second	775	"
Whole length of Flume	830	"
Height of walls.	64	"

Width from 9⁶⁄₁₂ to 35 ft.

The measurement of some scientific person
—according to Mr. Gurnsey who keeps the inn, and
furnishes these facts."

"Sept. 8th Walked from Franconia to Thomas J.
Crawford's."
"Sept. 9th at Crawfords"
"Sept 10th ascended the mountain and rode to Conway"
"Sept 11th rode to Concord."
"Sept 12th rode to Hooksett and rowed to Bedford N. H.
or rather to the northern part of Merrimack
—near the ferry—by a large Island near
which we camped."
"Sept 13th Rowed and sailed to Concord—about 50
miles."

I shall not soon forget my first night in a tent—how
the distant barking of dogs for so many still hours
revealed to me the riches of the night.— Who would not
be a dog and bay the moon?   —

I never feel that I am inspired unless my body is
also— It too spurns a tame and commonplace life. They
are fatally mistaken who think while they strive with
their minds, that they may suffer their bodies to stagnate

in luxury or sloth. The body is the first proselyte the
Soul makes. Our life is but the Soul made known by
its fruits—the body. The whole duty of man may be
expressed in one line— Make to yourself a perfect body.

{One-third page blank}

June 22nd 1840.

What a man knows that he does.

It is odd that people will wonder how Shakspeare
could write as he did without knowing Latin, or Greek,
or Geography—as if these were of more consequence
than to know how to whistle. They are not backward
to recognise Genius—how it dispenses with those
furtherances which others require—leaps where they
crawl—and yet they never cease to marvel that so it was
—that it was Genius, and helped itself.

Nothing can shock a truly brave man but dulness.
One can tolerate many things. What mean these sly
suspicious looks, as if you were an odd fish—a piece of
crockery ware to be tenderly handled? Surely people
forget how many rebuffs every man has experienced in
his day—perhaps has fallen into a horse pond—eaten
fresh water clams, or worn one shirt for a week without
washing. Cannot a man be as calmly tolerant as a
potatoe field in the sun—whose equanimity is not
disturbed by Scotch thistles over the wall, but there it
smiles and waxes till the harvest let thistles mount never
so high?
You cannot receive a shock unless you have an
electric affinity for that which shocks you. Have no
affinity for what is shocking.
Do not present a gleaming edge to ward off harm, for
that will oftenest attract the lightning, but rather be

the all-pervading ether which the lightning does not strike but purify. Then will the rudeness or profanity of your companion be like a flash across the face of your sky, lighting up and revealing its serene depths. Earth cannot shock the heavens; but its dull vapor and foul smoke make a bright cloud spot in the ether, and anon the sun, like a cunning artificer, will cut and paint it, and set it for a jewel in the breast of the sky.

When we are shocked at vice we express a lingering sympathy with it. Dry rot–rust–and mildew, shock no man, for none is subject to them.

June 23d 1840

We Yankees are not so far from right, who answer one question by asking another. Yes and No are lies – A true answer will not aim to establish anything, but rather to set all well afloat. All answers are in the future and day answereth to day–do we think we can anticipate them?

In Latin to respond–is to pledge oneself before the Gods to do faithfully and honorably, as a man should, in any case. This is good.

Music soothes the din of philosophy and lightens incessantly over the heads of sages.

How can the language of the poet be more expressive than nature! He is content that what he has already read in simple characters or indifferently in all, be translated into the same again.

He is the true artist whose life is his material–every stroke of the chisel must enter his own flesh and bone, and not grate dully on marble.

The Springs

"What is any man's discourse to me if I am not
sensible of something in it as steady and cheery as the
creak of the crickets? In it the words must be relieved
against the sky– Men tire me when I am not constantly
greeted and cheered in their discourse, as it were by
the flux of sparkling streams.

"I cannot see the bottom of the sky, because I cannot
see to the bottom of myself. It is the symbol of my own
infinity. My eye penetrates as far into the ether, as that
depth is inward from which my contemporary thought
springs.

"Not by constraint or severity shall you have access
to true wisdom, but by abandonment and childlike
mirthfulness. If you would know aught, be gay before it.

June 24th 1840

When I read Cudworth I find I can tolerate all
–atomists–pneumatologists–atheists, and theists–Plato
–Aristotle–Leucippus–Democritus–and Pythagoras
– It is the attitude of these men, more than any
communication, which charms me. It is so rare to
find a man musing.– But between them and their
commentators there is an endless dispute. But if it comes
to that–that you compare notes–then you are all wrong.

As it is, each takes me up into the serene heavens,
and paints earth and sky. Any sincere thought is
irresistible, it lifts us to the Zenith, whither the smallest
bubble rises as surely as the largest.

Dr. Cudworth does not consider that the belief in a
deity is as great a heresy as exists. Epicurus held that
the gods were "of human form, yet were so thin and
subtile, as that, comparatively with our terrestrial

bodies, they might be called incorporeal; they having
not so much *carnem* as *quasi-carnem*, nor *sanguinem*
as *quasi-sanguinem*, a certain kind of aerial or etherial
flesh and blood." This which Cudworth pronounces
"romantical", is plainly as good doctrine as his own.
– As if any sincere thought were not the best sort
of truth.

There is no doubt but the highest morality in the
books is rhymed or measured,–is in form as well as
substance–poetry. Such is the Scripture of all nations.
If I were to compile a volume to contain the condensed
wisdom of mankind, I should quote no rhythmless line.

Not all the wit of a college can avail to make one
harmonious line– It never *happens*. It may get so as
to jingle–but a jingle is akin to a jar–jars regularly
recurring.

So delicious is plain speech to my ears, as if I were
to be more delighted by the whistling of the shot–than
frightened by the flying of the splinters–I am content, I
fear, to be quite battered down and made a ruin off.– I
out-general myself when I direct the enemy to my
vulnerable points.
The loftiest utterance of love–is perhaps sublimely
satirical. Sympathy with what is sound makes sport of
what is unsound.

                              Cliffs.– Evening
"Though the sun set a quarter of an hour ago, his
rays are still visible, darting half way to the zenith. That
glowing morrow in the west flashes on me like a faint
presentiment of morning when I am falling asleep. A
dull mist comes rolling from the west–as if it were the

dust which day has raised– A column of smoke is rising
from the woods yonder to uphold heaven's roof till
the light comes again. The landscape, by its patient
resting there, teaches me that all good remains with
him that waiteth–and that I shall sooner overtake the
dawn by remaining here, than by hurrying over the hills
of the west.

"Morning and evening are as like as brother and
sister. The sparrow and thrush sing, and the frogs
peep–for both.

"The woods breathe louder and louder behind me
–with what hurry-skurry night takes place! The wagon
rattling over yonder bridge is the messenger which
day sends back to night–but the despatches are sealed.
In its rattle the village seems to say–This one sound,
and I have done.–

"Red, then, is Day's color–at least, it is the color
of his heel. He is "stepping westward"– We only notice
him when he comes and when he goes.

"With noble perseverance the dog bays the stars
yonder – – I too like thee walk alone in this strange
familiar night– My voice like thine beating against its
friendly concave, and barking I hear only my own
voice. 10. o'clock.

June 25th 1840

Let me see no other conflict but with prosperity– If
my path run on before me level and smooth, it is all
a mirage–in reality it is steep and arduous as a chamois
pass.– I will not let the years roll over me like a
Juggernaut car.

We will warm us at each other's fire. Friendship is
not such a cold refining process by a double sieve, but a
glowing furnace in which all impurities are consumed.

Men have learned to touch before they scrutinise—to shake hands, and not to stare.

June 26th 1840
The best poetry has never been written, for when it might have been, the poet forgot it, and when it was too late remembered it—or when it might have been, the poet remembered it, and when it was too late forgot it.

The highest condition of art is artlessness.

Truth is always paradoxical.

He will get to the goal first who stands stillest.

There is one let better than any help—and that is—*Let-alone*.

By sufferance you may escape suffering.

He who resists not at all will never surrender.

When a dog runs at you whistle for him.

Say—not so—and you will outcircle the philosophers.

Stand outside the wall and no harm can reach you —the danger is that you be walled in with it.

{*One-fifth page blank*}

June 27th 1840
I am living this 27th June 1840—a dull cloudy day —and no sun shining. The clink of the smith's hammer sounds feebly over the roofs, and the wind is sighing

gently as if dreaming of cheerfuller days. The farmer is ploughing in yonder field–craftsmen are busy in the shops–the trader stands behind the counter–and all works go steadily forward– But I will have nothing to do– I will tell fortune that I play no game with her, and she may reach me in my Asia of serenity and indolence if she can.

For an impenetrable shield stand inside yourself.

He was no artist but an artisan who first made shields of brass.

Unless we meet religiously we prophane one another – What was the consecrated ground around the temple we have used as no better than a domestic court.

Our friend's is as holy a shrine as any God's–to be approached with sacred love and awe. Veneration is the measure of Love– Our friend answers ambiguously, and sometimes before the question is propounded, like the oracle of Delphi. He forbears to ask explanation, but doubts and surmises darkly with full faith–as we silently ponder our fates.

In no presence are we so susceptible to Shame. Our hour is a sabbath–our abode a Temple–our gifts peace offerings–our conversation a communion–our silence a prayer. In prophanity we are absent–in holiness near–in sin estranged–in innocence reconciled.

June 28th 1840

The prophane never hear music–the holy ever hear it. It is God's voice–the divine breath audible. Where it is heard there is a sabbath. It is omnipotent–all things obey it as they obey virtue. It is the herald of virtue. It passes by sorrow–for grief hangs its harp on the willows.

{One-fifth page blank}

June 29th 1840

Of all phenomena my own race are the most
mysterious and undiscoverable— For how many years
have I striven to meet one; even on common manly
ground; and have not succeeded!

June 30th 1840

I sailed from Fair Haven last evening as gently and
steadily as the clouds sail through the atmosphere.
The wind came blowing blithely from the South west
fields, and stepped into the folds of our sail like a winged
horse—pulling with a strong and steady impulse. The
sail bends gently to the breeze as swells some generous
impulse of the heart—and anon flutters and flaps with
a kind of human suspense. I could watch the motions of
a sail forever, they are so rich and full of meaning.
I watch the play of its pulse as if it were my own blood
beating there. The varying temperature of distant
atmospheres is graduated on its scale. It is a free boyant
creature—the bauble of the heavens and the earth. A
gay pastime the air plays with it. If it swells and tugs, it
is because the sun lays his windy finger on it. —— The
breeze it plays with has been out doors so long— So thin
is it—and yet so full of life. So noiseless when it labors
hardest—so noisy and impatient when least servicible. So
am I blown on by God's breath— So flutter and flap,
and fill gently out with the breeze.
   In this fresh evening each blade and leaf looks as if it
had been dipped in an icy liquid greenness. Let eyes
that ache come here and look, the sight will be a
sovereign eye water, or else wait and bathe there in
the dark.

We go forth into the fields and there the wind blows
freshly onward; and still on, and we must make new

efforts not to be left behind. What does the dogged wind
intend–that like a wilful cur it will not let me turn
aside to rest or content? Must it always reproove and
provoke me, and never welcome me as an equal?

The truth shall prevail and falsehood discover itself,
as long as the wind blows on the hills.

A man's life should be a stately march to a sweet but
unheard music, and when to his fellows it shall seem
irregular and inharmonious, he will only be stepping to
a livelier measure; or his nicer ear hurry him into
a thousand symphonies and concordant variations.
There will be no halt ever but at most a marching on his
post, or such a pause as is richer than any sound,
when the melody runs into such depth and wildness, as
to be no longer heard, but implicitly consented to with
the whole life and being. He will take a false step
never, even in the most arduous times; for then the
music will not fail to swell into greater sweetness and
volume, and itself rule the movement it inspired.

I have a deep sympathy with war it so apes the
gait and bearing of the soul.

Value and effort are as much coincident as weight
and a tendency to fall. In a very wide but true sense,
effort is the deed itself, and it is only when these
sensible stuffs intervene, that our attention is distracted
from the deed to the accident. It is never the deed
men praise, but some marble or canvass which are only
a staging to the real work.

July 1st 1840

To be a man is to do a man's work– Always our
resource is to endeavor. We may well say success to our
endeavors– Effort is the prerogative of virtue–

The laborer is recompensed by his labor, not by his employer. Industry is its own wages. Let us not suffer our hands to lose one jot of their handiness by looking behind to a mean recompense, knowing that our true endeavor cannot be thwarted, nor we be cheated of our earnings unless by not earning them.

Some symbol of value may shape itself to the senses in wood, or marble, or verse, but this is fluctuating as the laborer's hire, which may or may not be withheld. Perhaps the hugest and most effective deed may have no sensible result at all on earth, but paint itself in the heavens in new stars and constellations. Its very material lies out of nature. When in rare moments we strive wholly with one consent, which we call a yearning, we may not hope that our work will stand in any artist's gallery.

July 2nd 1840

I am not taken up, like moses, upon a mountain to learn the law, but lifted up in my seat here, in the warm sunshine and genial light.

They who are ready to go are already invited.

Neither men nor things have any true mode of invitation but to be inviting.

Can that be a task which all things but alleviate?

July 3d 1840

When Alexander appears, the Hercynian and Dodonean woods seem to wave a welcome to him.

Do not thoughts and men's lives enrich the earth and change the aspect of things as much as a new growth of wood?

What are Godfrey and Gonzalve unless we breathe a
life into them, and reenact their exploits as a prelude to
our own? The past is only so heroic as we see it—it is
the canvass on which our idea of heroism is painted—the
dim prospectus of our future field. We are dreaming
of what we are to do.

The last sunrise I witnessed seemed to outshine
the splendor of all preceding ones, and I was convinced
that it behoved man to dawn as freshly, and with equal
promise and steadiness advance into the career of
life, with as lofty and serene a countenance to move
onward through his midday to a yet fairer and more
promising setting. Has the day grown old when it sets?
and shall man wear out sooner than the sun? In the
crimson colors of the west I discern the budding hues of
dawn—to my western brother it is rising pure and
bright as it did to me, but the evening exhibits in the
still rear of day the beauty which through morning
and noon escaped me. When we are oppressed by the
heat and turmoil of the noon, let us remember that the
sun which scorches us with brazen beams, is gilding
the hills of morning, and awaking the woodland quires,
to other men.

We will have a dawn—and noon—and serene sunset
in ourselves.

What we call the gross atmosphere of evening is the
accumulated deed of the day, which absorbs the rays of
beauty, and shows more richly than the naked promise
of the dawn. By earnest toil in the heat of the noon,
let us get ready a rich western blaze against the evening
of our lives.

Low thoughted plodding men have come and camped
in my neighbor's field to-night, with camp music and

bustle. Their bugle instantly finds a sounding board in the heavens, though mean lips blow it. The sky is delighted with strains which the connoiseur rejects. It seems to say—now is this my own earth.

In music are the centripetal and centrifugal forces. The universe needed only to hear a divine harmony that every star might fall into its proper place and assume a true sphericity.

July 4th 1840. 4 o'clock A.M.

The Townsend Light Infantry encamped last night in my neighbor's enclosure. – –
The night still breathes slumbrously over field and wood, when a few soldier's gather about one tent in the twilight, and their band plays an old Scotch air—with bugle and drum and fife attempered to the season. It seems like the morning hymn of creation. The first sounds of the awakening camp—mingled with the chastened strains which so sweetly salute the dawn, impress me as the morning prayer of an army.

And now the morning gun fires—the soldier awakening to creation and awakening it— I am sure none are cowards now. These strains are the roving dreams which steal from tent to tent,—and break forth into distinct melody—they are the soldiers morning thought. Each man awakes himself with lofty emotions; and would do some heroic deed. You need preach no homily to him —he is the stuff they are made of.

The whole course of our lives should be analogous to one day of the soldiers. His Genius seems to whisper in his ear what demeanor is befitting, and in his bravery and his march he yields a blind and partial obedience.

The fresher breeze which accompanies the dawn
rustles the oaks and birches, and the earth respires
calmly with the creaking of crickets. Some hazle leaf
stirs gently, as if anxious not to awake the day too
abruptly—while the time is hastening to the distinct line
between darkness and light. And soldiers issue from
their dewy tents, and as if in answer to expectant nature,
sing a sweet and far echoing hymn.

We may well neglect many things, provided we
overlook them.

When to-day I saw the "Great Ball" rolled majestically
along, it seemed a shame that man could not move like
it. All dignity and grandeur has something of the
undulatoriness of the sphere. It is the secret of majesty
in the rolling gate of the elephant and of all grace
in action and in art. The line of beauty is a curve.
Each man seems striving to imitate its gait, and
keep pace with it, but it moves on regardless and
conquers the multitude with its majesty. What shame
that our lives which should be the source of planetary
motion, and sanction the order of the spheres, are
full of abruptness and angulosity, so as not to roll, nor
move majestically.

July 5th 1840

Go where we will we discover infinite change in
particulars only—not in generals.

You cannot rob a man of anything which he will miss.

July 6th 1840

All this worldly wisdom was once the unamiable
heresy of some wise man.

I observe a truly wise practice on every hand, in
education, in religion, and the morals of society—enough
embodied wisdom to have set up many an ancient
philosopher.

This society, if it were a person to be met face to
face, would not only be tolerated but courted, with its
so impressive experience and admirable acquaintance
with things.

Consider society at any epoch, and who does not
see that heresy has already *prevailed* in it?

Have no mean hours, but be grateful for every hour,
and accept what it brings. The reality will make any
sincere record respectable. No day will have been
wholly misspent, if one sincere thoughtful page has
been written.

Let the daily tide leave some deposit on these pages,
as it leaves sand and shells on the shore. So much
increase of *terra firma*. This may be a calender of the
ebbs and flows of the soul; and on these sheets as a
beach, the waves may cast up pearls and seaweed.

July 7th 1840

I have experienced such simple joy in the trivial
matters of fishing and sporting formerly—as might
inspire the muse of Homer or Shakspeare. And now
when I turn over the pages, and ponder the plates,
of the "Angler's Souvenir"— I exclaim with the poet—
    "Can these things be, and overcome us like a summer's
    cloud?

When I hear a sudden burst from a horn, I am
startled, as if one had provoked such wildness as he

could not rule nor tame. He dares wake the echoes, which he cannot put to rest.

{One-fifth page blank}

July 8th 1840.
Doubt and falsehood are yet good preachers. They affirm roundly, while they deny partially.

I am pleased to learn that Thales was up and stirring by night not unfrequently, as his astronomical discoveries prove.

It was a saying of Solon that "it is necessary to observe a medium in all things."
The golden mean, in ethics as in physics, is the centre of the System, and that about which all revolve, and though to a distant and plodding planet it is the uttermost extreme yet when that planet's year is complete it will be found central. They who are alarmed lest virtue run into extreme good, have not yet wholly embraced her; but described only a slight arc about her—and from so small a curvature, you can calculate no center whatever, but their mean is no better than meanness, nor their medium than mediocrity.

The brave man while he observes strictly the golden mean, seems to run through all extremes with impunity —like the sun which now appears in the zenith, now in the horizon, and, again is faintly reflected from the moon's disk, and has the credit of describing an entire great circle, crossing the equinoctial and solstitial colures, without detriment to his steadfastness or mediocrity.

every planet asserts its own to be the center of the
system.

Only *meanness* is mediocre–*moderate*–but the true
medium is not contained within any *bounds*, but is
as wide as the ends it connects.

When Solon endeavored to prove that Salamis had
formerly belonged to the Athenians and not to the
Megarians, he caused the tombs to be opened, and
showed that the inhabitants of Salamis turned the faces
of their dead to the same side with the Athenians, but
the Megarians to the opposite side.
So does each fact bear witness to all, and the history
of all the past may be read in a single grain of its ashes.

July 9th 1840.

In most men's religion the ligature which should
be its muscle and sinew is rather like that thread which
the accomplices of Cylon held in their hands, when
they went abroad from the temple of Minerva, the other
end being attached to the statue of the goddess. But
frequently, as in their case, the thread breaks, being
stretched, and they are left without an asylum.

The value of many traits in Grecian history depends
not so much on their importance as history, as the
readiness with which they accept a wide interpretation,
and illustrate the poetry and ethics of mankind.
When they announce no particular truth, they are yet
central to all truth. They are like those examples–by
which we improve–but of which we never formally
extract the moral. Even the isolated and unexplained

facts—are like the ruins of the temples—which in imagination we restore, and ascribe to some Phidias, or other master.

The Greeks were boys in the sunshine on sea and land,—the Romans were men in the field—the Persians women in the house—the Egyptians old men in the dark.

He who receives an injury is an accomplice of the wrong doer.

July 10th 1840.

To myself I am as pliant as osier—and my courses seem not so easy to be calculated as Encke's comet—but I am powerless to bend the character of another—he is like iron in my hands. I could tame a hyena more easily than my friend. I contemplate him as a granite boulder.

He is material which no tool of mine will work. A naked savage will fall an oak with a fire brand; and wear a hatchet out of the rock, but I cannot hew the smallest chip out of my fellow.— There is a character in every one which no art can reach to beautify or deform.

Nothing was ever so unfamiliar and startling to me as my own thought.

We know men through their eyes. You might say that the eye was always original and unlike another— It is the feature of the individual, and not of the family—in twins still different. All a man's privacy is in his eye, and its expression he cannot alter more than he can alter his character. So long as we look a man in the eye, it seems to rule the other features, and make them too original. When I have mistaken one person for another, observing only his form, and carriage, and inferior features, the unlikeness seemed of the least consequence, but when I caught his eye, and my doubts were removed –it seemed to pervade every feature.

The eye revolves on an independent pivot which we can no more control than our own will. Its axle is the axle of the soul, as the axis of the earth is coincident with the axis of the heavens.

July 11th 1840.

The true art is not merely a sublime consolation and holiday labor which the gods have given to sickly mortals, to be wrought at in parlors, and not in stithies, amid soot and smoke, but such a masterpiece as you may imagine a dweller on the table lands of Central Asia might produce, with three score and ten years for canvass, and the faculties of a man for tools,–a human life–wherein you might hope to discover more than the freshness of Guido's Aurora, or the mild light of Titian's landscapes; not a bald imitation or rival of nature, but the restored original of which she is the reflection. For such a work as this whole galleries of Greece and Italy are a mere mixing of colors and preparatory quarrying of marble.

Not how is the idea expressed in stone or on canvass, is the question, but how far it has obtained form and expression in the life of the artist.

There is much covert truth in the old mythology which makes Vulcan a brawny and deformed smith, who sweat more than the other gods. His stithy was not like a modern studio.

Let us not wait any longer, but step down from the mountains on to the plain of earth Let our delay be like the sun's when he lingers on the dividing line of day

and night–a brief space when the world is grateful
for his light– We will make such haste as the morning
and such delay as the evening.

It concerns us rather to be something here present
than to leave something behind us.

It is the man determines what is said, not the words.
If a mean person uses a wise maxim, I bethink me
how it can be interpreted so as to commend itself to his
meanness; but if a wise man makes a common place
remark, I consider what wider construction it will admit.
When Pittacus says "it is necessary to accommodate
ones self to the time–and take advantage of the
occasion"–I assent. He might have considered that to
accommodate ones self to all times, and take advantage
of all occasions, was really to be independent, and
make our own opportunity.

July 12th 1840.
What first suggested that necessity was grim–and
made fate so fatal? The strongest is always the least
violent. Necessity is a sort of eastern cushion on which
I recline– I contemplate its mild inflexible countenance
–as the haze in October days. When I am vexed I only
ask to be left alone with it. Leave me to my fate. It
is the bosom of time and the lap of eternity–since to be
necessary is to be needful, it is only another name
for inflexibility of good. How I welcome my grim fellow
–and aspire to be such a necessity as he! He is so
flexile, and yields to me as the air to my body! I leap
and dance in his midst, and play with his beard till he
smiles. I greet thee, my elder Brother, who with thy
touch ennoblest all things. Must it be so, then is it good.
Thou commendest even petty ills by thy countenance.

Over Greece hangs the divine necessity ever a mellower heaven of itself, whose light too gilds the Acropolis and a thousand fanes and groves.

Pittacus said there was no better course than to endeavor to do well what you are doing at any moment.

Go where he will the wise man is proprietor of all things– Every thing bears a similar inscription, if we could but read it, to that on the vase found in the stomach of a fish in old times–"To the most wise."

When his impious fellow passengers invoked the gods in a storm, Bias cried "Hist–hist–lest the gods perceive that you are here, for we should all be lost."

A wise man will always have his duds picked up, and be ready for whatever may happen–as the prudent merchant, notwithstanding the lavish display of his wares–will yet have them packed or easy to be removed in emergencies. In this sense there is something sluttish in all finery. When I see a fine lady or gentleman dressed to the top of the fashion, I wonder what they would do if an earthquake should happen; or a fire suddenly break out, for they seem to have counted only on fair weather, and that things will go on smoothly and without jostling. Those curls and jewels so nicely adjusted expect an unusual deference from the elements. Let our dress be such as will hang conveniently about us, and fit equally well in good and in bad fortune; such as will approve itself of the right fashion and fabric–whether for the cotillion or the earthquake. In the sac of Priene when the inhabitants with much hurry and bustle were carrying their effects to a place of safety, someone asked Bias who remained tranquil

amid the confusion, why he was not thinking how
he should save something, as the others were. I do so,
said Bias, for I carry all my effects with me.

July 14th 1840.
Our discourse should be *ex tempore*, but not *pro
tempore*.

July 16th 1840
We are as much refreshed by sounds, as by sights—or
scents—or flavors—as the barking of a dog heard in
the woods at midnight, or the tinklings which attend the
dawn.
As I picked blackberries this morning by starlight,
the distant yelping of a dog fell on my inward ear, as the
cool breeze on my cheek.

July 19th 1840.
These two days that I have not written in my Journal
—set down in the calendar as the 17th and 18th of
July—have been really an aeon in which a Syrian empire
might rise and fall— How many Persias have been lost
and won in the interim— Night is spangled with
fresh stars.

July 26th 1840.
When I consider how, after sunset, the stars come out
gradually in troops from behind the hills and woods,
I confess that I could not have contrived a more curious
and inspiring night.

July 27th 184c
Some men, like some buildings, are bulky but not
great— The pyramids any traveller may measure with
his line, but the dimensions of the Parthenon in feet
and inches will seem to dangle from its entablature like
an elastic drapery.

Much credit is due to a brave man's eye. It is the
focus in which all rays are collected. It sees from within
—or from the centre—just as we scan the whole concave
of the heaven at a glance, but can compass only one
side of the pebble at our feet.

The grandeur of these stupendous masses of clouds,
tossed into such irregular greatness across the sky,
seems thrown away on the meanness of my employment.

{*Fourteen leaves missing*}

The drapery seems altogether too rich for such poor
acting.
 In vain the sun challenges man to equal greatness
in his career— We look in vain over earth for a Roman
greatness to answer the eternal provocation.
 We look up to the gilded battlements of the eternal
city, and are contented to be suburban dwellers outside
the walls.

{*Two-thirds page blank*}

By the last breath of the May air I inhale I am
reminded that the ages never go so far down as this
before. The wood thrush is more modern than Plato and
Aristotle. They are a dogma, but he preaches the
doctrine of this hour.

This systole—diastole of the heart—the circulation of
the blood from the centre to the extremeties—the
chylification which is constantly going on in our bodies
—are a sort of military evolution. A struggle to outgeneral
the decay of time by the skilfullest tactics.

When bravery is worsted it joins the peace society.

A word is wiser than any man–than any series of
words. In its present received sense it may be false, but
in its inner sense by descent and analogy it approves
itself. Language is the most perfect work of art in
the world. The chisel of a thousand years retouches it.

Nature refuses to sympathize with our sorrow.
She seems not to have provided for, but by a thousand
contrivances, against, it. She has bevelled the margins
of the eyelids that the tears may not overflow on the
cheek.

{*One-fifth page blank*}

We can conceive of a Bravery so wide that nothing
can meet to befall it–So omnipresent that nothing can
lie in wait for it–so permanent that no obstinacy
can seduce it. The stars are its silent sentries by night
–and the sun its pioneer by day. From its superflous
cheerfulness come flowers and the rainbow, and its
infinite humor and wantonness produce corn and vines.

{*One-half page blank*}

{*Back endpaper*}

· 3 ·

July 30, 1840–January 22, 1841
TRANSCRIBED 1841

I've heard my neighbor's pump at night,
Long after Lyra sunk her light,
As if it were a natural sound,
And proper utterance of the ground—
Perchance some bittern in a fen—
Or the squeak of a meadow hen.

Who sleeps by day and walks by night,
Will meet no spirit but some sprite.

{*One and three-fifths pages blank*}

{*Two leaves missing*}

July 30th 1840.

No fresher tints than this morning's witnessed the
valor of Hector and Idomeneus, and some such evening
as this the Greek fleet came to anchor in the bay of
Aulis; but alas, it is not to us the eve of a ten years' war,
but of a sixty years' idleness and defeat.

Our peace is proclaimed by the rust on our swords,
and our inability to draw them from their scabbards
— She does not so much work as to keep these swords
bright and sharp. Let not ours be such nonresistance as
the chaff that rides before the gale.

The time lapses without epoch or era, and only a
half score of mornings and evenings are remembered
— Almost the night grieves, and leaves her tears on
the forelock of the day.

Sometimes I think I could find a foe to combat in the morning mist, and fall on its rear as it withdraws sluggishly to its daylight haunts—.

July 31st 1840

The very dogs that sullenly bay the moon from farm yards o' these nights, evince more heroism than is tamely barked forth in all the civil exhortations and war sermons of the age.

Our actions should make the stars forget their sphere music, and chant an elegiac strain—that heroism should have departed out of their ranks, and gone over to humanity.

If want of patriotism be objected to us, because we hold ourselves aloof from the din of politics, I know of no better answer than that of Anaxagoras to those who in like case reproached him with indifference to his country because he had withdrawn from it, and devoted himself to the search after truth— "On the contrary" he replied pointing to the heavens, "I esteem it infinitely."

The very laughter and jokes of a sober man are sober in their effects— They shake the firmament.

Any melodious sound apprises me of the infinite wealth of God.

Aug. 1st 1840.

The divinity in man is the vestal fire of the temple, which is never permitted to go out, but burns as steadily, and with as pure a flame, on the obscure provincial altar, as in Numa's temple at Rome.

Aug. 4th 1840.
Why let our lives be a cheap and broken hour, which
should be an affluent eternity?

{Four-fifths page blank}

July & August, 1840.

Spes sibi quisque. Virgil.

The brave man is the elder son of creation, who steps
boyantly into his inheritance, while the coward, who is
the younger, waits patiently till he decease.

He is that sixth champion against Thebes, whom,
when the proud devices of the rest have been recorded,
the poet describes as "bearing a full-orbed shield of
solid brass,"

"But there was no device upon its circle,
For not to seem just but to be is his wish."

"Discretion is the wise man's soul" saith the poet. His
prudence may safely go many steps beyond the utmost
rashness of the fool.

There is as much music in the world as virtue– At
length music will be the universal language, and men
greet each other in the fields in such accents as a
Beethoven now utters but rarely and indistinctly.

It entails a surpassing affluence on the meanest thing.

Let not the faithful sorrow that he has no ear for
the more fickle and rabble harmonies of creation–if he
be awake to the slower measure of virtue and truth. If
his pulse does not beat in unison with the musician's
quips and turns–it may yet accord with *their* larger
periods.

We too are dwellers within the purlieus of the camp.
The soul is a sterner master than any King Frederick, for
a true bravery would subject our bodies to rougher
usage than even a grenadier can bear– When the sun
breaks through the morning mist I seem to hear the
din of war louder than when his chariot thundered on
the plains of Troy.

It behoves us to make our life a steady progression
and not be defeated by its opportunities The stream
which first fell a drop from heaven, should be filtered
by events, till it burst out into springs of greater purity,
and extract a diviner flavor from the accidents through
which it passes.

Our task is not such a piece of day labor that a man must
be thinking what he shall do next for a livelihood,
but such that as it began in endeavor, so will it end
only when nothing in heaven or on earth, remain to be
endeavored.

Of such sort then be our crusade, that, while it
inclines chiefly to the heartiness and activity of war,
rather than the insincerity and sloth of peace, it may set
an example to both of calmness and energy; We will
be as unconcerned for victory as careless of defeat, not
seeking to lengthen our term of service, nor to cut
it short by a reprieve, but earnestly applying ourselves
to the campaign before us. Nor let our warfare be a
boorish and uncourteous one, but a higher courtesy
attend its higher chivalry, though not to the slackening
of its sterner duties and severer discipline–that so
our camp may be a palaestra for the exercise of the
dormant energies of men.

Methinks I hear the clarion sound, and the clang of
corselet and buckler from many a silent hamlet of
the soul. The morning gun has long since sounded, and
we are not yet at our posts.

Oftener from lone caves and over bogs and fens
gleams the ray which cheers and directs us, than from
lighted saloons.

–The age is resigned. Everywhere it sounds a retreat,
and the word has gone forth to fall back on innocence.
Christianity only *hopes*. It has hung its harp on the
willow and cannot sing a song in a strange land. It has
dreamed a sad dream and does not yet welcome the
morning with joy.

Surely joy is the condition of life. Think of the young
fry that leap in ponds–the myriads of insects ushered
into being of a summer's evening–the incessant note of
the hyla with which the woods ring in the spring. the
non chalance of the butterfly carrying accident and
change painted in a thousand hues upon his wings
–or the brook-minnow stemming stoutly the current, the
lustre of whose scales worn bright by the attrition is
reflected upon the bank.

Let us hear no more of peace at present– There
is more of it in fiercest war than any Amiens or Utrecht
ever compounded.

We have need to be as sturdy pioneers still as Miles
Standish or Church. We are to follow on another
trail, perhaps, but one as convenient for ambushes, and
with not so much as a moccasin print to guide us.

What if the Indians are exterminated? Do not savage.
as grim defile down into the clearing to-day?
    The danger is that we be exterminated.

    What if our Music be the sough of the wind— In the
deepest silence, I hear the distant din of conflict, and
the sound of clarion and trumpet comes wafted to
me upon the breeze.

{*One-third page blank*}

                                      Aug. 7th 1840
    When my senses are awake, I hear a "Battle of
Prague" played in these tame fields.

    When sitting in my chair I hear "Hero's Quick-step"
played on the piano—I am convinced that music was
invented for a stirring bravery—and not for an arm chair
stateliness.

    A wave of happiness flows over us like sunshine over
a field.

    Society is fragrant.

                                      Aug. 8th 1840

    Music is a flitting maiden, who now lives just through
the trees yonder, and now at an oriental distance.

    Floating in still water, I too am a planet, and have
my orbit, in space, and am no longer a satellite of
the earth.

    As summer wanes the chirp of the crickets seems
to come from further under the sod, and the frogs

croak from beneath the pads, but more complacently, as if they had struck a league with time, and were unanxious for the future.

Just before sunset the light in the west is purer –deeper–and more memorable than the noon.

Far in the eastern horizon I seem to glimpse the domes and minarets of an oriental city– And men lead a stately, civil life there, as poetical as the pastoral.

We hear it muttered of some village far up amid the hills, and look to our chart and guide book to learn of its mountains, and caves, and rivers. For the livelong day there skirts the horizon the dark blue outline of Crotched Mountain, in Goffstown, as we are told. Every sweep of the oar brings us nearer to "the far blue mountain."

Art is that which two may know– It is not lonely as Genius is.

The rich man's house is a *sedes*–a place to sit in–the poor man's a *tectum*–a shelter. So in English we say a gentleman's *seat* or *residence*, but a poor man's *house* or *roof*.

Aug 10th 1840.
Between the hills, as in a crucible, a gleaming flood of light undulates.

Aug. 12th 1840
A brave soul will make these peaceful times dangerous –and dangerous times peaceful.

We strive to prolong our moments of comfort and leisure–as if that were life and not a stagnation of life

— Life is current and not stagnant, and cannot afford to repeat a certain past cheapness, to the sacrifice of a possible future affluence.

When the accents of wisdom and eloquence have died away–I discover that the chirp of the crickets is still clear in advance.

A good book will not be dropped by its author–but thrown up. It will be so long a promise that he will not overtake it soon. He will have slipped the leash of a fleet hound.

When I hear a strain of music from across the street, I put away Homer and Shakspeare, and read them in the original.

———

When with pale cheek and sunken eye I sang
Unto the slumbering world at midnights hour,
How it no more resounded with war's clang,
And virtue was decayed in Peace's bower;

———

How in these days no hero was abroad,
But puny men, afraid of war's alarms,
Stood forth to fight the battles of their Lord,
Who scarce could stand beneath a hero's arms;

———

A faint, reproachful, reassuring strain,
From some harp's strings touched by unskilful hands,
Brought back the days of chivalry again,
And the surrounding fields made holy lands.

———

A bustling camp and an embattled host
Extending far on either hand I saw,
For I alone had slumbered at my post,
Dreaming of peace when all around was war.

Aug. 13th 1840.
When I listen to the faint creaking of the crickets,
it seems as if my course for the future lay that way.

These continents and hemispheres are the prey of a
speedy familiarity–but always an unexplored and
infinite region makes off on every side from my mind
–as near as Cathay, and as far too. I can make no
high way or beaten track into it, but immediately the
grass springs up in the path.

To travel and "descry new lands" is to think new
thoughts, and have new imaginings. In the spaces
of thought are the reaches of land and water over
which men go and come. The landscape lies fair within.
The deepest and most original thinker is the farthest
travelled.

A man should be collected and earnest in his bearing
–moving like one and not several, like an arrow with
a feather for its rudder–and not like a handful of
feathers bound to a rod,–or a disorderly equipage which
does not move unanimously. Addison says somewhat
to the purpose, when lamenting the "Preference of
Wit and Sense to Honesty and Virtue".– "I lay it down
therefore for a rule, that the whole man is to move
together;"–otherwise, he says, a man "is hopping
instead of walking, he is not in his entire and proper
motion."

A worm is as good a traveller as a grasshopper or
cricket; with all their activity they do not hop away from
drought nor forward to summer. No hopping animal
migrates.

We do not avoid evil by hurry-skurry and fleetness
in extenso, but by rising above or diving below its plane.
As the worm escapes drought and frost, by boring a
few inches deeper, but the grasshopper is overtaken and
destroyed— By our suppleness and speed we only fly
before an evil, by the height or depth of our characters
we avoid it.

The geniuses have been a hard-favored race of
immigrants, who have had no landed interests.

Aug. 14th 1840.

How many miles of hill and valley and expanded
plain between George Minot and Mr. Alcott— Within the
hour I am in Scythia and in the στοα at Athens.

For my Tyre and Sidon, I have only to go a shopping.
The Penobscots by the river are my Britains come
to Rome.

I cannot attatch much importance to historical
epochs–or geographical boundaries–when I have my
Orient and Occident in one revolution of my body.

While one hour lapses I am conversing in George
Minot's barn while the sun is disappearing from the
prospect of its wide door, upon pigeons and raccoons,
and corn and potatoes, and snuffing the odor of new hay,
and the wholsome breath of the cow, and again, in
a parlor, hear discussed the philosophies of Greece and
Rome.

The day came on so forwardly that the morning
was without dawn. The sun vaulted with elastic step
into the heavens.– So clear and liquid was the air that
you could almost discover a pulse in the sky. The whole
heavens palpitated like a vast artery, wherein the

.ue blood circulated in floods. A deeper silence brooded
over the earth as at the approach of evening–and the
morning was as the eve of a deep blue night. The
sun shone reflectedly like the moon– Day slumbered
yet, but had left his candle lit–. We flowed as one
drop in the veins of the slumbering earth–and our
thoughts were dreams.

Aug. 16th 1840

A strain of music reminds me of a passage of the
Vedas.

Aug. 17th 1840

When Robert, afterwards Lord, Clive, with one
hundred and twenty Europeans, and two hundred
Sepoys, was invested in the fort of Arcot by ten thousand
native and French soldiers, and, after a siege of fifty
days, began to feel the pressure of hunger, "The Sepoys
came to Clive–not to complain of their scanty fare,
but to propose that all the grain should be given to the
Europeans, who required more nourishment than
the natives of Asia. The thin gruel, they said, which
was strained away from the rice, would suffice for
themselves."

When I revolve it again in my mind, looking into the
west at sunset, whether these ordinances of the Hindoos
are to be passed by as the whims of an Asiatic brain,
I seem to see the divine Brahma himself sitting in
an angle of a cloud, and revealing himself to his scribe
Menu, and imagine that this fair modern creation is
only a reprint of the Laws of Menu with the Gloss
of Culucca. Tried by a New England eye, or the mere
practical wisdom of modern times–they are simply
the oracles of a race already in its dotage, but held up to

the sky, which is the only impartial and incorruptibl
ideal, they are of a piece with its depth and serenity,
and I am assured that they will have a place and
significance, as long as there is a sky to test them by.
They are not merely a voice floating in space for my own
experience is the speaker.

Aug. 19th 1840

Some events in history are more remarkable than
momentous—like eclipses of the sun by which all
are attracted, but whose effects no one calculates.

Homer was a greater hero than Ajax or Achilles.

Sir Thomas Overbury, who says that Raleigh followed
the sherriff out of court "with admirable erection, but
yet in such a sort as became a man condemned", has a
share in that exploit by his discernment. We admire
equally him who could do the deed, and him who could
see it done.

When nobleness of soul is accompanied by grace and
dignity of action—then especially has it a current
stamp and value.

Aug 20th 1840.

The historian of Greece and Rome is usually disabled
and unmanned by his subject—as a peasant cringes
and crouches before Lords.— From specimens I should
judge that Raleigh had done better than this.— When
the best man takes up the pen then will the best history
be written. He will shake all men by the hand from
Adam down, looking them familiarly in the face. He
will stalk down through the aisles of the past as through
the avenues of a camp, with poets and historians for

his guides and heralds, and from whatever side the
faintest trump reaches his ear, that way will he turn
though it lead to the purlieus of the camp, to the
neglect of many a gaudy pavilion.

It was a maxim of Raleigh—"that good success admits
of no examination.

Aug. 21st 1840

In fact, good success can only spring from good
conduct.

The age in which Sir Water Raleigh lived was indeed
a stirring one. The discovery of America and the
successful progress of the reformation afforded a field
both for the intellectual and physical energies of his
generation. Its fathers were Calvin—and Knox—and
Cranmer, and Pizarro, and Garcilasso; and its immediate
forefathers Luther and Raphael, and Bayard, and
Angelo and Ariosto—and Copernicus—and Machiavel,
and Erasmus—and Cabot, and Ximenes—and Columbus.
Its device should have been an anchor—a sword—and
a quill. The Pizarro laid by his sword and took to his
letters. The Columbus set sail for newer worlds still, by
voyages which did not need the patronage of princes.
The Bayard alighted from his steed to seek adventures
no less arduous in the western world. The Luther
who had reformed religion began now to reform politics
and Science.

In his youth, however it might have concerned him,
Camoens was writing a heroic poem in Portugal, and the
arts still had their representative in Paul Veronese
of Italy. He may have been one to welcome the works
of Tasso and Montaigne to England, and when he
looked about him found such men as Cervantes and
Sidney, men of like pursuit and not altogether dissimilar

genius from himself—a Drake to rival him on the sea,
and a Hudson in western in western adventure—a Halley
—a Gallileo, and a Kepler—for his astronomers—a Bacon
—a Behmen—and a Burton, for his books of philosophy
—and a Spenser and Shakspeare for his refreshment
and inspiration.

He wields his pen as one who sits at ease in his
chair, and has a healthy and able body to back his wits,
and not a torpid and diseased one to fetter them. In
whichever hand is the pen, we are sure there is a
sword in the other.

He sits with his armor on, and with one ear open to
hear if the trumpet sound, as one who has stolen a
little leisure from the duties of a camp. We are confident
that the whole man sat down to the writing of his
books—as real and palpable as an Englishman can be,
and not some curious brain only. Such a man's mere
daily exercise in literature might well astonish us—and
Sir Robert Cecil has said,

"He can toil terribly".

The humane society will not make the hunter
despicable so soon as the butcher nor the grouse shooter
so soon as he who kills sparrows— I feel great respect
for the English deer stalker on reading that " 'His
muscles must be of marble, and his sinews of steel'. He
must not only 'run like the antelope, and breathe like
the trade wind;' but he must be able 'to run in a stooping
position with a grey-hound pace, having his back
parallel to the ground, and his face within an inch of
it for miles together' He must have a taste for running,
like an eel through sand, *ventre à terre*, and he should
be accomplished in skilfully squeezing his clothes
after this operation, to make all comfortable.' "

Aug. 24th 1840

Man looks back eastward upon his steps till they are
lost in obscurity, and westward still takes his way to
the completion of his destiny. Whence he came or
whither he is going nor history nor prophecy can tell
– He sprang where the day springs and his course is
parallel with the sun. History gives no more satisfactory
answer to the one inquiry than the sun which is the
latest messenger from those parts, nor prophecy a
clearer revelation than the sunset. In the east we expect
to see the earth scarred with his first footsteps. It is
that point in the horizon on which our eye finally rests.
No doubt there are as fit fields there as anywhere to be
inhabited by a primitive race and men who lived. like
gods.

Aug 25th 1840

In imagination I seem to see there the grey temples
and hoary brow of the earth. The great plain of India
lies like a cup between the Himmaleh and the ocean, on
the north and south–and the Indus and Brahmapoutra,
on the east and west, wherein the primeval race was
received,–as if it were the cradle of the human race.

Aug 28th 1840

I like to read of the "pine, larch, spruce, and silver
fir," which cover the southern face of the Himmaleh
range–of the "gooseberry, raspberry, strawberry", which
from an imminent temperate zone overlook the torrid
plains. So did this active modern life have even then a
foothold and linking place in the midst of the primeval
stateliness, and contemplativeness of the plain. In
another era the "lilly of the valley, cowslip, dandelion,"
were to work their way down onto the plain, and bloom
in a level zone of their own, reaching round the world.

Aready has the era of the temperate zone arrived,
the era of the pine, and the oak, for the palm and the
Banyan do not supply the wants of the foremost races.
The lichens too on the summits of the rocks are to
find their level ere long,

The fowls which are elsewhere domesticated run wild
in India, and so I think of these domestic thoughts
and fashions when I read the Laws of Menu.

{*One-third page blank*}

Sep. 21st 1840.
In the old Chinese book which the French call
"L'Invariable Milieu" occurs this sentence–"L'ordre
ètablie par le ciel s'appelle *nature*; ce qui est conforme
à la nature s'appelle *loi*; l'etablissement de la loi s'appelle
instruction."

God's order is nature–man's order is law–and the
establishment of law is the subject of instruction

Some of these old distinctions imply a certain
grandeur and completeness in the view, far better than
any modern acuteness and accuracy.– They are a
thought which darted through the universe and solved
all its problems.

The French call writing a dead speech–une parole
morte–and articulate language a living speech–une
parole vive.

To Thales is attributed the saying–"It is hard, but
good, to know oneself; virtue consists in leading a life
conformable to nature."

Sep. 25th 1840.

Social yearnings unsatisfied are the temporalness
of time.

Birds were very naturally made the subject of augury
–for they are but borderers upon the earth–creatures of a
subtler and more etherial element than our existence
can be supported in–which seem to flit between us and
the unexplored.

As I sat on the cliff to-day the crows, as with one
consent, began to assemble from all parts of the horizon
–from river and pond and field, and wood, in such
numbers as to darken the sky–as if a netting of black
beads were stretched across it. After some tacking and
wheeling the centre of the immense cohort was poised
just over my head. Their cawing was deafening, and
when that ceased the winnowing of their wings was like
the rising of a tempest in the forest. But their Silence
was more ominous than their din.– At length they
departed sullenly as they came.

Prosperity is no field for heroism unless it endeavor
to establish an independent and supernatural prosperity
for itself.

In the midst of din and tumult and disorder we
hear the trumpet sound.

Defeat is heaven's success. He cannot be said to
succeed to whom the world shows any favor. In fact it
is the hero's point d'appui, which by offering resistance
to his action ennables him to act at all. At each step
he spurns the world. He vaults the higher in proportion
as he employs the greater resistance of the earth.

It is fatal when an elevation has been gained by too
wide a concession–retaining no point of resistance, for
then the hero like the aeronaut, must float at the

mercy of the winds—or cannot sail for calm weather,
nor steer himself for want of waves to his rudder.

When we rise to the step above, we tread hardest
on the step below.

My friend must be my tent companion.

Saturday Sep. 26th 1840.

The day, for the most part, is heroic only when it
breaks.

Every author writes in the faith that his book is to be
the final resting place of the sojourning soul, and sets
up his fixtures therein as for a more than oriental
permanence—but it is only a caravansery which we soon
leave without ceremony— We read on his sign only
—refreshment for man and beast—and a drawn hand
directs us to Isphahan or Bagdad.

"Plato gives science sublime counsels, directs her
toward the regions of the ideal; Aristotle gives her
positive and severe laws, and directs her toward a
practical end." Degerando.

Sept 27th 1840.
Ideas which confound all things must necessarily
embrace all.

Virtue will be known ere long by her elastic tread.—
When man is in harmony with nature.

Monday Sep. 28th 1840
The world thinks it knows only what it comes in
contact with, and whose repelling points give it a
configuration to the senses—a hard crust aids its distinct

knowledge. But what we truly know has no points of repulsion, and consequently no objective form—being surveyed from within. We are acquainted with the soul and its phenomena, as a bird with the air in which it floats. Distinctness is superficial and formal merely.

We touch objects—as the earth we stand on—but the soul—as the air we breathe. We know the world superficially—the soul centrally.— In the one case our surfaces meet, in the other our centres coincide.

Tuesday Sep. 29th 1840.

Wisdom is a sort of mongrel between Instinct and Prudence, which however inclining to the side of the father, will finally assert its pure blood again—as the white race at length prevails over the black. It is minister plenipotentiary from earth to heaven—but occasionally Instinct, like a native born celestial, comes to earth and adjusts the controversy.

All fair action in man is the product of enthusiasm — There is enthusiasm in the sunset. The shell on the shore takes new layers and new tints from year to year with such rapture as the bard writes his poem. There is a thrill in the spring, when it buds and blossoms —there is a happiness in the summer—a contentedness in the autumn—a patient repose in the winter.

Nature does nothing in the prose mood, though sometimes grimly with poetic fury, as in earthquakes &c and at other times humorously.

Saturday Oct 3d 1840

No man has imagined what private discourse his members have with surrounding nature, or how much the tenor of that intercourse affects his own health and sickness.

While the head goes star gazing the legs are not
necessarily astronomers too, but are acquiring an
independent experience in lower strata of nature. How
much do they feel which they do not impart— How much
rumor dies between the knees and the ears! Surely
Instinct uses this experience.

I am no more a freeman of my own members than
of universal nature. After all the body takes care of
itself—it saves itself from a fall.— It eats—drinks—sleeps
—perspires—digests—grows—dies—and the best economy is
to let it alone in all these.

Why need I travel to seek a site and consult the
points of compass My eyes are south windows, and out
of them I command a southern prospect.

But pray what has seeing to do with the soul that
she must sit always at a window?— for I find myself
always in the rear of my eye.

The eye does the least drudgery of any of the senses.—
It oftenest escapes to a higher employment— The rest
serve, and escort, and defend it— I attach some
superiority even priority to this sense. It is the oldest
servant in the soul's household—it images what it
imagines—it ideates what it idealizes. Through it idolatry
crept in—which is a kind of *religion*. If any joy or
grief is to be expressed the eye is the swift runner that
carries the news. In circumspection double—in fidelity
single—it serves truth always, and carries no false news.
Of five casts it is the Brahmin—it converses with the
heavens. How man serves this sense more than any
—when he builds a house he does not forget to put
a window in the wall.

We *see* truth— We are children of *light* our destiny
is *dark*. No other sense has so much to do with the future

— The body of science will not be complete till every
sense has thus ruled our thought and language, and
action, in its turn.

Oct. 4th 1840

Every country man and dairy-maid knows that the
coats of the fourth stomach of the calf will curdle milk
—and what particular mushroom is a safe and nutritious
diet. You cannot go into any field or wood but it will
seem as if every stone had been turned, and the bark on
every tree ripped up. Surely men are busy and knowing
enough after their fashion. One would suppose that
he who had counted the eyes of a fly and the nerves of
a caterpillar, must have learned the whole duty of
man in his youth. But alas, it is easier to make a white
rose black, or pears grow on an apple tree, than to do
one's duty for five minutes. It is vastly easier to discover
than to see when the cover is off.

A true poem is not known by a felicitous expression,
or by any thought it suggests, so much as by the fragrant
atmosphere which surrounds it— Most have beauty
of outline merely, and stand distinct on the pages. They
are striking as the form and bearing of a stranger
but true verses come toward us indistinctly as the very
kernel of all friendliness. They have an air of loneliness
which makes us long to be with them:—but they do
not want our company.

Oct 5th 1840.

There is one thing which a man cannot wheedle
nor overawe, and that is his genius. It requires to be
conciliated by purer and loftier conduct than the world
asks or can appreciate.— The moon is on the path
of her unconscious duty, when the sun lets the light of
his genius fall on her.

The visitations of genius are unbribed as the dawn.
It is by patient and unanxious labor at the anvil that
fairer mornings are to be compelled.

A part of me which has reposed in silence all day,
goes abroad at night, like the owl, and has its day.

At night we recline, and nestle, and infold ourselves
in our being. Each night I go home to rest. Each night
I am gathered to my fathers. The soul departs out
of the body, and sleeps in God, a divine slumber. As she
withdraws herself, the limbs droop and the eyelids
fall, and nature reclaims her clay again. Men have
always regarded the night as ambrosial or divine. The
air is then peopled–fairies come out.

Tuesday Oct 6th 1840

If we were to see a man die naturally and greatly, we
should learn that the sunset is but a reflection of his
with-drawing aspect.

The revolution of the seasons–is a great and steady
flow–it reminds me of the undulation of the back
in animals of the cat kind–a graceful–peaceful–motion
like the swell on lakes and seas. No where does any
rigidity grow upon nature–no muscles harden, no
bones protrude–but she is supple-jointed now and
always. No rubbish accumulates from day to day, but
still does freshness predominate in her cheek, and
cleanliness in her attire. The dust settles on the fences
and the rocks–and pastures by the road-side–from
year to year–but still the sward is just as green, nay
greener, for all that. How clear the morning air is even
at this day– It is not begrimmed with all the dust
that has been raised. The dew makes all clean again.
Nature keeps her besom always wagging–she has

lumber room no dust hole in her house. No man was
er yet too nice to walk in her woods and fields. His
eligion allows the Arab to cleanse his body with sand,
when water is not at hand.

I have not read any just literary criticism yet–nothing
is considered simply as it lies in the lap of eternal
beauty. Love the truth and write earnestly needs to be
said. The flowing drapery of genius is too often tucked
up and starched lest it offend against the fashions
of the time. What is sacrificed to time is lost to eternity.
This architectural civility and refinement will disappear
with the plaster and white-wash–but depth and solidity
will abide with the granite. I want no politeness nor
ceremony in books–there is no laughing nor sneezing in
their company. Our thoughts as well as our bodies
are dressed after the latest Parisian fashion.

To the finest talent or genius it is the most expensive
to succumb and conform to the ways of the world.
That is the worst of lumber when not the best utensil.
The bird of paradise in consequence of his gay trappings
is obliged constantly to fly against the wind, else his
long feathers pressing close to his body, impede his
free movements. We can strike with gracefuller and
steadier wing in proportion as the atmosphere is more
palpable and offers greater resistance.
The great man fronts the storm and steers in the
eye of the wind–so that his greatness is expanded, and
floats around him, like the plumage of the bird of
paradise.

He is the best sailor who can steer within fewest
points of the wind, and make the least occasion fill his
sails longest. He so extracts a motive power out of

his obstacles. But most begin to veer and tack as soc
the wind changes from aft—and as the wind does not
blow from all points of the compass within the tropic:
—there are some harbors they can never reach.

If I were to write some account of history before it
had a muse assigned it, I should remember this sentence
in Alwákidi's Arabian chronicle. "I was informed by
Ahmed Almatîn Aljorhami, who had it from *Rephâa Ebn
Kais Alámiri*, who had it from *Saiph Ebn Fabalah
Alchátquarni*, who had it from *Thabet Ebn Alkamah*,
who said he was present at the action." Where was Clio?

Wednesday Oct 7th 1840
When one hears a strain of music he feels his blood
flow in his veins.

{*One-fifth page blank*}

Saturday Oct 10th 1840
All life must be seen upon a proper back ground—else,
however refined, it will be cheap enough— Only the
life of some anchorite or nun or moody dweller among
his fellows will bear to be considered— Our actions lack
grandeur in the prospect—they are not so impressive as
objects in the desert, a broken shaft or crumbling
mound against a limitless horizon.

The fuel on the hearth sings a requiem—its fine
strain tells of untrodden fields of virtue.

Oct 11th 1840
It is always easy to infringe the law—but the Bedouin
of the desert find it impossible to resist public opinion.

The traveller Stevens had the following conversation
with a Bedouin of Mount Sinai. "I asked him who

governed them; he stretched himself up and answerd
in one word, 'God'. I asked him if they paid tribute
to the pasha; and his answer was, 'No, we take tribute
from him.' I asked him how. 'We plunder his caravans.'
Desirous to understand my exact position with the
sheik of Akaba, under his promise of protection, I asked
him if they were governed by their sheik; to which he
answered, 'No, we govern him'.

The true man of science will have a rare Indian
wisdom—and will know nature better by his finer
organization. He will smell, taste, see, hear, feel, better
than other men. His will be a deeper and finer experience
We do not learn by inference and deduction, and the
application of mathematics to philosophy but by direct
intercourse. It is with science as with ethics—we cannot
know truth by method and contrivance—the Baconian
is as false as any other method. The most scientific
should be the healthiest man.

Deep are the foundations of all sincerity—even stone
walls have their foundation below the frost.
Aristotle says in his "Meteorics" "As time never fails,
and the universe is eternal, neither the Tanais, nor
the Nile, can have flowed forever."
Strabo, upon the same subject, says, "It is proper to
derive our explanations from things which are obvious,
and in some measure of daily occurrence, such as
deluges, earthquakes, and volcanic eruptions, and
sudden swellings of the land beneath the sea." —Geology.

Marvellous are the beginnings of philosophy— We can
imagine a period when "Water runs down hill" may have
been taught in the schools. That man has something
demoniacal about him who can discern a law, or couple
two facts.

Every idea was long ago done into nature as the
translators say— There is walking in the feet—mechanics
in the hand climbing in the loose flesh of the palms
—boxing in the knuckles &c, &c.

In a lifetime you can hardly expect to convince a
man of an error— You must content yourself with the
reflection that the progress of science is slow. If he is not
convinced his grand children may be. It took 100
years to prove that fossils are organic, and 150 more,
to prove that they are not to be referred to the Noachian
deluge.

Oct 12th 1840.

The springs of life flow in ceaseless tide down below,
and hence this greenness everywhere on the surface.
But they are as yet untapped—only here and there men
have sunk a well.

One of the wisest men I know, but who has no
poetic genius—has lead me round step by step in his
discourse this afternoon, up to the height of land in these
parts; but now that I am left alone, I see the blue
peaks in the horizon, and am homesick.

Tuesday Oct 13th 1840.

The only prayer for a brave man is to be a doing—this
is the prayer that is heard.

Why ask God for a respite when he has not given it.
Has he not done his work and made man equal to
his occasions, but he must needs have recourse to him
again? God cannot give us any other than self help.

The workers in stone polish only their chimney
ornaments, but their pyramids are roughly done
— There is a soberness in a rough aspect, as unhewn

ınite—which addresses a depth in us, but the polished
ırface only hits the ball of the eye.

In all old books the stucco has long since crumbled
away, and we read what was sculptured in the granite.

To study style in the utterance of our thoughts, is
as if we were to introduce Homer or Zoroaster to
a literary club thus,—Gentlemen of the societies—let me
make you acquainted with Sir Homer.— Think you if
Socrates were to come on earth, he would bring letters
to the prominent characters? But a better than Socrates
speaks through us every hour and it would be a poor
story if we did not defer as much to him by waving
impertinent ceremony.

True politeness does not result from a hasty and
artificial polishing, but grows naturally by a long
fronting of circumstances and rubbing on good and bad
fortune.

The elements are yet polishing the pyramids.

The draft of my stove sounds like the dashing of
waves on the shore, and the lid sings like the wind in
the shrouds.

The steady roar of the surf on the beach is as incessant
in my ear as in the shell on the mantelpiece— I see
vessels stranded—and gulls flying—and fishermen running
to and fro on the beach.

Wednesday Oct 14th 1840

I arose before light
To work with all my might,
With my arms braced for toil
Which no obstacle could foil,
For it robbed me of my rest
Like an anvil on my breast.

But as a brittle cup
I've held the hammer up,
And no sound from my forge
Has been heard in the gorge.

I look forward into night,
And seem to get some light;
E're long the forge will ring
With its ding-dong-ding,
For the iron will be hot
And my wages will be got.

Oct 15th 1840
There is not a chestnut in the wood but some worm
has found it out. He will seem to be at home there,
and not far from the highway. Every maggot lives down
town.

Men see God in the ripple but not in miles of still
water. Of all the two-thousand miles that the St.
Lawrence flows—pilgrims go only to Niagara

Saturday Oct 17th 1840.
In the presence of my friend I am ashamed of my
fingers and toes. I have no feature so fair as my love for
him. There is a more than maiden modesty between
us. I find myself more simple and sincere than in my
most private moment to myself. I am literally true
with a witness. We should sooner blot out the sun than
disturb friendship.

Sunday Oct 18th 1840
The era of greatest change is to the subject of it
the condition of greatest invariableness. The longer
the lever the less perceptible its motion. It is the slowest
pulsation which is the most *vital*. I am independent
of the change I detect.

My most essential progress must be to me a state of absolute rest. So in geology we are nearest to discovering the true causes of the revolutions of the globe, when we allow them to consist with a quiescent state of the elements. We discover the causes of all past change in the present invariable order of the universe.

The pulsations are so long that in the interval there is almost a stagnation of life. The first cause of the universe makes the least noise. Its pulse has beat but once–is now beating. The greatest appreciable revolutions are the work of the light-footed air–the stealthy-paced water–and the subterranean fire. The wind makes the desert without a rustle.

To every being consequently its own first cause is an insensible and inconceivable agent.

Some questions which are put to me, are as if I should ask a bird what she will do when her nest is built, and her brood reared.

I cannot make a disclosure–you should see my secret. – Let me open my doors never so wide, still within and behind there, where it is unopened, does the sun rise and set–and day and night alternate.– No fruit will ripen on the common.

Monday Oct 19th 1840.

My friend dwells in the distant horizon as rich as an eastern city there. There he sails all lonely under the edge of the sky, but thoughts go out silently from me and belay him, till at length he rides in my roadsted. But never does he fairly come to anchor in my harbor – Perhaps I afford no good anchorage. He seems to move in a burnished atmosphere, while I peer in upon him from surrounding spaces of Cimmerian darkness. His house is incandescent to my eye, while I have no house, but only a neighborhood to his.

Tuesday Oct 20th 1840.
My friend is the apology for my life. In him are the
spaces which my orbit traverses.

There is no quarrel between the good and the bad—but
only between the bad and the bad. In the former case
there is inconsistency merely, in the latter a vitious
consistency.

Men chord sometimes, as the flute and the pumpkin
vine—a perfect chord—a harmony—but no melody.
They are not of equal fineness of tone.
For the most part I find that in another man and
myself the key note is not the same—so that there are no
perfect chords in our gamuts. But if we do not chord
by whole tones, nevertheless his sharps are sometimes
my flats, and so we play some very difficult pieces
together, though the sameness at last fatigues the ear.
We never rest on a full natural note—but I sacrifice
my naturalness and he his. We play no tune though
—only chromatic strains—or trill upon the same note till
our ears ache

Sunday Oct 25th 1840.
To yield bravely is infinitely harder than to resist
bravely. In the one course our sin assists us to be brave,
in the other our virtue is alone. True bravery has no
ally yet all things are with it.

We do not see in a man all he promises, but certainly
all he is. Just as the aspirations do not completely
appear in the features, but they are always in a transition
state— The past is in the rind, but the future is in
the core. The promise of a man must have become
experience and character before it can be expressed in
his face.

So this outward expression is after all a fair index
of his present state, for virtue is not all van, but needs
to be viewed both before and behind. In his aspirations
virtue is but a superficies and I know not if it be thick
or thin—but the features are made up of successive
layers of performance—and show the thickness of the
character The past and future met together make the
present.— Virtue is not virtue's face.

{*One-fourth page blank*}

Nov. 1st 1840
The day is won by the blushes of the dawn

I thought that the sun of our love should have risen as
noiselessly as the sun out of the sea, and we sailors
have found ourselves steering between the tropics as if
the broad day had lasted forever. You know how the
sun comes up from the sea when you stand on the cliff,
and does'nt startle you, but every thing, and you too
are helping it.

Monday Nov 2nd 1840.
It is well said that the "attitude of inspection is
prone." The soul does not inspect but behold. Like the
lily or the crystal in the rock, it looks in the face of
the sky.

Francis Howell says that in garrulous persons "The
supply of thought seems never to rise much above
the level of its exit." Consequently their thoughts issue
in no jets, but incessantly dribble. In those who speak
rarely, but to the purpose, the reservoir of thought
is many feet higher than its issue. It takes the pressure
of a hundred atmospheres to make one jet of eloquence.
For the most part the thoughts subside like a sediment,

while the words break like a surf on the shore. They
are being silently deposited in level strata, or held
in suspension for ages, in that deep ocean within
– Therein is the ocean's floor whither all things sink,
and it is strewed with wrecks.

{*One-fourth page blank*}

Tuesday Nov. 3d 1840
The truth is only contained, never withheld– As a
feudal castle may be the head quarters of hospitality,
though the portal is but a span in the circuit of the wall.
So of the three circles on the cocoa nut one is always
so soft that it may be pierced with a thorn, and the
traveller is grateful for the thick shell which held the
liquor so faithfully.

Wednesday Nov. 4th 1840
By your few words show how insufficient would be
many words. If after conversation I would reinstate
my thought in its primary dignity and authority, I have
recourse again to my first simple and concise statement.
In breadth we may be patterns of conciseness, but
in depth we may well be prolix

We may have secrets though we do not keep them.

Dr. Ware Jr. said today in his speech at the meeting
house–"There are these three–Sympathy–Faith
–Patience"–then proceeding in ministerial style, "and
the greatest of these is," but for a moment he was
at a loss, and became a listener along with his audience,
and concluded with "Which is it? I do'nt know. Pray
take them all brethren, and God help you".

Nov 5th 1840

Truth is as vivacious and will spread it self as fast
as the fungi, which you can by no means annihilate
with your heel, for their sporules are so infinitely
numerous and subtle as to resemble "thin smoke; so
light that they may be raised into the atmosphere, and
dispersed in so many ways by the attraction of the
sun, by insects, wind, elasticity, adhesion, &c., that it is
difficult to conceive a place from which they may be
excluded."

Saturday Nov 7th 1840.

–I'm guided in the darkest night
By flashes of auroral light,
Which over-dart thy eastern home
And teach me not in vain to roam.
Thy steady light on t'other side
Pales the sunset, makes day abide,
And after sunrise stays the dawn,
Forerunner of a brighter morn.

There is no being here to me
But staying here to be.
When others laugh I am not glad,
When others cry I am not sad,
But be they grieved or be they merry
I'm supernumerary.
I am a miser without blame,
Am conscience striken without shame
An idler am I without leisure,
A busy body without pleasure.
I did not think so bright a day
Would issue in so dark a night,
I did not think such sober play
Would leave me in so sad a plight,
And I should be most sorely shent
When first I was most innocent.

I thought by loving all beside
To prove to you my love was wide,
And by the rites I soared above
To show you my peculiar love.

{*One-fifth page blank*}

Monday Nov. 9th 1840

Events have no abstract and absolute importance,
but only concern me as they are related to some man.
The biography of a man who has spent his days in
a library, may be as interesting as the Peninsular
campaigns. Gibbon's memoirs prove this to me. To my
mind he travels as far when he takes a book from
the shelf, as if he went to the barrows of Asia. If the
cripple but tell me how like a man he turned in his seat,
how he now looked out at a south window then a
north, and finally looked into the fire, it will be as good
as a tour on the continent or the prairies. For I measure
distance inward and not outward. Within the compass
of a man's ribs there is space and scene enough for
any biography.

My life passes warmly and cheerily here within
while my ears drink in the pattering rain on the sill. It
is as adventurous as Crusoe's—as full of novelty as
Marco Polo's, as dignified as the Sultan's, as momentous
as that of the reigning prince.

Thursday Nov. 12th 1840.

Mathematical truths stand aloof from the warm life
of man—the mere cold and unfleshed skeletons of truth.

Perhaps the whole body of what is now called moral
or ethical truth may have once existed as abstract

science, and have been only gradually won over to humanity.– Have gradually subsided from the intellect into the heart.

The eye that can appreciate the naked and absolute beauty of a scientific truth, is far rarer than that which discerns moral beauty. Men demand that the truth be clothed in the warm colors of life–and wear a flesh and blood dress. They do not love the absolute truth, but the partial, because it fits and measures them and their commodities best–but let them remember that notwithstanding these delinquencies in practice –Science still exists as the sealer of weights and measures.

Sunday Nov. 15th 1840.

Over and above a man's business there must be a level of undisturbed serenity, only the more serene as he is the more industrious–as within the reef encircling a coral isle, there is always an expanse of still water, where the depositions are going on which will finally raise it above the surface.

He must preside over all he does– If his employment rob him of a serene outlook over his life, it is but idle though it be measuring the fixed stars. He must know no distracting cares.

The bad sense is the secondary one.

{Three-fourths page blank}

Nov. 11th I obtained a levelling instrument and circumferentor combined, and have since ascertained the height of the cliff hill–and surveyed other objects.

Height of Cliff Hill above the River

Progress		Position	Eleva
1st rise	12.10		12.1
2nd	12.91		25.01
3d	12.63		37.64
	11.49		49.13
	12.80		61.93
	12.50		74.43
	13.26	Bars in wall	87.69
	12.41		100.10
	12.40		112.50
	11.80	Pointed Rock.	124.30
	12.18	Turned "	136.48
	13.20	Near split Rock	149.68
	12.47	stone in path.	162.15
	12.31		174.46
	11.44	Stone by bars	185.90
	13.26	Stone in path near rock on right.	199.16
	12.64	Two birches by wall	211.80
	12.		223.80
	7.29	Top of Rock in Woods	231.09

The river was about three feet above low water mark.

{*Nine-tenths page blank*}

Wednesday Dec. 2nd 1840

The lake is a mirror in the breast of nature, as if
there were there nothing to be concealed. All the sins of
the wood are washed out in it. See how the woods
form an amphitheatre about it—and it becomes an arena
for all the genialness of nature. It is the earth's liquid
eye—it is blue or grey, or black as I choose my time. In
the night it is my more than forty feet reflector. It is the
cynosure of the wood, all trees direct the traveller
to its brink—all paths seek it out—birds fly to it—and

quadrupeds flee to it—and the very ground inclines
toward it. It is nature's saloon, or where she has sat
down to her toilet. The sun dusts its surface each
morning by evaporation. Always a fresh surface wells
up. I love to consider the silent economy and tidiness
of nature, how after all the filfth of the wood, and
the accumulated impurities of the winter have been
rinsed herein, this liquid transparency appears in the
spring.

I should wither and dry up if it were not for lakes
and rivers. I am conscious that my body derives its juices
from their waters, as much as the muskrat or the
herbage on their brink. The thought of Walden in the
woods yonder makes me supple jointed and limber for
the duties of the day. Sometimes I thirst for it.

There it lies all the year reflecting the sky—and from
its surface there seems to go up a pillar of ether, which
bridges over the space between earth and heaven.

Water seems a middle element between earth and
air. The most fluid in which man can float.

Across the surface of every lake there sweeps a
hushed music.

My body is invigorated by the cones and needles of
the pine seen against this frosty air— This is no thin diet.

Dec 3d 1840

Music in proportion as it is pure is distant. The strains
I now hear seem at an inconceivable distance, yet
remotely within me. Remotes throws all sound into my
inmost being and it becomes music, as the slumbrous
sounds of the village, or the tinkling of the forge—from
across the water or the fields. To the senses that is
farthest from me which addresses the greatest depth
within me.

Friday Dec. 4th 1840.

Methinks I have experienced a joy sometimes like that with which yonder tree for so long, has budded and blossomed—and reflected the green rays.

The opposite shore of the pond seen through the haze of a September afternoon, as it lies stretched out in grey content, answers to some streak in me.

I love to look aslant up the tree tops from some dell, and finally rest myself in the blueish mistiness of the white pines.

Many's the pine I know—that's a greybeard and wears a cocked hat.

Thursday Dec 10th 1840.

I discover a strange track in the snow, and learn that some migrating otter has made across from the river to the wood, by my yard and the smith's shop, in the silence of the night.— I cannot but smile at my own wealth, when I am thus reminded that every chink and cranny of nature is full to overflowing.— That each instant is crowded full of great events. Such an incident as this startles me with the assurance that the primeval nature is still working and makes tracks in the snow.

It is my own fault that he must thus skulk across my premises by night.— Now I yearn toward him—and heaven to me consists in a complete communion with the otter nature.

Mere innocence will tame any ferocity.

He travels a more wooded path, by watercourses and hedgerows—I by the highway—but though his tracks are now crosswise to mine, our courses are not divergent, but we shall meet at last.

{*One-third page blank*}

Dec 11th 1840

A man who had failed to fulfil an engagement to
me, and grossly disappointed me, came to me tonight
with a countenance radiant with repentance, and
so behaved that it seemed as if I was the defaulter, and
could not be satisfied till he would let me stand in
that light.— How long a course of strict integrity might
have come short of such confidence and good will!
— Such a "Roman recovery" was worth a thousand tons
of coal. The crack of his whip was before attractive
enough, but such conciliatory words from that shaggy
coat and coarse comforter I had not expected. I saw
the meaning which lurked far behind his eye all the
better for the dark, as we see some faint stars better
when we do not look directly at them with the full
light of the eye. A true contrition when witnessed will
humble integrity itself.

Dec 12th 1840.

Society seems very natural and easy—can I not walk
among men as simply as in the woods? I am greeted
everywhere with mild looks and words, and it seems
as if the eaves were running and I heard the sough
of melting snow all around me.

The young pines springing up in the corn fields from
year to year are to me a much more agreeable fact
than the most abundant harvests. My last stronghold is
the forest.

{Two-fifths page blank}

Dec. 14th 1840

How may a man most cleanly and gracefully depart
out of nature? At present his birth and death are
offensive and unclean things. Disease kills him, and
his carcass smells to heaven. It offends the bodily

sense, only so much as his life offended the moral sense.
It is the odor of sin.

His carcass invites sun and moisture, and makes
haste to burst forth into new and disgusting forms of
life with which it already teemed. It was no better than
carrion before but just animated enough to keep off
the crows. The birds of prey which hover in the rear of
an army are an intolerable satire on mankind, and may
well make the soldier shudder. The mosquito sings
our dirge–he is charon come to ferry us over the styx
– He preaches a biting homily to us. He says put
away beef and pork–small beer and ale, and my trump
shall die away and be no more heard. The intemperate
cannot go nigh to any wood or marsh but he hears
his requiem sung– All nature is up in arms against him.
He who will dance must pay the fiddler. Gnats and
mosquitos are the original imps and demons.

Man lays down his body in the field and thinks from
it as a stepping stone to vault at once into heaven, as
if he could establish a better claim there when he had
left such a witness behind him on the plain.– Our
true epitaphs are those which the sun and wind write
upon the atmosphere around our graves so conclusively
that the traveller does not draw near to read the lie
on our tombstones. Shall we not be judged rather by
what we leave behind us, than what we bring into
the world? The guest is known by his leavings. When
we have become intolerable to ourselves shall we
be tolerable to heaven?– Will our spirits ascend pure
and fragrant from our tainted carcasses?

May we not suffer our impurities gradually to
evaporate in sun and wind, with the superfluous juices
of the body, and so wither and dry up at last like a
tree in the woods, which possesses a sort of embalmed
life after death, and is as clean as the sapling or fresh

buds of spring. Let us die by *dry* rot at least. The dead
tree still stands erect without shame or offence amidst its
green brethren, the most picturesque object in the wood.
The painter puts it into the foreground of his picture,
for its death is pleasant to be remembered.

When nature finds man returned on her hands, he is
not simply those pure elements she has contributed to
his growth, but with her floods she must wash away and
with her fires burn up the filfth that has accumulated,
before she can receive her own again. He poisons
her gales, and is a curse to the land that gave him
birth— She is obliged to employ her scavengers in self
defence to abate the nuisance.

May not man cast his shell with as little offence
as the muscle, and it perchance be a precious relic to be
kept in the cabinets of the curious? May we not amuse
ourselves with it, as when we count the layers of a
shell, and apply it to our ear, to hear the history of its
inhabitant in the swell of the sea–the pulsation of
the life which once passed therein still faintly echoed?

We confess that it was well done in nature thus
to let out her particles of lime to the muscle and coral,
to receive them back again with such interest.

The ancients were more tidy than we who subjected
the body to the purification of fire before they returned
it upon nature–for fire is the true washer, water only
displaces the impurity. Fire is thorough–water is
superficial.

Tuesday Dec. 15th 1840.
In the woods one bough relieves another, and we
look into them, not with strained, but relaxed, eyes.
Seeing has a holiday in their maze.– But as soon as
man comes into nature, by running counter to her,
and cutting her off where she was continuous, he makes

her angular and formal, and when we would bathe our eyes in the prospect it only makes them ache.

I saw today where some pines had been felled at various angles with the rest of the wood, and on that side nature offended me, as a diagram. It seemed as if man could not lay his tree gracefully along the earth as the wind does, but my eye as well as the squirrel's would detect it. I saw squares and triangles only.

When most at one with nature I feel supported and propped on all sides by a myriad influences, as trees in the plain and on the hill side are equally perpendicular – The most upright man is he that most entirely reclines–(the prone recline but partially). By his entire reliance he is made erect. Men of little faith stand only by their feet–or recline on the ground, having lost their reliance on the soul.

Nature is right, but man is straight. She erects no beams, she slants no rafters, and yet she builds stronger and truer than he. Every where she preaches not abstract but practical truth– She is no beauty at her toilet, but her cheek is flushed with exercise. The moss grows over her triangles. Unlike the man of science she teaches that skeletons are only good to wear the flesh, and make fast the sinews to–that better is the man than his bones.

There seem to be some qualities of the mind, which, like the size and strength of the bones–cannot be altered by the will of the possessor–while the most are less stubborn and in more rapid flux like the flesh.

In health all the senses are indulged and each seeks its own gratification.– it is a pleasure to see, and to walk, and to hear–&c

In the fields lights and shadows are my diet. How
all trees tell of the sun— It is almost the only game the
trees play at—this tit for tat—now this side in the sun,
then that.

It is pleasant to work out of doors— My pen knife
glitters in the sun—my voice is echoed from the woods,
if an oar drops I am fain to drop it again, if my cane
strikes a stone, I strike it again— Such are the acoustics
of my work shop.

Wednesday Dec 16th 1840.

Nothing is so beautiful as the tree tops. A pine or
two with a dash of vapor in the sky—and our elysium is
made.— Each tree takes my own attitude sometime.
Yonder pine stands like Caesar. I see Cromwell, and
Jesus, and George Fox in the wood, with many savages
beside. A fallen pine, with its green branches still freshly
drooping, lies like Tecumseh with his blanket about
him. So the forest is full of attitudes, which give it
character. In its infinite postures I see my own erectness,
or humbleness—or sneaking—I am posture-master to
the wood. I duck with the willow and hold up my head
with the pine. The fair proportions of a great man like
those of a tree are but the balancing of his accidents The
vicissitudes of fortune are his sun wind, and rain.

Speech is fractional, silence is integral.

Beauty is where it is perceived. When I see the sun
shining on the woods across the pond, I think this side
the richer which sees it.

The motion of quadrupeds is the most constrained
and unnatural; it is angular and abrupt, except in
those of the cat tribe, where undulation begins. That of

birds and fishes is more graceful and independent–they
move on a more inward pivot. The former move by
their weight or opposition to nature, the latter by their
boyancy, or yielding to nature. Awkwardness is a
resisting motion, gracefulness is a yielding motion. The
line which would express the motion of the former
would be a tangent to the sphere, of the latter a radius.
But the subtlest and most ideal and spiritual motion
is undulation. It is produced by the most subtle element
falling on the next subtlest–and the latter impelling
itself. Rippling is a more graceful flight. If you consider
it from the hill top you will detect in it the wings of
birds endlessly repeated. The two waving lines which
express their flight seem copied from the ripple.–
There is something analogous to this in our most
inward experience. In enthusiasm we undulate to the
divine spiritus–as the lake to the wind.

Thursday Dec. 17 1840

The practice of giving the feminine gender–to all
ideal excellence personified, is a mark of refinement,
observable in the mythologies even of the most
barbarous nations. Glory and victory even are of the
feminine gender, but it takes manly qualities to gain
them. Man is masculine, but his manliness (virtus)
feminine. It is the inclination of brute force to moral
power.

Dec. 18th 1840.

I find Gibbon to have been less a man and more of
a student than I had anticipated– I had supposed him
a person of more genius with as much learning, more
an enthusiast than a pedant, better fitted to influence an
active and practical people like the English, than to
lead in a German School.

He had very little greatness. His Roman History, by
his own confession, was undertaken from no higher
motive than the love of fame. In his religious views he
did not differ nobly from mankind, but rather apologized
and conformed. He was ambitious and vain. It was a quite
paltry ambition that inspired his first Essay—his
observations on the AEneid, and the Decline an Fall—and
vanity inspired his memoirs of his own life. In his letters
he was more literary than social, they are moments
grudgingly given to his friends, whom he kept in pay
to inform him how that world went on from which he
had retired.

I hear him smack his lips at the prospect of a pipe
of wine to be sent from England to Lausanne. There is
not recorded of him, that I know, a single reckless
and heroic action, which would have been worth a
thousand histories. That would have been to Rise and
Stand. He withdrew into retirement in Switzerland, not
to perfect his culture, but be more at leisure to build
up a reputation undisturbed. He respected and courted
the doctors and learned, not the learning. I think of
him only as the laborious ambitious student who wrote
the Decline & Fall, during those 56 years—which after
all it does not concern me to read.

Dec. 19th 1840.

This plain sheet of snow which covers the ice of the
pond, is not such a blancness as is unwritten, but such
as is unread. All colors are in white. It is such simple
diet to my senses as the grass and the sky. There is
nothing fantastic in them. Their simple beauty has
sufficed men from the earliest times.— they have never
criticised the blue sky and the green grass.

{*One-third page blank*}

Dec. 20th 1840.
When I see lines set to catch pickerel through the
ice, and men moving about over the white ground like
pieces of forest furniture, I am pleased to think how
they are domesticated in nature. The pond is their deal
table or sanded floor, and the woods rising abruptly
from its edge–their walls.

My home is as much of nature as my heart embraces,
if I only warm my house, then is that only my home. But
if I sympathize with the heats and colds–the sounds and
silence of nature and share the repose and equanimity
that reigns around me in the fields then are they my
house, as much as if the kettle sang–and the faggots
crackled, and the clock ticked on the wall.

I am as much moved and elevated when I consider
men fishing on Walden Pond in the winter, as when
I read the exploits of Alexander in history. Their actions
are very nearly related. The occasions and scenery
are so similar that the difference is unimportant.

I rarely read a sentence which speaks to my muse
as nature does.– Through the sweetness of his verse,
without regard to the sense, I have communion with
Burns. His plaint escapes through the flexure of his
verses. It was all the record it admitted.

Dec 21st 1840
Where ever I walk I seem to have come upon ground
where giants have been at play. Nature looks too big
to fit me, and I would fall contentedly into some crevice
along with leaves and acorns.

Thursday Dec 24th 1840.
The same sun has not yet shined on me and my
friend.– He would hardly have to look at me to recognise

me—but glimmer with half shut eye, like some friendly
distant taper when we are benighted.— I do not talk
to any intellect in nature, but am presuming an infinite
heart somewhere—into which I play— Nature has many
ryhmes, but friendship is the most heroic of all.

Dec 25th 1840.

The character of Washington has after all been
undervalued, simply because not valued correctly. He
was a proper Puritan hero. It is his erectness and
persistency which attract me. A few simple deeds with
a dignified silence for background and that is all.

He never fluctuated, nor lingered, nor stooped, nor
swerved, but was nobly silent and assured. He was
not the darling of the people, as no man of integrity
can ever be, but was as much respected as loved.
His instructions to his steward—his refusal of a crown
—his interview with his officers at the termination of the
war,—his thoughts after his retirement as expressed
in a letter to La Fayette—his remarks to another
correspondent on his being chosen President—his last
words to Congress—and the unparalled respect which
his most distinguished cotemporaries—as Fox and
Erskine, expressed for him—are refreshing to read in
these unheroic days.

His behavior in the field and in council, and his
dignified and contented withdrawal to private life—were
great. He could advance and he could withdraw.

But we are not sorry he is dead.

The thought there is in a sentence is its solid part,
which will wear to the latest times.

Sat. Dec. 26 1840.

There is as good as a mine under my feet wherever
I go.— When the pond is frozen and covered with
snow, I do not suspect the wealth under my feet. How

many pickerel are poised on easy fin fathoms below
the loaded wain.– The revolution of the seasons must
be a curious phenomenon to them. Now the sun and
wind brush aside their curtain and they see the heavens
again.

{*One-fifth page blank*}

Sunday Dec. 27th 1840
The wood gaily wears its burden of snow. It is glad
and warm always, sometimes even more genial in winter
than in summer. The snow melts round every tree.

In a little hollow between the hills, some twenty feet
higher than the village, lies Walden pond, the expressed
juice of the hills and trees whose leaves are annually
steeped in it. Its history is in the lapse of its waves,
in the rounded pebbles on its shore, and the pines which
have grown on its brink.

It has its precessions and recessions, its cycles and
epicycles–it has not been idle, though sedentary as
Abu Musa–who says that "Sitting still at home is the
heavenly way. The going out is the way of the world."
Yet in its evaporations and by a thousand unimagined
ways it has travelled as far as any.

Dec. 28th 1840.
The snow hangs on the trees as the fruit of the season.
In those twigs which the wind has preserved naked,
there is a warmer green for the contrast. The whole tree
exhibits a kind of interior and household comfort–a
sheltered and covert aspect– It has the snug inviting
look of a cottage on the moors, buried in snows.

How like your house are the woods, you voice rings
hollowly through them as through a chamber– The
twigs crackle under feet with private and household

echoes. All sound in the woods is private and domestic
still, though never so loud.

I have, observed of a clear winters morning that the
woods have their southern window as well as the house,
through which the first beams of the sun stream along
their aisles and corridors. The sun goes up swiftly
behind the limbs of the white pine, as the sashes of
a window.

The sun reflected from the red leaves of the shrub
oak on the hill side–and the green pine needles, is
as warm as a cottage fire. It has the ancient principle of
heat in it–a gentle simmering to eternity. There is a
Slumbering fire, an infinite eternal warmth in nature
which never goes out, and no cold can chill. It melts the
great snow

Only the fates intercede between friends.

Tuesday Dec 29th 1840

An echo makes me enunciate distinctly– So the
sympathy of a friend gives plainness and point to my
speech. This is the advantage of letter writing.

Dec. 30th 1840

In the sunrise I see an eastern city with its spires, in
the sunset a western forest.–

The woods are an admirable fence to the landscape
–every where skirting the horizon.

You see some trees in the fields which are but
overgrown bushes; no matter how large they are, for
character is of no dimensions.

The western landscape early of a winter's morning
reminds me of the shadowy realms of Pluto–it is clothed

in such a sombre Tartarean light. The trees stand very much as Dante and Virgil have described them. They are only infernal sounds that you hear—the crowing of cocks—the barking of dogs—the chopping of wood—the lowing of kine—all come from over the Styx.

The elegance of Virgil's digressions, though too often to flatter his age or patron, is admirable.

Our Golden Age must after all be a pastoral one, we would be simple men in ignorance, and not accomplished in wisdom. We want great peasants more than great heroes. The sun would shine along the highway to some purpose, if we would unlearn our wisdom and practise illiterate truth henceforth. The great dwell in cottages on the moor, whose windows the sun visits from day to day with his ray, and of their greatness none knoweth but that there they dwell. They write no Iliads nor Hamlets more than the Columbine at their doors.

Let us grow to the full stature of our humbleness —ere we aspire to be greater.

It is great praise in the poet to have made husbandry famous.—

"In the new spring, when cool moisture from the hoary mountains flows,
"And the mouldering clod is dissolved by the zephyr,
"Then straightway let the bull with deep pressed plough begin
"To groan, and the share, worn by the furrow, to shine.
Georg. 1st 43d.

And again when the husbandman conducts water down the slope to restore his thirsty crops.
"That falling makes a hoarse murmur among the

smooth rocks, and tempers the parching fields with its bubbling streams." ibid 109th.

Describing the end of the Golden Age and the commencement of the reign of Jupiter, he says—

"He shook honey from the leaves, and removed fire,
"And stayed the wine every where flowing in rivers;
"That experience by meditating might invent various arts
"By degrees, and seek the blade of corn in furrows,
"And strike out hidden fire from the veins of the flint.

131st

{One-fifth page blank}

Thursday Dec. 31st 1840.

To discover a gleam in the trenches, and hear a music in the rattling of the tool we work with—is to *have* an *eye* and an *ear*— We should not be sad on account of the sins of men, but glad in our own innocence. Another man's sin never made me sad, it was my own. A burnishing of spades and ploughshares the country over—would be symbolic of the true reform.

There must be respiration as well as aspiration— We should not walk on tiptoe, but healthily expand to our full circumference on the soles of our feet.

This sickly preaching of love, and a sympathy that will be tender of our faults, is the dyspepsia of the soul.

If aspiration be repeated long without intervals of respiration—it will be no better than expiration or simply losing one's breath— In the healthy for every aspiration there will be a respiration, which is to make his idea take shape, and give its tone to the character. Every time he steps boyantly up—he steps solidly down again, and stands the firmer on the ground for his independence

upon it. We should fetch the whole–heel–sole–and
toe–horizontally down to earth.

Let not ours be a wiped virtue, as men ago about with
an array of clean linnen, but unwashed as a fresh
flower. Not a clean sunday garment, but better as a
soiled work-day one.

{*One-fifth page blank*}

January–1841.

Friendship–in The Dial Dec. 28th 1840

Friends–
They cannot help,
They cannot hurt,
Nor in indifference rest,
But when for a host's service girt,
They are a mutual guest.

They are a single power
Plenipotentiary,
No minister of state,
Anxious and wary
Decides their fate.

Where interest's self is
There is no go-between,
But where another reaps,
They do but glean
In scanty heaps.

They have learned well to hate,
And never grant reprieve,
Nor e'er succumb to love,
But sternly grieve,
And look above.

—

If faults arise, my friend will send for me
As some great god,
Who will the matter try,
Holding the scales, even or odd,
Under the sky—

Who will award strict justice
All the while,
Confounding mine and thine,
And share his smile,
When they 'gainst me incline.

{*One-half page blank*}

When in some cove I lie,
A placid lake at rest,
Scanning the distant hills,
A murmur from the west,
And gleam of thousand rills
Which gently swell my breast,
Announce the friendly thought,
And in one wave sun-lit
I'm softly brought
Seaward with it.

{*One-half page blank*}

Jan 1st 1841.

All men and women woo me. There is a fragrance
in their breath—
"Nosque—equis oriens afflavit anhelis"
And if now they hate, I muse as in sombre cloudy
weather, not despairing of the absent ray.
"Illic sera rubens accendit lumina Vesper".

Jan 2nd 1841

My virtue loves to take an airing of a winter's morning
—it scents itself, and snuffs its own fragrance in the
bracing atmosphere of the fields—more than in the
sluggishness of the parlor.

The searching wind drives away all contagion, and
nothing can stand before it in the fields, but what
has a virtue in it, and so if I meet anything in very cold
and bleak places, as the tops of mountains, I respect
it for a sort of sturdy innocence, and Puritan toughness
— At such times it seems as if all God's creatures were
called in for shelter, and what stayed out must be
part of the original frame of the universe–, and of
such valor as God himself.– There is a very warm fire
under the traveller's fear-nought.

The shrub oaks rustling in the thin cold breeze are
a simmering crackling fire. They have more heat
than the pines. Green is a cold color.

The richness of the outline of the wood against the
sky is in proportion to the number of distinct interstices
through which the light straggles to us.

Every needle of the white pine trembles distinctly
in the breeze, which on the sunny side gives the whole
tree a shimmering seething aspect.
I stopped short in the path today to admire how the
trees grow up without forethought regardless of the
time and circumstances. They do not wait as men do
— Now is the golden age of the sapling– Earth, air, sun,
and rain, are occasion enough– They were no better
in primeval centuries. The "winter of their discontent"
never comes– Witness the buds of the native poplar,
standing gaily out to the frost, on the sides of its
bare switches– They express a naked confidence.

With cheerful heart I could be a sojourner in the
wilderness if I were sure to find there the catkins of the
alder. When I read of them in the accounts of Northern

adventurers, by Baffin's bay or Mackenzie's river, I
see how even there too I could dwell. They are my little
vegetable redeemer. Methinks my virtue will not flag
ere they come again. They are worthy to have had a
greater than Neptune or Ceres for their donor– Who was
the benignant goddess that bestowed them on mankind?

I saw a fox run across the pond today on the snow
with the carelessness of freedom. As at intervals I
traced his course in the sunshine as he trotted along the
ridge of a hill on the crust, it seemed as if the sun
never shone so proudly, sheer down on the hill side, and
the winds and woods were hushed in sympathy. I
gave up to him sun and earth, as to their true proprietor.
He did not go in the sunshine, but the sunshine seemed
to follow him. There was a visible sympathy between
him an it.

It would be worth the while to be a wood-chopper,
for every sound would echo to heaven.– Virgil says as
much.

Jan 4th 1841.

I know a woman who is as true to me and as incessant
with her mild rebuke as the blue sky– I stand under
her cope, and instantly all pretension drops off–for she
plys me like wind and rain, to remove all taint. I am
fortunate that I can pass and repass before her as a
mirror each day–and prove my strength in her glances.
She is far truer to me than to herself. Her eyes are
such bottomless and inexhaustible depths as if they
were the windows of nature, through which I caught
glimpses of the native land of the soul. The sun shines
for this inner and lower world, but through them gleams
a milder and steadier light than his. His rays are in
eclipse when they shine on me. Methinks in these *soular*
rays there is no refraction of the light.

Tuesday Jan 5th 1841.

I grudge to the record that lavish expenditure of
love and grace which are due rather to the spoken
thought—a man writes because he has no opportunity to
speak.— Why should he be the only mute creature,
and his speech no part of the melody of the grove? He
never gladdens the ear of nature—he ushers in no
spring with his lays.

We are more anxious to speak than to be heard.

Wednesday Jan 6th 1841.

We are apt to imagine that this hubbub of Philosophy
—Literature, and Religion—which is heard in pulpits
—Lyceums, & parlors—vibrates through the universe—and
is as catholic a sound as the creaking of the earth's
axle— But if a man sleep soundly he will forget it
all between sunset and dawn. It is the three inch swing
of some pendulum in a cubbord.— Which the great
pulse of nature vibrates clearly and through each
instant.— When we lift our lids—and open our ears—it
disappears, with smoke and rattle, like the cars on
the railroad.

Thursday Jan 7th 1841

There is no covert in nature but it covers a man—this
is what we mean by the genialness of nature.

There is a total disinterestedness and self
abandomment vein in fretfulness and despondency,
which few attain to. If there is no personality or
selfishness, you may be as fretful as you please. I
congratulate myself on the richness of human nature,
which a virtuous and even temper had not wholly
exhibited. May it not whine like a kitten or squeak like
a squirrel? Some times the weakness of my fellow
discovers a new suppleness, which I had not anticipated.

We are not inspired to speak, I guess, but to be silent.

Jan. 8th 1841.
Man finds himself in life, but with no hint for the
conduct of an hour.– Conscience only informs that
he must *behave*

Jan 9th 1841
Each hearty stroke we deal with these outward
hands, slays an inward foe.

Sunday Jan. 10th 1841
A perfectly healthy sentence is extremely rare,
Sometimes I read one which was written while the
world went round, while grass grew and water ran.

The church bell is not a natural sound to the church
goer.

> Who hears the parson
> Will not hear the bell,
> But if he deafly pass on
> He will hear of hell.

> I' faith the people go to church
> To leave the devil in the lurch,
> But since they've carpeted the pews
> To squat with hymn books he doth use.

The first beams of the sun are a sovereign remedy
for wrinkles.
He seems to come rolling his car over the slopes with
the faint clashing or swinging sound of cymbals.

I dont like people who are too good for this world.
Let a man reserve a good appetite for his peck of dirt,
and expect his chief wealth in unwashed diamonds. To
know nature and ourselves well, we must have acquired
a certain hardness and habitual equanimity.

The virtue of some is only an excessive refinement.—
In comparison with theirs the sternness and rigidity
of the Hebrew faith is refreshing.

Only the tender sex, and their hangers on, will mind
such a last trump as I have heard foretold, but men
of true mettle will prefer to buffet it here a spell longer.

{*One-fourth page blank*}

Monday Jan 11th 1841
"In the 'human face divine', portrait painters affirm
that the two sides never correspond; and even when
the external form of an animal exhibits an appearance
of bilateral or radiate symmetry, nature departs from
it in her arrangement of the internal structure."

> H. E. Strickland "on the Natural System"—in
> "The Annals and Magazine of Natural History"
> —No 36 for Nov. 1840. London.

{*One-fifth page blank*}

Wednesday Jan 13th 1841.
We should offer up our *perfect* thoughts to
the gods daily—our writing should be hymns and
psalms. Who keeps a journal is purveyor for the Gods.
There are two sides to every sentence; the one is
contiguous to me, but the other faces the gods, and no
man ever fronted it. When I utter a thought I launch a
vessel which never sails in my haven more, but goes
sheer off into the deep. Consequently it demands a
godlike insight—a fronting view, to read what was greatly
written.

Jan 14th 1841.
As for public speaking, diffidence may prompt us to
excessive circumspection, and to hold ourselves in our

own hands, and over see our own conduct in the debate, or we may throw ourselves on the occasion, and the sympathies of the audience, In the former case we are quite defenceless because prepared but for one thing, and may be discomfitted by any simple and natural accident, in the latter this will help us, and furnish an argument for the truth we are asserting.

Friday Jan. 15th 1841.

When men die they do not leave their works behind them—but they will find rather that they have gone before them.

Saturday Jan 16th 1841.

"Sic Vita"—in The Dial.

Sunday Jan 17th 1841.

A true happiness never happened, but rather is proof against all haps. I would not be a happy, that is, a lucky man, but rather a necessitated and doomed one.

After so many years of study I have not learned my duty for one hour. I am stranded at each reflux of the tide—and I who sailed as boyantly on the middle deep as a ship, am as helpless as a muscle on the rock.

I cannot account to myself for the how I live. Here time has given me a dull prosaic evening, not of kin to Vesper or Cynthia—a dead lapse—where time's stream seems settling into a pool—a stillness not as if nature's breath were held but expired. But let me know that such hours as this are the healthiest in time's gift— It is the insufficiency of the hour, which if we but feel and understand, we shall reassert our independence then.

{One-third page blank}

Monday Jan. 18th 1841

We must expect no income beside our outgoes—we must succeed now, and we shall not fail hereafter. So soon as we begin to count the cost the cost begins.

If our scheme is well built within, any mishap to the outbuilding will not be fatal.

The capital wanted is an entire independence upon all capital, but a clear conscience, and a resolute will.

When we are so poor that the howling of the wind shall have a music in it, and not declare war against our property—they proprietors may well envy us. We have been seeking riches not by a true industry or building within, but by mere accumulation, putting together what was without till it rose a heap beside us.— We should rather acquire them by the utter renunciation of them. If I hold a house and land as property am I not disinherited of sun, wind, rain, and all good beside? The richest are only some degrees poorer than nature.

It is impossible to have more property than we dispense— Genius is only as rich as it is generous, if it hoards it impoverishes itself.— What the banker sighs for the meanest clown may have, leisure and a quiet mind.

Tuesday Jan. 19th 1841

The mind which first contemplated the present order of things at some remote era—must have been visionary and Utopian.

Coleridge, speaking of the love of God, says—"He that loves, may be sure he was loved first." The love wherewith we are loved is already declared, and afloat in the atmosphere, and our love is only the inlet to it. It is an inexhaustible harvest—always ripe and ready for the sickle. It grows on every bush, and let not them

complain of their fates who will not pluck it. We need
make no beggarly demand for it, but pay the price, and
depart. No–transaction can be simpler– Loves accounts
are kept by single-entry.

When we are amiable, then is love in the gale, and in
sun, and shade, and day and night, and to sigh under
the cold cold moon for a love unrequited, is to put a
slight upon nature; the natural remedy would be to fall
in love with the moon and the night, and find our love
requited.

I anticipate a more thorough sympathy with nature
when my thigh-bones shall strew the ground like
the boughs which the wind has scattered.– These
troublesome humors will flower into early anemonies,
and perhaps in the very lachrymal sinus, nourished
by its juices, some young pine or oak will strike root.

What I call pain when I speak in the spirit of a
partizan, and not as a citizen of the body, would be
serene being if our interests were one. Sickness is civil
war– We have no external foes–even death will take
place when I make peace with my body–and set my
seal to that treaty which transcendent justice has so long
required. I shall at length join interest with it.

The mind never makes so great effort, without a
corresponding energy of the body– When great resolves
are entertained its nerves are not relaxed, nor its
limbs reclined.

Wednesday Jan 20th 1841.
Disappointment will make us conversant with the
nobler part of our nature, it will chasten us, and
prepare us to meet accident on higher ground the next

time— As Hannibal taught the Romans the art of war.
So is all misfortune only our stepping-stone to fortune.

The desultory moments—which are the grimmest
features of misfortune—are a step before me on which I
should set foot, and not stumbling blocks in the path.—
To extract its whole good I must be disappointed with
the best fortune, and not be bribed by sunshine nor
health.

Oh Happiness—what is the stuff thou art made of? Is
it not gossamer and floating spider's webs?—a crumpled
sunbeam—a coiled dew line settling on some flower?
What moments will not supply the reel from which
thou may'st be wound off?— Thou art as subtle as the
pollen of flowers—and the sporules of the fungi.

When I meet a person unlike me, I find myself
wholly in the unlikeness. In what I am unlike others,
in that I am.

When we ask for society—we do not want the double
of ourselves—but the complement rather.

Society should be additive and helpful, we would be
reinforced by its alliance. True friends will know
how to use each other in this respect, and never barter
or interchange their common-wealth, just as barter
is unknown in families. They will not dabble in the
general coffers, but each put his finger into the private
coffer of the other. They will be most familiar, they
will be most unfamiliar, for they will be so one and
single that common themes and things will have to be
bandied between them, but in silence they will digest
them as one mind; but they will at the same time
be so two and double, that each will be to the other as
admirable and as inaccessible as a star When my

friend comes I view his orb "through optic glass", "At
evening from the top of Fesolé."

After the longest earthly period he will still be in
apogee to me.

But we should so meet ourselves as we meet our
friends, and still ever seek for us in that which is above
us, and unlike us. So only shall we see the light of
our own

{*One leaf missing*}

countenances.

Jan 21st 1841.

We can render men the best assistance, by letting
them see how sore a thing it is to need any assistance.
I am not in haste to help men more than God is. If they
will not help themselves, shall I become their abettor?

If I have unintentionally injured the feelings of any
—or prophaned their sacred character, we shall be
necessitated to know each other better than before.—
I have gained a glorious vantage ground then. And
to the other, the shaft which carried the wound, will
bear its own remedy with it, for we cannot be prophaned
without the consciousness that we have a holy fane
for our asylum somewhere.

Would that sincere words might always drive men
thus to earth themselves!

Jan 22nd 1841.

I hear it complained of some modern books of genius,
that they are irregular, and have no flow, but we should
consider that the flow of thought is more like a tidal
wave than a prone river, and is the effect of a celestial

influence, or sort of ground swell, it may be, and not of
any declivity in its channel, each wave rising higher
than the former, and partially subsiding back on it.
But the river flows, because it runs down hill, and
descends faster, as it flows more rapidly. The one
obeys the earthly attraction, the other the heavenly
attraction. The one runs smoothly because it gravitates
toward the earth alone, the other irregularly because
it gravitates toward the heavens as well.

The reader who has been accustomed to expend all
his energy in the launching—as if he were to float down
stream for the whole voyage— may well complain of
nauseating ground swells, and choppings of the sea,
when his frail shore craft gets amidst the breakers of the
ocean stream—which flows as much to sun and moon,
as lesser streams to it— If he would appreciate the
true flow that is in these books, he must expect to see it
rise from the page like an exhalation—and wash away
the brains of most like burr-millstones. They flow
not from right to left, or from left to right, but to higher
levels, above and behind the reader.

{*One-third page blank*}

{*Back endpaper*}

·4·

January 23–March 27, 1841

TRANSCRIBED 1841

Jan. 23d 1841

A day is lapsing. I hear cockrils crowing in the yard,
and see them stalking among the chips in the sun. I
hear busy feet on the floors—and the whole house jars
with industry. Surely the day is well spent—and the
time is full to overflowing. Mankind is as busy as
the flowers in summer—which make haste to unfold
themselves in the forenoon, and close their petals
in the afternoon.

The momentous topics of human life are always of
secondary importance to the business in hand, just
as carpenters discuss politics between the strokes of the
hammer, while they are shingling a roof.

The squeaking of the pump sounds as necessary
as the music of the spheres.

The solidity and apparent necessity of this routine
—insensibly recommend it to me. It is like a cane or
a cushion for the infirm, and in view of it all are infirm.
If there were but one erect and solid standing tree in
the woods, all creatures would go to rub against it, and
make sure of their footing. Routine is a ground to
stand on, a wall to retreat to; we cannot draw on our
boots without bracing ourselves against *it*. It is the
fence over which neighbors lean when they talk. All
this cockcrowing and hawing and geeing, and business
in the streets, is like the spring board on which tumblers
perform, and develope their elasticity.

Our health requires that we should recline on it
from time to time. When we are in it, the hand stands
still on the face of the clock, and we grow like corn
in the genial dankness and silence of the night. Our
weakness wants it, but our strength uses it. Good for the

body is the work of the body, and good for the soul
the work of the soul, and good for either the work of the
other—let them not call hard names, nor know a divided
interest.

When I detect a beauty in any of the recesses of nature,
I am reminded by the serene and retired spirit in which
it requires to be contemplated, of the inexpressible
privacy of a life— How silent and unambitious it is— The
beauty there is in mosses will have to be considered
from the holiest—quietest nook.

The gods delight in stillness, they say 'st—'st. My truest
—serenest moments are too still for emotion—they have
woolen feet.— In all our lives we live under the hill,
and if we are not gone we live there still.

Sunday—Jan 24th 1841.
I almost shrink from the arduousness of meeting men
erectly day by day — —

Be resolutely and faithfully what you are—be humbly
what you aspire to be— Be sure you give men the best
of your wares, though they be poor enough, and the
gods will help you to lay up a better store for the future.
Man's noblest gift to man is his sincerity, for it embraces
his integrity also. Let him not dole out of himself
anxiously, to suit their weaker or stronger stomachs,
but make a clean gift of himself, and empty his coffers
at once.— I would be in society as in the landscape; in
the presence of nature there is no reserve, nor effrontery

Coleridge says of the "*ideas* spoken out everywhere in
the Old and New Testament," that they—"resemble the
fixed stars, which appear of the same size to the naked
as to the armed eye; the magnitude of which the
telescope may rather seem to diminish than to increase."

It is more proper for a spiritual fact to have suggested
an analogous natural one, than for the natural fact
to have preceded the spiritual in our minds.

By spells seriousness will be forced to cut capers,
and drink a deep and refreshing draught of silliness; to
turn this sedate day of Lucifer's and Apollo's, into
an all fool's day for Harlequin and Cornwallis. The sun
does not grudge his rays to either, but they are alike
patronised by the gods. Like overtasked school boys
all my members, and nerves and sinews, petition
thought for a recess,—and my very thigh bones itch
to slip away from under me, and run and join the
meleè— I exult in stark inanity, leering in nature and
the soul. We think the gods reveal themselves only
to sedate and musing gentlemen, but not so, the buffoon
in the midst of his antics, catches unobserved glimpses,
which he treasures for the lonely hour. When I have
been playing tom fool I have been driven to exchange
the old for a more liberal and catholic philosophy.

Monday Jan 25th 1841.
To-day I feel the migratory instinct strong in me,
and all my members and humors anticipate the breaking
up of winter. If I yielded to this impulse it would surely
guide me to summer haunts. This ill defined restlessness
and fluttering on the perch, do no doubt prophecy
the final migration of souls out of nature to a serener
summer, in long harrows and waving lines through
the spring weather, over what fair uplands and fertile
pastures winging their way at evening—and seeking
a resting place with loud cackling and uproar!—

Wealth, no less than knowledge, is power. Among
the Bedouins the richest man is the Sheik, among

Savages he who has most iron and wampum is chief—and in England and America he is the merchant prince.

We should strengthen, and beautify, and industriously mould our bodies to be fit companions of the soul.— Assist them to grow up like trees, and be agreeable and wholsome objects in nature.— I think if I had had the disposal of this soul of man—I should have bestowed it sooner on some antelope of the plains, than upon this sickly and sluggish body.

Tuesday Jan 26th 1841.
I have as much property as I can command and use.— If by a fault in my character I do not derive my just revenues, there is virtually a mortgage on my inheritance. A man's wealth is never entered in the regristrar's office. Wealth does not come in along the great thorough-fares, it does not float on the Erie or Pennsylvania canal, but is imported by a solitary track without bustle or competition—from a brave industry to a quiet mind.

I had a dream last night which had reference to an act in my life, in which I had been most disinterested and true to my highest instinct, but completely failed in realizing my hopes; and now, after so many months, in the stillness of sleep, complete justice was rendered me. It was a divine remuneration— In my waking hours I could not have conceived of such retribution; the presumption of desert, would have damned the whole. But now I was permitted to be not so much a subject as a partner to that retribution. It was the award of divine justice, which will at length be, and is even now accomplished.

Good writing as well as good acting will be obedience
to conscience. There must not be a particle of will or
whim mixed with it.– If we can listen we shall hear. By
reverently listening to the inner voice, we may reinstate
ourselves on the pinnacle of humanity.

Wednesday Jan 27th 1841.
In the compensation of the dream, there was no
implied loss to any, but immeasurable advantage to all.
The punishment of sin is not positive, as is the reward
of virtue.

For a flower, I like the name pansy–or pensèe, best
of any.

Jan 28th 1841.
No innocence can quite stand up under suspicion–if it
is conscious of being suspected– In the company of
one who puts a wrong construction upon your actions,
they are apt really to deserve a mean construction.
While in that society I can never retrieve myself.
Attribute to me a great motive, and I shall not fail to
have one, but a mean one, and the fountain of virtue will
be poisoned by the suspicion. Show men unlimited faith
as the coin with which you will deal with them, and
they will invariably exhibit the best wares they have.
I would meet men as the friends of all their virtue,
and the foes of all their vice, for no man is the partner
of his guilt.
If you suspect me you will never see me, but all
our intercourse will be the politest leavetaking, I shall
constantly defer and apologise, and postpone myself
in your presence. The self defender is acursed in the
sight of gods and men; he is a superfluous knight

who serves no lady in the land. He will find in the
end that he has been fighting windmills, and battered
his mace to no purpose.

The injured man with querulous tone resisting his
age, is like a tree struck by lightning, which rustles its
sere leaves the winter through, but being dead has
not vigor enough shake them off.

As for apologies—I must be off with the dew and the
frost, and leave mankind to repair the damage with
their gauze screens and straw.

Resistance is a very wholesome and delicious morsel
at times,

When Venus advanced against the Greeks with
resistless valor, it was by far the most natural attitude
into which the poet could throw his hero to make him
resist heroically. To a devil one might yield gracefully,
but a god would be a worthy foe, and would pardon
the affront.

It would be worth while once for all, fairly and
cleanly, to tell how we are to be used, as venders of
lucifer matches send directions in the envelope, both
how light may be readily procured, and no accident
happen to the user. — —

Let your mood determine the form of salutation, and
approach the creature with a natural nonchalance,
as though he were anything but what he is, and you
were anything but what you are,—as though he were
he, and you were you—in short, as though he were so
insignificant that it did not signify—and so important
that it did not import. — —

Depend upon it the timber is well seasoned and tough,
and will bear rough usage, and if it should crack there
is plenty more where it came from. I am no piece of

China ware that cannot be jostled against my neighbor,
without danger of rupture from the collision, and
must needs ring a scrannel strain to the end of my days
when once I am cracked, but rather one of the old
fashioned wooden trenchers, which one while stands at
the head of the table, and at another is a milking stool,
and at another a seat for children; And finally goes
down to its grave not unadorned with honorable scars,
and does not die till it is *worn* out. Use me for I am
useful in my way. I stand as one of many petitioners
from toadstool and henbane, up to dahlia and violet,
supplicating to be put to my use—if by any means
ye may find me servicible, whether for a medicated
drink or bath—as balm and lavender—or for fragrance, as
verbenum and geranium—or for sight, as cactus, or for
thoughts, as pansy.

If ye ask me for God's tropes and Divine rhymes, I
shall be more likely to give ye rumblings from the
infernal regions. Take me for all in all.

Jan 29th 1841.

There is something proudly thrilling in the thought,
that this obedience to conscience and trust in God,
which is so solemnly preached in extremities and
arduous circumstances, is only to retreat to ones self,
and rely on our own strength. In trivial circumstance
I find myself sufficient to myself, and in the most
momentous I have no ally but myself, and must silently
put by their harm by my own strength, as I did the
former. As my own hand bent aside the willow in my
path, so must my single arm put to flight the devil and
his angels. God is not our ally when we shrink and
neuter when we are bold.

If by trusting in God, you lose any particle of your
vigor—trust in him no longer. When you trust do not lay

aside your armor but put it on, and buckle it tighter.
If by reliance on the gods I have disbanded one of
my forces, then was it poor policy. I had better have
retained the most inexperienced tyro, who had straggled
into the camp, and let go the heavenly alliance. I
cannot afford to relax discipline, or neglect to lay up a
single munition, because the gods are on my side—for
they are those gods. And if the gods were only the
heavens I fought under, I would not care if they stormed
or were calm— I do not want a countenance but a
help.— And there is more of God, and divine help, in my
little finger, than in idle prayer and trust.

The best and bravest deed, is that which the whole
man—heart, lungs, hands, fingers, and toes, at any
time prompt. Each hanger on in the purlieus of the
camp, must strike his standard at the signal from the
Praetorian tent, and fall into the line of march; but if a
single suttler delay to make up his pack, then suspect
the fates and consult the omens again. This is the
meaning of integrity; this is to be an integer, and not
a fraction. Be even for all virtuous ends, but odd for all
vice. Be a perfect power, so that any of your roots
multiplied into itself may give the whole again.

Beauty is compared, not measured, for it is the
creature of proportions, not of size. Size must be subdued
to it. It is hard for a tall or a short person to be beautiful.
To graft the Persian lilac on the ash, is as if you were
to splice the thigh bones of the Venus de Medici.
Friends will have to be introduced each time they
meet. They will be eternally strange to one another,
and when they have mutually appropriated their value
for the last hour, they will go and gather a new measure
of strangeness for the next. They are like two boughs

crossed in the wood, which play backwards and forwards
upon one another in the wind, and only wear into
each other, but never the sap of the one flows into the
pores of the other, for then the wind would no more
draw from them those strains which enchanted the
wood. They are not two united, but rather one divided.

Of all strange and unaccountable—things this
journalizing is the strangest, it will allow nothing to be
predicated of it; its good is not good, nor its bad bad.
If I make a huge effort to expose my innermost and
richest wares to light, my counter seems cluttered with
the meanest homemade stuffs, but after months or
years, I may discover the wealth of India, and whatever
rarity is brought overland from Cathay, in that confused
heap, and what perhaps seemed a festoon of dried
apple or pumpkin, will prove a string of Brazilian
diamonds, or pearls from Corromandel.

Men lie behind the barrier of a relation as effectually
concealed as the landscape by a mist; and when at
length some unforeseen accident throws me into a new
attitude to them, I am astounded, as if for the first
time I saw the sun on the hill-side.— They lie out before
me like a new order of things.— As when the master
meets his pupil as a man.— Then first do we stand under
the same heavens—and master and pupil alike go down
the resistless ocean stream together.

Saturday Jan. 30th 1841.
Far over the fields, between the tops of yonder wood,
I see a slight cloud not larger than the vapor from a
kettle, drifting by its own inward purpose in a direction
contrary to the planet. As it flits across the dells and
defiles of the tree tops, now seen then lost behind a pine,

I am curious to know wherein its will resides, for to
my eye it has no heart, nor lungs, nor brain, nor any
interior and private chamber, which it may inhabit.
Its motion reminds me of those lines of Milton—

"As when far off at see a fleet descried
"Hangs in the clouds, by equinoctial winds
"Close sailing from Bengala, or the isles
"Of Ternate and Tidore, whence merchants bring
"Their spicy drugs; they on the trading flood,
"Ply stemming nightly toward the pole—

The snow collects upon the plumes of the pitch
pine in the form of a pineapple, which if you divide
in the middle will expose three red kernels like the
tamarind stone. So does winter with his mock harvest
jeer at the sincerity of summer. The tropical fruits
which will not bear the rawness of our summer, are
imitated in a thousand fantastic shapes by the whimsical
genius of winter.

In winter the warmth comes directly from the sun,
and is not radiated from the earth.— In summer I forget
to bless the sun for his heat, but when I feel his beams
on my back, as I thread some snowy dale, I am grateful
as for a special kindness, which would not be weary
of welldoing, but had pursued me even into that by place,

When the wind blows the fine snow comes filtering
down through all the aisles of the wood, in a golden
cloud.

The trees covered with snow admit a very plain and
clean light, but not brilliant, as if through windows
of ground glass—a sort of white darkness it is—all of the
sun's splendor that can be retained.

The fashions of the wood are more fluctuating than those of Paris—snow—rime—ice—green and dry leaves, incessantly make new patterns. There are all the shapes and hues of the kaleidiscope, and the designs and cyphers of books of heraldry in the outlines of the trees. Every time I see a nodding pine top, it seems as if a new fashion of wearing plumes had come into vogue.

I saw a team come out of a path in the woods, as though it had never gone in—but belonged there and only came out like Elisha's bears. It was wholly of the village, and not at all of the wood.

These particles of snow which the early wind shakes down, are what is stirring, or the morning news of the wood.
Sometimes it is blown up above the trees, like the sand of the desert.

You glance up these paths, closely imbowerd by bent trees, as through the side aisles of a cathedral, and expect to hear a quire chanting from their depths. You are never so far in them, as they are far before you. Their secret is where you are not, and where your feet can never carry you.

I tread in the tracks of the fox which has gone before me by some hours, or which perhaps I have started, with such a tiptoe of expectation, as if I were on the trail of the spirit itself which resides in these woods, and expected soon to catch it in its lair.
The snow falls on no two trees alike, but the forms it assumes are as various as those of the twigs and leaves which receive it. They are as it were predetermined

by the genius of the tree. So one divine spirit descends alike on all, but bears a peculiar fruit in each. The divinity subsides on all men, as the snow flakes settle on the fields, and ledges, and take the form of the various clefts and surfaces in which it lodges.

Here is the distinct trail of a fox stretching quarter of a mile across the pond. Now I am curious to know what has determined its graceful curvatures, its greater or less spaces and distinctness, and how surely they were coincident with the fluctuations of some mind. Why they now lead me two steps to the right, and then three to the left— If these things are not to be called up and accounted for in the Lamb's Book of Life, I shall set them down for careless accountants. Here was one expression of the divine mind this morning.

The pond was his journal, and last nights snow made a *tabula rasa* for him. I know which way a mind wended this morning.— what horizon it faced by the setting of these tracks—whether it moved slowly or rapidly; by the greater or less intervals and distinctness —for the swiftest step leaves yet a lasting trace.

Sometimes I come out suddenly upon a high plain, which seems to be the upper level and true surface of the earth—and by its very baldness aspires, and lies up nearer to the stars. A place where a decalogue might be let down or a saint translated.

I take a horse and oxen, standing among the woodpiles in the forest, for one of them, and when at length the horse pricks his ears, and I give him another name, where's the difference? I am startled by the possibility of such errors, and the indifference with they are allowed to occur.

Fair Haven Pond is *scored* with the trails of foxes,
and you may see where they have gambolled and
gone through a hundred evolutions, which testify to a
singular listlessness, and leisure in nature.

Suddenly looking down the river I saw a fox some
sixty rods off, making across to the hills on my left. As
the snow lay five inches deep, he made but slow progress,
but it was no impediment to me. So yielding to the
instinct of the chase, I tossed my head aloft, and
bounded away, snuffing the air like a fox hound; and
spurning the world and the humane society at each
bound. It seemed the woods rang with the hunter's horn,
and Diana and all the satyrs joined in the chace, and
cheered me on. Olympian and Elean youths were
waving palms on the hills.– In the meanwhile I gained
rapidly on the fox, but he showed a remarkable presence
of mind, for in stead of keeping up the face of the
hill which was steep and unwooded in that part, he
kept along the slope in the direction of the forest, though
he lost ground by it. Notwithstanding his fright he took
no step which was not beautiful– The course on his
part was a series of most graceful curves. It was a sort
of leopard canter, I should say, as if he were nowise
impeded by the snow, but were husbanding his strength
all the while. When he doubled I wheeled and cut
him off, bounding with fresh vigor, and Anteus like,
recovering my strength each time I touched the snow.
Having got near enough for a fair view, just as he
was slipping into the wood, I gracefully yielded him the
palm. He ran as though there were not a bone in his
back, occasionally dropping his muzzle to the snow
for a rod or two, and then tossing his head aloft, when
satisfied of his course. When he came to a declivity
he put his forefeet together and slid down it like a
cat. He trod so softly that you could not have heard it

from any nearness, and yet with such expression,
that it would not have been quite inaudible at any
distance. So hoping this experience would prove a useful
lesson to him—I returned to the village by the highway
of the river.

There is all the romance of my youthfullest moment
in music. Heaven lies about us as in our infancy.
There is nothing so wild and extravagant that it does
not make true. It makes a dream my only real experience,
and prompts faith to such elasticity, that only the
incredible can satisfy it. It tells me again to trust the
remotest, and finest, as the divinest instinct. All that I
have imagined of heroism, it reminds and reassures
me of. It is a life unlived, a life beyond life, where at
length my years will pass. I look under the lids of Time

Sunday Jan. 31st 1841.

At each step man measures himself against the
system. If he can not actually belay the sun, and make
it fast to this planet, yet the British man alone spins
a yarn in one year, which will reach fifty one times the
distance from the earth to the sun. So having his cable
ready twisted and coiled, the fixed stars are virtually
within his grasp. He carries his lasso coiled at his
saddlebow, but is never forced to cast it.

All things are subdued to me by virtue of that coiled
lasso I carry, and I lead them without the trouble of
a cast. It is the rope that lies coiled on the deck which
moors my ship, and I have never to bend a cable.

In God's hall hang cables of infinite length—and
in his entries stand bars of infinite strength, but

{One leaf missing}

those cables were never bent, nor those bars ever poised,
for all things have been subdued to the divinity from
the first, and these are the seals of his power.

The guilty never escape–for a steed stands ever ready saddled and bridled at God's door, and the sinner surrenders at last.

End of my Journal of 396 ps

{*One-half·page blank*}

Tuesday Feb. 2nd 1841.

It is easy to repeat but hard to originate. Nature is readily made to repeat herself in a thousand forms –and in the Daguerreotype her own light is amanuensis, and the picture too has more than a surface significance –a depth equal to the prospect–so that the microscope may be applied to the one as the spy-glass to the other. Thus we may easily multiply the forms of the outward, but to give the within outwardness, that is not easy.

That an impression may be taken, perfect stillness, though but for an instant, is necessary– There is something analogous in the birth of all rhymes.–
Our sympathy is a gift whose value we can never know –nor when we impart it. The instant of communion is when, for the least point of time, we cease to oscillate, and coincide in rest–by as fine a point as a star pierces the firmament.

The stars are the mountain peaks of the beyond country.

A child asked its father what became of the old moon, and he said it was cut up into stars.

There is always a single ear in the audience to which we address ourselves.

How much does it concern you, the good opinion of
your friend–therein is the measure of fame.– For the
herd of men multiplied many times will never come up
to the value of one friend.– In this society there is no
fame but love, for as our name may be on the lips
of men, so are we in each others hearts. There is no
ambition but virtue, for why should we go round about,
who may go direct?

All those contingences which the philanthropist
–statesman, and housekeeper write so many books to
meet, are simply and quickly settled in the intercourse of
friends.

For our aspirations there is no expression as yet,
but if we obey steadily, by another year, we shall have
learned the language of last year's aspirations.

When I read the other day the weight of some of the
generals of the Revolution, it seemed no unimportant
fact in their biography– It is at least one other means of
comparing ourselves with them– Tell me how much
Milton or Shakspeare weighed and I will get weighed
myself, that I may know better what they are to me.

Weight has something very imposing in it–for we can
not get rid of it. Once in the scales we must weigh
– And are we not always in the scales, and weighing
just our due, though we kick the beam, and do all
we can to heavy or lighten ourselves?

Wednesday Feb. 3d 1841.

The present seems never to get its due–it is the
least obvious–neither before, nor behind, but within us.
All the past plays into this moment, and we are what
we are. My aspiration is one thing, my reflection another,

but over all myself and condition–is and does. To men
and nature I am each moment a finished tool–a spade
–a barrow or a pick-axe. This immense promise is no
efficient quality– For all practical purposes I am done.

When we do a service to our neighbor, we serve our
next neighbor.

We are constantly invited to be what we are; as to
something worthy and noble. – – I never waited but
for myself to come round; none ever detained me, but I
lagged or tagged after myself.

It steads us to be as true to children and boors, as to
God himself. It is the only attitude which will suit all
occasions,–it only will make the earth yield her increase
–and by it do we effectually expostulate with the wind.
If I run against a post this is the remedy. I would meet
the morning and evening on very sincere ground–when
the sun introduces me to a new day, I silently say to
myself–let us be faithful all round, we will do justice and
receive it. Something like this is the secret charm of
nature's demeanor toward us, strict consciensciousness
and disregard of us when we have ceased to have regard
for ourselves.– So she can never offend us. How true she
is and never swerves– In her most genial moment her
laws are as steadfastly and relentlessly fulfilled–though
the decalogue is rhymed and set to sweetest music–as in
her sternest.

Any exhibition of affection–as an inadvertent
word–or act–or look–seems premature–as if the time
were not ripe for it–like the buds which the warm days
near the end of winter, cause to push out and unfold
before the frosts are yet gone.

My life must seem as if it were passing at a higher
level than that which I occupy. It must possess a dignity
which will not allow me to be familiar

The unpretending truth of a simile implies sometimes
such distinctness in the conception as only experience
could have supplied. Homer could not improve the
simile of a soldier who was careful enough to tell the
truth. If he knows what it was, he will know what
it was like.

As the ancient Britons were exhibited in Rome in
their native costume—and the Dacian came to display
his swordsmanship in the arena— So Tyrolese peasants
have come farther yet—even from the neighborhood of
Rome—to Concord—for our entertainment this night.

Thursday Feb. 4th 1841.
When you are once comfortably seated at a public
meeting, there is something unmanly in the sitting
on tiptoe, and *qui vive* attitude—the involuntarily rising
into your into throat—as if gravity had ceased to operate
—when a lady approaches with quite godlike presumption
to elicit the miracle of a seat where none is.

Music will make the most nervous chord vibrate
healthily.

Such a state of unrest becomes only a fluttered virtue
—when once I have learned my place in the sphere I
will fill it once for all—rather like a fixed star than a
planet—I will rest as the mountains do—so that your ladies
might as well walk into the midst of the Tyrol, And
look for nature to spread them a green lawn for their
disport in the midst of those solemn fastnesses—as that

I should fly out of my orbit at their approach, and go
about eccentric like a comet, to endanger other systems.

No—be true to your instincts—and sit—wait till you can
be genuinely polite—if it be till doomsday, and not
lose your chance everlastingly by a cowardly yielding
to young etiquette. By your look say unto them,—the
lines have fallen to me in pleasant places—and I will
fill that station God has assigned me. As well Miss
Cassiopeia up there—might ask the brazen fronted
Taurus to draw in his horns, that she might shine in
his stead— No—no—not till my cycle is completed.

How is it that motion will always find space to move
in—and rest a seat? Men hate antagonism—and the
weaker will always yield to the stronger. If a stranger
enter with sufficient determination into a crowded
assembly, as if commissioned by the gods to find a seat
there—as the falling stone by a divine impulse seeks
a resting place—each one will rise without thinking—to
offer his place.— Now we have only to be commissioned
to sit, and depend upon it the gods will not balk their
own work.— Ye came one day too late—as did the
poet after the world had been divided, and so returned
to dwell with the god that sent him.

When presumptuous womanhood demands to
surrender my position—I bide my time—though it be with
misgiving—and yield to no mortal shove, but expect a
divine impulse. Produce your warrant and I will retire
for not now can I give you a clear seat—but must
leave part of my manhood behind—and wander a
diminished man—who at length will not have length and
breadth enough to fill any seat at all. It was very kind
in the gods who gave us a now condition—or condition
of rest, in which we might unhurriedly deliberate,
before taking a step. When I give up my—now and here
without having secured my then and there—I am the

prodigal son of a kind father—and deserve no better than the husks which the swine eat, nor that the fatted calf be killed for me.

Rest forever,—when instinct comes to the rescue of your politeness, it will seat you securely still—though it be to hang by a rail—or poise yourself on a stick. To do otherwise is to be polite only as the soldier who runs away when the enemy demands his post. Politeness is rather when the generals interchange civilities before the fight—not when one returns a sword after the victory.

Not only in his cunning hand and brain, but when he speaks too does man assert his superiority—he conquers the spaces with his voice—as well as the lion. The voice of a strong man modulated to the cadence of some tune is more imposing than any natural sound. The keepers is the most commanding—and is heard over all the din of the menagerie.

A strong musical voice imposes a new order and harmony upon nature—from it as a centre—the law is promulgated to the universe. What it lacks in volume and loudness may always be made up in musical expression and distinctness. The brute growls to secure obedience—he threatens—the man speaks as though obedience were already secured.

Brave speaking is the most entire and richest sacrifice to the gods.

Friday Feb. 5th 1841

Only on rare occasions am I reminded that man too has a voice, as well as birds and quadrupeds, which breaks on the stillness of nature with its peculiar accent. The least sound pervades and subdues all space

to it as long as it fills my ear. Contrasted single with the
silence it is as wide as it. Music is the Crystalization of
Sound. There is something in the effect of a harmonious
voice upon the disposition of its neighborhood analogous
to the law of crystals—it centralizes itself—and sounds
like the published law of things. If the law of the
universe were to be audibly promulgated no mortal
lawgiver would suspect it—for it would be a finer melody
than his ears ever attended to. It would be sphere music.

When by tutoring their voices singers enhance one
anothers performance—the harmony is more complete
and essential than is heard. The quire is the family held
together by a very close bond. Hence the romance we
associate with Gypsies—and circus companies—and
strolling musicians. The idea of brotherhood is so
strong in them. Their society is ideal for that one end.

There is something in this brotherhood this feeling
of kind—or kindness—which insensibly elevates the
subjects of it in our eyes. However poor or mean they
have something which counterbalances our contempt.
This is that in the strolling pauper *family* which does
not court our charity—but can even bless and smile
on us, and make the kindness reciprocal.— It sanctifies
the place and the hour.
These Rainers if they are not brothers and sisters
—must be uncles and cousins at least. These Swiss
who have come to sing to us we have no doubt are the
flower of the Tyrol— Such is the instinctive kindness
with which the foreigner is always received, that he is
even presumed to be the fairest and noblest of his
race— The traveller finds that it is not easy to move
away from his friends after all—but all people whom he

visits are anxious to supply the place to him of his parents and brothers and sisters— To these swiss I find that I have attributed all Tell's patriotism—and the devotion of Arnold Winkelried—and whatever goodness or greatness belongs to the nation.

All costume off a man—when not simply doffed—is grotesque. There must be a heart inside it. When these swiss appear before me in gaiters and high crowned hats with feathers—I am disposed to laugh—but soon I see that their serious eye becomes these and they it. It is the sincere life passed within it which consecrates the costume of any people— A sufficiently sober eye will retrieve itself and subordinate any grotesqueness. Let Harlequin be taken with a fit of the colic in the midst of his buffoonery, and his trappings and finery will serve that mood too—and with this drooping sympathy enhance the sincerity of his misfortune. When the soldier is hit by a cannon ball rags are as becoming as purple. So soon as a man engages to eat—drink—sleep—walk—and sit—and meet all the contingences of life therein—his costume is hallowed and a theme for poetry—whether it be a bear's skin or ermine—a beaver hat—or a Turkish Turban. He will not wear any thing because it is blue or black or round or square—but from a necessity which can not be superseded.

I look into the face and manners for something familiar and homely ever, to be assured that the costume of the foreigner is not whimsical or finical.

In all emergencies there is always one step which you may take on firm ground where gravity—will assure you footing   So you hold a draft on Fate payable at sight.

{*One-fifth page blank*}

Saturday Feb. 6th 1841.

One may discover a new side to his most intimate
friend when for the first time he hears him speak
in public—he will be stranger to him as he is more
familiar to the audience. The longest intimacy could not
foretell how he would behave then. When I observe
my friend's conduct toward others, then chiefly I learn
the traits in his character, and in each case I am
unprepared for the issue.

When one gets up to address briefly a strange audience
—in that little he may have opportunity to say, he will
not quite do himself injustice. For he will instantly
and instinctively average himself to his audience, and
while he is true to his own character still—he will in
a few moments—make that impression—which a series
of months and years would but expand. Before he
answers his thought like lightning runs round the whole
compass of his experience, and he is scrupulous to
speak from that which he is—and with a more entire
truthfulness than usual.— How little do we know each
other then—who can tell how his friend would behave
on any occasion

As for those swiss, I think of the fields their hands
have ploughed and reaped, and respect their costume as
the memorial or rather cotemporary and witness of
this.— What is there in a toga but a Roman?— what but
a Quaker in a broad-brimmed hat?— He who describes
the dress of a Janisary going to war, does me a similar
service as when he paints the scenery of the battle
field It helps make his exploit picturesque.

Costume is not determined by whim—not even the
tattooing and paint of the savage— Sun—wind—rain—and
the form of our bodies—shape our hats and coats for
us, more even than taste. Good taste secures the utmost

gratification without sacrificing any conveniences. If all nations derived their fashions from Paris or London the world would seem like a vanity fair or all fools day—and the Tartar and Bedouin ride in it like jesters in a circus—and the Pawnee and Esquimaux hunt in masquerade.— What I am must make you forget what I wear. The fashionable world is content to be eclipsed by its dress, and never will bear the contrast. Only industry will reform *their* dress—they are idle—*exo*strious —building without.

The value of the recess in any public entertainment, consists in the opportunity for self-recovery which it offers. We who have been swayed as one heart, expanding and contracting with the common pulse, find ourselves in the interim—and set us up again, and feel our own hearts beating in our breasts— We are always a little astonished to see a man walking across the room through an attentive audience—with any degree of self possession— He makes himself strange to us. He is a little stubborn withal—and seems to say—I am self-sustained and independent as well as the performer —and am not to be swallowed up in the common enthusiasm— No—no—there are two of us—and John's as good as Thomas.
—In the recess the audience is cut up into a hundred little coteries—and as soon as each individual life has recovered its tone and the purposes of health have been answered, it is time for the performances to commence again.

In a public performer, the simplest actions—which at other times are left to unconscious nature—as the ascending a few steps in front of an audience—acquire a fatal importance—and become arduous deeds.

When I select one here and another there and strive
to join sundered thoughts, I make but a partial heap
after all— Nature strews her nuts and flowers broadcast,
and never collects them into heaps— A man does not
tell us all he has thought upon truth or beauty at a
sitting—but from his last thought on the subject wanders
through a varied scenery of upland meadow and
woodland to his next— Some times a single and casual
thought rises naturally and inevitably with a queenly
majesty and escort like the stars in the east. Fate has
surely enshrined it in this hour and circumstances for
some purpose— What she has joined together let not
man put asunder.— Shall I transplant the primrose
by the river's brim—to set it beside its sister on the
mountain? *This* was the soil it grew in—*this* the hour
it bloomed in—if sun wind and rain came *here* to cherish
and expand it—shall not we come here to pluck it?
— Shall we require it to grow in a conservatory for our
convenience?

I feel slightly complimented when nature condescends
to make use of me without my knowledge—as when I
help scatter her seeds in my walk—or carry burs and
cockles on my clothes from field to field— I feel as
though I had done something for the commonweal, and
were entitled to board and lodging.— I take such airs
upon me as the boy who holds a horse for the circus
company—whom all the spectators envy.

Lu ral lu ral lu—may be more impressively sung—than
very respectable wisdom talked—it is well timed—as
wisdom is not always.

All things prophecy but the prophet— In augury and
divination nature is put to the torture— In Ben Jonson's

tragedy of Cataline, Lentulus makes answer to Cataline, who has bribed the augurs to say that he is that third Cornelius who is to be king of Rome—
    "All prophecies, you know, suffer the torture". He who inspects the entrails is *always* bribed but they are unbribable. He who seeks to know the future by unlawful means has unavoidably subjected the oracle to the torture of *private* and *partial* interests The oracles of God—serve the *public* interest—without fee. To the just and benevolent mind—nature *declares* —as the sun lights the world.

Sunday Feb. 7th 1841.

    Without great coat or drawers I have advanced thus far into the snow banks of the winter, without thought and with impunity. When I meet my neighbors in muffs and furs and tippets—they look as if they had retreated into the interior fastnesses from some foe invisible to me.— They remind me that this is the season of winter in which it becomes a man to be cold— For feeling, I am a piece of clean wood of this shape which will do service till it rots, and though the cold has its physical effect on me—it is a kindly one, for it "finds its acquaintance there."
    My diet is so little stimulating, and my body in consequence so little heated, as to excite no antagonism in nature, but flourishes like a tree—which finds even the winter genial to its expansion and the secretion of sap.— May not the body defend itself against cold by its very nakedness—and its elements be so simple and single that they cannot congeal.?— Frost does not affect one but several— My body now affords no more pasture for cold than a leafless twig— I call it a protestant warmth.— My limbs do not tire as formerly, but I use

myself as any other piece of nature, and from mere
indifference and thoughtlessness may break the timber.

It is the vice of the last season which compels us to
arm ourselves for the next. If man always conformed to
nature, he would not have to defend himself against
her, but find her his constant nurse and friend—as do
plants and quadrupeds.

In the sunshine and the crowing of cocks I feel an
illimitable holiness, which makes me bless God and
myself. The warm sun casts his incessant gift at my
feet as I walk along—unfolding his yellow worlds—

Yonder sexton with a few cheap sounds makes me
richer than them who mind his summons.—

The true gift is as wide as my gratitude—and as
frequent—and the donor is as grateful as the recipient.

—There would be a new years gift indeed—if we
would bestow on each other our sincerity— We should
communicate our wealth, and not purchase that which
does not belong to us for a sign. Why give each other a
sign to keep? If we gave the thing itself there would
be no need of a sign.

I am not sure I should find out a really great person
soon—he would be simple Thomas or Oliver for some
centuries first— The lesser eminences would hide the
higher—and I should at last reach his top by a gentle
acclivity— I felt it would be necessary to remain some
weeks at the notch to be impressed by the grandeur
of the scenery.— We do not expect that Alexander will
conquer Asia the first time we are introduced to him
— A great man accepts the occasion the fates offer
him— Let us not be disappointed, we stand at first upon
the pampas which surround him— It is these mountains

round about, which makes the valleys here below.
– He is not a dead level, so many feet above low water
mark– Greatness is in the ascent.– But there is no
accounting for the little men

> "They must sweat no less
> To fit their properties, than t'express their parts."
> or the line before this
> "Would you have
> Such an Herculean actor in the scene,
> And not his hydra?"   Jonson.

The eaves are running on the south side of the
house– The titmouse lisps in the poplar–the bells are
ringing for church–while the sun presides over all
and makes his simple warmth more obvious than all
else.– What shall I do with this hour so like time
and yet so fit for eternity?– Where in me are these russet
patches of ground–and scattered logs and chips in the
yard?– I do not feel cluttered.– I have some notion
what the joohnswort and life-everlasting may be
thinking about–when the sun shines on me as on them
–and turns my prompt thought–into just such a seething
shimmer– I lie out indistinct as a heath at noon-day
– I am evaporating airs ascending into the sun.

Nothing stands in the way to success–but to failure. To
victory is all the way up hill–to defeat the simplest wight
that weighs may soon slide down.– Cowards would
not have victory but the fruits of victory–but she it is
that sweetens all the spoil– Thus by a just fate the
booty cannot fall to him who did not win it. There is
victory in every effort. In the least swing of the arm, in
indignant thought–in stern content–we conquer
our foes.

Great thoughts make great men–without these no
heraldry nor blood will avail.

The blood circulates to the feet and hands–but the thought never descends from the head.

The most I can do for my friend is simply to be his friend. I have no wealth to bestow on him– If he knows that I am happy in loving him–he will want no other reward– Is not Friendship divine in this?

I have myself to respect but to myself I am not amiable–but my friend is my amiableness personified.

And yet we walk the stage indifferent actors–not thinking what a sublime drama we might enact–if we would be joint workers–and a mutual material. Why go to the woods to cut timber to display our art upon–when here are men as trees walking?– The world has never learned what men can build each other up to be–when both master and pupil work in love.

He that comes as a stranger to my house will have to stay as a stranger– He has made his own reception. But persevering love was never yet refused.

"The vicious count their years, virtuous their acts."
                              Jonson
The former consider the length of their service–the latter its quality.

Wait not till I invite thee, but observe
I'm glad to see thee when thou com'st.

The most ardent lover holds yet a private court–and his love can never be so strong or etherial that there will not be danger that judgment may be rendered against the beloved.

I would have men make a *greater* use of me– Now I must belittle myself to have dealings with them.

My friend will show such a noble confidence that I
shall aspire to the society of his good opinion—never
presume men less that you may make them more. So far
as we respond to our ideal estimate of each other do
we have profitable intercourse.

A brave man always knows the way no matter how
intricate the roads.

Feb 8th 1841

All we have experienced is so much gone within us
—and there lies— It is the company we keep. One day, in
health or sickness, it will come out and be remembered.—
Neither body nor soul forgets anything— The twig
always remembers the wind that shook it, and the stone
the cuff it received— Ask the old tree and the sand.

To be of most service to my brother I must meet
him on the most equal and even ground—the platform
on which our lives are passing. But how often does
politeness permit this?

I seek a man who will appeal to me when I am in
fault— We will treat as gods settling the affairs of
men.— In his intercourse I shall be always a god today,
who was a man yesterday. He will never confound me
with my guilt—but let me be immaculate, and hold up my
skirts.— Differences he will make haste to clear up, but
leave agreements unsettled the while.

As time is measured by the lapse of ideas—we may
grow of our own force—as the muscle adds new circles to
its shell— My thoughts secrete the lime.— We may
grow old with the vigor of youth. Are we not always in
youth so long as we face heaven. We may always live
in the morning of our days. To him who seeks early the

sun—never gets over the edge of the hill, but his rays
fall slanting forever.— His wise sayings are like the
chopping of wood and crowing of cocks in the dawn.

My Journal is that of me which would else spill over
and run to waste.— gleanings from the field which
in action I reap. I must not live for it, but in it for the
gods— They are my correspondent to whom daily I send
off this sheet post-paid. I am clerk in their counting room
and at evening transfer the account from day-book to
ledger.

It is as a leaf which hangs over my head in the path
— I bend the twig and write my prayers on it then letting
it go the bough springs up and shows the scrawl to
heaven. As if it were not kept shut in my desk—but were
as public a leaf as any in nature—it is papyrus by the
river side—it is vellum in the pastures—it is parchment on
the hills— I find it every where as free as the leaves
which troop along the lanes in autumn— The crow—the
goose—the eagle—carry my quill—and the wind blows
the leaves—as far as I go— Or if my imagination does not
soar, but gropes in slime and mud—then I write with
a reed.

It is always a chance scrawl and commemorates
some accident—as great as earthquake or eclipse. Like
the sere leaves in yonder vase these have been gathered
far and wide—upland and lowland.— forest and field
have been ransacked.

In our holiest moment our devil with a leer stands
close at hand. He is a very busy devil.— It gains vice
some respect I must confess thus to be reminded
how indefatigable it is— It has at least the merit of
industriousness— When I go forth with zeal to some

good work—my devil is sure to get his robe tucked up
the first—and arrives there as soon as I—with a look
of sincere earnestness—which puts to shame my best
intent. He is as forward as I to a good work—and as
disinterested. He has a winning way of recommending
himself by making himself useful—how readily he
comes into my best project—and does his work with a
quiet and steady cheerfulness which even virtue may
take pattern from.

I never was so rapid in my virtue but my vice kept
up with me—it always came in by a hand, and never
panting, but with a curried coolness halted as if halting
were the beginning not the end of the course. It only
runs the swifter because it has no rider. It never was
behind me but when I turned to look—and so fell behind
myself.— I never did a charitable thing—but there he
stood—scarce in the rear, with hat in hand—partner on
the same errand—ready to share the smile of gratitude
Though I shut the door never so quick and tell it stay at
home like a good dog—it will out with me—for I shut
in my own legs so—and it escapes in the mean while
—and is ready to back and reinforce me in most virtuous
deeds.— And if I turn & say get thee behind me—he then
indeed turns too and takes the lead though he seems to
retire with a pensive and compassionate look—as much
as to say— Ye know not what ye do.

Just as active as I become to virtue just so active is
my remaining vice— Every time we teach our virtue a
new nobleness we teach our vice a new cunning. When
we sharpen the blade it will stab better as well as whittle
— The scythe that cuts will cut our legs. We are double
edged blades—and every time we whet our virtue the
return stroke straps our vice.

And when we cut a clean descending blow—our
vice on tother edge rips up the work.— Where is the

skilful swordsman that can draw his blade straight back
out of the wound?

Everyman proposes fairly and does not wilfully take
the devil for his guide–as our shadows never fall
between us and the sun– Go towards the sun and your
shadow will fall behind you.

Tuesday Feb. 9th 1841.

Cato. "Good Marcus Tullius, (which is more than great)
        Thou hadst thy education with the gods."
            Jonson.

Better be defamed than overpraised– Thou canst
then justly praise thyself.– What notoriety art thou that
can be defamed?– Who can be praised for what they
are not–deserve rather to be damned for what they are.
It is hard to wear a dress that is too long and loose
without stumbling
                Whoe'er is raised,
    For wealth he has not, he is tax'd, not prais'd,

says Jonson. If you mind the flatterer you rob yourself
–and still cheat him– The fates never exaggerate–men
pass for what they are– The state never fails to get a
revenue out of you without a direct tax.– Flattery
would lay a direct tax. What I am praised for what I
am not I put to the account of the gods– It needs a
skilful eye to distinguish between their coin and my
own– But however there can be no loss either way,
for what mede I have earned is equally theirs. Let
neither fame nor infamy hit you, but the one go as far
beyond as the other falls behind–let the one glance past
you to the gods, and the other wallow where it was
engendered.– The home thrusts are at helmets upon
blocks, and my worst foes but stab an armor through.

My life at this moment is like a summer morning
when birds are singing– Yet that is false–for nature's is
an idle pleasure in comparison–my hour has a more
solid serenity.

I have been breaking silence these twenty three years
and have hardly made a rent in it– Silence has no
end, speech is but the beginning of it. My friend thinks
I *keep* silence who am only choked with letting it out
so fast. Does he forget that new mines of secresy are
constantly opening in me?

If any scorn your love, let them see plainly that you
serve not them but another– If these bars are up, go
your way to other of God's pastures, and browse there the
while,– When your host shuts his door on you–he
incloses you in the dwelling of nature. He thrusts you
over the threshhold of the world.

My foes restore me to my friends.

I might say friendship had no ears as love has no
eyes–for no word is evidence in its court– The least act
fulfills more than all words profess. The most gracious
speech is but partial kindness–but the least genuine
deed takes the whole man. If we had waited till
doomsday it could never have been uttered.

Wednesday Feb. 10th 1841
That was fine praise which Ben Johnson gave to
Thomas Lord Chancelor–
"Whil'st thou art certain to thy words, once gone,
As is thy conscience, which is always one."
Words do not lose their truth by time or misinterpretation
but stand unscathed longer than he who spoke them.

Let our words be such as we may unblushingly behold
sculptured in granite on the walls–to the least syllable.

Our thoughts and actions may be very private for a long time—for they demand a more catholic publicity to be displayed in than the world can afford. Our best deeds shun the narrow walks of men, and are not ambitious of the faint light the world can shed on them, but delight to unfold themselves in that public ground between god and conscience.

Truth has for audience and spectator all the world. Within, where I resolve and deal with principles, there is more space and room, than any where without where my hands execute— Men should hear of your virtue only as they hear the creaking of the earths' axle and the music of the spheres. It will fall into the course of nature and be effectually concealed by publicness.

I asked a man to-day if he would rent me some land, and he said he had four acres as good soil "as any out doors." It was a true poets account of it— He and I, and all the world, went out doors to breathe the free air, and stretch ourselves. For the world is but out doors—and we duck behind a pannel.

Feb. 11th 1841.

True help for the most part—implies a greatness in him who is to be helped as well as in the helper — It takes a god to be helped even. A great person, though unconsciously, will constantly give you great opportunities to serve him, but a mean one will quite preclude all active benevolence— It needs but simply and *greatly* to want it for once, that all true men may contend who shall be foremost to render aid. My neighbors state must pray to heaven so devoutly yet disinterestedly as he never prayed in words, before my ears can hear. It must ask divinely. But men so cobble and botch their request, that you must stoop as low as they to give them aid. Their meanness would drag down your deed to be a compromise with conscience–and not leave it to be done on the high table land of the benevolent soul. They would have you doff your bright and knightly armor and drudge for them.– serve *them* and not God. But if I am to serve them I must not serve the devil.

What is called charity is no charity–but the interference of a third person. Shall I interfere with fate? shall I defraud man of the opportunities which God gave him–and so take away his life? Beggars and Silent poor cry–how often–get between me and my god. I will not stay to cobble and patch God's rents, but do clean new work where he has given me my hands full. This almshouse charity is like putting new wine into old bottles, When so many tuns in God's cellars stand empty. We go about mending the times–when we should be building the eternity.

I must serve a strong master, not a weak one. Help implies a sympathy of energy and effort–else no alleviation will avail.

Friday Feb 12th 1841.

Those great men who are unknown to their own generation and expect a tardy justice from posterity, are indeed already famous in the society of the great who have gone before them.

All worldly fame but subsides from their high estimate beyond the stars– We may still keep pace with those who have gone out of nature, for we run on as smooth ground as they.

The early and the latter saints are separated by no eternal interval.

The child may soon stand face to face with the best father.

Feb. 13th 1841

By the truthfulness of our story today we help explain
ourselves for all our life henceforth— How we hamper
and belay ourselves by the least exaggeration— The truth
is God's concern—he will sustain it—but who can afford
to maintain a lie? We have taken away one of the
pillars of Hercules—and must support the world on our
shoulders, who might have walked freely upon it.

My neighbor says that his hill-farm is poor stuff
and "only fit to hold the world together"— He deserves
that God should give him better for so brave a treating
of his gifts—more than for repining or a dogged putting
up therewith. It is a sort of stay, or gore, or gusset,—and
he will not be blinded by modesty or gratitude, but
sees it for what it is— Knowing his neighbors fertile
land he calls his by its right name. But perhaps my
farmer forgets, that his lean soil has sharpened his
wits. It is good for some crops— And beside you see the
heavens at a lesser angle from the hill than from
the vale.

We have nothing to fear from our foes— God keeps
a standing army for that service; but we have no ally
against our friends—those ruthless vandals—whose kind
intent is a subtler poison than the Colchian—a more
fatal shaft than the Lydian.

{One-fourth page blank}

Sunday Feb. 14th 1841.

I am confined to the house by bronchitis, and so seek
to content myself with that quiet and serene life there
is in a warm corner by the fireside, and see the sky
through the chimney top.— Sickness should not be
allowed to extend further than the body— We need only

to retreat further within us, to preserve uninterrupted the continuity of serene hours to the end of our lives.

As soon as I find my chest is not of tempered steel, and heart of adamant–I bid good bye to these and look out a new nature. I will be liable to no accidents.

I shall never be poor while I can command a still hour in which to take leave of my sin.

The jingling team which is creaking past reminds me of that verse in the Bible which speaks of God being heard in the bells of the horses.

Feb. 15th 1841.

There is elevation in every hour. No part of the earth is so low and withdrawn, that the heavens cannot be seen from it, but every part supports the sky. We have only to stand on the eminence of the hour, and look out thence into the empyrean, allowing no pinnacle above us, to command an uninterrupted horizon. The moments will be outspread around us like a blue expanse of mountain and valley, while we stand on the summit of our hour as if we had descended on eagle's wings. For the eagle has stooped to his perch on the highest cliff–and has never climbed the rock–he stands by his wings more than by his feet. We shall not want a foothold, but wings will sprout from our shoulders, and we shall walk securely self-sustained.

For how slight an accident shall two noble souls wait to bring them together–

Feb 17th 1841

Our work should be fitted to and lead on the time, as bud flower and fruit lead the circle of the seasons–

The mechanic works no longer than his labor will pay for lights—fuel—and shop rent.— Would it not be well for us to consider if our deed will warrant the expense of nature. Will it maintain the sun's light?

Our actions do not use time independently as the bud does— They should constitute its lapse— It is their room— But they shuffle after and serve the hour.

Thursday Feb. 18 1841

I do not Judge men by anything they can do— Their greatest deed is the impression they make on me — Some serene inactive men can do everything.

—Talent only indicates a depth of character in some direction.— We do not acquire the ability to do new deeds, but a new capacity for all deeds. My recent growth does not appear in any visible new talent—but its deed will enter into my gaze when I look into the sky —or vacancy— It will help me to consider ferns and everlasting.

Man is like a tree which is limited to no age, but grows as long as it has its root in the ground— We have only to live in the alburnum and not in the old wood.— The gnarled stump has as tender a bud as the sapling.

Sometimes I find that I have frequented a higher society during sleep, and my thoughts and actions proceed on a higher level in the morning.

A man is the hydrostatic paradox—the counterpoise of the system. You have studied flowers and birds cheaply enough, but you must lay yourself out to buy him.

Feb. 19th 1841.

A truly good book attracts very little favor to itself
— It is so true that it teaches me better than to read
it— I must soon lay it down and commence living on its
hint— I do not see how any can be written more, but
this is the last effusion of genius.

When I read an indifferent book—it seems the best
thing I can do, but the inspiring volume hardly leaves
me leisure to finish its latter pages— It is slipping out
of my fingers while I read. It creates no atmosphere in
which it may be perused, but one in which its teachings
may be practised— It confers on me such wealth that
I lay it down with the least regret— What I began
by reading I must finish by acting.

—So I cannot stay to hear a *good* sermon, and applaud
at the conclusion, but shall be half way to Thermopylae
before that.

When any joke or hoax traverses the Union in
the newspapers—it apprizes me of a fact which no
geography or guide book contains—of a certain leisure
and nonchalance pervading society— It is a piece of
information from over the Alleghanies which I know
how to prize—though I did not expect it. And it is just so
in nature— I sometimes observe in her—a strange
trifling almost listlessness which conducts to beauty
and grace— The fantastic and whimsical forms of
snow and ice— The unaccountable peaks which the
tracks of rabbits exhibit.

I know now why all those busy speculators do not
die of fever and ague.

Coleridge observed the "landscapes made by damp
on a white-washed wall" and so have I.

We seem but to linger in manhood to tell the dreams
of our childhood, and they vanish out of memory ere
we learn the language.

It is the unexplored grandeur of the storm which
keeps up the spirits of the traveller. When I contemplate
a hard and bare life in the woods, I find my last
consolation in its untrivialness— Shipwreck is less
distressing because the breakers do not trifle with us.
We are resigned as long as we recognise the sober and
solemn mystery of nature. The dripping mariner
finds consolation and sympathy in the infinite sublimity
of the storm— It is a moral force as well as he. With
courage he can lay down his life on the strand, for
it never turned a deaf ear to him–nor has he ever
exhausted its sympathy.

In the love of narrow souls I make many short
voyages, but in vain–I find no sea room–but in great
souls I sail before the wind without a watch, and never
reach the shore.

You demand that I be less your friend that you
may know it.

Nothing will reconcile friends but love. They hinder
nature when they go about like foes to explain and
treat with one another— It is a mutual mistake— None
are so unmanageable.

Saturday Feb. 20th 1841
I suspect the moral discrimination of the oldest and
best authors. I doubt if Milton distinguished greatly
between his Satan and his Raphael. In Homer and
Aeschylus and Dante I miss a nice *dis*crimination of
the *important* shades of character.

When I am going out for an evening I arrange the fire in my stove, so that I do not fail to find a good one when I return, though it would have engaged my frequent attention present. So that when I know I am to be at home, I sometimes make believe that I may go out, to save trouble. And this is the art of living too—to leave our life in a condition to go alone, and not to require a constant supervision. We will then sit down serenely to live as by the side of a stove.

When I sit in earnest—nothing must stand—all must be sedentary with me.

I hear the faint sound of a viol and voices from the neighboring cottage—and think to myself I will believe the muse only forevermore— It assures me that no gleam which comes over the serene soul is deceptive—it warns me of a reality and substance, of which the best that I see is but the phantom and shadow. O music—thou tellest me of things of which memory takes no heed, thy strains are whispered aside from memory's ear.

This is the noblest plain of earth over which these sounds are borne—the plain of Troy or Eleusis.

Thou openest all my senses to catch thy least hint, and givest me no thought— It would be good to sit at my door of summer evenings forever—and hear thy strains. Thou makest me to toy with speech—or walk content without it—not regretting its absence. I am pleased to think how ignorant and shiftless the wisest are— My imperfect sympathies with my friend is cheerful glimmering light in the valley.

Sunday Feb. 21st 1841

It is hard to preserve equanimity and greatness on that debateable ground between love and esteem.—

There is nothing so stable and unfluctuating as love.
The waves beat steadfast on its shore forever, and its
tide has no ebb– It is a resource in all extremities,
and a refuge even from itself– And yet love will not be
leaned on.

Feb 22d 1841
Love is the tenderest mood of that which is tough
–and the toughest mood of that which is tender. It
may be roughly handled as the nettle, or gently as the
violet. It has its holidays, but is not made for them.
The whole of the day should not be day time, nor of
the night night time, but some portion be rescued from
time to oversee time in. All our hours must not be
current–all our time must not lapse. There must be one
hour at least which the day did not bring forth–of
ancient parentage and long established nobility–which
will be a serene and lofty platform overlooking the
rest. We should make our notch every day on our
characters as Robinson Crusoe on his stick. We must
be at the helm at least once a day–we must feel the tiller
rope in our hands, and know that if we sail, we steer.

Friends will be much apart–they will respect more
each others privacy than their communion–for therein
is the fulfillment of our high aims and the conclusion
of our arguments.– That we know and would associate
with not only has high intents–but goes on high
errands, and has much private business.
The hours he devotes to me were snatched from
higher society. He is hardly a gift level to me, but
I have to reach up to take it. My imagination always
assigns him a nobler employment in my absence than
ever I find him engaged in.
We have to go into retirement religiously, and enhance

our meeting by rarity and a degree of unfamiliarity.
Would you know why I see thee so seldom my friend
— In solitude I have been making up a packet for thee.

The actions which grow out of some common but
natural relations affect me strangely— As sometimes
the behavior of a mother to her children. So quiet and
noiseless an action often moves me more than many
sounding exploits.

Tuesday Feb. 23d 1841.
Let all our stores and munitions be provided for
the lone state.

The care of the body is the highest exercise of
prudence. If I have brought this weakness on my lungs,
I will consider calmly and disinterestedly how the thing
came about, that I may find out the truth, and render
justice. Then after patience I shall be a wiser man
than before.

Let us apply all our wit to the repair of our bodies
as we would mend a harrow, for the body will be dealt
plainly and implicitly with. We want no moonshine
nor surmises about it. This matter of health and sickness
has no fatality in it, but is a subject for the merest
prudence. If I know not what ails me I may resort to
amulets and charms and moon struck die of dysentery.

We do wrong to slight our sickness and feel so ready
to desert our posts when we are harassed.— So much
the more should we rise above our condition, and make
the most of it, for the fruit of disease may be as good
as that of health.

There is a subtle elixir in society which makes it a
fountain of health to the sick— We want no consolation

which is not the overflow of our friend's health.– We
will have no condolence who are not dolent ourselves.–
We would have our friend come and respire healthily
before us–with the fragrance of many meadows and
heaths in his breath–and we will inhabit his body while
our own recruits.

Nothing is so good medicine in sickness as to witness
some nobleness in another which will advertise us of
health.– In sickness it is our faith that ails, and noble
deeds reassure us.

To know that anybody has thought of you on some
indifferent occasion implies more good will than you
had reason to expect– You have henceforth a higher
motive for conduct. We do not know how many amiable
thoughts are current.

{*One-fifth page blank*}

Friday Feb. 26th 1841
My prickles or smoothness are as much a quality of
your hand as of myself– I cannot tell you what I am
more than a ray of the summer's sun– What I am–I am
–and say not. Being is the great explainer. In the
attempt to explain shall I plane away all the spines,
till it is no thistle but a cornstalk.

If my world is not sufficient without thee, my friend,
I will wait till it is and then call thee– You shall come
to a palace not to an almshouse.

My homeliest thought, like the diamond brought
from farthest within the mine, will shine with the
purest lustre.

Though I write every day yet when I say a good thing,
It seems as if I wrote but rarely.

To be great we do as if we would be tall merely—be longer than we are broad, stretch ourselves and stand on tiptoe. But greatness is well proportioned—unstrained, and stands on the soles of the feet.

How many are waiting for health and warm weather but they wait for none—

In composition I miss the hue of the mind. As if we could be satisfied with the dews of the morning and evening—without their colors—or the heavens without their azure.

This good book helps the sun shine in my chamber. The rays fall on its page as if to explain and illustrate it.

I who have been sick hear cattle low in the street, with such a healthy ear as prophecies my cure.— These sounds lay a finger on my pulse to some purpose— A fragrance comes in at all my senses which proclaims that I am still of nature the child. The threshing in yonder barn, and the tinkling of the anvil—come from the same side of styx with me.

If I were a physician I would try my patients thus — I would wheel them to a window and let nature feel their pulse— It will soon appear if their sensuous existence is sound.

—These sounds are but the throbbing of some pulse in me.

Nature seems to have given me these hours to pry into her private drawers— I watch the shadow of the insensible perspiration rising from my coat or hand on the wall.

I go and feel my pulse in all the recesses of the house
—and see if I am of force to carry a homely life and
comfort into them.

Sat. Feb. 27th 1841.

Life looks as fair at this moment as a summers sea
—or a blond dress in a saffron light—with its sun and
grass—and walled towns—so bright and chaste—as fair
as my own virtue which would adventure therein.
Like a Persian city or hanging gardens in the distance
—so washed in light—so untried—only to be thridded by
clean thoughts. All its flags are flowing and tassels
streaming—and drapery flapping like some gay pavilion.

The heavens hang over it like some low screen, and
seem to undulate in the breeze.

Through this pure unwiped hour—as through a crystal
glass—I look out upon the future, as a smooth lawn
for my virtue to disport in. It shows from afar as
unrepulsive as the sunshine upon walls and cities—over
which the passing life moves as gently as a shadow I see
the course of my life—like some retired road—wind on
without obstruction into a country maze.

I am attired for the future so—as the sun setting
presumes all men at leisure and in contemplative
mood—and am thankful that it is thus presented blanc
and indistinct— It still oertops my hope. My future
deeds bestir themselves within me and move grandly
towards a consummation—as ships go down the Thames.
A steady onward motion I feel in me as still as that
—or like some vast snowy cloud, whose shadow first is
seen across the fields.— It is the material of all things
loose and set afloat, that makes my sea.

These various words are not without various meanings
— The combined voice of the race makes nicer

distinctions than any individual. There are the words diversion and amusement. It takes more to amuse than to divert. We must be surrendered to our amusements, but only turned aside to our diversions. We have no will in the former–but oversee the latter. We are oftenest diverted in the street–but amused in our chambers. We are diverted from our engagements–but amused when we are listless.

We may be diverted from an amusement–and amused by a diversion.– It often happens that a diversion becomes our amusement–and our amusement our employment.

Feb 28 1841

Nothing goes by luck in composition–it allows of no trick. The best you can write will be the best you are. Every sentence is the result of a long probation.– The author's character is read from title page to end–of this he never corrects the proofs–we read it as the essential character of a handwriting without regard to the flourishes.

And so of the rest of our actions, it runs as straight as a ruled line through them all,–no matter how many curvets about it. Our whole life is taxed for the least thing well done–it is its net result. How we eat, drink, sleep, and use our desultory hours now in these indifferent days, with no eye to observe, and no occasion excite us–determines, determines our authority and capacity for the time to come.

March 3d 1841

I hear a man blowing a horn this still evening–and it sounds like the plaint of nature in these times. In this which I refer to some man there is something greater

than any man It is as if the earth spoke. It adds a
great remoteness to the horizon, and its very distance is
grand, as when one draws back the head to speak.
That which I now hear in the west seems like an
invitation to the east, It runs round the earth as a
whisper gallery. It is the spirit of the West calling to the
spirit of the East or else it is the rattling of some team
lagging in Days' train coming to me through the darkness
and silence   all things great seem transpiring there. It
is friendly as a distant hermits taper. When it is trilled;
or undulates the heavens are crumpled into time, and
successive waves flow across them.

It is a strangely healthy sound for these disjointed
times.– It is a rare soundness when cow-bells and horns
are heard from over the fields– And now I see the
beauty and full meaning of that word sound. Nature
always possesses a certain sonorousness, as in the hum
of insects–the booming of ice–the crowing of cocks
in the morning and the barking of dogs in the night
–which indicates her sound state. God's voice is but a
clear bell sound. I drink in a wonderful health–a cordial
–in sound. The effect of the slightest tinkling in the
horizon measures my own soundness. I thank God
for sound it always mounts, and makes me mount. I
think I will not trouble myself for any wealth, when
I can be so cheaply enriched, Here I contemplate to
drudge that I may own a farm–and may have such a
limitless estate for the listening. All good things are
cheap–all bad are very dear.

As for these communities–I think I had rather keep
batchelor's hall in hell than go to board in heaven.–
Dost think thy virtue will be boarded with you? It will
never live on the interest of your money, depend upon it.

The boarder has no home. In heaven I hope to bake
my own bread and clean my own linen.– The tomb
is the only boarding house in which a hundred are served
at once–in the catacomb we may dwell together and
prop one another without loss.

March 4th 1841

Ben Johnson says in his epigrams–He makes himself
a thorough-fare of Vice."

This is true–for by vice the substance of a man is
not changed, but all his pores, and cavities–and avenues
are profaned by being made the thorough-fares of vice.
He is the highway of his vice. The searching devil
courses through and through him. His flesh and blood
and bones are cheapened. He is all trivial–a place where
three highways of sin meet.

So is another the thorough-fare of virtue, and virtue
circulates through all his aisles like a wind, and he
is hallowed.

We reprove each other unconsciously by our own
behavior. Our very carriage and demeanor in the streets
should be a reprimand that will go to the conscience
of every beholder. An infusion of love from a great soul
gives a color to our faults, which will discover them
–as lunar caustic detects impurities in water.

The best will not seem to go contrary to others–but
as if *they* could afford to travel the same way, they
go a parallel but higher course–a sort of upper road.
Johnson says
> "That to the vulgar canst thyself apply,
> Treading a better path not contrary."

Their way is a mountain slope–a river valley's course
–a tide which mingles a myriad lesser currents.

Friday March 5th 1841.

How can our love increase—unless our loveliness
increase also. We must securely love each other as
we love God, with no more danger that our love be
unrequited or ill-bestowed There is that in my friend
before which I must first decay and prove untrue
— Love is the least moral and the most— Are the best
good in their love—or the worst bad?

March 6th 1841.

An honest misunderstanding is often the ground
of future intercourse.

March 7th 8th 9th 10th 1841.

"The Sphinx"

The Sphinx is man's insatiable and questioning spirit,
which still as of old, stands by the roadside in us and
proposes the riddle of life to every passer.

The ancients represented this by a monster who
was a riddle of herself, having a body composed of
various creatures, as if to hint that she had no individual
existence, but was nearly allied to and brooded over
all. They made her devour those who were unable
to explain her enigmas, as we are devoured by doubt,
and struggle towards the light, as if to be assured of our
lives. For we live by confidence and our bravery is in
some moment when we are certain—to that degree that
our certainty cannot be increased, as when a ray
bursts through a gap in a cloud, it darts as far, and
reaches the earth as surely as the whole sun could have
done.

1 In the first four lines is described the mood in
which the Sphinx bestirs herself in us. We must look on

the world with a drowsy and half shut eye, that it may
not be too much in our eye, and rather stand aloof
from than within it. When we are awake to the real
world, we are asleep to the actual. The sinful drowse to
eternity–the virtuous to time. Menu says–that the
"supreme omnipresent intelligence" is "a spirit which
can only be conceived by a mind *slumbering.*" Wisdom
and holiness always slumber–they are never active
in the ways of the world. As in our night-dreams we are
nearest to awakening–so in our daydreams we are
nearest to a supernatural awakening, and the plain and
flat satisfactoriness of life becomes so significant as
to be questioned.

The Sphinx hints that in the ages her secret is kept
–but in the annihilation of ages alone is it revealed.
So far from solving the problem of life, Time only
serves to propose and keep it in. Time waits but for its
solution to become eternity. Its lapse is measured
by the successive failures to answer the incessant
question, and the generations of men are the unskilful
passengers devoured.

2. She hints generally at man's mystery. He knows
only that he is, not what–nor whence. Not only is he
curiously and wonderfully wrought, but with Daedalian
intricacy. He is lost in himself as a labyrinth and has
no clue to get out by. If he could get out of his humanity
–he would have got out of nature. Daedalian expresses
both the skill and the inscrutable design of the builder.

The insolubleness of the riddle is only more forcibly
expressed by the lines–
"Out of sleeping a waking,
Out of waking a sleep,"
They express the complete uncertainty–and renunciation
of knowledge of the propounder.

3-4-5-6. In these verses is described the integrity of all animate and inanimate things but man—how each is a problem of itself and not the solution of one—and presides over and uses the mystery of the universe as unhesitatingly as if it were the partner of God. How by a sort of *essential and practical faith* each understands all—for to see that we understand—is to know that we misunderstand. Each natural object is an end to itself— A brave undoubting life do they all live, and are content to be a part of the mystery which is God—and throw the responsibility on man of explaining them and himself too.

3— The outlines of the trees are as correct as if ruled by God on the sky— The motions of quadrupeds and birds nature never thinks to mend but they are a last copy—and the flourishes of his hand.

4— The waves lapse with such a melody on the shore as shows that they have long been at one with nature. Theirs is as perfect play as if the heavens and earth were not—they meet with a sweet difference and independently—as old play-fellows. Nothing do they lack more than the world—the ripple is proud to be a ripple and balances the sea.— The atoms which are in such a continual flux notwithstanding their minuteness—have a certain essential valor and independence— They have the integrity of worlds, and attract & repel firmly as such. The least has more manhood than Democritus.

5— So also in nature the perfection of the whole is the perfection of the parts— And what is itself perfect serves to adorn and set off all the rest. Her distinctions are but reliefs. Night veileth the morning for the morning's sake, and the vapor adds a new attraction to the hill. Nature looks like a conspiracy for the advantage of all her parts—when one feature shines all the rest

seem suborned to heighten its charm. In her circle each
gladly gives precedence to the other— Day gladly
alternates with night— Behind these the vapor atones
to the hill for its interference, and this harmonious
scene is the effect of that at-one-ment.

6— In a sense the babe takes its departure from
nature as the grown man his departure out of her, and
so during its nonage is at one with her, and as a part
of herself. It is indeed the very flower and blossom
of nature—

> "Shines the peace of all being
> Without cloud in its eyes,
> And the *sum* of the world
> In soft *miniature* lies."

To the charming consistency of the palm and thrush,
this universal and serene beauty is added—as all the
leaves of the tree flower in the blossom.

7 But alas, the fruit to be matured in these petals
is fated to break the stem which holds it to universal
consistency. It passes *through nature* to manhood,
and becomes unnatural—without being as yet quite
supernatural. Man's most approved life is but conformity
—not a simple and independent consistency, which
would make all things conform to it. His actions do not
adorn nature nor one another, nor does she exist in
harmony but in contrast with them. She is not their
willing scenery. We concive that if a true action were to
be performed it would be assisted by nature—and
perhaps be fondled and reflected many times as the
rainbow. The sun is a true light for the trees in a picture,
but not for the actions of men. They will not bear so
strong a light as the stubble—the universe has little
sympathy with them, and sooner or later they rebound
hollowly on the memory. The April shower should be

as reviving to our life as to the garden and the grove, and the scenery in which we live reflect our own beauty, as the dew drop the flower. It is the actual man, not the actual nature that hurts the romance of the landscape. "He poisons the ground". The haymakers must be lost in the grass of the meadow. They may be Faustus and Amyntas here–but near at hand they are Reuben and Jonas. The wood cutter must not be better than the wood lest he be *worse*– Neither will bear to be considered as a distinct feature. Man's works must lie in the bosom of nature, cottages be buried in trees, or under vines and moss, like rocks, that they may not outrage the landscape. The hunter must be dressed in Lincoln green, with a plume of eagles feathers–to imbosom him in nature. So the skilful painter secures the distinctness of the whole by the indistinctness of the parts.– We can endure best to consider our repose and silence. Only when–the city–the hamlet–or the cottage–is viewed from a distance does man's life seem in harmony with the universe, but seen closely his actions have no eagles feathers or Lincoln green to redeem them– The sunlight on cities at a distance is a deceptive beauty, but foretells the final harmony of man with nature.

Man as he is is not the subject of any art, strictly speaking– The naturalist pursues his study with love –but the moralist persecutes his with hate– In man is the material of a picture, with a design partly sketched –but nature is such a picture drawn and colored.– He is a studio–nature a gallery. If men were not idealists no sonnets to beautiful persons, nor eulogies on worthy ones would ever be written. We wait for the preacher to express *such* love for his congregation as the Botanist for his herbarium.

8 Man, however, detects something in the lingering ineradicable sympathy of nature which seems to side with him against the stern decrees of the soul. Her essential friendliness is only the more apparent to his waywardness, (for disease and sorrow are but a rupture with her). In proportion as he renounces his will, she repairs his hurts—and if she burns, does oftener warm, if she freezes oftener refreshes. This is the motherliness which the poet personifies—and the Sphinx or wisely inquiring man, makes express a real concern for him. Nature shows us a stern kindness and only we are unkind. She endures long with us, and though the serenity of her law is unrelaxed, yet its evenness and impartiality look relenting, and almost sympathize with our fault.

9-10-11-12-13-14. But to the poet there are no riddles, they are "pleasant songs" to him—his faith solves the enigmas which recurring wisdom does not fail to repeat. Poetry is the only solution time can offer. But the poet is soonest a pilgrim from his own faith. Our brave moments may still be distinguished from our wise. Though the problem is always solved for the soul, still does it remain to be solved by the intellect. Almost faith puts the question, for only in her light can it be answered. However true the answer it does not prevent the question—for the best answer is but plausible—and man can only tell his relation to truth, but render no account of truth to herself.

9.— Believe, and ask not—says the poet—

"Deep love lieth under
These pictures of time,
They fade in the light of
Their meaning sublime."

Nothing is plain but love.

10-11-12-13. Man comes short because he seeks
perfection. He adorns no world while he is seeking to
adorn a better. His best actions have no reference to
their actual scenery. For when our actions become
of that worth that they might confer a grace on nature
–they pass out of her into a higher arena–where they
are still mean and awkward.

So that the world beholds only the rear of great deeds
and mistakes them often for inconsistencies, not
knowing with what higher they consist. Nature is
beautiful as in repose–not promising a higher beauty
tomorrow. Her actions are level to one another, and so
are never–unfit or inconsistent. Shame and remorse,
which are so unsightly to her, have a prospective beauty
and fitness which redeem them. We would have our
lover to be nobler than we, and do not fear to sacrifice
our love to his greater nobleness Better the disagreement
of noble lovers than the agreement of base ones. In
friendship each will be nobler than the other, and so
avoid the cheapness of a level and idle harmony. Love
will have its chromatic strains–discordant yearnings for
higher chords–as well as symphonies. 13 Let us expect
no finite satisfaction–who looks in the sun–will see
no light else–but also he will see no shadow. Our life
revolves unceasingly–but the centre is ever the same and
the, same–and the wise will regard only the seasons
of the soul.

14 The poet concludes with the same trust he began
with, and jeers at the blindness which could inquire.
But our sphinx is so wise as to put no riddle that can
be answered. It is a great presumption–to answer
conclusively a question which any sincerity has put.
The wise answer no questions–(nor do they ask
them–) She silences his jeers with the conviction that
she is the eyebeam of his eye. Our proper eye never

quails before an answer. To rest in a reply—as a response
of the oracle—that is error—but to suspect time's reply,
because we would not degrade one of God's meanings to
be intelligible to us—that is wisdom. We shall never
arrive at his meaning, but it will ceaselessly arrive
to us. The truth we seek with ardor and devotion will
not reward us with a cheap acquisition. We run
unhesitatingly in our career—not fearing to pass any goal
of truth in our haste. We career toward her eternally.—
A truth rested in stands for all the vice of an age—and
revolution comes kindly to restore health.

16 The cunning Sphinx who had been hushed into
stony silence and repose in us—arouses herself and
detects a mystery in all things—in infancy—the moon
—fire—flowers—sea—mountain—and,

17 in the spirit of the old fable, declares proudly—
"Who telleth one of my meanings
Is master of all I am.".

When some OEdipus has solved one of her enigmas,
she will go dash her head against a rock.

—

You may find this as enigmatical as the Sphinx's
riddle— Indeed I doubt if she could solve it herself.

Thursday March 11th 1841
Every man understands why a fool sings.

Saturday March 13th 1841.
There is a sort of homely truth and naturalness in
some books, which is very rare to find, and yet looks
quite cheap.
There may be nothing lofty in the sentiment—or

polished in the expression—but it is careless—countrified talk. The scholar rarely writes as well as the farmer talks. Homeliness is a great merit in a book—it is next to beauty and a high art. Some have this merit only—a few homely expressions redeem them.— Rusticity is pastoral—but affectation merely civil— The scholar does not make his most familiar experience come gracefully to the aid of his expression—and hence, though he live in it—his books contain no tolerable pictures of the country and simple life. Very few men can speak of nature with any truth— They confer no favor—they do not speak a good word for her. Most cry better than they speak— You can get more nature out of them by pinching than by addressing them. It is naturalness, and not simply good nature, that interests. I like better the surliness with which the wood chopper speaks of his woods, handling them as indifferently as his axe —than the mealy mouthed enthusiasm of the lover of nature. Better that the primrose by the river's brim be a yellow primrose and nothing more, than the victim of his bouquet or herbarium—to shine with the flickering dull light of his imagination, and not the golden gleam of a star.

Aubrey relates of Thomas Fuller that his was "a very working head, in so much, that walking and meditating before dinner, he would eat up a penny loaf, not knowing that he did it. His natural memory was very great, to which he added the art of memory: He would repeat to you forwards and backwards all the signs from Ludgate to Charing-cross." These are very good and wholesome facts to know of a man—as copious as some modern volumes.

He also says of Mr John Hales, that—"He loved Canarie"—and was buried "under an altar monument

of black marble – – with a too long epitaph." Of
Edmund Halley, that he "at sixteen could make a dial,
and then he said he thought himself a brave fellow." Of
William Holder, who wrote a book upon his curing
one Popham who was deaf and dumb–"he was beholding
to no author; did only consult with nature." For the most
part an author but consults with all who have written
before upon any subject–and his book is but the advice
of so many. But a true book will never have been
forestalled but the topic itself will be new–and by
consulting with nature–it will consult not only with
those who have gone before, but with those who may
come after. There is always room and occasion enough
for a true book on any subject–as there is room for more
light the brightest day–and more rays will not interfere
with the first.

How alone must our life be lived– We dwell on
the sea-shore and none between us and the sea– Men
are my merry companions–my fellow pilgrims–who
beguile the way, but leave me at the first turn in the
road–for none are travelling *one* road so far as myself.
Each one marches in the van. The weakest child is
exposed to the fates henceforth as barely as its parents
– Parents and relations but entertain the youth–they
cannot stand between him and his destiny. This is
the one bare side of every man– There is no fence–it
is clear before him to the bounds of space

What is fame to a living man– If he live aright the
sound of no man's voice will resound through the
aisles of his secluded life. His life is a hallowed silence
–a fane. The loudest sounds have to thank my little
ear that they are heard.

March 15th 1841

When I have access to a man's barrel of sermons,
which were written from week to week, as his life
lapsed–though I now know him to live cheerfully and
bravely enough–still I cannot conceive what interval
there was for laughter and smiles in the midst of so
much sadness. Almost in proportion to the sincerity and
earnestness of the life–will be–the sadness of the
record. When I reflect that twice a week for so many
years he pondered and preached such a sermon–I think
he must have been a splenetic and melancholy man,
and wonder if his food digested well. It seems as if the
fruit of virtue was never a careless happiness–

A great cheerfulness have all great wits possessed
–almost a prophane levity–to such as understood them
not–but their religion had the broader basis in proportion
as it was less prominent. The religion I love is very
laic. The clergy are as diseased, and as much possessed
with a devil as the reformers– They make their topic
as offensive as the politician–for our religion is as
unpublic and incommunicable as our poetical vein–and
to be approached with as much love and tenderness.

Wednesday March 17th 1841

The stars go up and down before my only eye
– Seasons come round to me alone. I cannot lean so
hard on any arm as on a sunbeam– So solid men are
not to my sincerity as is the shimmer of the fields.

Friday March 19th 1841

No true and brave person will be content to live on
such a footing with his fellow and himself as the laws
of every household now require. The house is the
very haunt and lair of our vice. I am impatient to

withdraw myself from under its roof as an unclean spot. There is no circulation there—it is full of stagnant and mephitic vapors.

March 20th 1841.

Even the wisest and best are apt to use their lives as the occasion to do something else in than to live greatly. But we should hang as fondly over this work as the finishing and embellishment of a poem.

It is a great relief when for a few moments in the day we can retire to our chamber and be completely true to ourselves. It leavens the rest of our hours. In that moment I will be nakedly as vicious as I am—this false life of mine shall have a being at length.

Sunday March 21st 1841

To be associated with others by my friend's generosity when he bestows a gift—is an additional favor to be grateful for.

Sat. March 27th 1841

Magnanimity—though it looks expensive for a short course, is always economy in the long run. Be generous in your poverty if you would be rich. To make up a great action there are no subordinate mean ones. We can never afford to postpone a true life to-day to any future and anticipated nobleness. We think if by tight economy we can manage to arrive at independence —then indeed we will begin to be generous without stay— We sacrifice all nobleness to a little present meanness. If a man charges you 800 pay him 850, and it will leave a clean edge to the sum. It will be like nature—overflowing and rounded like the bank of a river —not close and precise like a drain or ditch.

It is always a short step to peace—of mind.

I must be a farmer—and not

{Back flyleaf missing}

Under this line there is or has been life as when I
see the mole's raised gallery in the meadow I know that
he hass passed underneath.

I must not lose any of my freedom by being a farmer
and land holder. Most who enter on any profession
are doomed men—the world might as well sing a dirge
over them forthwith. The farmer's muscles are rigid
—he can do one thing long not many well. His pace
seems determined henceforth—he never quickens it.
A very rigid Nemesis is his fate. When the right wind
blows or a star calls, I can leave this arable and grass
ground, without making a will or settling my estate.
I would buy a farm as freely as a silken streamer.
Let me not think my front windows must face east
henceforth because a particular hill slopes that way. My
life must undulate still. I will not feel that my wings
are clipt when once I have settled on ground which
the law calls my own—but find new pinions grown to the
old—and talaria to my feet beside.

{Two-thirds page blank}

{Back endpaper}

· 5 ·

March 30–September 30, 1841
TRANSCRIBED 1841

Tuesday March 30th 1841.

I find my life growing slovenly when it does not exercise a constant supervision over itself. Its deeds accumulate. Next to having lived a day well—is a clear and calm overlooking of all our days.

Friendship—
Now we are partners in such legal trade,
We'll look to the beginnings, not the ends,
Nor to pay day—knowing true wealth is made
For current stock and not for dividends.

I am amused when I read how Ben Johnson engaged that the ridiculous masks with which the royal family and nobility were to be entertained—should be "grounded upon antiquity and solid learning."

April 1st 1841.

On *The Sun coming out in the Afternoon.*
Methinks all things have travelled since you shined,
But only Time, and clouds, Time's team, have moved;
Again foul weather shall not change my mind,
But In the shade I will believe what in the sun I loved.

In reading a work on agriculture I skip the author's moral reflections, and the words "Providence" and "He" scattered along the page, to come at the profitable level of what he has to say. There is no science in men's religion—it does not teach me so much as the report of the committee on Swine. My author shows he has dealt in corn and turnips—and can worship God with the hoe and spade—but spare me his morality.

April 3d 1841.
Friends will not only live in harmony but in melody.

Sunday April 4th 1841.
The rattling of the tea-kettle below stairs reminds
me of the cow bells I used to hear when berrying in the
Great Fields many years ago–sounding distant and deep
amid the birches   That cheap piece of tinkling brass
which the farmer hangs about his cow's neck–has been
more to me than the tons of metal which are swung
in the belfry.

> They who prepare my evening meal below
> Carelessly hit the kettle as they go
> With tongs or shovel,
> And ringing round and round,
> Out of this hovel
> It makes an eastern temple by the sound.
>
> At first I thought a cow bell right at hand
> Mid birches sounded o'er the open land,
> Where I plucked flowers
> Many years ago,
> Spending midsummer hours
> With such secure delight they hardly seemed to flow.

April 5th 1841.
This long series of desultory mornings does not
tarnish the brightness of the prospective days. Surely
faith is not dead. Wood–water–earth–air–are essentially
what they were–only society has degenerated– This
lament for a golden age is only a lament for golden men.

I only ask a clean seat. I will build my lodge on the
southern slope of some hill, and take there the life
the gods send me– Will it not be employment enough

to accept gratefully all that is yielded me between sun &
sun?– Even the fox digs his own burrow– If my jacket
and trowsers–my boots and shoes are fit to worship
God in–they will do.

Wednesday April 7th 1841
My life will wait for nobody–but is being matured
still irresistibly while I go about the streets, and chaffer
with this man and that to secure it a living– It will
cut its own channel–like the mountain stream which by
the longest ridges–and by level prairies is not kept
from the sea finally. So flows a man's life–and will
reach the sea water, if not by an earthy channel–yet in
dew and rain overleaping all barriers–with rainbows
to announce its victory. It can wind as cunningly and
unerringly as water that seeks its level, and shall I
complain if the gods make it meander. This staying to
buy me a farm is as if the Mississipi should stop to
chaffer with a clam-shell.

What have I to do with plows– I cut another furrow
than you see– Where the off ox treads, there is it not
–it is nigher–where the nigh ox walks will it not be–it is
nigher still. If corn fails, so do not all crops fail. What
of drought–what of rain– Is not my sand well clayed
–my peat well sanded. Is it not underdrained and
watered.

My ground is high,
But t'is not dry,
What you call dew
Comes filtering through;
Though in the sky,
It still is nigh;
Its soil is blue
And virgin too.
—

If from your price ye will not swerve,
Why then I'll think the gods reserve
A greater bargain there above,
Out of their sup'rabundant love
Have meantime better for me cared,
And so will get my stock prepared,
Plows of new pattern—hoes the same—
Designed a different soil to tame,
And sow my seed broadcast in air,
Full sure to reap my harvest there.

{*One-fifth page blank*}

April 8th 1841.

Friends are the ancient and honorable of the earth. The oldest men did not begin friendship. It is older than Hindostan, and the Chinese empire. How long has it been cultivated, and is still the staple article— It is a divine league struck forever—warm serene days only bring it out to the surface. There is a friendliness between the sun and the earth in pleasant weather—the grey content of the land is its color.

You can tell what another's suspicions are by what you feel forced to become— You will wear a new character, like a strange habit, in their presence.

Friday April 9th 1841.

It would not be hard for some quiet brave man to leap into the saddle to-day—and eclipse Napoleon's career by a grander.— Show men at length the meaning of war. One reproaches himself with supineness, that he too has sat quiet in his chamber, and not treated the world to the sound of the trumpet, that the indignation which has so long rankled in his breast, does not take to horse, and to the field. The bravest warrior will have to fight his battles in his dreams—and no earthly war note can arouse him. There are who would not

run with Leonidas—only the third rate Napoleons and
Alexanders does history tell of. The brave man does
not mind the call of the trumpet—nor hear the idle
clashing of swords—without, for the infinite din within
War is but a training compared with the active service
of his peace—

Is he not at war? Does he not resist the ocean swell
within him—and walk as gently as the summer's sea?
Would you have him parade in uniform, and maneuver
men, whose equanimity is his uniform—and who is
himself maneuvered?

The times have no heart. The true reform can be
undertaken any morning before unbarring our doors.
It calls no convention. I can do two thirds the reform of
the world myself.—

When two neighbors begin to eat corn bread, who
before ate wheat—then the gods smile from ear to ear,
it is very pleasant. When an individual takes a sincere
step, then all the gods attend, and his single deed
is sweet.

Saturday April 10th 1841.
I dont know but we should make life all too tame if
we had our own way, and should miss these impulses in
a happier time.

How much virtue there is in simply seeing— The
hero has striven in vain for any preeminency when the
student over sees him. The woman who sits in the
house and *sees* is a match for a stirring captain. Those
still piercing eyes as faithfully exercised on their talent
will keep her even with Alexander or Shakspeare.
They may go to Asia with parade—or to fairy land, but
not beyond her ray. We are as much as we see— Faith is

sight and knowledge. The hands only serve the eyes.
The farthest blue streak in the horizon I can see, I may
reach before many sunsets. What I saw alters not—in
my night when I wander it is still steadfast as the
star which the sailor steers by. Whoever has had one
thought quite lonely—and could consciously digest
that in solitude, knowing that none might accept it, may
rise to the height of humanity—and overlook all living men
as from a pinnacle.

Speech never made man master of men, but the
eloquently refraining from it.

Sunday April 11th 1841

A greater baldness my life seeks, as the crest of some
bare hill, which towns and cities do not afford— I want
a directer relation with the sun.

Friendship's Steadfastness

True friendship is so firm a league
That's maintenance falls into the even tenor
Of our lives, and is no tie,
But the continuance of our lifes thread.

If I would safely keep this new got pelf,
I have no care henceforth but watch myself,
For lo! it goes untended from my sight,
Waxes and wanes secure with the safe star of night.

See with what liberal step it makes its way,
As we could well afford to let it stray
Throughout the universe, with the sun & moon,
Which would dissolve allegiance as soon.

Shall I concern myself for fickleness,
And undertake to make my friends more sure,
When the great gods out of sheer kindliness,
Gave me this office for a sinecure?

Death cannot come too soon
Where it can come at all,
But always is too late
Unless the fates it call.

Thursday April 15th 1841.

The Gods are of no sect–they side with no man.
When I imagined that nature inclined rather to some
few earnest and faithful souls, and specially existed for
them–I go to see an obscure individual who lives
under the hill letting both gods and men alone and
find that strawberries and tomatos grow for him too in
his garden there, and the sun lodges kindly under
his hill side–and am compelled to allow the grand
catholicism of nature, and the unbribable charity of the
gods.

Any simple unquestioned mode of living is alluring
to men. The man who picks peas steadily for a living
is more than respectable.

April 16th 1841.

I have been inspecting my neighbors' farms to-day
–and chaffering with the land holders–and I must
confess I am startled to find everywhere the old system
of things so grim and assured. Wherever I go the
farms are run out, and there they lie, and the youth
must buy old land and bring it to– Every where the
relentless opponents of reform are a few old maids and
batchelors, who sit round the kitchen fire, listening to
the singing of the tea kettle, and munching cheese rinds.

Sunday April 18th 1841.

We need pine for no office for the sake of a certain
culture, for all valuable experience lies in the way
of a man's duty.– My necessities of late have compelled
me to study nature as she is related to the farmer–as

she simply satisfies a want of the body.– Some interests have got a footing on the earth which I have not made sufficient allowance for– That which built these barns –and cleared the land thus had some valor.

We take little steps, and venture small stakes, as if our actions were very fatal and irretrievable. There is no swing to our deeds. But our life is only a retired valley where we rest on our packs awhile. Between us and our end there is room for any delay. It is not a short and easy southern way–but we must go over snow-capped mountains to reach the sun.

April 20th 1841.
You cant beat down your virtue–so much goodness it must have.

When a room is furnished–comfort is not furnished.

Great thoughts hallow any labor– To day I earned seventy five cents heaving manure out of a pen, and made a good bargain of it. If the ditcher muses the while how he may live uprightly, the ditching spade and turf knife, may be engravd on the coat of arms of his posterity.

There are certain current expressions–and blasphemous moods of viewing things–as when we say "he is doing a good business"–which is more prophane than cursing and swearing– There is death and sin in such words–let not the children hear them.
Thursday April 22d 1841.
There are two classes of authors– The one write the history of their times– The other their biography.

Friday April 23d 1841.

Any greatness is not to be mistaken– Who shall cavil
at it? It stands once for all on a level with the heroes
of history. It is not to be patronised, It goes alone.

When I hear music, I flutter, & am the scene of life,
as a fleet of merchantmen when the wind rises.

April 24th 1841.

Music is the sound of the circulation in nature's
veins.– It is the flux which melts nature–men dance
to it–glasses ring and vibrate–and the fields seem to
undulate.– The healthy ear always hears it–nearer or
more remote.

It has been a cloudy drizzling day with occasional
brightenings in the mist, when the trill of the
tree-sparrow seemed to be ushering in sunny hours.

April 25th 1841.

A momentous silence reigns always in the woods
–and their meaning seems just ripening into expression.
But alas! they make no haste– The rush sparrow
–nature's minstrel of serene hours–sings of an immense
leisure and duration.

When I hear a robin sing at sunset–I cannot help
contrasting the equanimity of nature with the bustle
and impatience of man We return from the lyceum and
caucus with such stir and excitement–as if a crisis
were at hand but no natural scene or sound sympathizes
with us, for nature is always silent and unpretending
as at the break of day. She but rubs her eye lids.

I am struck with the pleasing friendships and
unanimities of nature in the woods–as when the moss
on the trees takes the form of their leaves.

There is all of civilized life in the woods—their wildest
scenes have an air of domesticity and homeliness, and
when the flicker's cackle is heard in the clearings, the
musing hunter is reminded that civilization has imported
nothing into them.

The ball room is represented by the catkins of the
alder at this season—which hang gracefully like a
ladies ear drops.

All the discoveries of science are equally true in their
deepest recesses—nature there too obeys the same laws.
Fair weather and foul concern the little red bug upon
a pine stump—for him the wind goes round the right
way and the sun breaks through the clouds.

{*One-fifth page blank*}

Monday April 26th 1841.
At R.W.E's.

The charm of the Indian to me is that he stands free
and unconstrained in nature—is her inhabitant—and
not her guest—and wears her easily and gracefully. But
the civilized man has the habits of the house. His
house is a prison in which he finds himself oppressed
and confined, not sheltered and protected. He walks
as if he sustained the roof—he carries his arms as
if the walls would fall in and crush him—and his feet
remember the cellar beneath. His muscles are never
relaxed— It is rare that he overcomes the house, and
learns to sit at home in it—and roof and floor—and walls
support themselves—as the sky—and trees—and earth.

It is a great art to saunter.

April 27th 1841.
It is only by a sort of voluntarry blindness, and
omitting to see that we know our selves—as when we
see stars with the side of the eye. The nearest approach

to discovering what we are is in dreams. It is as hard
to see onesself as to look backwards without turning
round. And foolish are they that look in glasses with
that intent.

The porters have a hard time, but not so hard as
he that carries his own shoulders— That beats the
Smyrna Turks. Some men's broad shoulders are load
enough. Even a light frame can stand under a great
burden, if it does not have to support itself— Virtue is
boyant and elastic–it stands without effort and does not
feel gravity–but sin plods and shuffles— Newton
needed not to wait for an apple to fall to discover the
attraction of gravitation–it was implied in the fall
of man.

Wednesday April 28th 1841.

We falsely attribute to men a determined character
–putting together all their yesterdays–and averaging
them–we presume we know them— Pity the man who
has a character to support–it is worse than a large
family–he is silent poor indeed.— But in fact character
is never explored, nor does it get developed in time
–but eternity is its development–time its envelope. In
view of this distinction, a sort of divine politeness
and heavenly good breeding suggests itself–to address
always the enveloped character of a man. A large
soul will meet you as not having known you–taking
you for what you are to be, a narrow one for what you
have been–for a broad and roaming soul is as uncertain
–what it may say or be–as a scraggy hill side or pasture.
I may hear a fox bark–or a partridge drum–or some
bird new to these localities may fly up. It lies out there
as old, and yet as new. The aspect of the woods varys
every day–what with their growth–and the changes of
the seasons–and the influence of the elements–so that
the eye of the forester never twice rests upon the same
prospect— Much more does a character show newly and

variedly, if directly seen. It is the highest compliment
to suppose that in the intervals of conversation your
companion has expanded and grown— It may be a
deference which he will not understand, but the nature
which underlies him will understand it—and your
influence will be shed as finely on him as the dust in
the sun settles on our clothes. By such politeness we may
educate one another to some purpose. So have I felt
myself educated sometimes— I am expanded and
enlarged.

April 29th 1841.

Birds and quadrupeds pass freely through nature
—without prop or stilt. But man very naturally carries
a stick in his hand—seeking to ally himself by many
points to nature.— as a warrior stands by his horse's side
with his hand on his mane. We walk the gracefuller
for a cane—as the juggler uses a leaded pole to balance
him when he dances on a slack wire.

Better a monosyllabic life—than a ragged and muttered
one—let its report be short and round, so that it may
hear its own echo in the surrounding silence.

April 30th 1841.

Where shall we look for standard English but to the
words of any man who has a depth of feeling in him?
—not in any smooth and leisurely essay. From the
gentlemanly windows of the country seat no sincere
eyes are directed upon nature—but from the peasants
horn windows a true glance and greeting occasionally.
— — "For summer being ended, all things," said the
pilgrim, "stand in appearance with a weather-beaten
face, and the whole country full of woods and thickets
represented a wild and savage hue."
Compare this with the agricultural report.

Sat. May 1st 1841.

Life in gardens and parlors is unpalatable to me–it
wants rudeness and necessity to give it relish– I would
at least strike my spade into the earth with as good
will as the woodpecker his bill into a tree.

May 2nd 1841.

Wachusett

Especial–I remember thee,
Wachusett, who like me
Standest alone without society.
Thy far blue eye–
A remnant of the sky–
Seen through the clearing or the gorge,
Or from the windows of the forge,
Doth leaven all it passes by.
Nothing is true but stands
But stands tween me and you,
Thou western pioneer,
Who know'st not shame nor fear,
By venturous spirit driven
Under the eaves of heaven,
And can'st expand thee there?
And breathe enough of air?
Upholding heaven, holding down earth,
Thy pastime from thy birth,
Not steadied by the one nor leaning on the other,
May I approve myself thy worthy brother.

Monday May 3d 1841.

We are all pilots of the most intricate Bahama
channels– Beauty may be the sky overhead–but Duty
is the water underneath. When I see a man with serene
countenance in the sunshine of summer–drinking in
peace in the garden or parlor, it looks like a great inward
leisure that he enjoys–but in reality he sails on no
summer's sea, but this steady sailing comes of a heavy
hand on the tiller.

We do not attend to larks and blue birds so leisurely

but that conscience is as erect as the attitude of the
listener. The man of principle gets never a holiday. Our
true character silently under lies all our words and
actions—as the granite underlies the other strata. Its
steady pulse does not cease for any deed of ours—as the
sap is still ascending in the stalk of the fairest flower.

Thursday May 6th 1841.

The fickle person is he that does not know what is
true or right absolutely—who has not an ancient wisdom
for a life time—but a new prudence for every hour. We
must sail by a sort of dead reckoning on this course
of life—not speak any vessel—nor spy any headland—but
in spite of all phenomena come steadily to port at
last. In general we must have a catholic and universal
wisdom—wiser than any particular—and be prudent
enough to defer to it always. We are literally wiser than
we know. Men do not fail for want of knowledge—but
for want of prudence to give wisdom the preference.
These low weather-cocks on barns and fences show not
which way the general and steady current of the wind
sets—which brings fair weather or foul—but the vane
on the steeple—high up in another stratum of atmosphere
tells that— What we need to know in any case is very
simple. I shall not mistake the direction of my life—if I
but know the high land and the main—on this side
the Cordilleras on that the pacific— I shall know how
to run. If a ridge intervene I have but to seek or make
a gap to the sea.

Sunday May 9th 1841.

The pine stands in the woods like an Indian—untamed
—with a fantastic wildness about it even in the clearings.
If an Indian warrior were well painted, with pines in
the back ground—he would seem to blend with the

es, and make a harmonious expression.– The pitch
nes are the ghosts of Philip and Massassoit– The
vhite pine has the smoother features of the squaw.

The poet speaks only those thoughts that come
unbidden like the wind that stirs the trees–and men
cannot help but listen. He is not listened to but heard.
The weather-cock might as well dally with the wind–as
a man pretend to resist eloquence.– The breath that
inspires the poet has traversed a whole campagna–and
this new climate here indicates that other latitudes
are chilled or heated.

Speak to men as to gods and you will not be insincere.

Westward-ho!
—

The needles of the pine
All to the west incline.

The Echo of the Sabbath Bell–
heard in the Woods.
—

Dong–sounds the brass in the east–
As if for a civic feast,
But I like that sound the best
Out of the fluttering west.

The steeple rings a knell,
But the fairies' silvery bell
Is the voice of that gentle folk–
Or else the horizon that spoke.

Its metal is not of brass,
But air and water and glass,
And under a cloud it is swung,
And by the wind is rung,
With a slim silver tongue

When the steeple tolls the noon
It soundeth not so soon,
Yet it rings an earlier hour,
And the sun has not reached its tower.

{*One-fifth page blank*}

Monday May 10th 1841.

A good warning to the restless tourists of these days
is contained in the last verses of Claudian's Old Man
of Verona.

Erret, et extremos alter scrutetur Iberos.
Plus habet hic vitae, plus habet ille viae.

Sunday May 23d 1841.– Barn.

The distant woods are but the tassels of my eye.

Books are to be attended to as new sounds merely.
Most would be put to a sore trial if the reader should
assume the attitude of a listener. They are but a new note
in the forest. To our lonely sober thought the earth
is a wild unexplored Wildness as of the jay and muskrat
reign over the great part of nature. The oven bird and
plover are heard in the horizon. Here is a new book
of heroes–come to me like the note of the chewink
from over the fen–only over a deeper and wider fen. The
pines are unrelenting sifters of thought–nothing petty
leaks through them. Let me put my ear close, and
hear the sough of this book–that I may know if any
inspiration yet haunts it. There is always a later edition
of every book than the printer wots of–no matter
how recently it was published.– All nature is a new
impression every instant.

The aspects of the most simple object are as various
as the aspects of the most compound– Observe the
same sheet of water from different eminences. When I

have travelled a few miles I do not recognize the
profile of the hills which hang over my native village.

Thursday May 27th 1841

I sit in my boat on walden—playing the flute this
evening—and see the perch, which I seem to have
charmed, hovering around me—and the moon travelling
over the ribbed bottom—and feel that nothing but the
wildest imagination can conceive of the manner of
life we are living. Nature is a wizzard. The Concord
nights are stranger than the Arabian nights.

We not only want elbow room, but eye room in this
grey air which shrouds all the fields. Sometimes my
eyes see over the county road by day light to the tops of
—yonder birches on the hill—as at others by moonlight.

Heaven lies above because the air is deep.

In all my life hitherto I have left nothing behind.

Monday May 31st 1841.

That title—The Laws of Menu—with the Gloss of
Culucca—comes to me with such a volume of sound as if
it had swept unobstructed over the plains of Hindostan,
and when my eye rests on yonder birches—or the sun
in the water—or the shadows of the trees—it seems
to signify the laws of them all.

They are the laws of you and me—a fragrance wafted
down from those old times—and no more to be refuted
than the wind.

When my imagination travels eastward and backward
to those remote years of the gods—I seem to draw near
to the habitation of the morning—and the dawn at
length has a place. I remember the book as an hour
before sunrise.

We are height and depth both—a calm sea—at the foot of a promontory— Do we not overlook our own depths?

June 1st 1841.

To have seen a man out of the east or west is sufficient to establish their reality and locality. I have seen a Mr. Wattles to-day from Vermont—and now know where that is and that it is—a reformer—with two soldier's eyes and shoulders—who began to belabor the world at ten years—a ragged mountain boy—as fifer of a company —with set purpose to remould it from those first years.

The great person never wants an opportunity to be great—but makes occasion for all about him.

Wednesday June 2nd 1841.

I am brought into the near neighborhood—and am become a silent observer of the moon's paces to-night by means of a glass—while the frogs are peeping all around me on the earth—and the sound of the accordion seems to come from some bright saloon yonder. I am sure the moon floats in a human atmosphere—it is but a distant scene of the world's drama. It is a wide theater the gods have given us, and our actions must befit it. More sea and land—mountain and valley here is—a further West—a freshness and wildness in reserve when all the land shall be cleared.

I see three little lakes between the hills near its edge—reflecting the sun's rays.— The light glimmers as on the water in a tumbler. So far off do the laws of reflection hold. I seem to see the ribs of the creature. This is the aspect of their day its outside—their heaven above their heads, towards which they breathe their prayers. So much is between me and them. It is noon there perchance and ships are at anchor in the havens

or sailing on the seas. and there is a din in the streets
—and in this light or that shade some leisurely soul
contemplates.

But now dorr-bugs fly over its disk and bring me
back to earth and night.

{One-fourth page blank}

Monday June 7th 1841

The inhabitants of those eastern plains seem to
possess a natural and hereditary right to be conservative
—and magnify forms and traditions. "Immemorial
custom is transcendent law" says Menu— That is, it was
the custom of gods before men used it. The fault of
our New England custom is that it is memorial— What
is morality but immemorial custom—? it is not manner
but character—and the conservative conscience
sustains it.

We are acccustomed to exaggerate the immobility
and stagnation of those eras—as of the waters which
levelled the steppes.— but those slow revolving "years of
the gods" were as rapid to all the needs of virtue as
these bustling and hasty seasons. Man stands to revere
—he kneels to pray. Methinks history will have to be
tried by new tests to show what centuries were rapid and
what slow. Corn grows in the night. Will this bustling
era detain the future reader longer? Will the earth
seem to have conversed more with the heavens during
these times? Who is writing better Vedas? How science
and art spread and flourished—how trivial conveniences
were multiplied That which is the gossip of the world,
is not recorded in them—and if they are left out of
our scripture too what will remain?

Since the Battle of Bunker Hill we think the world
has *not* been at a standstill.

When I remember the treachery of memory, and the manifold accidents to which tradition is liable—how soon the vista of the past closes behind—as near as night's crescent to the setting day—and the dazzling brightness of noon is reduced to the faint glimmer of the evening star, I feel as if it were by a rare indulgence of the fates—that any traces of the past are left us. — That my ears which do not hear across the interval over which a crow caws should chance to hear this far travelled sound — — With how little cooperation of the societies after all is the past remembered.

I know of no book which comes to us with grander pretensions than the Laws of Menu—and this immense presumption is so impersonal and sincere that it is never offensive or ridiculous. Observe the modes in which modern literature is advertised—and then consider this Hindoo prospectus. Think what a reading public it addresses—what criticism it expects— What wonder if the times were not ripe for it.

June 8th 1841.

Having but one chair—I am obliged to receive my visitors standing—and now I think of it—those old sages and heroes must always have met erectly.

July 10th to 12th 1841.

This town too lies out under the sky—a port of entry and departure for souls to and from Heaven.

A slight sound at evening lifts me up by the ears—and makes life seem inexpressibly serene and grand.— It may be in Uranus—or it may be in the shutter.— It is the original sound of which all literature is but the echo — It makes all fear superfluous— Bravery comes from further than the sources of fear.

{*One-fifth page blank*}

{*Eight leaves blank*}

Sunday Aug. 1st 1841.

I never met a man who cast a free and healthy glance over life–but the best live in a sort of sabbath light–a Jewish gloom. The best thought is not only without sombreness–but even without morality. The universe lies outspread in floods of white light to it. The moral aspect of nature is a disease caught of man–a jaundice imported into her– To the innocent there are no cherubims nor angels. Occasionally we rise above the necessity of virtue into an unchangeable morning light–in which we have not to choose in a dilemma between right and wrong–but simply to live right on and breathe the circumambient air.

There is no name for this life unless it be the very vitality of *vita*– Silent is the preacher about it–and silent must ever be. for he who knows it will not preach.

Wednesday Aug. 4th 1841.

My pen is a lever which in proportion as the near end stirs me further within–the further end reaches to a greater depth in the reader.

Nawshawtuct.

Far in the east I read *Natures Corn Law Rhymes* – Here in sight of Wachusutt and these rivers and woods, my mind goes singing to itself of other themes than taxation. The rush sparrow sings still unintelligible as from beyond a depth in me which I have not fathomed–where my future lies folded up–

I hear several faint notes–quite outside me–which populate the waste.

This is such fresh and flowing weather–as if the waves of the morning had subsided over the day.

Aug. 6th 1841.

If I am well then I see well. The bulletins of health are twirled along my visual rays–like pasteboards on a kite string.

I cannot read a sentence in the book of the Hindoos without being elevated as upon the table land of the Gauhts–it has such a rythm as the winds of the desert– such a tide as the Ganges–and seems as superior to criticism as the Himaleh mounts. Even at this late hour–unworn by time–it wears the English dress with a native and inherent dignity as indifferently as the Sanscrit.

The great tone of the book is of such fibre–and such severe tension, that no time nor accident can relax it. The great thought is never found in a mean dress but is of virtue to ennoble any language.– let it issue from the lips of the Woloffs–or from The forum of Rome–the nine muses will seem to have been purveyors for it. Its education is always liberal–it has all the graces of oratory and of poetry. The lofty tone which is its indispensable breath–is grace to the eye and music to the ear. It can endow a college.

So supremely religious a book imposes with authority on the latest age.– The very simplicity of style of the ancient lawgiver–implying all in the omission of all –proves an habitual elevation of thought–which the multiplied glosses of later days strive in vain to slope up to. The whole book by noble gestures and inclinations seems to render words unnecessary. The abbreviated sentence points to the thing for explanation – As the sublimest thought is most faithfully printed in the face, and needs the fewest interpreting words – The page nods toward the fact and is silent.

As I walk across the yard from The barn to the House –through the fog–with a lamp in my hand, I am reminded of the Merrimack nights–and seem to see the sod between tent ropes. The trees seen dimly through the mist suggest things which do not at all belong

to the past, but are peculiar to my fresh New England
life. It is as novel as green peas. The dew hangs every
where upon the grass—and I breathe the rich damp
air in slices.

Sat. Aug. 7th 1841
The impression which those sublime sentences
made on me last night has awakened me before any
—cock-crowing— Their influence lingers around me
like a fragrance or as the fog hangs over the earth late
into the day.

The very locusts and crickets of a summer day are
but later or older glosses on the Dherma Sástra of the
Hindoos—a continuation of the sacred code.

Aug. 9th 1841.
It is vain to try to write unless you feel strong in the
knees.

Any book of great authority and genius seems to our
imagination to permeate and pervade all space Its
spirit like a more subtle ether sweeps along with the
prevailing winds of the country. Its influence conveys
a new gloss to the meadows and the depths of the
wood—and bathes the huckleberries on the hills—as
sometimes a new influence in the sky washes in waves
over the fields and seems to break on some invisible
beach in the air.—
All things confirm it— It spends the mornings and
the evenings.
Everywhere the speech of Menu demands the widest
apprehension and proceeds from the loftiest plateau of
the soul— It is spoken unbendingly to its own level
—and does not imply any contemporaneous speaker.

I read history as little critically as I consider the
landscape–and am more interested in the atmospheric
tints and various lights and shades which the intervening
spaces create than in its groundwork and composition
It is the morning now turned evening and seen in the
west–the same sun but a new light and atmosphere
– Its beauty is like the sunset–not a frescoe painting on
a wall flat and bounded, but atmospheric and roving
–or free. But in reality history fluctuates as the face
of the landscape from morning to evening. What is
of moment in it is its hue and color. Time hides no
treasures–we want not its then–but its now. We do not
complain that the mountains in the horizon are blue
and indistinct–they are the more like the heavens.

Of what moment are facts that can be lost–which
need to be commemorated?– The monument of death
will outlast the memory of the dead– The pyramids do
not tell the tale confided to them.

The living fact commemorates itself– Why look in
the dark for light–look in the light rather.

Strictly speaking the Societies have not recovered one
fact from oblivion, but they themselves are instead of
the fact that is lost.– The researcher is more memorable
than the researched. The crowd stood admiring the
mist and the dim outline of the trees seen through it–&
when one of their number advanced to explore the
phenomenon, with fresh admiration all eyes were
turned on his dimly retreating figure– Critical acumen
is exerted in vain to uncover the past– The past cannot
be presented.– we cannot know what we are not– But
one veil hangs over past–present–and future.– And
it is the province of the historian to find out not what
was, but what is. When a battle has been fought you
will find nothing but the bones of men and beasts–where
a battle is being fought there are hearts beating. We

will sit on a mound and muse, and not try to make
these skeletons stand on their legs again. Does nature
remember, think you, that they were men, or not
rather that they are bones? Ancient history has an
air of antiquity—it should be more modern. It is written
as if the spectator should be thinking of the back side
of the picture on the wall—as if the author expected the
dead would be his readers, and wished to detail to
them their own experience. Men seem anxious to
accomplish an orderly retreat through the centuries
—earnestly rebuilding the works behind as they are
battered down by the incroachments of time—but while
they loiter—they and their works both fall a prey to
the enemy. (See p. 322 for an omission)

Aug. 12th 1841.

We take pleasure in beholding the form of a mountain
in the horizon as if by retiring to this distance we had
then first conquered it by our vision, and were made
privy to the design of the architect— So when we behold
the shadow of our earth on the moon's disk. When
we climb a mountain—and observe the lesser irregularities
—we do not give credit to the comprehensive and general
intelligence which shaped them; but when we see the
outline in the horizon—we confess that the hand which
moulded those opposite slopes—making one balance
the other—worked round a deep centre, and was privy to
the plan of The universe. The smallest of nature's
works fits the farthest and widest view, as if it had been
referred in its bearings to every point in space— It
harmonizes with the horizon line and the orbits of the
planets.

{One-third page blank}

Friday Aug. 13th 1841.

I have been in the swamp by Charles Miles' This afternoon, and found it so bosky and sylvan–that Art would never have freedom or courage to imitate it– It can never match The luxury and superfluity of nature. In Art all is seen–she cannot afford concealed wealth –and in consequence is niggardly–but nature–even when she is scant and thin outwardly–contents us still by the assurance of a certain generosity at the roots Surely no stinted hand has been at work here for these centuries to produce these particular tints this summer. The double spruce attracts me here, which I had hardly noticed in the gardens–and now I understand why men try to make them grow about their houses–

Nature has her luxurious and florid style as well as Art. Having a pilgrim's cup to make, she gives to the whole–stem–bowl–handle and nose–some fantastic shape–as if it were to be the car of a fabulous marine deity– A Nereus or Triton. She is mythical and mystical always–and spends her whole genius upon the least work.

Aug. 16th 1841.

There is a double virtue in the sound that can wake an echo–as in the lowing of the cows this morning– Far out in the horizon that sound travels quite round the town–and invades each recess of the wood–advancing at a grand pace, and with a sounding eastern pomp.

Aug. 18th 1841.

I sailed on the north river last night with my flute –and my music was a tinkling stream which meandered with the river–and fell from note to note as a brook from rock to rock. I did not hear the strains after they had issued from the flute, but before they were breathed

into it—for the original strain precedes the sound—by
as much as the echo follows after—and the rest is the
perquisite of the rocks—and trees—and beasts.

Unpremeditated music is the true gage which
measures the current of our thoughts—the very undertow
of our life's stream.

Of all the duties of life it is hardest to be in earnest
—it implies a good deal both before and behind. I sit
here in the barn this flowing afternoon weather, while
the school bell is ringing in the village—and find that
all the things immediate to be done are very trivial— I
could postpone them to hear this locust sing.— The
cockrils crow and the hens cluck in the yard—as if time
were dog cheap.— It seems something worth detaining
him—the laying of an egg. Cannot man do something
to comfort the gods, and not let the world prove such a
piddling concern? No doubt they would be glad to
sell their shares at a large discount by this time. Eastern
rail-road stock promises a better dividend.

The best poets, after all, exhibit only a tame and
civil side of nature— They have not seen the west side
of any mountain.

Day and night—mountain and wood are visible from
the wilderness as well as the village— They have their
primeval aspects—sterner savager—than any poet
has sung. It is only the white man's poetry—we want
the Indian's report. Wordsworth is too tame for the
Chippeway.

The landscape contains a thousand dials which
indicate the natural divisions of time—the shadows of a
thousand styles point to the hour. The afternoon is
now far advanced, and a fresh and leisurely wind is

blowing on the river—causing long reaches of serene ripples. It has done its stent—and seems not to flow—but lie at its length reflecting the light.

The haze over the woods seems like the breath of all nature, rising from a myriad pores into the attenuated atmosphere. It is sun smoke—the woof he has woven —his day's toil displayed.

If I were awaked from a deep sleep I should know which side the meridian the sun might be by the chirping of the crickets. — — Night has already insidiously set her foot in the valley in many places, where the shadows of the shrubs and fences begin to darken the landscape. There is a deeper shading in the colors of the afternoon landscape. Perhaps the forenoon is brighter than the afternoon, not only because of the greater transparency of the atmosphere then, but because we naturally look most into the west—as we look forward into the day—and so in the forenoon see the sunny side of things, but in the afternoon the shadow of every tree.

What a drama of light and shadow from morning to night.— Soon as the sun is over the meridian—in deep ravines under the east side of the cliffs— Night forwardly plants her foot—and as day retreats steps into his trenches—till at length she sits in his citadel.— For long time she skulks behind the needles of the pine—before she dares draw out her forces into the plain. Sun—moon —wind—and stars—are the allies of one side or the other.

{*One-third page blank*}

(Aug 9th 1841—omitted on p. 319)
Biography is liable to the same objection—it should be autobiography. Let us not leave ourselves empty

that so vexing our bowels—we may go abroad and be
somebody else to explain him— If I am not I—who will
be?— As if it were to dispense justice to all— But
the time has not come for that.

———

Friday Aug. 20th 1841.
It seems as if no cock lived so far in the horizon but
a faint vibration reached me here—spread the wider
over earth—as the more distant.
In the morning the crickets snore—in the afternoon
they chirp—at midnight they dream.

{One and three-fifths pages blank}

Aug. 24th 1841.
Let us wander where we will the universe is built
round about us, and we are central still. By reason
of this if we look into the heavens they are concave—and
if we were to look into a gulf as bottomless it would
be concave also— The sky is curved downward to the
earth in the horizon—because I stand in the plain.
I draw down its skirts. The stars so low there seem
loth to go away from me—but by a curcuitous path to be
remembering and returning to me.

Sat. Aug. 28th 1841.
A great poet will write for his peers alone—and indite
no line to an inferior.— He will remember only that
he saw truth and beauty from his position—and calmly
expect the time when a vision as broad shall overlook
the same field as freely.
Johnson can no more criticise Milton—than the
naked eye can criticise Herschel's map of the sun.

The Art which only gilds the surface—and demands
merely a superficial polish—without reaching to the
core—is but varnish and filigree. But the work of genius
is rough hewn from the first—because it anticipates
the lapse of time—and has an ingrained polish—which
still appears when fragments are broken off—an essential
quality of its substance. Its beauty is its strength. It
breaks with a lustre—and splits in cubes and diamonds
— Like the diamond, it has only to be cut to be polished
—and its surface is a window to its interior splendors.

True verses are not counted on the poet's fingers—but
on his heart strings.
> *My life hath been the poem I would have writ,*
> *But I could not both live and live to utter it.*

In the Hindoo scripture the idea of man is quite
illimitable and sublime—there is nowhere a loftier
conception of his destiny—he is at length lost in Brahma
himself—"the divine male". Indeed the distinction of
races in this life is only the commencement of a series
of degrees which ends in Brahma.

The veneration in which the Védas are held is itself
a remarkable fact— Their code embraced the whole
moral life of the Hindoo, and in such a case there is no
other truth than sincerity. Truth is such by reference
to the heart of man within not to any standard without
— There is no creed so false but faith can make it true.

In inquiring into the origin and genuineness of
this scripture it is impossible to tell when the divine
agency in its composition ceased, and the human began.
"From fire, from air, and from the sun"—was it "milked
out."—

There is no grander conception of creation any where
— It is peaceful as a dream—and so is the annihilation

of the world— It is such a beginning and ending as
the morning and evening.— for they had learned that
God's methods are not violent. It was such an awakening
as might have been heralded by the faint dreaming
chirp of crickets before the dawn.

The very indistinctness of its theogony—implies a
sublime truth. It does not allow the reader to rest in
any supreme first cause—but directly hints of a supremer
still which created the last.— The creator is still behind
increate.— The divinity is so fleeting that its attributes
are never expressed.

Aug. 30th 1841.
What is a day—if the day's work be not done? What
are the divisions of time to them who have nothing to
do. What is the present or the future to him who has
no occasion for them—who does not create them by
his industry?

It is now easy to apply to this ancient scripture such
a catholic criticism, as it will become the part of some
future age to apply to the Christian—wherein the
design and idea which underlies it is considered, and
not the narrow and partial fulfilment.—

These verses are so eminently textual, that it seems
as if those old sages had concentrated all their wisdom
in little fascicles—of which future times were to be
the commentary— As the light of this lower world—is
only the dissipated rays of the sun and stars.— They
seem to have been uttered with a sober morning
prescience, in the dawn of time.— There is a sort of
holding back, or withdrawal of the full meaning, that
the ages may follow after and explore the whole.— The
sentence opens unexpensively and almost unmeaningly
—as the petals of a flower.

To our nearsightedness this mere outward life seems a constituent part of us, and we do not realize that as our soul expands it will cast off the shell of routine and convention–which afterward–will only be an object for the cabinets of the curious.– But of this people the temples are now crumbled away–and we are introduced to the very hearth of Hindoo life–and to the primeval conventicle where–how to eat–and to drink –and to sleep–were the questions to be decided.

The simple life herein described confers on us a degree of freedom even in the perusal–we throw down our packs and go-on our way unencumbered.– Wants so easily and gracefully satisfied that they seem like a more refined pleasure and repleteness.

Wednesday Sep. 1st 1841.

When I observe the effeminate taste of some of my contemporaries in this matter of poetry–and how hardly they bear with certain incongruities, I think if this age were consulted it would not choose granite to be the back bone of the world–but Bristol spar–or Brazilian diamonds. But the verses which have consulted the refinements even of a golden age–will be found weak and nerveless for an iron one.– The poet is always such a Cincinnatus in literature as with republican simplicity to raise all to the chiefest honors of the state.

Each generation thinks to inhabit only a west end of the world, and have intercourse with a refined and civilized nature–not conceiving of her broad equality and republicanism. They think her aristocratic and exclusive because their own estates are narrow.

But the sun indifferently selects his rhymes, and with a liberal taste weaves into his verse–the planet and the stubble.

Let us know and conform only to the fashions of eternity.

The very austerity of these Hindoos is tempting
to the devotional as a more refined and nobler luxury.
They seem to have indulged themselves with a certain
moderation and temperance in the severities which
their code requires, as divine exercises not to be
excessively used as yet.

One may discover the root of a Hindoo religion in
his own private history.— when in the silent intervals
of the day or the night he does sometimes inflict on
himself like austerities with a stern satisfaction.

The Laws of Menu are a manual of private devotion
—so private and domestic—and yet so public and universal
a word as is not spoken in the parlor or pulpit in these
days. It is so impersonal that it exercises our sincerity
more than any other. It goes with us into the yard
and into the chamber—and is yet later spoken than the
advice of our mother and sisters.

Thursday Sep. 2nd 1841.

There is but one obligation and that is the obligation
to obey the highest dictate.— None can lay me under
another which will supersede this. The Gods have given
me these years without any incumbrance—society has
no mortgage on them. If any man assist me in the
way of the world, let him derive satisfaction from the
deed itself—for I think I never shall have dissolved
my prior obligations to God.

Kindness repaid is thereby annulled I would let
his deed lie as fair and generous as it was intended.
The truly beneficent never relapses into a creditor—his
great kindness is still extended to me and is never
done. Of those noble deeds which have me for their
object I am only the most fortunate spectator, And
would rather be the abettor of their nobleness, than stay
their tide with the obstructions of impatient gratitude.
As true as action and reaction are equal, that nobleness

which was as wide as the universe will rebound not
on him the individual, but on the world. If any have been
kind to me, what more do they want—I cannot make
them richer than they are— If they have not been kind,
they cannot take from me the privilege which they
have not improved. My obligations will be my lightest
load—for that gratitude which is of kindred stuff in me
—expanding every pore will easily sustain the pressure.
We walk the freest through the air we breathe.

The sublime sentences of Menu carry us back to a
time—when purification—and sacrifice—and self devotion
—had a place in the faith of men, and were not as
now a superstition — — They contain a subtle and
refined philosophy also—such as in these times is not
accompanied with so lofty and pure a devotion.

I saw a green meadow in the midst of the woods
to-day which looked as if dame nature had set her foot
there, and it had bloomed in consequence. It was the
print of her moccasin.

Sometimes my thought rustles in mid-summer—as
if ripe for the fall— I anticipate the russet hues and
the dry scent of autumn as the feverish man dreams of
balm and sage.

I was informed to-day that no Hindoo tyranny
presided at the framing of the world— That I am a
freeman of the universe, and not sentenced to any cast.

When I write verses I serve my thoughts as I do
tumblers— I rap them to see if they will ring.

{*One-fourth page blank*}

Friday Sep. 3d 1841.

Next to nature it seems as if man's actions were
the most natural—they so gently accord with her. The
small seines of flax or hemp stretched across the shallow
and transparent parts of the river—are no more intrusion
than the cobweb in the sun. It is very slight and refined
outrage at most. I stay my boat in mid current and
look down in the sunny water to see the civil meshes
of his nets—and wonder how the blustering people of the
town could have done this elvish work. The twine
looks like a new river weed—and is to the river like a
beautiful memento of man—man's presence in nature
—discovered as silently and delicately as Robinson
discovered that there savages on his island by a foot
print in the sand.

The moonlight is the best restorer of antiquity— The
houses in the village have a classical elegance as of
the best days of Greece—and this half finished church
reminds me of the Parthenon, or whatever is most
famous and excellent in art. So serene it stands reflecting
the moon, and intercepting the stars with its rafters,
as if it were refreshed by the dews of the night equally
with me. By day Mr. Hosmer—but by night Vitruvius
rather. If it were always to stand in this mild and sombre
light it would be finished already. It is in progress
by day but completed by night—and already its designer
is an old master.

The projecting rafter so carelessly left on the tower
—holding its single way through the sky is quite
architectural, and in the unnecessary length of the
joists and flooring of the staging around the walls there
is an artistic superfluity and grace— In these fantastic
lines described upon the sky there is no trifling or
conceit. Indeed the staging for the most part is the

only genuine native architecture—and deserves to stand longer than the building it surrounds.

In this obscurity there are no fresh colors to offend —and the light and shade of evening adorn the new equally with the old.

Sat Sept. 4th 1841.

I think I could write a poem to be called Concord— For argument I should have the River—the Woods—the Ponds —the Hills—the Fields—the Swamps and Meadows—the Streets and Buildings—and the Villagers. Then Morning —Noon—and Evening—Spring Summer—Autumn and Winter—Night—Indian Summer—and the Mountains in the Horizon.

A book should be so true as to be intimate and familiar to all men—as the sun to their faces. Such a word as is occasionally uttered to a companion in the woods in summer, and both are silent.

As I pass along the streets of the village on the day of our annual fair—when the leaves strew the ground, I see how the trees keep just such a holiday all the year.— The lively spirits of their sap mount higher than any plow-boy's let loose that day.— A walk in the Autumn woods, when, with serene courage they are preparing for their winter campaign—if you have an ear for the rustling of their camp—or an eye for the glancing of their armor—is more inspiring than the Greek or Peninsular war. Any grandeur may find society as great as itself in the forest.

Pond Hill.

I see yonder some men in a boat which floats boyantly amid the reflections of the trees—like a feather poised

in mid air–or a leaf wafted gently from its twig to the
water without turning over– They seem very delicately
to have availed themselves of the natural laws–and
their floating there looks like a beautiful and successful
experiment in philosophy.

It reminds me how much more refined and noble
the life of man might be made–how its whole economy
might be as beautiful as a Tuscan villa– A new and
more catholic art–the art of life–which should have its
impassioned devotees–and make the schools of Greece
and Rome to be deserted.

Sat. Sep. 5th 1841. Barn.

> Greater is the depth of Sadness
> Than is any height of gladness.

I cannot read much of the best poetry in prose or
verse–without feeling that it is a partial and exaggerated
plaint–rarely a carol as free as nature's– That content
which the sun shines for between morning and evening
is unsung. The Muse solaces herself–she is not delighted
but consoled. But there are times when we feel a
vigor in our limbs–and our thoughts are like a flowing
morning light–and the stream of our life without
reflection shows long reaches of serene ripples. And if
we were to sing at such an hour, There would be no
catastrophe contemplated in our verse–no tragic
element in it–nor yet a comic–for the life of the gods
is not in any sense dramatic–nor can be the subject of
the drama– It is epic without beginning or end–an
eternal interlude without plot.– not subordinate one
part to another, but supreme as a whole–at once–leaf
and flower–and fruit.– At present the highest strain is
Hebraic– the church bell is the tone of all religious

thought—the most musical that men consent to sing. In the youth of poetry men love to praise the lark and the morning—but they soon forsake the dews and skies —for the nightingale and evening shades. Without instituting a wider comparison I might say that in Homer there is more of the innocence and serenity of youth, than in the more modern and moral poets. The Iliad is not sabbath but morning reading—and men cling to this old song, because they have still moments of unbaptized and uncommitted life which give them an appetite for more. There is no cant in him—as there is no religion—we read him with a rare sense of freedom and irresponsibleness, as though we trod on native ground, and were autochthones of the soil.

Through the fogs of this distant vale we look back and upward to the source of song—whose crystal stream still ripples in the clear atmosphere of the mountain's side, and casts a silver gleam afar.

Some hours seem not to be occasion for any thing —unless for great resolves to draw breathe and repose in—so religiously do we postpone all action therein — We do not straight go about to execute our thrilling purpose—but shut our doors behind us, and saunter with prepared mind, as if the half were already done.

Sometimes a day serves only to hold time together.

{Four-fifths page blank, five and one-half leaves blank}

Sunday Sep. 12th 1841.

Where I have been
There was none seen.

Sep. 14th 1841.

No Bravery is to be named with that which can face its own deeds

In religion there is no society.

Do not dissect a man till he is dead.

Love does not analyze its object.

Ye do not know the number of muscles in a caterpillar
dead—much less the faculties of a man living.
You must believe that I know before you can tell me.
To the highest communication I can make no reply
—I lend only a silent ear.

Sat. 18th 1841. Barn
It is a great event—the hearing of a bell ring in one of
the neighboring towns—particularly in the night. It
excites in me an unusual hilarity—and I feel that I am
in season wholly—and enjoy a prime and leisure hour.

Monday Sep. 20th 1841.

Visited Sampson Wilder of Bolton. His method of
setting out peach trees is as follows.
Dig a hole six feet square and two deep, and remove
the earth—cover the bottom to the depth of six inches
with lime and ashes in equal proportions, and upon this
spread another layer of equal thickness of horn parings
—tips of horns—bones—and the like—then fill up with
a compost of sod and strong animal manure—say four
bushels of hog manure to a cart load of sod— Cover the
tree—which should be budded at two years old—but
slightly, and at the end of two years dig a trench round
it three feet from the tree and six inches deep, and
fill it with lime and ashes.

For grapes.
Let your trench be twelve feet wide and four deep

—cover the bottom with paving stones six inches—then
old bricks with mortar attached or loose six inches more
—then beef bones horns—&c six more (capt. Bobadil)
then a compost similar to the preceding. Set your roots
one foot from the north side—the trench running east
and west— —and bury eight feet of the vine crosswise
the trench, not more than eight inches below the surface.
Cut it down for three or four years that root may
accumalate—and then train it from the sun up an
inclined plane.

Sep. 30th 1841.

Better wait
Than be too late.

Tuesday Sep. 28th 1841.
I anticipate the coming in of spring as a child does
the approach of some pomp through a gate of the city.

{One and one-fifth pages, thirteen leaves blank}

{Six leaves missing}

{One leaf blank}

{Six leaves missing}

{Back endpaper}

·6·

November 29, 1841–April 3, 1842

Cambridge Nov. 29th 1841.

One must fight his way, after a fashion, even in the
most civil and polite society; the most truly kind and
gracious have to be won by a sort of valor–for the seeds
of suspicion seem to lurk in every spade-ful of earth,
as well as those of confidence. The President and
Librarian turn the cold shoulder to your application
–though they are known for benevolent persons– They
wonder if you can be anything but a thief, contemplating
frauds on the Library. It is the instinctive and salutary
principle of self-defence, that which makes the cat
show her talons. when you take her by the paw.

Certainly that valor which can open the hearts of
men is superior to that which can only open the gates
of cities.

You must always let people see that they serve
themselves more than you–not by your ingratitude, but
by sympathy and congratulation.

The 21st volume of Chalmers' English Poets contains
Hoole's and Mickle's Translations. In the shape of a
note to the 7th Book of the Lusiad–Mickle has written a
long–"Inquiry into the religious Tenets and Philosophy
of the Bramins."

Cambridge Tuesdday Nov 30th

When looking over the dry and dusty volumes of
the English poets, I cannot believe that those fresh and
fair creations I had imagined are contained in them.
English poetry from Gower down collected into one

alcove—and so from the library window compared wit
the commonest nature seems very mean.

Poetry cannot breath in the scholar's atmosphere.
The Aubreys and Hickeses, with all their learning,
prophane it yet indirectly by their zeal.

You need not envy his feelings who for the first
time has cornered up poetry in an alcove. I can hardly
be serious with myself when I remember that I have
come to Cam. after poetry—and while I am running over
the catalogue, and collating and selecting—I think if
it would not be a shorter way to a complete volume—to
step at once into the field or wood, with a very low
reverence to students and librarians. Milton did not
foresee what company he was to fall into. On running
over the titles of these books—looking from time to time
at their first pages or farther—I am oppressed by an
inevitable sadness. One must have come in to a library
by an oriel window as softly and undisturbed as the
light which falls on the books through a stained window,
and not by the Librarians door else all his dreams will
vanish.

Can the Valhalla be warmed by steam and go by
clock and bell?

Good poetry seems so simple and natural a thing
that when we meet it we wonder that all men are not
always poets. Poetry is nothing but healthy speech.
Though the speech of the poet goes to the heart of
things—yet he is that one especially who speaks civilly
to nature as a second person—and in some sense is the
patron of the world. Though more than any he stands in
the midst of nature—yet more than any he can stand
aloof from her. The best lines perhaps only suggest to
me that that man simply saw or heard or felt, what
seems the commonest fact in my experience.

One will know how to appreciate Chaucer best who
has come down to him the natural way through the
very meagre pastures of saxon and ante-Chaucerian
poetry. So human and wise he seems after such diet
–that we are as liable to misjudge him so as usually.

{*One-fourth page missing*}

vulgar–lies very near to them.

{*Three-fourths page blank*}

{*One-fourth page missing*}

The Saxon Poetry extant seems of a more serious
and philosophical cast than the very earliest that can be
called English– It has more thought, but less music.
It translates Boethius, it paraphrases the Hebrew
Bible, it solemnly sings of war of life–and Death–and
chronicles events– The Earliest English poetry is
tinctured with romance through the influence of the
Normans as the Saxon was not– The ballad and
Metrical Romance belong to this period. Those old
singers were for the most part imitators or translators
– Or will it not appear when viewed at a sufficient
distance–that our brave new poets are also secondary
as they, and refer the eye that reads them and their
poetry too, back and backward without end?

Nothing is so attractive and unceasingly curious as
character– There is not plant that needs such tender
treatment–there is not that will endure so rough.
It is the violet and the oak– It is the thing we mean
let us say what we will
We mean our own character or we mean yours. It
is divine and related to the heavens as the earth is by the

flashes of the Aurora. It has no acquaintance and no companion—it goes silent and unobserved longer than any planet in space—but when at length it does show itself in slight gleams it seems like the flowering of all the world—and its before unseen orbit is suddenly lit up like the trail of a meteor.

I hear no good news ever but some trait of a noble character. It reproaches me plaintively. I am mean in contrast but again am thrilled and elevated that I can see my own meanness—and again still—that my own aspiration is realized in that other. You reach me my friend not by your kind or wise words to me here or there, but as you retreat perhaps after years of vain familiarity some gesture or unconscious action in the distance speaks to me with more emphasis than all those years. I am not concerned to know what eigth planet is wandering in space up there—or when venus or Orion rises—but if in any cot to east or West and set behind the woods—there is any planetary character—illuminating the earth.

> Packed in my mind lie all the clothes
> Which outward nature wears
> For as its hourly fashions change
> It all things else repairs
>
> My eyes look inward not without
> And I but hear myself—
> And this new wealth which I have got
> Is part of my own pelf.
>
> For while I look for change abroad
> I can no difference find
> Till some new ray of peace uncalled
> Lumines my inmost mind
>
> As when the sun streams through the wood
> Upon a winter's morn
> Wher'eer his silent beams may stray
> The murky night is gone.

How could the patient pine have known
The morning breeze would come
Or simple flowers anticipate
The insect's noonday hum?—

Till that new light with morning cheer
From far streamed through the aisles
And nimbly told the forest trees
For many stretching miles?

Sunday Nov. 12th 1841

All music is only a sweet striving to express character.
Now that lately I have heard of some traits in the
character of a fair and pure maiden whom I had only
known superficially, but who has gone hence to make
herself more known by distance—they sound like
strains of a wild harp music— They make these parts
all retrospective. Every maiden conceals a fairer
flower—and more luscious fruit than any calix in the
field.— And if she go with averted face confiding in her
own purity and high resolves—all nature will humbly
confess its queen.

There is apology enough for all the deficiency and
shortcoming in the world—in the patient waiting of any
bud of character to unfold itself.

Only character can command our reverent love—it is
all mysteries in itself.

What is it gilds the trees and clouds
And paints the heavens so gay
But yonder fast abiding light
With its unchanging ray.

I've felt within my inmost soul
Such cheerful morning news
In the horizon of my mind
Ive seen such morning hues

As in the twilight of the dawn
When the first birds awake
Is heard within some silent wood
When they the small twigs break.

Or in the eastern skies is seen
Before the sun appears
Foretelling of the Summer heats
Which far away he bears.

{*One-fifth page blank*}

Walden P.m.

I seem to discern the very form of the wind when
blowing over the hills it falls in broad flakes upon the
surface of the pond— This subtle element obeying the
same law with the least subtle— As it falls it spreads
itself like a mass of lead dropped upon an anvil— I
cannot help being encouraged by this blithe activity in
the elements—in these degenerate days of men. Who
hears the rippling of the rivers will not utterly despair
of anything.

The wind in the wood yonder sounds like an incessant
waterfall—the water dashing and roaring among rocks.

Monday Nov. 13th

We constantly anticipate repose— Yet it surely can
only be the repose that is in entire and healthy activity.
It must be a repose without rust. What is leisure but
opportunity for more complete action— Our energies
pine for exercise— That time we spend in our duties is so
much leisure—so that there is no man but has sufficient
of it.

I make my own time I make my own terms— I cannot
see how God or nature can ever get the start of me

This ancient Scotch poetry at which its cotemporaries
so marvelled sounds like the uncertain lisping of a
child—when man's speech flows freest it but stutters and
stammers. There is never a free and clear deliverance

–but read now when the illusion of smooth verse is
destroyed by the antique spelling–the sense is seen to
stammer and stumble all the plainer. To how few
thoughts do all these sincere efforts give utterance– An
hours conversation with these men would have done
more. I am astonished to find how meagre that diet is
which has fed so many men. The music of sound which
is all sufficient at first is speedily lost and then the fame
of the poet must rest on the music of the sense. A great
philosopical and moral poet would give permanence
to the language–by making the best sound convey the
best sense–

Tuesday Nov. 14th 1841
   To hear the sunset described by the Old Scotch Poet
Douglas–as I have seen it–repays me for many weary
pages of of antiquated Scotch. Nothing so restores and
humanizes antiquity–and makes it blithe–as the discovery
of some natural sympathy between it and the present. Why
is it that there is some thing melancholy in antiquity– We
forget that it had any other future than our present–as
if it were not as near to *the* future as ourselves. No
thank heavens, these ranks of men to right and left
–posterity–and ancestry are not to be thridded–by any
earnest mortal– The heavens stood over the heads of
our ancestors as near–as to us.– Any living word
in these books abolishes the difference of time– It need
only be considered from the present stand point

Wednesday Nov. 15th 1841
   A mild summer sun shines over forest and lake– The
earth looks as fair this morning as the valhalla of the
gods– Indeed our spirits never go beyond nature. In the
woods there is an inexpressible happiness– Their
mirth is jusst repressed.

In winter, when there is but one green leaf for many
rods, what warm content is in them– They are not rude
but tender even in the severest cold. Their nakedness
is their defence. All their sounds and sights are elixir
to my spirit. They possess a divine health　God is not
more well. Every sound is inspiriting–and frawght
with the same mysterious assurance from the creaking
of the boughs in January to the soft sugh of the wind
in July.

How much of my well being think you depends on
the condition of my lungs and stomach–such cheap
pieces of nature as they which indeed she is every day
reproducing with prodigality– Is the arrow indeed fatal
which wrankles in the breast of the bird on the bough
–in whose eye all this fair landscape is reflected–and
whose voice still echoes through the wood?

The trees have come down to the bank to see the
river go by. This old familiar river is renewed each
instant–only the channel is the same. The water which
so calmly reflects the fleeting clouds and the primeval
trees I have never seen before–it may have washed
some distant shore–or formed a glacier or iceberg at the
north when I last stood here.– Seen through a mild
atmosphere–the works of the husbandman–his plowing
and reaping–have have a beauty to the beholder which
the laborer never sees

I seem to see somewhat more of my own kith and kin
in the lichens on the rocks than in any books　It does
seem as if mine were a peculiarly wild nature–which so
yearns toward all wildness–. I know of no redeeming
qualities in me–but a sincere love for some things– And
when I am reproved I have to fall back on to this
ground.

This is my argument in reserve for all cases. My
love is invulnerable　meet me on that ground, and

you will find me strong. When I am condemned and
condemn myself utterly–I think straightway–but I rely
on my love for some things.

Therein I am whole and entire. Therein I am
God-propt.

When I see the smoke curling up through the woods
from some farmhouse invisible–it is more suggestive
of the poetry of rural and domestic life than a nearer
inspection can be.– Up goes the smoke as quietly as the
dew exhales in vapor from these pine leaves and oaks
–as busily disposing itself in circles–and in wreathes
as the housewife on the hearth below– It is cotemporary
with a piece of human biography–and waves as a
feather in some *man's* cap– Under that rod of sky there
is some plot a-brewing–some ingenuity has planted
itself, and we shall see what it will do– It tattles of
more things than the boiling of the pot.

It is but one of man's breaths– All that is interesting
in history or fiction is transpiring beneath that cloud.

The subject of all life and death–of happiness and
grief–goes thereunder

When the traveller in the forest attaining to some
eminence, descries a column of smoke in the distence,
it is a very gentle hint to him of the presence of man.
It seems as if it would establish friendly relations
between them without more ado.

Sat Nov. 18th 1841.

Some men make their due impression upon their
generation–because a petty occasion is enough to call
forth all their energies–but are there not others who
would rise to much heigher levels whom the world has
never provoked to make the effort– I believe there are
men now living who have never opened their mouths in

a public assembly in whom nevertheless there is such
a well of eloquence that the appetite of any age could
never exhaust it. Who pine for an occasion worthy of
them, and will pine till they are dead— Who can admire
as well as the rest at the flowing speech of the orator
–but do yet miss the thunder and lightning, and visible
sympathy of the elements which would garnish their
own utterance

If in any straight I see a man fluttered and his ballast
gone–then I lose all hope of him–he is undone–but if
he reposes still though he do nothing else worthy of him
–if he is still a man in reserve–then is there everything
to hope of him.– The age may well go pine itself that
it cannot put to use this gift of the gods. He lives on
still unconcerned not needing to be used– The greatest
occasion will be the slowest to come

Sometimes a particular body of men do unconsciously
assert that their will is fate–that the right is decided
by their fiat without appeal–and when this is the case
they can never be mistaken. As when one man is
quite silenced by the thrilling eloquence of another and
submits to be neglected as to his fate–because such is
not the willfull vote of the assembly but their instinctive
decision.

Concord Thursday Dec 23d
The best man's spirit makes a fearful sprite to haunt
his tomb. The ghost of a priest is no better than that of
a highwayman. It is pleasant to hear of one who has
blest whole regions after his death by having frequented
them while alive–who has prophaned or tabooed no
place by being buried in it. It adds not a little to the fame
of Little John that his grave was long "celebrous for
the yielding of excellent whetstones".

A forest is in all mythologies a sacred place– As the oaks among the druids–and the grove of Egeria–and even in more familiar and common life, a celebrated wood is spoken of with respect–as "Barnsdale wood" and "Sherwood"–. Pan himself lives in the wood. Had Robin Hood no Sherwood to resort it would be difficult to invest his story with the charms it has got– It is always the tale that is untold–the deeds done. and the life lived in the unexplored secresy of the wood, that charm us and make us children again, to read his ballads, and hear of the greenwood tree.

Friday Dec 24th 1841.

I want to go soon and live away by the pond where I shall hear only the wind whispering among the reeds – It will be success if I shall have left myself behind, But my friends ask what I will do when I get there? Will it not be employment enough to watch the progress of the seasons?

Sat Dec 25th 1841

It does seem as if Nature did for a long time gently overlook the prophanity of man–the wood still kindly echoes the strokes of the axe–and when the strokes are few and seldom–they add a new charm to a walk– All the elements strive to *naturalize* the sound.

Such is our sympathy with the seasons that we experience the same degrees of heat in the winter as in the summer.

It is not a true apology for any coarseness to say that it is natural. The grim woods can afford to be very delicate and perfect in the details.

I dont want to feel as if my life were a sojourn any longer–that philosophy cannot be true which so paints it. It is time now that I begin to live.

Sunday Dec 26 1841

He is the rich man who in summer and winter for ever–could find delight in the contemplation of his own soul. I could look as unweariedly up to that cope–as into the heavens of a summer day–or a winter night. When I hear this bell ring–I am carried back to years and sabbaths when I was newer and more innocent I fear than now–and it seems to me as if there were a world within a world. Sin I am sure is not in overt acts or indeed in acts of any kind, but is in proportion to the time which has come behind us and displaced eternity. That degree to which our elements are mixed with the elements of the world– The whole duty of life is contained in this question   How to respire and aspire both at once

Wednesday Dec. 29th 1841.

One does not soon learn the trade of life. That one may work out out a true life requires more art–and delicate skill than any other work– There is need of the nice fingers of the girl as well as the tough hand of the farmer– The daily work is too often toughening the pericarp of the heart as well as the hand– Great familarity with the world must be nicely managed–lest it win away and bereave us of some susceptibility

     Experience bereaves us of our innocence
     Wisdom bereaves us of our ignorance

Let us walk in the world without learning its ways. Whole weeks or months of my summer life slide away in thin volumes like mist or smoke–till at length some warm morning perchance I see a sheet of mist blow down the brook to the swamp–it shadow flitting across the fields which have caught a new significance from that accident, And as that vapor is raised above the

earth so shall the next weeks be elevated above the plane
of the actual— Or when the setting sun slants across
the pastures—and the cows low to my inward ear—and
only enhance the stillness—and the eve is as the dawn—a
beginning hour and not a final one—as if it would never
have done— With its clear western amber inciting
men to lives of as limpid purity— Then do other parts
of my days work shine than I had thought at noon—for
I discover the real purport of my toil— As when the
husbandman has reached the end of the furrow and
looks back—he can best tell where the pressed earth
shines most.

All true greatness runs as level a course and is as
unaspiring as the plough in the furrow— It wears the
homeliest dress and speaks the homeliest language Its
theme is gossamer and dew lines—Johns-wort and
loosestrife for it has never stirred from its repose and is
most ignorant of foreign parts. Heaven is the inmost
place. The Good have not to travel far. What cheer
may we not derive from the thought—that our courses do
not diverge, and we wend not asunder—but as the web
of destiny is woven it is fulled—and we are cast more and
more into to the centre. And our fates even are Social.
There is no wisdom which can take place of humanity
—and I find that in old Chaucer—that love sings longest
which rhymes best with some saw of Milton's or
Edmund's. I wish I could be as still as God is. I can
recall to my mind the stillest summer hour—in which the
grasshopper sings over the mulleins—and there is a
valor in that time the memory of which is armor that
can laugh at any blow of fortunes. A man should go out
nature with the chirp of the cricket, or the trrill of the
veery ringing in his ear. These earthly sounds should

only die away for a season, as the strains of the harp
rise and swell– Death is that expressive pause in
the music of the blast. I would be as clean as ye oh woods
– I shall not rest till I be as innocent as you. I know
that I shall sooner or later attain to an unspotted
innocence–for when I consider that state even now I am
thrilled.–

If we were knowing enough we should see to what
virtue we were indebted for any happier moment we
might have, Nor doubt we had earned this at some time.

These motions every where in nature must surely
the circulations of God. The flowing sail–the running
stream–the waving tree–the roving wind–whence else
their infinite health and freedom–

I can see nothing so holy as unrelaxed play and
frolic in this bower God has built for us– The suspicion
of sin never comes to this thought–

Oh if men felt this they would never build temples
even of marble or diamond, but it would be sacrilege and
prophane–but disport them forever in this paradise–

In the coldest day it melts somewhere

It seems as if only one trait–one little incident in
human biography–need to be said or written–in some era
that all readers may go mad after it–and the man
who did the miracle is made a demigod henceforth
What we all do not one can tell–and when some lucky
speaker utters a truth of our experience and not of
our speculation–we think he must have had the nine
muses and the three graces to help him. I can at length
stretch me when I come to Chaucers breadth–and I
think well I could be *that* mans' acquaintance– For he
walked in that low and retired way that I do and was
not too good to live. I am grieved when they hint of
any unmanly submissions he may have made for that
subtracts from his breadth and humanity.

Thursday Dec 30th 1841.

I admire Chaucer for a sturdy English wit— The easy
height he speaks from in his Pro. to the Canterbury
tales is as good as any thing in it—as if he were indeed
better than any of the company there assembled.—

The poet does not have to go out of himself—and
cease to tattle of his domestic affairs, to win our
confidence, but is so broad that we see no limits to his
sympathy.

Great delicacy and gentleness of character is every
where constantly displayed in Chaucer's verse—the
simplest and humblest words come readily to his lips
The natural innocence of the man appears in the
simple and pure spirit in which the Prioresses Tale is
conceived in which the child sing O *Alma Redemptoris
mater*—and in The account of the departure of Custance
with her child upon the sea—in The Man of Lawes Tale.

The whole story of Chanticlere and Dame Partlet in
the Nonnes Preestes Tale is genuine humanity— I know
nothing better in its kind. The poets seem to be only
more frank and plain-spoken than other men— Their
verse is but confessions They always confide in the
reader—and speak privily with him keeping nothing back.

I know of no safe rule by by which to judge of the
purity of a former age but that I see that the impure of
the present age are not apt to rise to noble sentiments
when they speak or write.— and suspect therefore that
there may be more truth than is allowed in the apology
that such was the manner of the age.

> Within the circuit of this plodding life
> There are moments of an azure hue—
> And as unspotted fair as is the violet
> Or anemonie—when the spring strews them
> By some south woodside— Which make untrue
> The best philosophy, which has so poor an aim

But to console man for his grievance here
I have remembered when the winter came
High in my chamber in the frosty nights
How in the summer past some
unrecorded beam–slanted across
Some upland pasture–where the John's
wort grew– Or heard amidst
the verdure of my mind the bees long
smothered hum, So by the cheap economy
of God made rich to go upon my
wintry work again.
In the still cheerful cold of winter nights
When in the cold light of the moon
On every twig and rail and jutting spout
The icy spears are doubling their length
Against the glancing arrows of the sun.
And the shrunk wheels creak along the way–
Some summer accident long past
of lakelet gleaming in the July beams–
or hum of bee under the blue flag
Loitering in the meads–or busy rill
which now stands dumb and still
its own memorial–purling at its
play–along the slopes–and through
the meadows next–till that its
sound was quenched in the staid
current of its parent stream.

In Memory is the more reality. I have seen how the
furrows shone but late upturned, and where the field
fare followed in the rear–when all the fields stood
bound–and hoar–beneath a thick integument of snow.

When the snow is falling thick and fast–the flakes
nearest you seem to be driving straight to the ground
–but the more distant seem to float in the air in a
quivering bank like feathers–more like birds at play, and
not as if sent on any errand. So at a little distance all
the works of nature proceed with sport and frolic– They
are more in the eye and less in the deed.

Friday Dec 31st 1841

Books of natural history make the most cheerful
winter reading. I read in Audubon with a thrill of delight
when the snow covers the ground of the magnolia and
the Florida keys and their warm sea breezes—of the
fence rail and the cotton tree and the migrations of the
rice bird—or of the breaking up of winter in Labrador.
I seem to hear the melting of the snow on the forks of
the Missouri as I read. I imbibe some portion of health
from these reminiscences of luxuriant nature.

There is a singular health for me in those words
Labrador and East Main—which no desponding creed
recognizes.

How much more than federal are these States—!
If there were no other vicissitude but the seasons—with
their attendent and consequent changes our interest
would never flag. Much more is adoing than Congress
wots of in the winter season What journal do the
Persimon and Buckeye keep—or the sharp shinned
hawk? What is transpiring from summer to winter in
the Carolinas—and the great Pine forest, and the valley
of the Mohawk? The merely political aspect of the
land is never very cheering— Men are degraded when
considered as the members of a political organization

As a nation the people never utter one great and
healthy word— From side all nations present only the
symptoms of disease. I see but Bunkers Hill and Sing
sing— The district of Columbia—and Sullivans Island
—with a few avenues connecting them. But paltry are all
these beside one blast of the east or south wind which
blow over them all.

In society you will not find health but in nature— You
must converse much with the field and woods if you
would imbibe such health into your mind and spirit
as you covet for your body— Society is always diseased

and the best is the sickest– There is no scent in it it
so wholsome as that of these pines–nor any fragrance
so penetrating and restorative as that of everlasting
in high pastures.

Without that our feet at least stood in the midst of
nature all our faces would be pale and livid.

I should like to keep some book of natural history
always by me as a sort of elixir–the reading of which
would restore the tone of my system–and secure me true
and cheerful views of life. For to the sick nature is
sick but to the well a fountain of health. To the soul
that contemplates some trait of natural beauty no harm
nor disappointment can come. The doctrines of despair
–of spiritual or political servitude–no priestcraft nor
tyranny–was ever taught by such as drank in the
harmony of nature

Jan. 1st 1842

Virtue is the deed of the bravest. It is that art which
demands the greatest confidence and fearlessness. Only
some hardy soul ventures upon it–it deals in what
it has no experience in. The virtuous soul possess a
fortitude and hardihood which not the grenadier nor
pioneer can match It never shrunk.

It goes singing to its work. Effort is its relaxation.
The rude pioneer work of this world has been done by
the most devoted worshippers of beauty. Their resolution
has possessed a keener edge than the soldier's. In
winter is their campaign, they never go into quarters.
They are elastic under the heaviest burden–under
the extremest physical suffering.

Methinks Good courage will not flag here on the
Atlantic border as long as we are outflanked by the *Fur
Countries*. There is enough in that sound to cheer one
under any circumstances. The Spruce the Hemlock and

the pine will not countenance despair— Methinks some creeds in vestries and churches do forget the hunter wrapped in furs by the great Slave lake, or how the Esquimaux sledges are drawn by dogs—and in the twilight of the northern night the hunter does not give over to follow the seal and walrus over the ice.

These men are sick and of diseased imaginations who would toll the worlds knell so soon— Cannot these sedentary sects do better than them prepare the shrouds and write the epitaphs of those other busy living men? — The practical faith of men belies the preachers consolation— This is the creed of the hypochondriac.

There is no infidelity so great as that which prays —and keeps the Sabbath—and founds churches. The sealer of the south pacific preaches a truer doctrine. The church is the hospital for men's souls, but the reflection that he may one day occupy a ward in it should not discourage the cheerful labors of the able-bodied man. Let him remember the sick in their extremities—but not look thither as to his goal.

Sunday Jan 2nd 1841

The ringing of the church bell is a much more melodious sound than any that is heard within the church. All great values are thus public, and undulate like sound through the atmosphere. Wealth can not purchase any great private solace or convenience — Riches are only the means of sociality. I will depend on the extravagance of my neighbors for my luxuries—for they will take care to pamper me if I will be over fed.

The poor man who sacrificed nothing for the gratification—seems to derive a safer and more natural enjoyment from his neighbor's extravagance than he does himself— It is a new natural product from the contemplation of which he derives new vigor and solace as from a natural phenomenon.

In moments of quiet and leisure my thoughts are more apt to revert to some natural than any human relation

Chaucer's sincere sorrow in his latter days for the grossness of his earlier works—and that he "cannot recall and annull" what he had "written of the base and filthy love of men towards women: but alas they are now continued from man to man," says he, "and I cannot do what I desire"—is all very creditable to his character.

Chaucer is the make weight of his century—a worthy representative of England while Petrach and Bocacio lived in Italy and Tell and Tamerlane in Switzerland and Asia and Bruce and Rienzi in Europe and Wickliffe and Gower in his own land Edward III and John of Gaunt and the Black Prince complete the company. The fame of Roger Bacon came down from the preceding century —and Dante though just departed still exerted the influence of a living presence.

With all his grossness he is not undistinguished for the tenderness and delicacy of his muse. A simple pathos and feminine gentleness is peculiar to him which not even Wordsworth can match.

And then his best passages of length are marked by a happy and healthy wit which is rather rare in the poetry of any nation. On the whole he impresses me as greater than his reputation—and not a little like Homer and Shakespeare for he would have held up his head in their company. Among the earliest English poets he is their landlord and host, and has the authority of such. We read him with affection and without criticism for he pleads no cause but speaks for us his readers always. He has that greatness of trust and reliance which compels popularity, He is for a whole country and country to know and to be proud of.

The affectionate mention which succeeding early

poets make of him—coupling him with Homer and
Virgil is also to be taken into the account in estimating
his character. King James and Dunbar of Scotland
speak with more love and reverence of him than any
cotemporary poet of his predecessors of the last century.
That childlike relation indeed does not seem to exist
now which was then.

Monday Jan 3d 1841

It is pleasant when one can relieve the grossness of
the kitchen and the table by the simple beauty of his
repast so that there may be any thing in it to attract
the eye of the artist even.

I have been popping corn tonight—which is only a
more rapid blossoming of the seed under a greater than
July heat. The popped Corn is a perfect winter flower
hinting of anemonies and houstonias. For this little
grace man has mixed in with the vulgarness of his repast
he may well thank his stars. The law by which flowers
unfold their petals seems only to have operated more
suddenly under the intense heat. It looks like a sympathy
in this seed of the corn with its sisters of the vegetable
kingdom—as if by preference it assumed the flower
form rather than the crystalline—

Here has bloomed for my repast such a delicate
blossom as will soon spring by the wallsides, and this is
as it should be— Why should not nature revel sometimes,
and genially relax and make herself familiar at my
board   I would have my house a bower fit to entertain
her. It is a feast of such innocence as might have snowed
down by my warm hearth sprang these Cerealious
blossoms—here was the bank where they grew

Methinks some such visible token of approval would
always accompany the simple and healthy repast— There
would be such a smiling and blessing upon it. Our
appetite should always be so related to our taste—and

the board we spread for its gratification be an epitome of
the universal table which Nature sets by hill and wood
and stream for her dumb pensioners.

                              Wednesday Jan 5th 1842
I find that whatever hindrances may occur I write
just about the same amount of truth in my Journal–for
the record is more concentrated– And usually it is some
very real and earnest life after all that interrupts– All
flourishes are omitted. If I saw wood from morning to
night, though I grieve that I could not observe the train
of my thoughts during that time, yet in the evening the
few scrannel lines which discribe my days occupations
will make the creaking of the saw more musical than
my freest fancies could have been.– I find incessant
labor with the hands which engrosses the attention also,
the best method to remove palaver out of one's style.

One will not dance at his work who has wood to
cut and cord before the night falls in the short days of
winter–but every stroke will be husbanded and ring
soberly through the wood– And so will his lines ring
and tell on the ear when at evening he settles the
accounts of the day.

I have often been astonished at the force and precision
of style to which busy laboring men unpractised in
writing easily attain when they are required to make
the effort– It seems as if their sincerity and plainness
were the main thing to be taught in schools–and yet not
in the schools but in the fields in actual service I should
say. The scholar not unfrequently envies the propriety
and emphasis with which the farmer calls to his team
–and confesses that if that lingo were written it would
surpass his labored sentences.

Who is not tired of the weak and flimsy periods of the
politician and scholar and resorts not even to the
farmers almanack, to read the simple account of the

month's labor—to restore his tone again? I want to see a
sentence run clear through to the end, as deep and
fertile as a well drawn furow—which shows that the
plowgh was pressed down to the beam. If our scholars
would lead more earnest lives we should not witness
those lame conclusions to their ill-sown discourses—but
their sentences would pass over the ground like loaded
rollers—and not mere hollow and wooden ones, to press
in the seed and make it germinate.

A well built sentence in the rapidity and force with
which it works may be compared to a modern corn
planter which furrows out—drops the seed and covers
it up at one movement

The scholar requires hard labor as an impetus to
his pen—he will learn to grasp it as firmly and wield it as
gracefully and effectually as an axe or a sword. When
I consider the labored periods of some gentleman
scholar who perchance in feet and inches comes up to
the standard of his race—and is nowise deficient in
girth—I am amazed at the immense sacrifice of thewes
and sinewes—what these proportions and these bones
and this their work. How these hand hewed this fragile
matter—mere filagree or embroidery fit for ladies' fingers.
Can this be a stalwarts man's work who has marrow
in his back bone and a tendon achilles in his heel.

They who set up Stonehenge did somewhat— Much
in comparison—if it were only there strength—was once
fairly laid out—and they stretched themselves.

I discover in Raleigh's verses the vices of the courtier
— They are not equally sustained—as if his noble genius
were warped by the frivolous society of the court. He
was capable of rising to a remarkable elevation—his
poetry has for the most part a heroic tone and vigor as
of a knight errant—but again there seems to have been

somewhat unkindly in his education, and as if he
had by no means grown up to be the man he promised.
He was apparently too genial and loyal a soul or rather
he was incapable of resisting temptations from that
quarter,   If to his genius and culture he could have
added the temperament of Fox or Cromwell— The world
would have had cause longer to remember him. He
was the pattern of nobility.

One would have said it was by some lucky fate that he
and Shakespeare flourished at the same time in England,
and yet what do we know of their acquaintanceship?

Friday Jan 7th 1842

I am singularly refreshed in winter when I hear tell
of service berries—poke-weed—Juniper— Is not heaven
made up of these cheap summer glories?

The great God is very calm withall. How superfluous
is any excitement in his creatures! He listens equally
to the prayers of the believer and the unbeliever—

The moods of man should unfold and alternate as
gradually and placidly as those of nature The sun
shines for aye! The sudden revolutions of these times
and this generation, have acquired a very exaggerated
importance— They do not interest me much—for they are
not in harmony with the longer periods of nature.
The present, in any aspect in which it can be presented
to the smallest audience, is always mean. God does
not sympathize with the popular movements.

Sat. Jan 8th 1842

When, as now, in January a southwind melts the
snow and the bare ground appears covered with sere
grass and occasionally wilted green leaves, which seem
in doubt whether to let go their greenness quite or
absorb new juices against the coming year— In such a
season a perfume seems to exhale from the earth itself

and the south wind melts my integuments also. Then
is she my mother earth. I derive a real vigor from the
scent of the gale wafted over the naked ground as
from strong meats—and realize again how man is the
pensioner of nature. We are always conciliated and
cheered when we are fed by an influence—and our needs
are felt to be part of the domestic economy of nature.

What offends me most in my compositions is the
moral element in them The repentant say never a
brave word—their resolves should be mumbled in
silence. Strictly speaking morality is not healthy. Those
undeserved joys, which come uncalled, and make us
more pleased than grateful, are they that sing.

One music seems to differ from another chiefly in its
more perfect time— In the steadiness and equanimity
of music lies its divinity. It is the only assured tone
When men attain to speak with as settled a faith—and
as firm assurance their voices will sing and march
as do the feet of the soldier. Because of the perfect time
of this music box—its harmony with itself—is its greater
dignity and stateliness. This music is more nobly related
for its more exact measure—so simple a difference as
this more even pace raises it to the higher dignity.

Man's progress in nature should have an
accompaniment of music It relieves the scenery—which
is seen through it as a subtler element—like a very
clear morning air in autumn. Music wafts me through
the clear sultry valleys—with only a light grey vapor
against the hills.

Of what manner of stuff is the web of time wove
—when these consecutive sounds called a strain of music
can be wafted down through the centuries from Homer
to me— And Homer have been conversant with that

same unfathomable mystery and charm, which so newly tingles my ears.– These single strains–these melodious cadences which plainly proceed out of a very deep meaning–and a sustained soul are the interjections of God.

Am I so like thee my brother that the cadence of two notes affects us alike?

Shall I not sometime have an opportunity to thank him who made music? I feel very when I hear these lofty strains because there must be something in me as lofty that hears– Doest it not rather hear me? If my blood were clogged in my veins I am sure it would run more freely– God must be very rich who for the turning of a pivot can pour out such melody on me.– It is a little prophet–it tells me the secrets of futurity   where are its secrets wound up but in this box? So much hope had slumbered.– There are in music such strains as far surpass any faith in the loftiness of man's destiny – He must be very sad before he can comprehend them – The clear liquid note, from the morning fields beyond seems to come through a vale of sadness to man which gives all music a plaintive air– It hath caught a higher pace than any virtue I know. It is the arch reformer. It hastens the sun to his setting It invites him to his rising. It is the sweetest reproach, a measured satire.

I know there is a people somewhere this heroism has place– Or else things are to be learned which it will be sweet to learn. This cannot be all rumor. When I hear this I think of that everlasting and stable something which is not sound but to be a thrilling reality and can consent to go about the meanest work for as many years of time as it pleases even the Hindo penance–for a year of the gods were as nothing to that which shall come after– What then can I do to hasten that other time or that space where there shall be no time and

these things be a more living part of my life. Where
there will be no discords in my life?

Sunday Jan 9th 1842.
One cannot too soon forget his errors and
misdemeanors—for dwell long upon them is to add to
the offence—and repentance and sorrow can only be
displaced by somewhat better—and which is as free and
original as if they had not been.

Not to grieve long for any action but to go immediately
and do freshly and otherwise subtracts so much from
the wrong— Else we may make the delay of repentence
the punishment of the sin— But a greatnes will not
consider its sins as its own, but be more absorbed in the
prospect of that valor and virtue for the future which
is more properly it, than in those improper actions which
by being sins discover themselves to be not it

{*One-fifth page blank*}

Sir W Raleigh's faults are those of a courtier and
a soldier— In his counsels and aphorisms we see not
unfrequently the haste and rashness of a boy. His
philosophy was not wide nor deep but continually giving
way to the generosity of his nature— What he touches
he adorns by his greater humanity—and native nobleness
—but he touches not the true nor original. He thus
embellishes the old but does not unfold the new. He
seems to have been fitted by his genius for short flights
of impulsive poetry—but not for the sustained loftiness
of Shakespeare or Milton. He was not wise nor a seer
in any sense—but rather one of nature's nobility— The
most generous nature which can be spared to linger
in the purlieus of the court.

His was a singularly perverted genius with such an

inclination to originality and freedom–and yet who
never steered his own course. Of so fair and susceptible
a nature rather than broad or deep–that he delayed
to slake his thirst at the nearest and even more turbid
wells of truth & beauty Whose homage to the least
fair or nobler left no space for homage to the all fair
– The misfortune of his circumstances or rather of the
man–appears in the fact that he was the author of
Maxims of State and The Cabinet Council and The
Souls' Errand.

{*One-half page blank*}

Saturday Feb. 20th 1842
I never yet saw two men sufficiently great to meet
as two. In proportion as they are great the differences
are fatal–because they are felt not to be partial but total.
Frankness to him who is unlike me–will lead to
the utter denial of him.– I begin to see how that the
preparation for all issues is to do virtuously.–
When two approach to meet they incur no petty
dangers, but they run terrible risks.
Between the sincere there will be no civilities.– No
greatness seems prepared for the little decorum, even
savage unmannerliness it meets from equal greatness.

{*One-fifth page blank*}

Sunday Feb. 20 1842
"Examine animal forms geometrically, from man,
who represents the perpendicular, to the reptile which
forms the horizontal line, and then applying to those
forms the rules of the exact sciences, which God himself
cannot change, we shall see that visible nature contains
them all; that the combinations of the seven primitive
forms, are entirely exhausted, and that, therefore, they

.1 represent all possible varieties of morality." From
.he True Messiah; or the Old and New Testaments,
.xamined according to the principles of the Language
of Nature. By G. Oegger–" Translated from French
by Gratér.

I am amused to see from my window here how
busily man has divided and staked off his domain. God
must smile at his puny fences running hither and
thither everywhere over the land. I seem to see how all
this lies see p. 368

{Two leaves missing}

{One-eighth page missing}

Feb. 21st

I must confess there is nothing so strange to me as
my own body– I love any other piece of nature, almost,
better.

I was always conscious of sounds in nature which
my ears could never hear–that I caught but the prelude
to a strain– She always retreats as I advance– Away
behind and behind is she and her meaning– Will not
this faith and expectation make to itself ears at length.

I never saw to the end nor heard to the end–but the
best part was unseen–and unheard.

I am like a feather floating in the atmosphere, on
every side is depth unfathomable

I feel as if years had been crowded into the last month
–and yet the regularity of what we call time has been
so far preserved as that I

{One-eighth page missing}

will be welcome in the present.

I have lived ill for the most part because too near
myself— — I have tripped myself up—so that there was
no progress for my own narrowness— I cannot walk
conveniently and pleasantly but when I hold myself
far off in the horizon— And the soul dilutes the body and
makes it passable— My soul and body have tottered
along together of late tripping and hindering oneanother
like unpractised Siamese twins— They two should
walk as one that no obstacle may be nearer than the
firmament—

There must be some narrowness in the soul that
compels one to have secrets.

Wednesday Feb. 23d 1842

Every Poets muse is circumscribed in her wanderings
—and may be well said to haunt some favorite spring
or mountain. Chaucer seems to have been the poet
of gardens   he has hardly left a poem in which some
retired and luxurious retreat of the kind is not described,
to which he gains access by some secret port, and
there by some fount or grove is found his hero and the
scene of his tale. It seems as if by letting his imagination
riot in the matchless beauty of an ideal garden, he thus
fed his fancy on to the invention of a tale which would
fit the scene. The muse of the most universal poet
retires into some familiar nook, whence it spys out the
land as the eagle from his eyrie—for he who sees so
far over plain and forest is perched in a narrow cleft of
the crag. Such pure childlike love of nature is nowhere
to be matched. And it is not strange that the poetry of so
rude an age should contain such polished praise of
nature For the charms of nature are not enhanced by
civilization, as society is—but she possesses a permanent
refinement—which at last subdues and educates men.

The reader has great confidence in Chaucer— He tells

no lies– You read his story with a smile as if it were
the circumlocution of a child, and yet you find that he
has spoke with more directness and economy of words
than a sage. He is never heartless. So new was all his
theme in those days that had not to invent but only
to tell

The language of poetry is *infantile* It cannot talk.

{*One leaf missing*}

We are not what we are, nor do we treat or esteem
each other for what we are–but for what we are capable
of being–and pray that we may never meet on the low
ground of our actual natures. It is the charm and
greatness of all society from friendship to the drawing
room–that it takes place on a level slightly higher than
the actual characters of the parties would warrant–it is·
an expression of faith. True politeness is only hope
and trust in men. It never addresses a fallen or falling
man–but salutes a rising generation– It does not
flatter but only congratulates

The rays of light come to us in such a curve that
every fellow in the street appears higher than he really
is– It is the innate civility of nature.

I am glad that it was so because it could be.

March 2nd 1842.

The greatest impression of character is made by
that person who consents to have no character. He who
sympathizes with and runs through the whole circle
of attributes can not afford to be an individual. Most
men stand pledged to themselves–so that their narrow
and confined virtue has no suppleness. They are like
children who cannot walk in bad company and learn the
lesson which even it teaches without their guardians

for fear of contamination. He is a fortunate man who gets through the world without being burthened by a name and reputation—for they are at any rate but his past history and no prophecy and as such concern him no more than another. Character is Genius settled — It can maintain itself against the world—and if it relapses it repents— It is as a dog set to wattch the property of Genius. Genius, strictly speaking, is not responsible for it is not moral.

{Four-fifths page missing}

March 8 1842

I live in the perpetual verdure of the globe— I die in the annual decay of nature.

We can understand the phenomenon of death in the animal better if we first consider it in the order next below us—the vegetable

The death of the flea and the Elephant are but phenomena of the life of nature.

{Four-fifths page missing}

Feb 20th 1842

possible and may have a spiritual meaning.

My path hitherto has been like a road through a diversified country, now climbing high mountains then descending into the lowest vales. From the summits I saw the heavens—from the vales I looked up to the heights again.

In prosperity I remember God—or memory is one with consciousness—in adversity I remember my own elevations, and only hope to see God again.

It is vain to talk–what do you want?– To bandy
words–or deliver some grains of truth which stir within
you? Will you make a pleasant rumbling sound after
feasting for digestion's sake?–or such music as the
birds in spring-time?

The death of friends should inspire us as much as
their lives.

If they are great and rich enough they will leave
consolation to the mourners before the expenses of
their funerals.

It will not be hard to part with any worth because
it is worthy. How can any good depart. It does not go and
come but we. Shall we wait for it? is it slower than we?

March 1st 1842.

Whatever I learn from any circumstances that
especially I needed to know–events come out of God
–and our characters determine them and constrain
fate–as much as they determine the words and tone of
a friend to us.– Hence are they always acceptable in
experience, and we do not see how we could have done
without them.

March 8th 1842.

Most lecturers preface their discourses on music with
a history of music–but as well introduce a virtue with
a history of virtue. As if the possible combination
of sound–the last wind that sighed a melody that waked
the wood had any history other than a perceptive ear
might hear in the least and latest sound of nature. A
history of music would be like the history of the future
–for so little past is it and capable of record that it is
but the hint of a prophecy. It is the history of gravitation.

It has no history more than God. It circulates and
resounds for us—and only flows like the sea or air. There
might be a history of men or of hearing, but not of the
unheard.

Why if I should sit down to write its story the west
wind would rise to refute me.

Properly speaking there can be no history but natural
history, for there is no past in the soul but in nature.

So that the history of anything is only the true
account out it—which will be always the same—

I might as well write the history of my Aspirations
— Does not the last and highest contain them all?

Do the lives of the great composers contain the facts
which interested them

What is this music—why thinner and more evanescent
than ether. Subtler than sound—for it is only a disposition
of sound. It is to sound what color is to matter— It is
the color of a flame—or of the rainbow—or of water. Only
one sense has known it.

The least profitable the least tangible fact—which
cannot be bought or cultivated but by virtuous methods
—and yet our ears ring with it like shells left on the
shore.

{*Three leaves missing*}

sky or landscape, but seemed a Sybbilline arm stretched
over the wood.

Friday March 11th 1842

Chaucers familiar, but innocent way of speaking of
God is of a piece with his character. He comes readily
to his thoughts without any false reverence.

If nature is our mother is not God much more? God
should come into our thought with no more parade than

the zephyr into our ears—only strangers approach him
with ceremony. How rarely in our English tongue do
we find expressed any affection for God. No sentiment is
so rare as love of God—universal love. Herbert is almost
the only exception. "Ah my dear God"—&c

Chaucers was a remarkably affectionate genius.
There is less love and simple trust in Shakspeare.

When he sees a beautiful person or object he almost
takes a pride in the "maistry" of his God. The protestant
church seem to have nothing to supply the place of
the Saints of the catholic calendar—who were at least
channels for the affections. Its God has perhaps too
many of the attributes of a scandinavian deity.

We can only live healthily the life the gods assign
us. I must receive my life as passively as the willow leaf
that flutters over the brook. I must not be for myself,
but God's work and that is always good. I will wait the
breezes patiently—and grow as nature shall determine
— My fate cannot but be grand so. We may live the
life of a plant or an animal—without living an animal
life. This constant and universal content of the animal
—comes of resting quietly in God's palm.

I feel as if could at any time resign my life and the
responsibility of living into Gods hands—and become
an innocent free from care as a plant or stone.

My life my life—why will ye linger? Are the years
short are the months of no account? How often has long
delay quenched my aspirations— Can God afford that
I should forget him— Is he so indifferent to my career
— Can heaven be postponed with no more ado—.

Why were my ears given to hear those everlasting
strains—which haunt my life—and yet to be prophaned
much more by these perpetual dull sounds!

Our doubts are so musical that they persuade themselves.

Why God did you include me in your great scheme? Will ye not make me a partner at last?

Did it need there should be a conscious material–

My friend–my friend I'd speak so frank to thee that thou wouldst pray me to keep back some part for fear I robbed myself. To address thee delights me there is such cleanness in the delivery.– I am delivered of my tale, which told to strangers still would linger on my lips as if untold–or doubtful how it ran.

March 12th 1842

Consider what a difference there is between living and dying–

To die is not to *begin* to die–and *continue*–it is not a state of continuance but of transientness–but to live is a condition of continuance and does not mean to be born merely– There is no continuance of death–it is a transient phenomenon– Nature presents nothing in a state of death.

Sunday March 14th 1842.

The sad memory of departed friends is soon incrusted over with sublime & pleasing thoughts–as their monuments are overgrown with moss. Nature doth thus kindly heal every wound.

By the mediation of a thousand little mosses and fungi–the most unsightly objects become radiant of beauty. There seem to be two sides to this world presented us at different times–as we see things in growth or dissolution–in life or death– For seen with the eye of a poet–as God sees them, all are alive and beautiful, but seen with the historical eye, or the eye of the memory, they are dead and offensive. If we see

nature as pausing immediately all mortifies and decays
–but seen as progressing she is beautiful

I am startled that God can make me so rich even
with my own cheap stores– It needs but a few wisps of
straw in the sun–as some small word dropped, or that
has long laid silent in some book. When heaven begins
and the dead rise, no trumpet is blown–perhaps the
southwind will rise– What if you or I be dead– God is
alive still.

March 14th

Chaucer's genius does not soar like Miltons–but is
genial and familiar. It is only a greater portion of
humanity–with all its weakness. It is not Heroic as
Raleigh–or pious as Herbert–or philosophical as
Shakspeare–but the child of the English nation but that
child that is "father of the man." His genius is only
for the most part an exceeding naturalness. It is perfect
sincerity though with the behavior of a child–rather
than of a man. He can complain as in the Testament
of Love, but yet so truly and unfeignedly–that his
complaint does not fail to interest– All England has his
case at heart.

He shows great tenderness and delicacy but not
the heroic sentiment. His genius was feminine not
masculine–not but such is rarest to find in woman
–(though the appreciation of it is not)–but less manly
than the manliest.

It is not easy to find one brave enough to play the
game of love quite alone with you, but they must get
some third person or world to countenance them. They
thrust others between.

Love is so delicate and fastidious that I see not how
can ever begin. Do you expect me to love with you,

unless you make my love secondary to nothing else? Your words come tainted, if the thought of the world darted between thee and the thought of me. Ye are not venturous enough for love. It goes alone unscared through wildernesses.

As soon as I see people loving what they see merely –and not their own high hopes that they form of others–I pity and do not want their love. Such love delays me. Did I ask thee to love me who hate myself – No–love that I love. and I will love thee that loves it.

The love is faint hearted and short-lived, that is contented with the past history of its object. It does not prepare the soil to bear new crops lustier than the old.

I would I had leisure for these things, sighs the world–when I have done my quilting and baking–then I will not be backward.

Love never stands still–nor does its object. It is the revolving sun–and the swelling bud. If I know what I love, it is because I *remember* it.

Life is grand–and so are its environments of Past and Future. Would the face of nature be so serene and beautiful–if man's destiny were not equally so?

What I am I good for now–who am still reaching after high things but to hear and tell the news–to bring wood and water–and count how many eggs the hens lay? In the meanwhile I expect my life will begin.–

I will not aspire longer–I will see what it is I would be after–I will be unanimous.

{*One-fourth page blank*}

Tuesday March 15th 1842.
It is a new day the sun shines. The poor have come out to employ themselves in the sunshine–the old and feeble to scent the air once more.– I hear the blue

bird and the song-sparrow—and the robin—and the note
of the lark leaks up through the meadows, as if its bill
had been thawed by the warm sun.

As I am going to the woods I think to take some
small book in my pocket whose author has been there
already.— whose pages will be as good as my thoughts
—and will eke them out—or show me human life still
gleaming in the horizon—when the woods have shut out
the town. But I can find none—none will sail as far
forward into the bay of nature as my thought—they stay
at home—I would go home. When I get to the wood
their thin leaves rustle in my fingers. They are bare and
obvious and there is no halo or haze about them.
Nature lies far and fair behind them all.

I should like to meet the great and serene sentence
—which does not reveal itself—only that it is great.
— which I may never with my utmost intelligence pierce
through and beyond—(more than the earth itself)—which
no intelligence can understand— There should be a
kind of life and palpitation to it—under its rind a kind
of blood should circulate forever—communicating
freshness to its countenance.

Cold Spring

I hear nothing but a phoebe, and the wind, and the
rattling of a chaise in the wood. For a few years I stay
here—not knowing—taking my own life by degrees
—and then I go. I hear a spring bubbling near—where
I drank out of a can in my earliest youth. The birds—the
squirrels—the alders—the pines—they seem serene and
in their places— I wonder if my life looks as serene
to them too— Does no creature then see with the eyes of
its own narrow destiny—but with God's? When God
made man, he reserved some parts and some rights to
himself— The eye has many qualities which belong
to God more than man— It is his lightening which

flashes in them– When I look into my companions eye,
I think it is Gods private mine. It is a noble feature–it
cannot be degraded. For God can look on all things
undefiled.

Pond

Nature is constantly original–and inventing new
patterns, like a mechanic in his shop. When the
overhanging pine drops into the water, by the action
of the sun and the wind rubbing it on the shore–its
boughs are worn white and smooth–and assume
fantastic forms, as if turned by a lathe.

All things indeed are subjected to a rotary motion
–either gradual and partial or rapid and complete
– From the planet and system to the symplest shell fish
and pebbles on the beach. As if all beauty resulted from
an object turning on its own axis–or others turning
about it. It establishes a new centre in the universe. As
all curves have reference to their centres or foci–so
all beauty of character has reference to the soul–and
is a graceful gesture of recognition a waving of the body
toward it.

The great and solitary heart will love alone without
the knowledge of its object. It cannot have society in its
love. It will, expend its love as the cloud drops rain
upon the fields over which floats–

The only way to speak the truth is to speak lovingly
–only the lovers words are heard. The intellect should
never speak–it–is not a natural sound.

How trivial the best actions are!– I am led about from
sunrise to sunset by an ignoble routine–and yet can
find no better road. I must make a port of the planet. I
must obey the law of nature.

Wednesday March 16th

Raleigh's Maxims are not true and impartial, but yet

are expressed with a certain magnanimity, which
was natural to the man—as if this selfish policy could
easily afford to give place in him to a more human and
generous. He gives such advice that we have more faith
in his conduct than his principles.

He seems to have carried the courtiers life to the
highest-pitch of magnanimity and grace it was—capable
of— He is liberal and generous as a prince—that is
within bounds—brave—chivalrous—heroic—as the knight
in armor—and not as a defenceless man.

His was not the heroism of Luther, but of Bayard.
— There was more of grace than of truth in it. He had
more taste than character. There may be something
petty in a refined taste—it easily degenerates into
effeminacy—it does not consider the broadest use. It
is not content with simple good and bad—and so is
fastidious and curious—or nice only.

The most attractive sentences are not perhaps the
wisest, but the surest and soundest. He who uttered
them had a right to speak. He did not stand on a rolling
stone—but was well assured of his footing—and naturally
breathed them without effort. They were spoken in
the nick of time.

With rare fullness were they spoken as a flower
expands in the field—and if you dispute their doctrine
—you will say but there is truth in their assurance.
Raleghs are of this nature—spoken with entire
satisfaction and heartiness. They are not philosophy
but Poetry.

With him it was always—well done—and nobly said.

That is very true which Ralegh says about the equal
necessity of war and law— —that "The necessity of
war, which among human actions is most lawless, hath
some kind of affinity and near resemblance with the

necessity of law;" for both equally rest on force as their
basis—and war is only the resource of law—either on a
smaller or larger scale—its authority asserted. In war
in some sense lies the very genius of law—it is law
creative and active—it is the first principle of the law.

What is human warfare but just this an effort to
make the laws of God and nature take sides with
one party. Men make an arbitrary code and because it
is not right, they try to make it prevail by might. The
moral law does not want any champion—its asserters to
not go to war—it was never infringed with impunity.

It is inconsistent to decry war and maintain law—for
if there were no need of war there would be no need
of law.

I must confess I see no resource but to conclude
that conscience was not given us to no purpose, or for
a hindrance but that however flattering order and
expediency may look—it is but the repose of a lethargy
—and we will choose rather to be awake though it be
stormy and maintain ourselves on this earth and in this
life as we may—without signing our death warrant in
the outset.— What does the law protect my rights?
or any rights—my right or the right? If I avail myself
of it, it may help my sin, it cannot help my virtue— Let
us see if we cannot stay here where God has put us
on his own conditions.

Does not his law reach to the earth?

While the law holds fast the thief and murderer—for
my protection—(I should say its own) it lets itself go
loose.!

Expediencies differ—they may clash—

English law may go to war with American law—that is
English interest with American interest—but what is
expedient for the whole world will be absolute right—and

synonymous with the law of God— So the law is only partial right–it is selfish, and consults for the interest of the few.

Somehow strangely the vice of men gets well represented and protected but their virtue has none to plead its cause–nor any charter of immunities and rights. The Magna Charta is not chartered rights–but chartered wrongs.

Thursday March 17th

I have been making pencils all day–and then at evening walked to see an old–schoolmate who is going to help make the Welland canal navigable for ships round Niagara.–

He cannot see any such motives and modes of living as I– Professes not to look beyond the securing of certain "Creature comforts." And so we go silently different ways–with all serenity–I in the still moon light through the village this fair evening to write these thoughts in my journal–and he forsooth to mature his schemes to ends as good maybe but different.

So are we two made while the same stars shine quietly over us. If I or he be wrong–nature yet consents placidly – She bites her lip and *smiles* to see how her children will agree.

So does the Wellland canal get built–and other conveniences while I live. Well and good I must confess. Fast sailing ships are hence not detained.

What means this changing sky–that now I freeze and contract & go within myself to warm me–and now I say it is a south wind, and go all soft and warm along the way? I sometimes wonder if I do not breathe the south wind.

Friday, March 18th 1842

Whatever book or sentence will bear to be read twice, we may be sure was thought twice. I say this thinking

of Carlyle—who write pictures or first impressions
merely—which consequently will only bear a first
reading. As if any transient—any *new*, mood of the
best man deserved to detain the world long. I should
call Carlyle's writing essentially dramatic—excellent
acting—entertaining especially to those who see rather
than those who hear Not to be repeated more than
a joke If he did not think who made the joke—how
shall we think who hear it. He never consults the
oracle—but thinks to utter oracles himself— There
is nothing in his books for which he is not, and does
not feel, responsible. He does not retire behind the
truth he utters—but stands in the foreground. I wish
he would just think and tell me what he thinks— Appear
to me in the attitude of a man with his ear inclined.
— who comes as silently and meekly as the morning
star which is unconscious of the dawn it heralds
— Leading the way up the steep as though alone and
unobserved in its observing—without looking behind
— He is essentially a humorist—but humors will not
feed a man— They are the least satisfactory morsel to
the healthy appetite— They circulate— I want rather
to meet that about which they circulate. The heart is
not a humor—nor do they go to the heart, as the blood
does.

Saturday March 19th 1842
When I walk in the fields of Concord and meditate
on the destiny of this prosperous slip of the Saxon
family—the unexhausted energies of this new country
—I forget that this which is now Concord was once
Musketaquid and that the *American race* has had its
destiny also. Everywhere in the fields—in the corn and
grain land—the earth is strewn with the relics of a race
which has vanished as completely as if trodden in
with the earth.

I find it good to remember the eternity behind me as
well as the eternity before. Where ever I go I tread in the
tracks of the Indian– I pick up the bolt which he has
but just dropped at my feet. And if I consider destiny I
am on his trail. I scatter his hearth stones with my feet,
and pick out of the embers of his fire the simple but
enduring implements of the wigwam and the chace– In
planting my corn in the same furrow which yielded its
increase to his support so long–I displace some memorial
of him.

I have been walking this afternoon over a pleasant
field planted with winter rye–near the house. Where this
strange people once had their dwelling place. Another
species of mortal men but little less wild to me than
the musquash they hunted– Strange spirits–daemons
–whose eyes could never meet mine. With another nature
–and another fate than mine– The crows flew over
the edge of the woods, and wheeling over my head
seemed to rebuke–as dark winged spirits more akin to
the Indian than I. Perhaps only the present disguise
of the Indian– If the new has a meaning so has the old.

Nature has her russet hues as well as green– Indeed
our eye splits on every object, and we can as well take
one path as the other– If I consider its history it is
old–if its destiny it is new– I may see a part of an
object or the whole– I will not be imposed on and think
nature is old, because the season is advanced I will
study the botany of the mosses and fungi on the decayed
–and remember that decayed wood is not old, but has
just begun to be what it is. I need not think of the
pine almond or the acorn and sapling when I meet the
fallen pine or oak–more than of the generations of
pines and oaks which have fed the young tree.

The new blade of the corn–the third leaf of the
melon–these are are not green but gray with time, but
sere in respect of time.

The pines and the crows are not changed but instead
that Philip and Paugus stand on the plain—here are
Webster and Crocket. Instead of the council-house is the
legislature

What a new aspect have new eyes given to the
land. Where is this country but in the hearts of its
inhabitants   why there is only so much of Indian
America left—as there is of the American Indian in the
character of this generation.

A blithe west wind is blowing over all. In the fine
flowing haze men at a distance seem shadowy and
gigantic— As ill-defined and great as men should always
be.— I do not know if yonder be a man or a ghost.

What a consolation are the stars to man—so high
and out of his reach as is his own destiny.

I do not know but my life is fated to be thus low and
grovelling always— I cannot discover its use even to
myself— But it is permitted to see those stars in the sky
equally useless, yet highest of all and deserving of
a fair destiny. My fate is in some sense linked with that
of the stars— And if they are to persevere to a great
end—shall I die who could conjecture it? It surely
is some encouragement to know that the stars are my
fellow creatures—for I do not suspect but they are
reserved for a high destiny.

Has not he who discovers and names a planet in the
heavenes as long a date as it? I do not fear that any
misadventure will befal *them*

Shall I not be content to disappear with the missing
stars? Do I mourn their fate?—

Man's moral nature is a riddle which only eternity
can solve.

I see laws which never fail—of whose failure I never conceived— Indeed I cannot detect failure any where but in my fear. I do not fear that right is not right—that good is not good—but only the annihilation of the present existence— But only that can make me incapable of fear.

My fears are as good prophets as my hopes.

Sunday March 20 1842

My friend is cold and reserved because his love for me is waxing and not waning These are the early processes—the particles are just beginning to shoot in crystals. If the mountains came to me I should no longer go to the mountains— So soon as that consummation takes place which I wish—it will be past— Shall I not have a friend in reserve? Heaven is to come   I hope this is not it.

Words should pass between friends as the lightning passes from cloud to cloud. I dont know how much I assist in the economy of nature when I declare a fact— Is it not an important part in the history of the flow that I tell my friend where I found it.— We do not wish friends to feed and clothe our bodies—neighbors are kind enough for that,—but to do the like offices to ourselves.— We wish to spread and publish ourselves—as the sun spreads its rays and we toss the new thought to the friend and thus it is dispersed. Friends are those twain who feel their interests to be one— Each knows that the other might as well have said what he said All beauty—all music—all delight springs from apparent dualism—but real unity. I see his nature groping yonder so like mine— Does there go one whom I know then I go there.

The field where friends have met is consecrated forever— Man seeks friendship out of the desire to

realize a home here. As the Indian thinks he receives
in to himself the courage and strength of his conquered
enemy—so we add to ourselves all the character and
heart of our friend. He is my creation I can do what I
will with him. There is no possibility of being thwarted
—the friend is like wax in the rays that fall from our
own hearts

The friend does not take my word for any think—but
he takes me— He trusts me as I trust myself— We only
need be as true to others as we are to ourselves that
there may be ground enough for Friendship.

In the beginnings of friendship—for it does not grow
—we realize such love and justice as are attributed to God.

Very few are they from whom we derive any
*in*formation— The most only announce and tell tales
—but the friend *in*-forms

What is all nature and human life at this moment
—what the scenery and vicinity of a human soul—but the
song of an early sparrow from yonder fences—and the
cackling hens in the barn— So for one while my destiny
loiters within ear-shot of these sounds— The great
busy dame nature is concerned to know how many
eggs her hens lay.

The soul—the proprietor of the world has an interest
in the stacking of hay—the foddering of cattle—and
the draining of neat meadows— Away in Scythia, away
in India, they make butter and cheese for its behoof.

I wish that in some page of the Testament there
were something like Charlemagne's egg account—was
not Christ interested in the setting hens of Palestine?

Nature is very ample and roomy—she has left us
plenty of space to move in. As far as I can see from this
window how little life in the landscape—the few birds
that flit past do not crowd—they do not fill the valley. The

traveller on the highway has no fellow traveller for mile before or behind him. Nature was generous and not niggardly certainly.

How simple is the natural connexion of events. We complain greatly of the want of flow and sequence in books—but if the journalist only move himself—from Boston to New York—and speaks as before—there is link enough. And so there would be—if he were as careless of connexion and order when he stayed at home, and let the incessant progress which his life makes be the apology for abruptness. Do I not travel as far away from my old resorts though I stay here at home as though though I were on board the steam boat? Is not my life riveted together—has not it sequence? Do not my breathings follow each other naturally?

Set the Red Hen Sunday March 21st

March 21st 1842
Who is old enough to have learned from experience?
Tuesday March 22d 1842
Nothing can be more useful to a man than a determination not to be hurried.

I have not succeeded if my antagonist fails— It must be humanity's success

I cannot think nor utter my thought unless I have infinite room— The cope of heaven is not too high—the sea is not too deep for him whould unfold a great thought— It must feed me & warm & clothe me— It must be an entertainment to which my whole nature is invited— I must know that the Gods are to be my fellow guests.

We cannot well do without our sins, they are the highway of our virtue.

Wednesday March 23 1842

Plain speech is always a desideratum. Men write in a
florid style only because they would match the simple
beauties of the plainest speech.

They prefer to be misunderstood—rather than come
short of its exuberance.

Hussein Effendi praises the epistolary style of Ibrahim
Pasha to the French traveller Botta, because of "the
difficulty of understanding it: there was, he said, but
one person at Jidda who was capable of understanding
and explaining the Pasha's correspondence"

A plain sentence where every word is rooted in the
soil is indeed flowery and verdurous. It has the beauty
and variety of mosaic with the strength and compactness
of masonry.

All fullness looks like exuberance— We are not rich
without superfluous wealth— But the imitator only
copies the superfluity.

If the words were sufficiently simple and answering
to the thing to be expressed our sentences would be
as blooming as wreaths of evergreen and flowers.

You cannot fill a wine glass quite to the brim without
heaping it.

Simplicity is exuberant

When I look back eastward over the world it seems
to be all in repose Arabia—Persia—Hindostan—are
the land of contemplation. Those eastern nations have
perfected the luxury of idleness. Mount Sabér according
to the French traveller and naturalist Botta is celebrated
for producing the Kát tree   "The soft tops of the twigs
and tender leaves are eaten," says his reviewer, "and
produce an agreeable soothing excitement, restoring
from fatigue, banishing sleep, and disposing to the
enjoyment of conversation."

What could be more dignified than to browse the
tree tops with the camelopard. Who would not be a
rabbit or partridge sometimes–to chew mallows–and
pick the apple tree buds? It is not hard to discover
an instinct for the opium and betel and tobacco chewers.

After all I believe it is the style of thought entirely and
not the style of expression which makes the difference
in books. For if I find any thought worth extracting
I do not wish to alter the language Then the author
seems to have had all the graces of eloquence and poetry
given him.

I am pleased to discover myself as much a pensioner
in nature as mole and tit-mice, In some very direct
and simple uses to which man puts nature he stands in
this relation to her. Oriental life does not want this
grandeur. It is in Sadi and the Arabian Nights and the
Fables of Pilpay– In the New England noon tide I
have discovered more materials of oriental history than
the Sanscrit contains or Sir W. Jones has unlocked. I
see why it is necessary there should be such history at
all.– Was not Asia mapped in my brain before it was
in any geography?

In my brain is the sanscrit which contains the history
of the primitive times. The Vedas and their Angas are
not so ancient as my serenest contemplations. My mind
contemplates them– As Brahma his scribe.

I occasionally find myself to be nothing at all, because
the gods give me nothing to do. I cannot brag, I can
only congratulate my masters.

In idleness I am of no thickness I am thinnest
wafer– I never compass my own ends– God schemes
for me.

We have our times of action and our times of
reflection–the one mood caters for the other– Now I am
Alexander–and then I am Homer. One while my hand
is impatient to handle an axe or hoe, and at another
to pen. I am sure I write the tougher truth for these
calluses on my palms They give firmness to the sentence.
The sentences of a laboring man are like hardened
thongs–or the sinews of the deer–or the roots of the pine.

Thursday March 24th 1842

Those authors are successful who do not *write down*
to others, but make their own taste and judgment
their audience. By some strange infatuation we forget
that we do not approve what yet we recommend to
others.–

It is enough if I please myself with writing– I am
then sure of an audience.

If hoarded treasures can make me rich–have I not
the wealth of the planet in my mines and at the bottom
of the sea?

It is always singular to meet common sense in very
old books as the Veeshnoo Sarma–as if they could
have dispensed with the experience of later times. We
had not given space enough to *their* antiquity for the
accumulation of wisdom.

We meet even a trivial wisdom in them, as if truth
were already hacknied– The present is always younger
than antiquity.– A playful wisdom which has eyes
behind as well as before and oversees itself.

This pledge of sanity cannot be spared in a book–that
it sometime reflect upon itself–that it pleasantly behold
itself–that it hold the scales over itself.

The wise can afford to doubt in his wisest moment
–the easiness of doubt is the ground of his assurance.

Faith keeps many doubts in her pay. If I could not doubt I should not believe.

It is seen in this old Scripture how wisdom is older than the talent of composition It is a simple and not a compound rock– The story is as slender as the thread on which pearls are strung–it is a spiral line growing more and more perplexed till it winds itself up and dies like the silk worm in its cocoon. It is an interminable labyrinth.

It seems as if the old philosopher could not talk without moving–and each motion were made the apology or occasion for a sentence–but this being found inconvenient–the fictitious progress of the tale was invented. The story which winds between and around these sentences these barrows in the desert–these oases–is as indistinct as a camel track between Mourzuk to Darfur–between the pyramids and the Nile.– from Gaza to Jaffa.

The great thoughts of a wise man seem to the vulgar who do not generalize to stand far apart like isolated mounts–but Science knows that the mountains which rise so solitary in our midst are parts of a great mountain chain–dividing the earth– And the eye that looks into the horizon–toward the blue sierra melting away in the distance may detect their flow of thought– look below 3 ps

These sentences which take up your common life so easily–are not seen to run into ridges–because they are the table land on which the spectator stands.

I do not require that the mountain peaks be chained together, but by the common basis on which they stand –nor that the path of the muleteer be kept open at so much pains, when they may be bridged by the milky way.

That they stand frowning upon one another or

mutually reflecting the suns rays, is proof enough of their common basis.

The book should be found where the sentence is—and its connexion be as inartificial— It is the inspiration of a day and not of a moment— The links should be gold also— Better that the good be not united than that a bad man be admitted into their society. When men can select they will—if there be any stone in the quarry better than the rest—they will forsake the rest because —of it. Only the good will be quarried.

In these fables the story goes unregarded—while the reader leaps from sentence to sentence— As the travller leaps from stone to stone—while the water rushes unheed between them.

Friday March 25th 1842

Great persons are not soon learned not even their outlines—but they change like the mountains in the horizon as we ride along.

A mans life should be as fresh as a river—it should be the same channel but a new water every instant. Some men have no inclination—they have no rapids nor cascades—but marshes, and aligators and miasma instead.

How insufficient is all wisdom without love— There may be curtesy—there may be good will—there may be even temper there may be wit—and talent and sparkling conversation—and yet the soul pine for life. Just so sacred—and rich as my life is to myself—will it be to another. Ignorance and bungling with love is better than wisdom and skill without— Our life without love is

like coke and ashes–like the cocoa nut in which the
milk is dried up. I want to see the sweet sap of living
wood in it.

Men may be pure as alabaster and Parian marble
—elegant as a Tuscan villa–sublime as Terni–but if they
are not in society as retiring and inexperienced as
children– We shall go join Alaric and the Goths and
Vandals.

There is no milk mixed with the wine at the
entertainment.

Enthusiasm which is the formless material of thought
– I wish by the behavior of my friend toward me to be
led to have such regard for myself as for a box of
precious ointment. I shall not be so cheap to myself
if I see that another values me.

We talk much about education and yet none will
assume the office of our educator– I never gave anyone
the whole advantage of myself– I never afforded him
the culture of my love. How can I talk of Charity–who
at last withhold the kindness which alone makes charity
desirable.–

The poor want nothing less than me myself–and I
shirk charity by giving rags and meat–

Very dangerous is the talent of composition–the
striking out the heart of life at a blow–as the Indian
takes off a scalp– I feel as if my life had grown more
outward since I could express it.

What can I give–or what deny to another but myself?

The stars are God's dream–thoughts remembered
in the silence of his night.

In company that person who alone can understand
you you cannot get out of your mind.

The artist must work with indifferency–too great
interest vitiates his work.

Saturday March 26th 1842

The wise will not be imposed on by wisdom– You can tell–but what do you know?

I thank God that the cheapness which appears in time and the world–the trivialness of the whole scheme of things–is in my own cheap and trivial moment.

I am time and the world.

I assert no independence.

In me are summer and winter–village life and commercial routine–Pestilence and famine and refreshing breezes–joy and sadness–life & death. How near is yesterday– How far to-morrow! I have seen nails which were driven before I was born. Why do they look old and rusty?–

Why does not God make some mistake to show to us that time is a delusion. Why did I invent Time but to destroy it.

Did you ever remember the moment when you was not mean?

Is it not a satire–to say that life is organic?–

Where is my heart gone–they say men cannot part with it and live.

Are setting hens troubled with ennui Nature is very kind–does she let them reflect? These long march days setting on and on in the crevice of a hayloft with no active employment–

Do setting hens sleep?

But the eye that looks into the horizon and sees the blue line melting away in the distance–knows that the nearer hills too make a part of the chain.

A book should be a vein of gold ore–as the sentence is a diamond found in the sand or a pearl fished out of the sea.

He who does not borrow trouble does not lend it.

I must confess I have felt mean enough when asked how I was to act on society—what errand I had to mankind—undoubtedly I did not feel mean without a reason—and yet my loitering is not without defence— —

I would fain communicate the wealth of my life to men—would really give them what is most precious in my gift— I would secrete pearls with the shellfish—and lay up honey with the bees for them. I will sift the sunbeams for the public good—

I know no riches I would keep back. I have no private good—unless it be my peculiar ability to serve the public—this is the only individual property— Each one may thus be innocently rich— I enclose and foster the pearl till it is grown.

I wish to communicate those parts of my life which I would gladly live again myself.

It is hard to be a good citizen of the world in any great sense—but if we do render no interest or increase to mankind out of that talent God gave us—we can at least preserve the principal unimpaired.

One would like to be making large dividends to society out that deposited capital in us—but he does well for the most part if he proves a secure investment only —without adding to the stock.

In such a letter as I like there will be the most naked and direct speech—the least circumlocution.

Sunday March 27th 1842

The eye must be firmly anchored to this earth which beholds birches and pines waving in the breeze in a certain light—a serene rippling light.

Cliffs—

Two little hawks have just come out to play—like butterflies rising one above the other in endless alternation far below me— They swoop from side to

side in the broad basin of the tree tops–with wider and
wider surges–as if swung by an invisible pendulum.
They stoop down on this side and scale up on that–

Suddenly I look up and see a new bird–probably an
eagle–quite above me laboring with the wind not
more than forty rods off– It was the largest bird of the
falcon kind I ever saw– I was never so impressed by
any flight. She sailed the air–and fell back from time
to time like a ship on her beam ends–holding her talons
up as if ready for the arrows– I never allowed before
for the grotesque attitudes of our national bird–

The eagle must have an educated eye.

See what a life the Gods have given us–set round
with pain and pleasure– –it is too strange for sorrow
it is too strange for joy– One while it looks as shallow
though as intricate as a Cretan labyrinth–and again it is
a pathless depth– I ask for bread incessantly–that
my life sustain me–as much as meat my body.– No
man knoweth in what hour his life may come.– Say not
that nature is trivial–for to-morrow she will be radiant
with beauty. I am as old as old as the Alleghanies– I
was going to say Wachusett– –but it excites a youthful
feeling–as I were but too happy to be so young.

Monday March 28th 1842.

How often must one feel as he looks back on his
past life that he has gained a talent but lost a character.–

My life has got down into my fingers. My inspiration
at length is only so much breath as I can breathe.

Society does nominally estimate men by their talents
–but really feels and knows them by their characters.

What a man does compared with what he is is but a
small part.– To require that our friend possesss a certain
skill–is not to be satisfied till he is something less than
our friend.

Friendship should be a great promise—a perennial spring-time.

I can conceive how the life of the gods may be dull and tame—if it is not disappointed and insatiate.

One may well feel chagrined when he finds he can do nearly all he can conceive.

Some books ripple on like a stream and we feel that the author is in the full tide of discourse— Plato and Jamblichus and Pythagoras and Bacon—halt beside them — Long stringy—slimy thoughts which flow or run together.

They read as if written for military men—or men of business—there is such a dispatch in them.— and a double-quick time a Saratoga march—with beat of drum. But the grave thinkers and philosophers seem not to have got their swaddling clothes off—they are slower than a Roman army on its march—the rear encamping to-night where the van camped last night— The wise Jamblichus eddies and gleams like a watery slough—

But the reviewer seizes the pen and shouts forward! Alamo and Fanning! and after rolls the tide of war.

Immediately the author discovers himself launched —and if the slope was easy and the grease good does not go to the bottom.

They flow as glibly as mill streams sucking under a race-way.

The flow is ofttimes in the poor reader who makes such haste over their pages—as to the traveller the walls and fences seem to travel. But the most rapid trot is no flow after all.

If I cannot chop wood in the yard—can I not chop wood in my journal? Can I not give vent to that appetite so? I wish to relieve myself of superfluous energy— How poor is the life of the best and wisest—the petty side

will appear at last— Understand once how the best in
society live—with what routine—with what tedium
and insipidity—with what grimness and defiance—with
what chuckling over an exaggeration of the sunshine
— Altogether are not the actions of your great man—poor
—even pitiful and ludicrous?

I am astonished I must confess that man looks so
respectable in nature— Considering the littlenesses
Socrates must descend to in the twenty four hours—that
he yet wears a serene countenance And even adorns
nature—

Tuesday March 29th 1842.
Wednesday " 30th

Though nature's laws are more immutable than any
despot's yet to our daily life they rarely seem rigid, but
we relax with license in summer weather— We are not
often nor harshly reminded of the things we may not
do. I am often astonished to see how long and with what
manifold infringments of the natural laws—some
men I meet in the highway, maintain life. She does not
deny them quarter they do not die without priest.— all
the while she rejoices for if they are not one part of
her they are another.

I am convinced that consistency is the secret of
health— How many a poor man striving to live a pure
life pines and dies after a life of sickness—and his
successors doubt if nature is not pitiless—while the
confirmed and consistent sot, who is content with
his rank life like mushrooms—a mass of corrruption still
dozes comfortably under a hedge.— He has made his
peace with himself—there is no strife.

Nature is really very kind and liberal to all persons
of vicious habits—they take great licenses with her.
She does not exhaust them with many excesses.

How hard it is to be greatly related to mankind!– they are only my uncles and aunts and cousins– I hear of some persons greatly related, but only he is so who has all mankind for his friend. Our intercourse with the best grows soon shallow and trivial– They no longer inspire us. After enthusiasm comes insipidity and blancness– The sap of all noble schemes drieth up–and the schemers return again and again in despair to "common sense and labor." If I could help infuse some life and heart into society–should I not do a service? Why will not the Gods mix a little of the wine of nobleness with the air we drink–? Let virtue have some firm foothold in this earth. Where does she dwell?– who are the salt of the earth– May not Love have some resting place on the earth as sure the sunshine on the rock.– The crystals imbedded in the cliff sparkle and gleam from afar–as if they did certainly enrich our planet–but where does any virtue permanently sparkle and gleam?– She was sent forth over the waste too soon before the earth was prepared for her.

Rightfully we are to each other the gate of heaven–and redeemers from sin–but now we overlook these lowly and narrow ways–we will go over the bald mountain tops without going through the valleys.

Men do not meet on the ground of their real acquaintance and actual understanding of one another –but degrade themselves immediately into the puppets of convention– They do as if in given circumstances they had agreed to know each other only so well–they rarely get to that that they inform one-another gratuitously–and use each other like the sea and woods for what is new and inspiring there.

At present all the intercourse or communion we have

is in silence above and behind our speech– We should
be very simple to rely on words–as it is what we knew
before always interprets a man's words– I cannot easily
remember what any man has said to me–but how can
I forget what he is to me? Not only do we know
each-other better than we tell to one another but
better than we tell to ourselves,–for really no person
is quite unknown to us whose body we have met–and in
some emergency we shall find how well we knew him.
When society fears thee man of new views–the reformer
–she is not mistaken–he is fearful to her.

Thursday March 31st 1842.

I cannot forget the majesty of that bird at the cliff
– It was no sloop or smaller craft hove in sight but a
ship of the line–worthy to struggle with the elements. It
was a great presence– As of the master of river and
forest. His eye would not have quailed before the owner
of the soil–none could challenge his rights. And then
his retreat, sailing so steadily away, was a kind of
advance– How is it that man always feels like an
interloper in nature as if he had intruded on the domains
of bird and beast.

The really efficient laborer will be found not to crowd
his day with work but will saunter to his task surrounded
by a wide halo of ease and leisure– There will be a
wide margin for relaxation to his day– He is only
earnest to secure the kernels of time–and does not
exaggerate the value of the husk.

Why should the hen set all day–she can lay but
one egg–and besides she will not have picked up
materials for a new one.– Those who work much do
not work hard.

Nothing is so rare as sense—very uncommon sense
is poetry—and has a heroic or sweet music. But in verse
for the most part the music now runs before and then
behind the sense, but is never coincident with it. Given
the true metre and one will make music while another
makes sense. But good verse, like a good soldier, will
make its own music—and it will march to the same
with one consent.

In most verse there is no inherent music—the man
should not march—but walk like a citizen—it is not
time of war but peace— Boys study the metres to write
Latin verses, but it does not help them to write English.

Lydgate's "Story of Thebes," intended for a Canterbury
Tale, is a specimen of most unprogressive unmusical
verse— Each line rings the knell of its brother—as if it
were introduced but to dispose of him. No mortal
man could have breathed to that cadences without long
intervals of relaxation—the repetition would have been
fatal to the lungs.— No doubt there was much healthy
exercise taken in the meanwhile— He should forget
his ryhme and tell his story—or forget his story and
breathe himself.—

In Shakspeare and elsewhere the climax may be
somewhere along the line—which runs as varied and
meandering as a country road—but in Lydgate it is
no-where but in the ryhme— The couplets slope headlong
to their confluence.

Set the grey hen Ap. 1st

                                    Saturday April 2nd 1842
The Prologue to the Canterbury Tales is full of good
sense and humanity—but is not transcendent poetry.

It is so good that it seems like fault-finding to esteem it second to any other For pictursque description of persons it is without a parallel. It did not need inspiration –but a cheerful and easy wit– It is essentially humorous –as no inspired poetry is– Genius is so serious as to be grave and sublime rather Humor takes a narrower vision–however broad and genial it may be–than enthusiasm. Humor delays and looks back

Sunday April 3d 1842.

I can remember when I was more enriched by a few cheap rays of light falling on the pond side–than by this broad sunny day.

Riches have wings–indeed. The weight of present wo will express the sweetness of past experience.– When sorrow comes how easy it is to remember pleasure – When in winter the bees cannot make new honey–they consume the old.

Experience is in the head and fingers. The heart is inexperienced.

Sorrow singeth the sweetest strain– –The Daughters of Zion–the Last Sigh of the Moor–

Joy is the nectar of flowers–sorrow the honey of bees.

I thank God for sorrow– It is hard to be abused– Is not he kind still–who lets this south wind blow–this warm sun shine on me?

I have just heard the flicker among the oaks on the hill side ushering in a new dynasty.– It is the age and youth of time– Why did nature set this lure for sickly mortals– Eternity could not begin with more security and momentousness than the spring– The summer's eternity is reestablished by this note.

All sights and sounds are seen and heard both in time and eternity. And when the eternity of any sight or sound strikes the eye or ear–they are intoxicated with delight.

Sometimes as through a dim haze we see objects in their eternal relations. And they stand like Stonehenge and The Pyramids.

The destiny of the soul can never be studied by the reason–for its modes are not extatic– In the wisest calculation or demonstration I but play a game with myself– I am not to be taken captive by myself.

I cannot convince myself–God must convince– I can calculate a problem in arithmetic–but not any morality.

Virtue is incalculable, as it is inestimable. Well man's destiny is but Virtue–or manhood–it is wholly moral –to be learned only by the life of the soul. God cannot calculate it–he has no moral philosophy–no ethics The reason before it can be applied to such a subject will have to fetter and restrict it–how can he step by step perform that long journey–who has not conceived whither he is bound– How can he expect to perform an arduous journey without interruption who has no passport to the end?

On one side of man is the actual and on the other the ideal– The former is the province of the reason   it is even a divine light when directed upon it–but it cannot reach forward into the ideal without blindness. The moon was made to rule by night, but the sun to rule by day. Reason will be but a pale cloud like the moon when one ray of divine light comes to illumine the soul.

How rich and lavish must be the system which can afford to let so many moons burn all the day as well as the night–though no man stands in need of their light– There is none of that kind of economy in nature that husbands its stock–but she supplies inexhaustible means to the most frugal methods. The poor may learn of her frugality–and the rich generosity.– Having carefully determined the extent of her charity—she establishes it for ever—her almsgiving is an annuity.

She supplies to the bee only so much wax as is necessary for its cell—so that no poverty could stint it more— But the little economist which fed the evangelist in the desert—still keeps in advance of the immigrant, and fills the cavities of the forest for his repast.

Transcripts, 1840–1842

TRANSCRIBED 1842

{Front endpaper}

{Three leaves missing}

{Nine-tenths page blank, one-tenth page missing}

Any book of great authority and genius would seem
to our imagination to permeate and pervade all space.
Its spirit like a more subtle ether would sweep along with
the prevailing winds of a country–conveying a new
gloss to the meadows, and the depths of the wood, and
bathing the huckleberries on the hills, as sometimes
a subtle influence in the sky washes in waves over
the fields, and seems to break on some invisible beach in
the air. It would spend the mornings and the evenings
–and all things would confirm it.

{Two-fifths page blank, one-tenth page missing}

As I am going to the woods I think to take some
book with me whose author has been there already
–whose sentences will be as good as my thoughts, and
will eke them out–or show me human life still gleaming
in the horizon when the hills have shut out the town.
But I can find none, none will sail as far forward into
the bay of nature as my thought–they stay at home
— When I get to the woods their thin leaves rustle in my
fingers. They are bare and obvious, and have no halo
or haze about them. Nature lies far and fair behind
them all.

I should like to meet the great and serene sentence,
which does not reveal itself–only that it is great, which
I may never with my utmost intelligence pierce through

and beyond—more than the sky itself—which no
intelligence can understand. There should be a kind
of life and palpitation to it; under its rind a kind of
blood should circulate forever, communicating freshness
to its countenance.

A book should be so true as to be intimate and familiar
to all men as the sun to their faces. Such a serene word
as is occasionally uttered to a companion in a summer
ramble, and both are silent. It will help the sun shine
in the fields, and the rays will fall on its page as if to
explain and illustrate it, It will take in the mosses and
the rocks as if addressed to them, if read in their midst,
It will color the scenery, and explain the greenness
of the spring, and the russet of the autumn.

A book is to be attended to as a new sound merely—a
new note in the forest— Most indeed would be put to a
sore trial if the reader should assume the attitude of
a listener— To any lonely and sober thought the earth
is a wild unexplored— Wildness as of the jay and
muskrat reigns over the great part of nature, the crow
and the upland plover sound out of the horizon— Let us
take the road which leads to the hill top if by any means
we may spy out what manner of earth we inhabit— East
west north and south it is hill and valley forest and plain
this earth of ours—one may see how at convenient interva'
men have settled themselves—without thought for the
universe— But How little matters it all men have built
and delved there in the valley, it is but a feature in the
landscape. Still the vast impulse of nature breathes over
all;—the eternal winds sweep across the interval to-day,
bringing mist and haze to shut out their works. Still the

crow caws from hill to hill—as no feeble tradesman nor smith may do—and in all swamps the hum of mosquitoes drowns this modern hum of industry.

{*One-fifth page blank*}

There is always a later edition of every book than the printer thinks of—no matter how recently it was issued. All nature is a newer impression with which it is to be compared. The pines are unrelenting sifters of thought, nothing petty leaks through them. Let me put my ear close and hear the sough of this book, that I may know if any inspiration yet haunts it.

That title—The Laws of Menu with the Gloss of Culluca—comes to me with such a volume of sound as if it had swept unobstructedly over the plains of Hindostan, and when my eye rests on yonder birches—or the sun in the water—or the shadows of the trees—it seems to signify the laws of them all. They are the laws of you and me—a fragrance wafted down from those old-times, and no more to be refuted than the wind.

{*One-fifth page blank*}

The impression which those sublime sentences made on me last night, has awakened me before any cock-crowing— Their influence lingers around me like a fragrance or as the fog hangs over the earth late into the day. When my imagination travels eastward and backward to those remote years of the gods, I seem to draw near to the habitation of the morning—and the dawn at length has a place. I remember the book as an hour before sunrise.

How thrilling is a noble sentiment in the oldest books
–in Homer–the Zendavesta–or Confucius! A strain
of music reminds me of the védas– They are a strain
wafted down to us on the breeze of time through the
aisles of innumerable ages. By its very nobleness it is
made near and audible to us.

{*One-fifth page blank*}

I know of no book which comes to us with grander
pretensions than this–and its immense presumption is
so impersonal and sincere, that it is never offensive
or ridiculous. Observe the modes in which modern
literature is advertised–and then consider this Hindoo
prospectus– Think what a reading public it addresses
what criticism it expects. What wonder if the times
were not ripe for it.

Every where it demands the widest apprehension–and
proceeds from the loftiest plateau of the soul–it is
spoken unbendingly to its own level, and does not imply
any contemporaneous speaker.

I cannot read a sentence without being elevated as
upon the table land of the Gauhts–it has such a rhythm
as the winds of the desert, such a tide as the Ganges,
and seems as superior to criticism as the Himaleh
mounts. So supremely religious a book imposes with
authority on the latest age. The very simplicity of style
of the ancient lawgiver–implying all in the omission
of all–proves an habitual

{*Two leaves missing*}

in the primeval race was received–as if it were the
cradle of the human race.

I like to read of the "pine, larch, spruce, and silver
fir," which cover the southern face of the Himmaleh
range—of the "gooseberry, raspberry, strawberry", which
from an imminent temperate zone overlook the torrid
plains. So did this active modern life have even then a
foothold and lurking place in the midst of the primeval
stateliness and contemplativeness of the plain.

In another era the "lily of the valley, cowslip,
dandelion," were to work their way down into the
plain, and bloom in a level zone of their own, reaching
round the earth. Already has the era of the temperate
zone arrived, the era of the pine and the oak, for the
palm and the banyan do not supply the wants of this
generation. The lichens too on the summits of the rocks
are to find their level ere long.

The fowls which are elsewhere domesticated run
wild in India—and so I think of these domestic thoughts
and fashions when I read the laws of Menu—

Arabia—Persia—Hindostan—are the native land of
contemplation.

If the Roman—the Greek—and the Jew have a character
in history—so has the Hindoo— He may help to balance
Asia which is all too onesided with its Palestine.

{*Two-fifths page blank*}

It was not an unfitting nor unpleasing contrast that
the impetuous macedonian should be met—at this which
he thought the eastern boundary of the world, by the
calm philosophy of the Brahmens. We cannot but make
the most of the transient and solitary gleam of Indian
philosophy afforded to the nations of the west by the

expedition of Alexander Having reached this point
he sends forward Onesicritus to meet certain of the sect
of gymnosophists a little without the city, and learn
their tenets and manner of life— At first they refuse
to answer to answer his inquiries though he came from
Jupiter himself unless he will strip and throw himself
on the stones with themselves. But at length they
condescend to show courtesy to the stranger and
becoming interested in those new philosophers of Greece
—Pythagoras—Socrates—Diogenes—whose doctrines he
assures them are similar to their own—one of them
named Dandamis expresses their stern sympathy with
their western bretheren—saying "They appeared to
him to have been men of genius, but to have lived with
too passive a regard for the laws," reflecting with proud
confidence upon the independent simplicity of their
own lives. Another of them called Calanus is said to
have afterward given this advice to Alexander "He laid
a dry and shrivelled hide before him, and first trod
upon its edges. This he did all round; and still as he trod
on one side, it started up on the other. At last, he placed
his feet upon the middle, and then it lay still. By this
emblem he showed him, that he should fix his residence
and plant his principal force in the heart of his empire,
and not wander to its extremities".

{One-third page blank}

There is nothing in sight but alders and pines— I hear
a phoebe from the depths of the wood—and a spring
bubbling near where I drank out of a can in my earliest
youth—for p 415

{Four-fifths page blank}

It seems to me we are accustomed to exaggerate the immobility and stagnation of those eras, as of the waters which levelled the steppes; but those slow revolving "years of the gods" were as rapid to all the needs of virtue as these bustling and hasty seasons. Man stands to revere—he kneels to pray. Methinks history will have to be tried by new tests to show what centuries were rapid and what slow. Corn grows in the night. Will this bustling era detain the future reader longer? Will the earth seem to have conversed more with the heavens during these times? Who is writing better Vedas? How science and art spread and flourished, how trivial conveniences were multiplied, that which is the gossip of this age—is not recorded in them, and if it is left out of our scripture too what will remain? Since the battle of Bunker hill we think the world has not been at a stand still.

They have perfected the luxury of idleness—.

Some events in history are more remarkable than momentous—like eclipses of the sun by which all are attracted, but whose effects—no one takes the trouble to calculate.

The era of greatest change is to the subject of it the condition of greatest invariableness. The longer the lever—the less perceptible its motion. It is the slowest pulsation which is the most vital. I am independent of the change I detect. My most essential progress must be to me a state of absolute rest. So in geology we are nearest to discovering the true causes of the revolutions of the globe, when we allow them to consist with a quiescent state of the elements. We discover the causes

of all past change in the present invariable order of
the universe.– The pulsations are so long that in
the interval there is almost a stagnation of life. The
first cause of the universe makes the least noise. Its
pulse has beaten but once, is now beating. The greatest
appreciable revolutions are the work of the light footed
air—the stealthy paced water—and the subterranean
fire. The winds make the desert without a rustle.

To every being consequently its own first cause is an
insensible and inconceivable agent.

{*Two-thirds page blank*}

We will not quarrel with the Hindoos because
they assert an immortallity *post* as well as *ante*. The
Athenians wore a golden grasshopper as an emblem
that they sprang from the earth, and the Arcadians
pretended that they were προϲεληνοι, or before the moon.
In the absence of direct testimony this is authentic
history enough. Plato might as well have considered this
back reaching tendency of the human mind.

{*One-fifth page blank*}

It would be vain to trouble ourselves with the much
vexed question respecting the antiquity of the Hindoo
scripture—whether prior or posterior to this or that
other— If the reader cannot judge by internal evidence,
no external will avail. One might as well investigate
the chronology of light and heat. Let the sun shine.

Menu understood this matter best when he said.
"Those persons best know the divisions of days and
nights, who understand, that the day of Brahmá, which
endures to the end of a thousand such ages, gives rise

to virtuous exertions; and that his night endures as
long as his day."

What is a day if the day's work be not done? What
are the divisions of time to them who have nothing
to do? What is the present or the future to him who has
no occasion for them who does not create them by
his industry!

4. 320,000,000 years says Murray form "the grand
anomalistic period called a calpa, and fantastically
assigned as a day of Brama."

"the Maha Yug, or great divine age, through which
mankind are now passing, consists of four human
ages, the last and worst of which is at present revolving.
These ages, of unequal and continually decreasing
length, are the

Satya Yug, which lasted	– –	1,728,000 years
Treta Yug,	– –	1,296,000
Dwapar Yug,	– –	864,000
Cali Yug, which is to last		432,000

Of the dark era in which we live, only about five
thousand years have yet elapsed."

But their chronology or any chronology is of small
moment.

We will not complain of absurd and contradictory
statements, but be thankful that we have any. When
I remember the treachery of memory, and the manifold
accidents to which tradition is liable—how soon the
vista of the past closes behind, as near as night's crescent
to the setting day, and the dazzling brightness of noon
is reduced to the faint glimmer of the evening star,
I feel as if it were by a rare indulgence of the fates,
that any traces of the past are left us—that my ears

which do not hear across the interval over which a cro
caws, should chance to hear this far travelled sound.

I read history as little critically as I consider the
landscape, and am more interested in the atmospheric
tints, and various lights and shades which the
intervening spaces create, than in its groundwork and
composition. It is the morning now turned evening
and seen in the west—the same sun but a new light and
atmosphere. Its beauty is like the sunset—not a fresco
painting on a wall—flat and bounded by the actual,
but atmospheric and roving or free. In reality history
fluctuates as the face of the landscape from morning to
evening. What is of moment is its hue and color. Time
hides no treasures—we want not its then, but its now.
We do not complain that the mountains in the horizon
are blue and indistinct, they are the more like the
heavens.

Of what moment are facts that can be lost—which
need to be commemorated? The monument of death
will outlast the memory of the dead. The pyramids do
not tell the tale that was confided to them. The living
fact commemorates itself— Why look in the dark
for light—look in the light rather. Strictly speaking the
societies have not recovered one fact from oblivion, but
they themselves are instead of the fact that is lost.
The researcher is more memorable than the researched.
The crowd stood admiring the mist and the dim outline
of the trees seen through it—when one of their number
advanced to explore the phenomenon, and with fresh
admiration all eyes were turned on his dimly retreating
figure. Critical acumen is exerted in vain to uncover
the past—the past cannot be presented—we cannot know
what we are not— But one veil hangs over past—present

—and future— And it is the province of the historian
to find out not what was but what is. Where a battle has
been fought you will find nothing but the bones of
men and beasts, where a battle is being fought there
are hearts beating. We will sit on a mound and muse,
and not try to make these skeletons stand on their
legs again. Does nature remember, think you, that they
were men, or not rather that they are bones?

What is all nature and human life at this moment
—what the scenery and vicinity of one human soul—but
the song of an early sparrow from yonder fence—and
the cackling of hens in a distant barn So for one while
my destiny loiters within ear shot of these sounds.
The great busy dame nature is concerned to know how
many eggs her hens lay.

The soul the proprietor of the world has an interest
in the stacking of hay—the foddering of cattle—and
the draining of peat meadows— Away in Scythia—away
in India they make butter and cheese for its larder— I miss
in the New Testament something like Charlemagne's
egg account— Was not Christ interested in the setting
hens of Palestine?

Ancient history has an air of antiquity, it should
be more modern. It is written as if the spectator should
be thinking of the back side of the picture on the wall,
as if the author expected the dead would be his readers,
and wished to detail to them their own experience.
Men seem anxious to accomplish an orderly retreat
through the centuries, earnestly rebuilding the works
behind as they are battered down by the incroachments
of time but while they loiter they and their work both
fall a prey to the arch enemy.

Biography is liable to the same objection–it should be autobiography. Let us not leave ourselves empty that so vexing our bowels we may go abroad and be somebody else to explain him. If I am not I who will be?–as if it were to dispense justice to all– But the time has not come for that.– There are two classes of authors the one write their biography–the other the history of their times.

With how little cooperation of the societies after all is the past remembered– At first history had no muse–but a kind fate watched over her–some garrulous old man with tenacious memory told it to his child– There is a good instance of this in Alwákidis Arabian chronicle –translated by Occleve– "I was informed by *Ahmed Almatîn Aljorhami*, who had it from *Rephâa Ebn Kais Alámiri*, who had it from *Saiph Ebn Fabalah Alchâtquarmi*, who had it from *Thabet Ebn Alkamah*, who said he was present at the action"

It has neither the venerableness of antiquity–nor the freshness of novelty.

It does as if it would go to the beginning of things –which Natural history might with reason assume to do – But consider the universal history, and then tell me, when did burdock and plantain sprout first.

It has been so written for the most part that those times it describes–are with remarkable propriety called dark ages– They are dark as one has observed because we are so in the dark with respect to them. The sun rarely shines in history– It has no leisure nor opportunity what with the din and the smoke– And when we meet with any cheering fact which implies the presence of that luminary we excerpt and modernize it– As

when we read in the history of the Saxons how Edwin
of Northumbria "caused stakes to be fixed in the
highways where he had seen a clear spring," and that
"brazen dishes were chained to them, to refresh the
weary sojourner, whose fatigues Edwin had himself
experienced." This is worth all Arthur's twelve battles.
The sun again shines along the highway—and the
landscape presents us sunny glades, and occasional
cultivated patches as well as dark primeval forests.

I find on seeing a painting of our village as it appeared
a hundred years ago with a fair open aspect—and a light
on trees and river, as if it were mid noon—that I had
not thought the sun shone in those days—or that men
lived in broad day light then. When I have been reading
the Indian wars or the early history of the colonies, I
do not remember to have seen the sun once—but a dim
twilight or night did their events transpire in. I cannot
imagine the sun shining on hill or valley during Philip's
war—or on the war path of Paugus—or Standish or
Church or Lovell—with serene summer weather.
But it is fit the past should be dark—and yet it is
not altogether the fault of the past but equally of
tradition— It is not a distance of time but a distance
of rotation which makes thus dusky the memorials of the
past— What is near to the heart of this generation is
present and bright. Greece lies outspread fair and
sunshiny in floods of light—for there is the sun and
daylight in her literature and art— Homer does not allow
me to forget that the sun shone—nor Phidias—nor the
Parthenon.
I must confess I am a little incredulous when I hear
of the excessive sultriness of the weather—during
some of those toilsome Indian marches, and how the
troops sweated, and their tongues were swollen in their

mouths– I do not question the fatigue–but it implies
such a glare of light on the landscape.– They could
have fought in the shade of their own dusky deeds.

But no era has been wholly dark nor will we too
hastily submit to history–and congratulate ourselves
upon a blaze of light– If we could pierce the obscurity
of those remote years we should find it light enough
–some creatures are made to see in the dark.
The eyes of the oldest fossil remains, they tell us,
indicate that the same laws of light prevailed then that
do now–yes always the laws of light are the same–but
the modes and degrees of seeing vary. The Gods are
partial to no era–but steadily shines their light in the
heavens while the eye of the beholder is turned to stone
– There was but the eye and the sun from the first
–the ages have not added a new ray–nor altered a fibre
of the eye.

But enough upon this subject   the reader will
have learned by this time that we do not intend to be
hampered by what is called the history of this people.

{*One leaf missing*}

Penobscots by the river are my Britons come to Rome.

The true India is neither east nor west–who has not
lived under the Mussalman and Tartar dynasty? You
will not have to pierce far into the summer day to come
to these.
I sometimes hear an anecdote told of my neighbors
and these modern days which is true but for its scenery–
It should have been told of Scythia and the east– A
certain behavior and expression we call oriental– I

have seen a man—a seer—hold up one finger to express individuality—and then two for dualism, without injuring the effect of his action by speech—in a way which he could only have learned in the east.

Having but one chair I am obliged to receive my visitors standing—and now I think of it—those old sages and heroes must always have met thus erectly.

In the New England noontide I have discovered more materials for oriental history than the sanscrit contains, or Sir William Jones has unlocked. In my brain is the sanscrit— Was not Asia mapped there before it was in any geography? The Vedás and their Angas are not so ancient as serene Contemplation— My mind contemplates them as Brahmá his scribe.

{Two-thirds page blank, one leaf missing}

"the Véda with its Angas, or the six compositions deduced from it, the revealed system of medicine, the Puránas, or sacred histories, and the code of Menu," according to Vyása, "were four works of supreme authority, which ought never to be shaken by arguments merely human." The last, which is in blank verse—and is one of the oldest compositions extant—has been translated by Sir William Jones— It is believed by the Hindoos "to have been promulged in the beginning of time, by Menu, son or grandson of Brahmá," and "first of created beings." Brahmá is said to have "taught his laws to Menu in a hundred thousand verses, which Menu explained to the primitive world in the very words of the book now translated."

Others affirm that they have undergone successive abridgments for the convenience of mortals, "while the gods of the lower heaven, and the band of celestial musicians, are engaged in studying the primary code."

"A number of glosses or comments on Menu were composed by the Munis, or old philosophers, whose treatises, together with that before us, constitute the Dherma Sastra, in a collective sense, or Body of Law." Culluca Bhatta was one of the more modern commentators— His gloss however is for the most part omitted in the following selections, but when retained is printed in Italics.

{*Two-thirds page blank*}

The conception of Creation is peaceful as a dream. They had learned that God's methods are not violent. It was such an awakening as might have been heralded by the faint dreaming chirp of crickets before the dawn. And so of the annihilation of the world—a beginning and ending as the morning and evening.

{*Two-thirds page blank*}

"Menu *sat* reclined, with his attention fixed on one object, God; when the divine Sages approached" to learn the law. "He, whose powers were measureless,—gave them a comprehensive answer."

"This," that is the universe, "existed only in darkness, imperceptible, undefinable, undiscoverable, undiscovered, as if it were wholly immersed in sleep".

"Then the self existing power, himself undiscerned, but making this world discernible, with five elements and other principles, appeared with undiminished glory, dispelling the gloom."

"He, whom the mind alone can perceive, whose essence eludes the external organs, who has no visible parts, who exists from eternity, even HE, the soul of all beings, whom no being can comprehend, shone forth in person."

"He, having willed to produce various beings from his own divine substance, first with a thought created the waters, and placed in them a productive seed:"

"That *seed* became an egg bright as gold, blazing like the luminary with a thousand beams; and in that egg he was born himself, Brahmá, the great forefather of all spirits."

{*One-fourth page blank*}

He then creates Menu, and heaven—and earth, and ether—and mind—and consciousness, and all qualities and creatures and inferior gods, and declares the fate of various souls, the origin of sex, and of various races of animals.

"He, whose powers are incomprehensible, having thus created both me and this universe, was again absorbed in the supreme Spirit, changing *the* time *of energy* for *the* time *of repose*"

"When that power awakes, then has this world its full expansion; but, when he slumbers with a tranquil spirit, then the whole system fades away;"

"For, while he reposes in calm sleep, embodied spirits, endued with principles of action, depart from their several acts, and the mind itself becomes inert;"

"And, when they once are absorbed in that supreme essence, then the divine soul of all beings withdraws his energy, and placidly slumbers;"

"Thus that immutable Power, by waking and reposing alternately, revivifies and destroys in eternal succession this whole assemblage of locomotive and immoveable creatures."

Menu then appoints his son Bhrigu to declare his laws to the sages.

{*One leaf missing*}

And yet there is something in this routine and desultoriness of our lives not quite vulgar nor useless—its solidity and apparent necessity insensibly recommend it to us. It is like a cane or a cushion for the infirm, and in view of it all are infirm. If there were but one erect and solid standing tree in the woods, all creatures would go to rub against it, and make sure of their footing. It is the ground we stand on a wall to retreat to, we cannot draw on our boots without bracing ourselves against it. It is the fence over which neighbors lean when they talk—it is like the spring board on which tumblers perform and develope their elasticity. Health requires that we should recline on it from time to time. When we are in it—the hand stands still on the face of the clock, and we grow like corn in the genial darkness and silence of the night. Our weakness wants, but our strength uses it. Good for the body is the work of the body, good for the soul the work of the soul—and good for either the work of the other—let them not call hard names nor know a divided interest.

In some of these verses we seem to be dabbling in

the very elements of our present conventional and actual life. Here is a history of the forms which humanity has in all ages assumed. To our contracted view this mere outward life seems a constituent part of us, and we do not realize that as the soul expands it will cast off the shell of routine and convention— But of this people the temples are already crumbled away, and we are introduced to the very hearth of Hindoo life—and to the primeval conventicle where—how to eat—and to drink —and to sleep—were the questions to be decided. The old lawgiver seems to have foreseen all the possible conditions and relations of man, and provided that they be maintained with adequate dignity and sincerity. The sacred importance attached to trivial and indifferent things makes a great part of the charm of the book.

{*One leaf, one-third page missing*}

"The staff of a priest must be of such a length as to reach his hair; that of a soldier, to reach his forehead; and that of a merchant, to reach his nose."

"Let a learned man ask a priest, when he meets him, if his devotion prospers; a warrior, if he is unhurt; a merchant, if his wealth is secure; and one of the servile class, if he enjoys good health;—"

"Way must be made for a man in a wheeled carriage, or above ninety years old, or afflicted with disease, or carrying a burden; for a woman; for a prince just returned from the mansion of his preceptor; for a prince, and for a bridegroom."

"Among all these, if they be met at one

{*One-third page missing*}

manysided and practical Genius—for such is its descent —which always has possession of the world of the present moment.

I observe a truly wise practice on every hand, in education—in religion—and in the morals of society —enough embodied wisdom to have set up many an ancient philosopher. This Society—if it were a person to be met face to face, would not only be tolerated but courted, with its so impressive experience and admirable acquaintance with things.

Consider society at any epoch—and who does not see that heresy has already prevailed in it? All this worldly wisdom was once the unamiable heresy of some wise man. The mind which

{Six leaves missing}

Any moral philosophy is exceedingly rare This of Menu springs from so inward and fine an experience —that almost it cannot be uttered— It is addressed to our privacy most of all. We wonder how so minute and delicate a discrimination—could have been preserved unscathed through so many ages and so many tongues.

It is a manual of private devotion—so private and domestic—and yet so public and universal a word as is not spoken in parlor or pulpit now adays. It is so impersonal that it exercises our sincerity more than any other. It goes with us into the yard and into the chamber, and is yet later spoken than the advice of our mother and sisters.

It is not merely a voice floating in space for my own experience is the speaker.

Nowhere is the dignity of the teacher's office so nobly asserted, and secured by so many observances.

Yet it seems to be uttered more publicly than other truth as if it were made to be spoken out of doors— I think I do not apprehend the full breadth of these sentences in a low or narrow place— As I go through the woods I revolve them in my mind, and all the while they expand with my horizon as I advance–but not till I come out on the cliff–do they spread out before me –and unfold themselves fully. They are not only true but true for the widest horizon–and as far as I can see does their truth hold. The horizon line jagged with its dim mountains is their rhyme. Here they are native and aboriginal again–and they can afford to be ingenuous even

{*Two leaves missing*}

As for the Bráhmen who keeps house "Let him say what is true, but let him say what is pleasing; let him speak no disagreeable truth, nor let him speak agreeable falsehood: this is a primeval rule."
"Let him say "Well and good," or let him say "well" only; but let him not maintain fruitless enmity and altercation with any man".

{*Three-fifths page blank*}

is never offensive or ridiculous. Observe the modes in which modern literature is advertised, and then consider this Hindoo prospectus. Think what a reading public it addresses, what criticism it expects. Everywhere it demands the widest apprehension, and proceeds from the loftiest plateau of the soul. It is spoken unbendingly to its own level and does not imply any contemporaneous speaker. I cannot read a sentence without being elevated as upon the table land of the Gauhts; it has such a rhythm as the winds of the desert, such a tide as the Ganges, and seems as superior to criticism as the Himaleh mounts. So supremely religious is it that it imposes with authority on the latest age. The simple style of the ancient lawgiver implying all in the omission of all, proves a natural elevation of thought which the multiplied glosses of later days have striven in vain to slope up to. The whole book by noble gestures and inclinations seems to render words unnecessary. The

{*Three leaves missing*}

The Bráhmen is the ideal man. There is thus much to recommend the priesthood of all nations—that the priest represents in a degree that condition of virtue or true manhood to which the multitude aspire. The Druids like the Bráhmens paid no taxes, and were exempted from warfare and enjoyed many other privileges and immunities The clergy are even now a privileged class. The truth that poetry—religion and philosophy are one seems to have been obscurely expressed in the division of the Druidical order into Bards—Druids and Ouates.

The idea of man as expressed in the life of the Brahmen—is quite illimitable and sublime—there is no where a loftier conception of his destiny—he is at length lost in Brahmá himself—"the divine male." Indeed the distinction of races in this life is only the commencement of a series of degrees which ends in Brahmá.

With them life was an art—

He is the true artist whose life is his material—every stroke of the chisel must enter his own flesh and blood —and not grate dully on marble.

They were anxious to perform nobly and purely the most trivial actions—and banish vulgarity and grossness from their lives.

Some simple actions and conditions suggest
occasionally how this might be I see yonder some men
in a boat which floats boyantly amid the reflections
of these trees—like a feather poised in mid air or a
leaf wafted gently from its stem to the water without
once turning over. They seem very delicately to have
availed themselves of the natural laws—and their
floating there looks like a beautiful and successful
experiment in natural philosophy. It reminds me how
much more refined and noble the life of man might
be made—how its whole economy might be as beautiful
as a Tuscan villa—a new and more catholic art—

{*Ten leaves missing*}

These sublime passages as they proceeded from so
do they address what is most abiding and deepest
in human nature. In solitude and silence whether in
England or Arkansas their old dynasty and dispensation
begins again There is an orientalism in the most
restless pioneer The farthest west is the farthest east.
They belong to the noontide of the day the midsummer
of the year. When the snow has melted and the waters
evaporated in the spring—still their truth speaks fresh
and fair amid the drought. They are not new they
are not old, but wherever the sun shines or the night
broods they are true. They harmonize with the fragrance
of decayed pine leaves in sultry weather— The very
locusts and crickets of a summer day are but later
or earlier glosses on the Dherma Sástra of the Hindoos
—a continuation of the sacred code. In the New England
noontide I have discovered more materials of Oriental
history than the sanscrit contains or Sir W. Jones
has unlocked.

In my brain is the sanscrit. Was not Asia mapped
in my brain before it was in any geography?

The Védas and their Angas are not so ancient as serene contemplation. My mind contemplates them—as Brahmá his scribe.

{Three-fourths page blank, five leaves missing}

As for the tenets of the Brahmens I am not so much concerned to know what doctrines they held as what held them.— I find I can tolerate all the philosophies —atomists—pneumatologists—atheists—and theists—Plato —Aristotle—Leucippus—Democritus and Pythagoras —Zoroaster and Confucius. It is the attitude of these men more than any communication that charms me. — It is so rare to find a man musing. But between them and their commentators there is an endless dispute; but if it come to that—that you compare notes then you are all wrong.

As it is each takes me up into the serene heavens —and paints earth and sky afresh. Any sincere thought is irresistible—it lifts us to the zenith whither the smallest bubble rises as surely as the largest.

Every author—be he ancient lawgiver or modern philosopher—writes in the faith that his book is to be the final resting place of the sojourning soul and sets up his fixtures therein as for a more than oriental permanence, but it is only a caravansary—which we soon leave without ceremony. We read on his sign only —refreshment for man and beast—and a drawn hand directs to Isphahan or Bagdat.

I thank God that no Hindoo tyranny presided at the framing of the world—that I am a freeman of the universe and not sentenced to any caste

{One-half page blank, five leaves missing}

We have no divination or prospective memory.— but live as if it were impossible we should ever oversee ourselves again. So soon as we want more light it will inevitably come.

In view of the possible and future—we should live quite laxly—and be more straightened behind than before. If there were a true and natural development we should be all undefined in front our outlines dim and shadowy on that side—as the crown of a rising flower shows newly from day to day—and from hour to hour.

{*One and one-half pages blank, fifteen leaves missing*}

{*Back endpaper*}

· 7 ·

July 1842–April 13, 1843

{*Ninety pages missing*}

pulse out at that north eastern angle of the town.
In the south west part on either side of the stream
and a mile or more apart—like tanks or reservoirs of
water in the midst of the forest, at different elevations
above the river, lie White, Walden and Flints Ponds.

Today the pollywogs are in the different stages
of their transformation into frogs— Some with with
complete tails and only the rudiments of legs some with
their tails partially shrunk away and turned black,
some with perfect legs—and contracted heads, with only
a slight black projection half an inch long to mark
where the tail was.

Monday July 18th 1842

If the strong scent of the sweet fern does make
us faint at this season while climbing the bare hills
—the cool fragrance of swamp pink restores us when
threading the vallies between.

He who traverses the woodland paths will have
occasion to remember the small drooping bell-like
flowers, and slender red stem of the dog's-bane—which
were the subject of his study while resting from his
walk. And later in the year the coarse stem and berries
of the poke—which are both to be found in the remotest
and wildest scenes.

> One more is gone
> Out of the busy throng
> That treads these paths
> The church bell tolls
> Sadly its knell rolls
> To many hearths

But flowerbells toll not
Their echoes roll not

{Ten pages missing}

referred to some prior age of experience—of action
—they are the western reflections of an older day, but
they throw no substantial light over his morning.

He has to make a new experience however mean
which will be the basis of his manhood's success. The
fates are kind to none. Where there is any success
I am sure there has been a proportionate outlay of life.

In this view the youth is still of the party of the
old and has still to begin the new career.

The failures and reverses which await men—and one
after another sadden the brow of youth—add a dignity
to the prospect of human life, which no Arcadian
success would do.

No experience is so gross but it may bear etherial
fruit.

The heroic actions are performed by such as are
oppressed by the meanness of their lives. As in thickest
darkness the stars shine the brightest

Sir Philip Sidney seems to have been a man whose
many excellencies blinded men to his deficiencies as a
poet.

The praise of him which is in all books, and on
all men's lips is very vague and indiscriminate. As for
instance his "Arcadia" was "said by one living at or near
the time" of its publication to be "A book most famous
for rich conceits, and splendor of courtly expressions."

This reason is assigned why no monument should
be erected over him. That "he is his own monument,
whose memory is eternized in his writings, and who was

born into the world to shew unto our Age a sample
of antient virtue."

Another says of him "It was he whom Queen Elizabeth
called Her Philip, the Prince of Orange His master;
and whose friendship my Lord Brooks was so proud of,
that he would have no other epitaph on his grave than
this,

Here lieth Sir Philip Sidney's Friend."

Monday Aug. 8th 1842.

Gray was not a poet only a lover of poetry. He
cultivated poetry but the plant did not thrive.

He did no doubt possess a natural vein of poetry,
but this was not so rich or deep but that it was all
expended upon the imagery and ornament. Enough to
smooth the sound but not to gild the sense.

In the Churchyard the muse was a little more
prevalent with him and it will always be popular,
though the machinery is bare, because it retains the
atmosphere and tone of poetry.

How grand are mountains—by their elevation they
are placed at an infinite distance.

In the morning you see the distinct form of every
tree and creep happily along the dank roads like some
new creation of her exuberance. The morning hour is as
private as the evening— Not such privacy as the day
leaves but such as the day has not prophaned.

Tuesday Aug 9th 1842

There is then much to console the most wayworn
traveller upon the dustiest and dullest road that the
path his feet travel is so perfectly typical of human life.

Now climbing the highest mountains now descending
into the lowest vales. From the summits we see the
heavens and the horizon from the vales we look up to

the heights again. He is treading his old lessons still
— This which is such a wearines at

{*Twelve pages missing*}

so little earth. A blue Atlantic island where who knows
what islanders inhabit. While we sail near its shores
we see the waving of the trees and hear the lowing kine.
Voyagers of an etherial Polynesia

Tennyson's poems are polished harmonious–beautiful
–but they are for holidays not for work-days–they are
art not nature– I miss the warm breath of the man
upon my cheek– I must know that the breath in which
the poet utters his verse is the breath by which he
lives. That it was the inspiration of his natural life.
The poet only possesses a more earnest frank and public
nature, and tells the secrets of his race.

I would not disparage the exquisite sweetness of
these rhymes, but only regret that it is too often the
sweetness of sugar merely and not such as toil gives
to sour bread.– No pulses beat no human breath stirs
the leaves. I am not concerned about this man's life– I
feel no sympathy with his fate.

Tuesday 23d 1842

We were soon after reminded how every man has
his use–and what what one remembers another forgets
–what one knows another has not thought of The
man in the field could not tell us the name of the brook
only that it was *the* brook–but the young man going to
his work knew that it was Great Brook– Neither the
farmer nor the farmer's clock could tell us the hour but
the barefoot boy knew how near it was to schooltime.
In some remote village two shall grow up together
helpful and sufficient to each other, and yet with
information as various as if they were natives of different

hemispheres. They shall not even suspect each others reserved knowledge till the stranger comes by. Truely men do not have to travel to seek knowledge—for if they stay at home—she will travel to find them. Of as much learning as a man was born to be patron—so much shall find him out

{*Thirty pages missing*}

> In some withdrawn untraversed mead
> Let me sigh upon a reed
> In my place I still will stand
> A pattern unto the firm land
> Until revolving spheres come round
> To embrace my stable ground.

Gower writes like a man of common sense and good parts who had undertaken with steady rather than high purpose to do narrative with rhyme.

With little or no invention—merely following in the track of the old fablers—he employs his leisure and his pen-craft to entertain his readers, and speak a good word for the right side.

He has no fire or rather no blaze in him though occasionally some brands end peeps out from the ashes especially if in time of darkness you approach the heap—and if you extend your hands over him you experience a slight warm—more than else where— And even in fair weather you may see a slight smoke go

He narrates what Chaucer sometimes sings. With a fair understanding of the original he tells his story—and sometimes it gains a little in directness and point—or perhaps I should say in blunt plainness, in his hands.

The poet is partaker of a repose which is akin to the central law of the universe— No excitement is the mode in which he acts— He is perfectly poised, and rests as it were on the axis of the universe. He cannot but be wise and holy and brave.

There is a great significance in the fact—that we can never permit the man to cease to be a child. We say he must at any rate be a grown child.

There is a littleness in him who is made aware of antagonism The opposition I feel reproaches me.

{*Eight pages missing*}

He writes to impatient readers who wish to learn the facts

He might have been a teamster and written his rhymes on his wagon seat, he speaks with bar-room bluntness.

> Oh ye proud days of Europes middle age
> Transfer your pomp to this my humble page
> > The moon hung low in Provence vales
> > Twas night upon the midland sea
> > Sweet France was wooed by Afric gales
> > And paid her—in her minstrelsy.
> > Along the Rhone there moves a band
> > Their banner floating to the breeze
> > Of mail-clad men with iron hand
> > And steel on breast and knees.
> > The herdsman following his droves
> > Far in the night alone
> > Read faintly through the olive groves
> > > T'was Godfrey of Boulogne.
>
> > The mist still slumbered on the heights
> > The glaciers rested in the shade
> > The stars withdrew with faded lights
> > The moon went down the glade
> > Proud Jura saw the day from far
> > And whispered it to Europes plain.
> > She heard the din of coming war
> > But told it not again.
> > The goat herd seated on the rocks
> > Dreaming of peace of battles none
> > Was wakend by his startled flocks
> > > T'was Godfrey of Boulogne.

Night hung upon the Danube's stream
Deep midnight on the vales
Along the shore no beacons gleam
No sound is on the gales
The Turkish Lord has banished care
The Harem sleep a sleep profound
Save one fair Georgian sitting there
As if she heard a waking sound
The lightning flashed a transient gleam
A glancing banner shone
A host swept swiftly down the stream
Twas Godfrey of Boulogne

Twas noon upon Byzantium
On street and tower and sea
On Europes edge a warlike hum

{*Thirty pages missing*}

Silently we unlatch the door—letting the drift fall
in— And step forth like knights encased in steel—to
sport with the cutting air. Still through the drifts I see
the farmers early candle—like a paled star—emitting a
lonely beam from the cottage windows—as one by one the
sluggish smokes begin to ascend from the chimneys
of the farm houses from midst the trees from midst the
snows—from midst the town— Thus from each domestic
altar does incense go up each morning to heaven. Anon
the stars lose some of their sparkle and a deep blue
mist skirts the eastern horizon— A lurid and brazen
light foretels the approaching day. You hear the sound
of woodchopping at the farmer's door—the baying of
the house dog and the distant clarion of cocks. The
frosty air seems to convey only and with new distinctness
the finer particles of sound to our ears. It comes clear
and round like a bell. as if there were fewer impediments
than in the green atmosphere of summer to make it
faint and ragged. And besides all nature is tight-drawn

and sonorous like seasoned wood. Sounds now come
to our ears from a greater distance in the horizon
than in the summer– For then nature is never silent
–and the chirp of crickets is incessant but now the
farthest and faintest sound takes possession of the
vacuum.

Even the barking of dogs and lowing of kine is
melodious. The jingling the ice on the trees is sweet
and liquid.– I have heard a sweeter music in some
lone dale where flowed a rill released by the noonday sun
from its frosty fetters–while the icicles were melting
upon the apple trees, and the ever present chic-a-dee–and
nuthatch flitted about.

> Now melts the snow
> In this warm sun
> The meadows flow
> The streamlets run.

> The chic a dee
> Lisps in the tree
> The winter bee
> not fearing frost
> The nuthatch creeps
> The marmot sleeps

> The flag out peeps
> The rabbit leaps
> Beside the brook
> The mouse out-creeps

> The apples thaw
> The ravens caw
> The squrrels gnaw
> The frozen fruit

> To their retreat
> I track the feet
> Of mice that eat
> The apples root.

The spring is born
The wild bees bum
The insects hum
And trees drop gum
And winter's gone
And summer's come

The ferret weeps
The marmot sleeps
The owlet keeps
    In his snug nook

The small nuthatch
The bark doth scratch
Some worm to catch
    At any cost.

I melt I flow
    And fuming run
Like melting snow
    In this warm sun.

The willows droop
The alders stoop
The pheasants group
    Beneath the snow

Friday Oct 14th 1842

The snow dust falls
The otter crawls
The partridge calls
    Far in the wood

The traveller dreams
The tree-ice gleams
The blue-jay screams
    In angry mood

The fishes glide
From side to side
In the clear tide
    The ice below

The catkins green
     Cast o'er the scene
     A summer sheen.
          A genial glow

The axe resounds
And bay of hounds
And tinkling sounds
     Of wintry fame.

The hunters horn
     Awakes the dawn
On fields forlorn
          And frights the game.

The tinkling air
Doth echo bear
To rabbit's lair
     With dreadful din

She scents the air
And far doth fare
Returning where
     She did begin

The fox stands still
upon the hill
Not fearing ill
     From trackless wind.

But to his foes
     The still wind shows
          In treacherous snows
               His tracks behind

{One-fifth page blank}

Sat Oct 15th 1842.

Thursday I went over to Nawshawtuct only to look
into the horizon, for as long as I have lived here, and as
many times as I have been there, I could not have
told how it appeared. When I discovered over how many

miles of Bedford and Carlisle and Acton my eye ranged,
even into Billerica and Framingham—which had never
occurred to me before—though I was familar with
the roads leading thither— The inward horizon seemed
proportionally to extend itself, and embrace Many
Actons and Carlisles, and I thought I would not travel
to see these places, and balk the fates who placed
them thus under my eyes. The most familiar and best
known facts leave no distinct impression on our minds,
no man can tell at evening how his horizon looks.
We do not know till the time comes which way the river
runs and the hills range. Or that the hill takes in our
homestead in its sweep. At first our birth and existence
sunders all things, as if like a wedge we had been
thrust up through nature—and not till the scar heals,
do we begin to see her unity.

{*Sixteen pages missing*}

And again we find him participating heartily and
bearing off the palm even in the birth day tournaments
or tilting matches of the Queen. Of this sort was his
greatness— The greatness of a man with the littleness
of a boy.

His Behavior towards the Earl is the foulest stain
upon his escutcheon—it is the one which it is hardest to
reconcile with his natural nobleness and generosity.
Nor are the terms on which he was the *friend* of Cecil
any more tolerable to consider. His greatnes herein
deserted him as in his feigning himself sick. He is said
to have remembered his behavior toward Essex with
regret. There was here the spirit of revenge—which is
most unheroic—

He is said to have first introduced the potatoe from
Virginia and the cherry from the Canaries into Ireland
where was his own garden.

On his trial "He answered with that temper, wit,
learning, courage, and judgment, that save that it went
with the hazzard of his life, it was the happiest day
that ever he spent– The two first that brought the
news to the king were Roger Ashton, and a Scotsman,
whereof one affirmed that never any man spake so
well in times past, nor would do in the world to come:
And the other said, that whereas when he saw him
first, he was so led with the common hatred, that he
would have gone a hundred miles to have seen him
hanged, he would, ere he parted, have gone a thousand
to have saved his life."

In connexion with his behavior to Essex it should
be said that by his behavior on his own trial he in a
great measure removed the ill will which existed against
him on that account.– One says he "behaved himself
so worthily, so wisely, and so temperately, that in
half a day the mind of all the company was changed
from the extremest hate to the extremest pity."

Another–"to the lords humble, but not prostrate; to
the jury affable, but not fawning; to the king's counsel
patient, but not yielding to the imputations laid upon
him, or neglecting to repel them with the spirit which
became an injured and honorable man."

He said he had been "a soldier, a sea-captain and a
courtier,"

In the tower he is said to have "spent

{Twenty-two pages missing}

Friday Nov 11th 1842

I am charmed when in midsummer traversing some
remote fields set round with birchen leafy woods–where
under the low rustle of leaves is heard the faint
twittering of all birds–the old-fashioned farmer describes
to me the pranks of the red-mavis–for so long has the

classic name survived, It is like a fresh line of very
old English poetry.

The farmers boys thus interpret this bird's song
when seated on some birch in the neighboring copse
it entertains them in cornplanting– They will tell you
that the bird says drop it–drop it–drop-it–cover it
up–cover it up–plow it plow it plow–harrow it harrow
it–pull it up–pull it up. pull it up.

What a revelation and influx of life it is in the winter
months to be carried back to midsummer–and genial
spring by such hints as the "larvae of beetles". I do
not often listen to the "goodness of God" with so much
happiness.

To know that while the earth is thus frost-bound
the larvae of beetles are still to be found about the roots
of all plants

To hear of the curlew

When you have most talent you have least genius
– The equilibrium is always preserved. When least is
done most is adoing.

Wednesday Nov 16th 1842

In many parts the merrimack is as fresh and natural
as ever– In many parts of its course the shore and
surrounding scenery exhibit only the revolutions of
nature– The pine stands up erect on its brink–and the
alders and willows fringe its edge–and only the beaver
and the redman are wanting to complete the picture.
Though it the lumberer that wakes the echoes, still
they are the everlasting and natural echoes that are
waked. The immense unseen back ground which
reflects the sound is as primitive as ever. The round
timber rolling down the steep banks or of the distant
scow just

{Sixteen pages missing}

Tuesday Jan 3d 1843

I hardly know of any subject upon which so little
to the purpose has been said as Musick–few ever have
indicated their sense of this inadequacy so that I am
inclined to mark a passage which expressess any such
feeling– Richter's single line is a gem. De Quincey
shows that he heard music in the lines– "Music is an
intellectual or a sensual pleasure, according to the
temperament of him who hears it. And, by the bye, with
the exception of the fine extravaganza on that subject
in Twelfth Night, I do not recollect more than one
thing said adequately on the subject of music in all
literature: it is a passage in the Religio Medici of
Sir T. Browne; and, though chiefly remarkable for its
sublimity, has also a philosophic value, inasmuch as it
points to the true theory of musical effects."

The whole of the passage referred to is this. "It is
my temper, and I like it the better, to affect all harmony;
and sure there is music, even in the beauty and the
silent note which Cupid strikes, far sweeter than the
sound of an instrument. For there is a music wherever
there is a harmony, order, or proportion; and thus
far we may maintain "the music of the spheres": for
those well-ordered motions, and regular paces, though
they give no sound unto the ear, yet to the understanding
they strike a note most full of harmony. Whatsoever
is harmonically composed delights in harmony, which
makes me much distrust the symmetry of those heads
which declaim against all church-music. For myself, not
only from my (Catholic)* obedience, but my particular
genius, I do embrace it: for even that vulgar and
tavern-music, whicch makes one man merry, another

*not in most editions

mad, strikes in me a deep fit of devotion, and a profound
contemplation of the first composer. There is something
in it of divinity more than the ear discovers: it is an
hieroglyphical and shadowed lesson of the whole
world, and creatures of God,–such a melody to the ear,
as the whole world, well understood, would afford
the understanding. In brief, it is a sensible fit of that
harmony which intellectually sounds in the ears of God.
[It unties the ligaments of my frame, takes me to
pieces, dilates me out of myself, and by degrees methinks
resolves me into heaven.)* I will not say, with Plato,
the soul is an harmony, but harmonical, and hath
its nearest sympathy unto music: thus some, whose
temper of body agrees, and humors the constitution of
their souls, are born poets, though indeed all are
naturally inclined unto rhythm."

Monday Jan. 16 1843

  I would fain describe myself though I am a rather
uninterresting object to myself– I force myself even now
to write this. What am I at present? A diseased bundle
of nerves standing between time and eternity like a
withered leaf that still hangs shivering on its stem. A
more miserable object one could not well imagine–but
still very dull very insipid to think of. I suppose I
may live on not a few years–trailing this carcass
after me–or perhaps trailing after it– Healthy I have
been–for periods perhaps healthier than most– But
there were short

*'omitted in most editions'

{Ninety-four pages missing}

Fog

Dull water spirit—and Protean god
Descended cloud fast anchored to the earth
That drawest too much air for shallow coasts
Thou ocean branch that flowest to the sun
Incense of earth, perfumed with flowers—
Spirit of lakes and rivers—seas and rills
Come to revisit now thy native scenes
Night thoughts of earth—dream drapery
Dew cloth—and fairy napkin
Thou wind-blown meadow of the air

Tuesday April 11th 1843.

Wednesday

Poetry is a purer draught of life.

Thursday

I am pleased with the manner in which Quarles
and his contemporaries speak of nature. The utmost
poetry of their expression is after all a sort of gallantry
—as of a knight to his lady— They do not speak as
sincere lovers of nature or as very conversant with her
—but as preserving a thorough respect for her, and
a good title to her acquaintance. They can speak of and
to her well and manfully because their lips are not
closed by affection

"The pale-faced lady of the black-eyed light,"
says Quarles.

I do not think there was in that age an unusual
devotion to nature—but she certainly held her court
then, and all authors were her gentlemen and esquires
then and had always ready an abundance of courtly
expressions.

Quarles is always full-mouthed—he is not often weak
or shallow though he is coarse and untasteful. He writes
lines which it employs the whole tongue to utter.

He runs into conceits as well as Herbert He uses many able bodied and strong-backed words—which have a certain rustic fragrance and force like country men come to town—as if now first devoted to literature, after having served sincere and stern purposes:

{Remaining leaves of MS Volume 7 missing}

·8·

April–September 1, 1843

{*142 pages missing*}

find my thought more warm and cheery than when
I remember the summer–and yet not by reason of the
contrast–but a very positive genialness it is. All things
upon the surface of the earth are still as if they were
not–it is a slumber–not the earth's last sleep but its
first. The meadow mice have crept into their snug
galleries in the sod–the owl sits in a hollow tree in the
depth of the swamp–the rabbit the marmot are all
housed. The watch lies by the hearth–and cattle are
hushed in the stalls– But while the earth thus slumbers
all the air is alive with feathery flakes descending.
Some Ceres or minerva reigns–showering the silvery
grain on all the fields and in every nook. How kind
this work. I have seen a few whose spirits it would
delight to perform this fairy work. Perhaps it will be so
–that nature will say you shall snow over hamlet and
wood–now plastering the roofs now dallying with the
twigs of the alder and willow by the river-side.– You
shall rain–and you shall blow. &c. These are the environs
of our life. I recognise in my thoughts all seasons the
difference of the seasons–now a snug inward cheer
then a summer luxuriousnes and greenness. From our
comfortable pillows we lend our warm sympathy to
the Siberian traveller on whose morning route the
sun–is even then rising–we make one of the group with
the Kanskalkan and his dogs–we hie us to dreariest
moor–or to warm boudoirs. We are transported in
imagination to the encampment of the lonely fur trader
on lake winnipeg or Athabasca–we climb the Ural
mountains or the Jura in our dreams– And the cold frigid

zones seems to melt and is another torrid zone for us.
Now for a three months the human destiny is wrapped
in furs.

{Thirty-four pages missing}

All the water on the globe insulates us in a kettle—and
is either hastening to become ice and snow or ocean
and steam. The tropical waves are hastening to become
polar ice and the polar ice to lapse under the equator.

The foot of the skater passes swiftly oer the deep dark
waters where the stately pickerel lurked in the long
corridors formed by the bulrush—enjoying the dim light.

Quarles is not to be passed by because he has
indubitably the pronounciation of a poet though he
stutters— If he could speak out smooth and plain it
would be verse. He can with far more pleasure be read
than criticised. He certainly speaks the English tongue
with a right manly accent—only he has not refined
his speech enough. He has not been sufficiently chary
of his words.

He is one of those whose claim to be styled poet is
based upon their skill in the use of the English language.
His poetry is a "confessions" It is repentance. There
is as much death as life in them—a musty odor.

Wednesday Ap. 19th 1843
I should prefer that my farm be bounded by a river
— It is to live on the outside of the world—and to be
well flanked on one side— It would increase my sense
of security and my energy and boyancy when I would
take any step, as the Geometer cannot proceed without
his base line is given.

You may go far up within the country and meet no
town— By a perfectly level road such as no engineer

constructs–never climbing a hill– But from the interior
to the sea-shore does the river like a judicious and
patient conduct us by gentle imperceptible gradation
without any abrupt descents but by a most gently
inclined plane by the easiest steps descending into the
vales by broad and easy stairs– The tired though
unhasty traveller could not choose more skilfully his
path. And thus the most yielding and easily influenced
of all the elements, holds the evenest and steadiest

{Ten pages missing}

end of the tongue– I may have a good deal still without
having any thing to say.– Indeed the largest allowance
of any thing unless it be nonsense is none to speak of.

It is harder to write great prose than to write verse,
it implies a life of practical elevation– The whole
man must have been pervaded with the grandeur of
his thought. It shows how he lives every day. It is a
conscious power.

Thursday Ap 27th

The dumb erect fisherman made to be enveloped in
clouds and snows. His lines set in some retired cove
We skate now near to to where the blackbird the king
bird the pewee hung their nests over the water–and
there yet they hang empty. We can go near to the
hornets in these meadows suspended from the maple.
In the winter nature is a cabinet of curiosities She
is full of dried specimens in their natural order and
positions– The meadows and forests everywhere are a
hortus siccus.

The leaves and grass stand perfectly pressed by
the winters air without bands or gum arabick. The birds

nests are hung on no artifical peg but where the builder placed them.

We go about to inspect the summer's work. See what a growth have got the alders the willows and maples –testifying of how many warm suns and fertilizing dews and showers And now they rest– See what strides they took in the luxuriant summer–and anon one of these dormant buds will carry the bough upward another span into the trackless atmosphere– In this hollow tree the wood duck reared her brood–and slid away to feed every day among the reeds of yonder fen.

Where now we skim lightly over glare ice ice–lately "the mower whet his scythe." In this forked willow twig hangs the nest of the Maryland yellow-throat

How many gay warblers now following the sun, have radiated from this nest of silver birch and thistle-down — on the swamps' outer edge hang these deserted cities, where no foot penetrated in summer– These super-marine villages

All man's aspirations are symbolized by some part of nature– He wishes to sail away from winter–and enjoy perennial summer– The birds do this. It is not very hard. They do not go into the ground but when the cold comes they fly away.

Scholars have for the most part a diseased way of looking at the world– For by the world frequently they mean a few uneasy men or women in New York or London who take up very little room in the universe –who might all be concealed in the grass of one prairie.

They describe their world as old or new–healthy or diseased–when it should seem to be like their old and new books–a little dust more or less in their library. Their history is but a troubled dream– What do they know of the *old world*? I read their books sometimes sad

and earnest or confident and congratulatory and then
go abroad from under this roof of cedar shingles
and eastern boards—and find several things which they
did not consider— Their conclusions seem imperfect

In winter summer is in the heart of man— Thither
have all birds and beasts and insects migrated— Round
the warm spring in his breast are gathered the robin
and the lark still— Man is a summer. All the greenness
of vegetation is there. A healthy man is the complement

{*Two pages missing*}

Thursday May 19th 1843.
The serene and innocent beauty of the fields on
a winter's day is not to be parallelled by the most
luxuriant summer. Fine crystals of a thousand hues—and
stubble dangling with jewels suggest an unspeakable
tenderness in nature. How near and real is that Love
and Elysium of which the poets dream!—which way did
the vision disappear! To the bad there is no memory
of good. Young God is there
June 19th
Marlowe had many of the qualities of a great poet.
He had the poetic madness, as Drayton justly says
— And we read his Dr Faustus—Dido Queen of Carthage
—and Hero & Leander with great pleasure. Especially
the last. He was even worthy in some respects to
preceeded Shakespeare. Such a poet seems to have run
to waste mainly for want of seclusion and solitude—as if
mere pause and deliberation would have added a new
element of greatness to his poetry—

In his unquestionable fine and heroic tone it seems as
if he had the raresst part of genius—and education
could have added the rest. I do not know but the Hero and
Leander is purely imagined throughout— It can be

read so—which is the best evidence—it is like Shakspere's
Venus and Adonis—in this—and tells much better for
the author's character than the anecdotes that survive.

{One-half page blank, 252 pages missing}

Tonight while I am arranging these sprigs of white
cedar in my scrap-book I am reminded by their fragrance
of the pines and hemlocks which over hang the river
in my native town. I love the whole race of pines They
address my senses with the authority of a revelation
— The pine is a sacred tree

Men no where live as yet a natural life. The poets
even have not described it. Man's life must be of equal
simplicity and sincerity with nature, and his action's
harmonize with her grandeur and beauty. I do not
know of any reformer who is ultra plus ne one unworthy
to speak with critical reserve on this subjects.

Shall we suffer a single action to be mean? We have
now our sabbaths and our moments of inspiration
—as if these could be too protracted or constant. I see
plainly that my own meanness is that which which
robs me of my birth-right—and shuts me out from the
society of the gods.

The life of men will ere long be of such purity and
innocence, that it will deserve to have the sun to light it
by day and the moon by night.— to be ushered in by
the freshness and melody of spring—to be entertained by
the luxuriance and vigor of summer—and matured
and solaced by the hues and dignity of Autumn.

Monday 14th

When we withdraw a little from the village—and
perceive how it is embosomed in nature—where perhaps
its roofs are gleaming in the setting sun— We wonder
if the life of its inhabitants might not also be thus

natural and innocent reflecting the aspects of nature.
We are apt to view again the life of the haymaker
of such simplicity and innocence as his occupation
Do not the gleaming crops—the verdant lawns—the
springing groves—the flocks and herds—suggest what
kind of a man the farmer should be?

In the first place his life must be serene and calm.

{*Ten pages missing*}

No where east or west is man living a fair natural
life—around which the vine clings—and which the
elm shadows— The witch hazel late into October?
putting forth its yellow Autumnal flowers blooms in
no garden of man's. The natural world alas has no
inhabitants— The sun and moon rise and set in vain.

For the most part our authors are like vines pruned
late in the spring which bleed to death in the endeavor
to heal their wounds.

Friday 25th

He who is not touched by the poetry of Channing
—Very—Emerson and the best pieces of Bryant may be
sure he has not drunk deep of the Pierian spring.
Channing's might very properly as has been suggested
be called poetry for poets—it is so fine a vein that it
floats in the common air and is not perceived. It is a
richer and deeper tone than Tennyson's with its
own melody—but the melody of the language will be
sought in vain without the melody of the thought for a
guide.

We read Marlowe as so much poetical pabulum
—it is food for poets it is water from the Castalian
spring.   some of the atmosphere of Parnassus raw and
crude indeed and at times breezy but pure, / and bracing.

Quarles has a sturdy fibre—a true poet though not

polished—an austere and savage Eremite. He did stand
cheek by jowl with nature and reality—and sturdily lived
a man's life—fighting the devil and his angels.

Spenser was not an *actual* poet. He is not sublime—or
morally grand and inspired—but led a life of imagination
above the vulgar. His are not words for a dying man
to hear, but to be sung in a summer bower—sweet,
and graceful, and full of hope.

one should not read the whole of Marvell who wishes
to enjoy a part He will be disappointed to find him
so frivolous and mean—at times.

{End of MS Volume 8}

Sat Aug 26 1843—

The future will no doubt be a more natural life
than this. We shall be acquainted and shall use flowers
and stars, and sun and moon, and occupy this nature
which now stands over and around us. We shall reach
up to the stars and pluck fruit from many parts of
the universe. We shall purely use the earth and not
abuse it— God is in the breeze and whispering leaves
and we shall then hear him. We live in the midst of
all the beauty and grandeur that was ever described or
conceived.

We have hardly entered the vestibule of Nature.
It was here be assured under these heavens that the
gods intended our immortal life should pass—these stars
were set to adorn and light it—these flowers to carpet it

Monday 28th

I would have the man who is coming to see me
pause by the way and consider if he is prompted by a
laudable curiosity—if he has anything to communicate

and really wishes to stand over against me come
what may. I shall be truly glad to ram him if he will
not run.

Sep. 1st 1843

Some of Spensers shorter pieces in which there is
no affectation of an antique style are a relief after the
perusal of the Fairie Queene—and they make us regret
that he was not equally simple and natural in that
greater poem.

I have made a discovery in Quarles. Even the
Shepheards Oracles which I read yesterday at the Soc.
Library yielded an almost unaccountable pleasure—for
they thus might offend the taste in many respects— It
was like conversing with a man of strong unaffected
sense. The words he speaks are made of the very breath
by which he lives, and not of some passing wind for
any artful purpose. They are a vital breath. He is
admirable for his language. When he is unhappy and
coarse or ungraceful he oftimes but uttters what
the poet of more taste represses. He does not distrust the
muse— Here and there there are things memorable
and entirely uttered—born but to be expressed as it
were, as there are not in many a finer poet. But such
a master of speech is extremely rare—one who could use
his mother-tongue. It is delightful to hear with what
a sound and relish he utters his words. Such sturdiness
must be forever respectable. Perhaps culture would
only have drawn the pen over the ruder parts without
increasing the number of brilliant passages.— If
he is coarse and unpoetic we may say at any rate that
it costs him no labor—he is never elaborate nor is his
grace more expensive. It is most freely borne—it is

twice blest—it blesseth him that gives and him that takes.

He has sense enough to stock a dozen poets we could name formed after a classic model— It is like the strong and often soaring flight of a vulture—   Compared compared with the fastidious wing of blue jay or parroket. Some times he soars near to the sun though again he gorges himself with carrion.

And after all do we actually get abroad— Alas! we only postpone staying at home.

{*One page blank*}

·9·

September 24, 1843–after January 7, 1844

{*Four pages missing*}

Sunday 24th

The poet is he that hath fat enough like bears and marmots to suck his claws o' winters. He feeds on his own marrow. He hybernates in this world, till spring breaks. He records a moment of pure life. Who can see these cities and say that there is any life in them. I walked through New York yesterday—and met no real and living person.

I love to think of dormice and all that tribe of dormant creatures—who have such a superfluity of life while man is pining—enveloped in thick folds of life—impervious to winter. I love to think as I walk over the snowy plain of those happy dreamers that lies in the sod

The poet is a sort of dormouse, early in the autumn he goes in to winter quarters till the sun shall fetch the year about.

But most men lead a starved existence like hawks that would fain keep on the wing, and catch but a sparrow now and then.

I hate museums, there is nothing so weighs upon the spirits. They are catacombs of Nature. They are preserved death. One green bud of Spring one willow catkin, one faint trill from some migrating sparrow, might set the world on its legs again.

I know not whether I muse most at the bodies stuffed with cotton and sawdust—or those stuffed with bowels and fleshy fibre.

The life that is in a single green weed is of more worth than all this death. They are very much like the written history of the world—and I read Rollin and Ferguson with the same feeling

It is one great and rare merit in the old tragedy that it says something The words slide away very fast but toward some conclusion— It has to do with things and not words—   And the reader feels as if he were advancing. It does not seem to make much odds what the author has to say at this distance of time, if he only deliver himself of it in a downright and manly way. We like Marlowe because he is so plain spoken and direct and does not waste the time.

I think that the mythological system interwoven as it is with the astronomical, points to time when a grander and mightier genius inhabited the earth than now. There is a grandeur and perfection about this scheme which match with the architecture of the heavens themselves.

The villager crossing the bridge stood awhile to gaze at us gliding swiftly from his sight—following our other fates.

We stopped awhile at a place called the holt, a sort of bayou or cove on the side of the river—to look for blue-berries in a swamp near by—but we were too late.

They say that Carew was a laborious writer but his poems do not show it— They are finished but do not show the marks of the chisel. Drummond was indeed a quiddler—with little fire and fibre Rather a taste for poetry—than a taste of it

Monday 25th 1843

How tremendously moral is our life. After all no man can be said to live much in the senses, but every moment is the product of so much character. What

painters of scenery we are. We impart to the landscape
the perfect colors of our minds

26th

After all we draw on very gradually in English
literature to Shakspeare–through Peele and Marlowe
–to say nothing of Raleigh and Spenser–and Sidney. We
hear the same great tone already sounding–to which
Shakspeare added a deeper strain of wisdom Its chief
characteristics of reality and unaffected manliness
are there and they constitute even a more important
distinction than the greater or less wisdom–for the least
wisdom of the most foolish is mysterious enough The
more one reads of the literature of those times the
more does acquaintance divest the genius of shakspeare
of the false mystery which has thickened around it
and leave it shrouded in the grander mystery of daylight.
The critic of Shakspeare has for the most part, made
his contemporaries less that he might make shakspeare
more–but we have no doubt there were mystics in
England in that day whose faith was darkness to
shakspeare himself

A cheerful wit marrked that age far enough removed
from the solemn wisdom of this– The men of genius
were at the same time the merriest and most full of life,
as they would ever naturally be. See what another
thing was fame and a name then than now–they were
Kit Marlowe and George (Peele) and Will (Shakspeare)
and Ben Jonson.– Great fellows–chaps–

Thursday 28th

We have never conceived how many natural
phenomena would be revealed to a simpler and more
natural life. Rain, wind, sunshine, day, and night,
would be very different to experience if we were always
true. We cannot deceive the ground under our feet.

We never try. But we do not treat each other with the same sincerity. How much more wretched would the life of man be if there was the same formality, and reserve between him and his intercourse with nature that there is in human society.

It is a strange world we live in— With this incessant dream of friendship and love where is any? Genius can not do without these—it pines and withers. I believe that the office of music is to remind us continually of the reality and necessity of the fine elements of love and friendship. One mood always forgets another.— and till we have loved we have not imagined the heights of love. Love is an incessant inspiration. By the dews of love the arid desert of life is made as fragrant and blooming as a paradise.

The world waits yet to see man act greatly and divinely upon man— What are social influences as yet? The poor human flower wouuld hold up its drooping head at once if this sun should shine on it. That is the dyspepsia with which all men ail.

In purer more intellectual moods we translate our gross experiences in to fine moralities.

Sometimes we would fain see events as merely material—wooden—rigid—dead—but again we are reminded that we actually inform them with little life by which they live. That they are the slaves and creatures of our conduct.

When dull and sensual I believe these are cornstalks good for cattle no more nor less— The laws of nature are science but in an enlightened moment they are morality and modes of divine life. In a medium intellectual state they are aesthetics.

What makes us think that time has lapsed is that we have relapsed.

Strictly speaking there can be no criticism of poetry

other than a separating of that which is poetry from
that which is not—a detecting of falsehood. From the
remotest antiquity we detect in the literature of all
nations here and there words of a loftier tone and
purport than are required to transact the daily business
of life. As Scott says they float down the sea of time
like the fragments of a parted wreck. Sounds which
echo up among the stars rather than through the vallies
of earth but yet are heard plainly enough to remind
men of other spheres of life and activity.

Perhaps I may say that I have never had a deeper
and more memorable experience of life—its great
serenity, than when listening to the trill of a tree-sparrow
among the huckleberry bushes after a shower. It is a
communication to which a man must attend in solitude
and silence, and may never be able to tell to his brother.

The least sensual life is that experienced through
pure senses. We sometimes hear—and the dignity of that
sense is asserted—

Friday 29th

I am winding up my music box and as I pause
meanwhile the strains burst forth like a pent up fountain
of the middle ages. Music is strangely allied to the
past—every era has its strain. It awakens and colors my
memories.

The first sparrow of spring. The year beginning
with younger hope than ever. The first silvery warblings
heard over the bare dank fields—as if the last flakes
of winter tinkled. What then are histories, chronologies
—traditions, and written revelations. Flakes of warm
sunlight fall on the congealed earth—the brooks and rills
sing carols and glees for the spring.

The marsh hawk already seeks the first slimy life

that awakes– The sough of melting snow is heard in the
dells of the wood, by the sunny river banks, and the
ice dissolves in the seething ponds, evaporating hourly.
The earth sends forth as it were an inward green
heat and the grass flames up on the warm hill sides
like a green spring fire. Methinks the sight of the first
sod of fresh grass in the spring would make the reformer
reconsider his schemes, the faithless and despairing
man revive– The grass blade is a perpetual growth a
long green ribbon–streaming from the sod into the
summer–checked in deed by the frost–but anon pushing
on again lifting its withered hay with fresh life below
– I have seen where early in spring the clumps of grass
stood with their three inches of new green upholding
their withered spears of the last autumn, and from
year to year the herds browse and the mower cuts from
this never failing out-welling supply–what their needs
require.

So the human life but dies down to the surface, but
puts forth a green blade to eternity.

The grass blade is as steady a growth as the rill
which leaks out of the ground–indeed it is almost
identical with that, for in the vigorous fertile days
of June–when the rills are dry the grass blades are their
channel.

When the ground is completely bare of snow and
a few warm days have dried its surface– It is pleasant
to compare the faint tender signs of the infant year just
peeping forth–with the stately beauty of the withered
vegetation which has withstood the winter–the various
thistles which have not yet sown their seeds– The
graceful reeds and rushes, whose winter is more gay and
stately than their summer–as if not till then was their
beauty ripe.

I never tire of admiring their arching drooping

sheaf like tops. It is like summer to our winter memories.
One of the forms which art loves to perpetuate. Wild
oats perchance—and life ever lasting—whose season has
now arrived. These with their seeds entertain the
earliest birds these unexhausted granaries of the winter.

We are obliged to respect that custom which stamps
the loaf of bread with the sheaf of wheat and the
sickle. Men have come at length after so many centuries
to regard these gifts properly. The gift of bread even
to the poor is perhaps better received than any other
—more religiously given and taken and is not liable to be
a stone. The manner in which men consider husbandry
—is marked and worthy of the race. They have slowly
learned thus much.

Let the desparing race of men know that there is in
Nature no sign of decay—but universal uninterrupted
vigor— All waste and ruin has a speedy period. Who ever
detected a wrinkle on her brow—or a weather seam
—or a grey hair on her crown or a rent in her garment.
No one sees nature, who sees her not as young and
fresh—without history. We may have such intercourse
today as we imagine to constitute the employment
of gods. We live here to have intercourse with rivers
forests mountains—beasts and men.

How few do we see conversing with these things.
We think the ancients were foolish who worshipped
the sun. I would worship it forever if I had grace to do
so. Observe how a New England farmer moves in
the midst of nature—his potato and grain fields—and
consider how poets have dreamed that the more religious
shepherd lived—and ask which is the wiser, which
made the highest use of nature.

As if the Earth were made to yield pumpkins mainly
— Did you never observe that the seasons were ripening
another kind of fruit?

Men have a strange taste for death who prefer to
go to museums to behold the cast off garments of life
—rather than handle the life itself. Where is the proper
Herbarium—the cabinet of shells—the museum of
skeletons but in the meadow—where the flower bloomed
—or by the sea-side where tide cast up the fish—or on
the hills where the beast laid down his life. Where the
skeleton of the traveller reposes in the grass there
may it profitably be studied. What right has mortal man
to parade any skeleton on its legs when once the
gods have unloosed its sinews—what right to imitate
heaven with his wires—or to stuff the body with sawdust
—which nature has decreed shall return to dust again?

All the fishes that swim in the ocean can hardly atone
for the wrong done by stuffing and varnishing and
encasing under glass the relics of one inhabitant of the
deep.— Go to Italy and Egypt if you would behold
these things where bones are the natural product of
the soil which bears tombs and catacombs. Would you
live in a dried specimen of a world? a pickled world.
Embalming is a sin against heaven and earth—against
heaven who has recalled the soul—and set free the
servile elements—against earth who is robbed of her dust.

I have had my right perceiving senses so disturbed
in these haunts as for long to mistake a veritable living
man, in the attitude of repose musing like myself
as the place requires, for a stuffed specimen. So are men
degraded in consequence.

                                        Monday Oct 2nd.

There must be all degrees of life from a stone if we
can find any starting point—to God. There are very few
fibres in the stone—very little organism. Sometimes
we are conscious of the simple but slow and insensate
life which it lives. We are mere pudding stone or scoriae
in the world. But suddenly we may be informed with

new life—and pass through all the scales of being up to
the most complex and nearest to God—furnished with
countless nerves and imbibing more and more of
vital air or inspiration.

How suddenly and silently do all the eras which
we call history awaken and glimmer in us— All the
dynasties that have past away are still passing in our
memory. There is room for Alexander to march and
for Hannibal to Conquer— The grand three act drama
of past present and future where does its scene lie
but within the compass of this same private life which
beats within its ribbed wall?

We may say that our knowledge is infinite—for we
never discovered its limits—and what we know of
infinity is a part of our knowledge still.

History is the record of my experience I can read
only my own story, never a syllable of another man's.

{*Two pages missing*}

Friday 6th

Gleams of life and a wise serenity pass over us from
time like flakes of sunlight over the fields in cloudy
weather. In some happier moment when more sap
flows in the withered stalk of my life I recognize myself
as a part of the hour and Syria or India stretch away
from my present, as they do in history.

Sunday 8th

Daniel does really sometimes deserve praise for
his moderation, and you find him risen into poetry before
you know it. Some strong sense appears in his epistles
—but you have to remember so often in what age he
wrote, and yet that Shakspeare was his contemporary.
In his style, and what may be called the tricks of the
trade, he is really in advance of his age—much of it.

He strikes us like a retired scholar who has a small
vein of poesy which he is ambitious to work– He
woulld keep himself shut up in his house two whole
months together–they say.

Thursday 12th

It is hard to read a contemporary poet critically–for
we go within the shallowest verse and inform it with
all the life and promise of this day. We are such a
near and kind and knowing audience as he will never
have again– We go within the fane of the temple
and hear the faint music of the worshippers–but
posterity will have to stand without and consider the
vast proportions and grandeur of the building. It will be
solidly and conspicuously great and beautiful for the
multitudes who pass at a distance as well as for the few
pilgrims who enter in to its shrine.

The Poet will prevail and be popular in spite of his
faults and in spite of his beauties too–he will be careful
only that you feel the hammer hit without knowing
whether the head be square or round. No man is enough
his overseer (and not himself ever) to take cognizance
of *all* the particulars which impress men in his actions
– The impression will always proceed from a more
general influence than he can ever dream of. We may
count our steps but we must not count our breaths
– We must be careful not to mix consciousness with
the vital functions– May the gods deliver us from too
critical an age–when cross-eyed near sighted men
are born–who instead of looking out and bathing their
eyes in the deep heaven introvert them–and think to
walk erect and not to stumble by watching their feet and
not by preserving pure hearts.

Saturday 13th

What an impulse was given some time or other to the principle of vegetation that now nothing can stay it. I understand why one said he thought he could write an epic to be called the leaf. What is a leaf—and how much does it cover? In the veins and fibres of the leaf see the future tree. —the grove. It is the print of nature's footstep—this form. See how nature works and produces leaves—wherever she has been she leaves her patterns. Whether in ice or in vegetable or in coral—she works the same figure. Set away a jar in the dark, and mould leaves make haste to grow over it —and clothe the naked omnipresent and everlasting law. Nature has only to breathe on the glass and the form of leaves appears. Nature loves these forms and has not tired of repeating them for how many centuries.

Monday 15

We often hear the expression the natural life of man—we should rather say the unnatural life of man. It is rare indeed to find a man who has not long ago departed out of nature. We only have a transient glimpse of some solitary feature in a serener moment.—

If anything ails a man that he does not perform his functions—especially if his digestion be poor—though he has considerable nervous strength still— What does he do? why he sets about reforming the world.

If he learned that life is short—errare est humanum and has faild in all undertakings hitherto—what does he do—why he reforms the world.

If he has committed some heinous sin and repented —that is having done it—is now thinking that he has done it—what does he do? he reforms the world.

Do ye hear–the world is going to be reformed. formed again–made over–formed rather–made for once. Well well strike away old boy But wait till I've explained it – So long gone unformed–or rather uninformed Do you hear it ye Woloffs–ye Patagonians–ye Tartars–ye Nés Percés– The world is going to be changed presto –change.

Publish it over the green prairies of the west–over the silent pampas of the South american continent–to the parched African deserts and the stretching Siberian wests. Through the populous Indian and chinese villages–along the Indus Ganges and Hydaspes.

We had resolved to travel to those White mountains –whither the old colonists went in search of the great carbuncles–the Crystal hills which one John Field an Irish man had visited–as Winthrop says.

On foot indeed we continued up along its banks –till it became the Pemmiggewasset that leaped by our Side–and later still the Wild Ammonusuck that murmured in our ears, whose puny current we crossed at a stride. Wondering that it should be so rapid to forsake the pleasant land of its birth.

Why should we take the reader who may be gentle and tender, through this rude tract–where the ways are steep and the views none of the best for such as are tenderly bred– Rude men and rough paths would he have to encounter–and many a cool blast over the mountain side.

The wind goes hurrying down the country–gleaning dry loose straw that is left in the fields–while every farmer lad has scud away from out the fields in his best pea jacket and pepper and salt waist coat, his unbent outstanding rigging of duck or kersymere and his furry

–hat–to county fairs and cattleshows. All the land
over they go leaping the fences with their tough idle
palms–which have never learned to hang by their sides
amid the low of calves and the bleating of sheep–to
that Rome, among the villages where the trreasures
of the year are gathered– I love to see these sons
of earth mothers' sons every one give vent to their great
hearty hearts–rushing tumultuously in heards first
to this spectacle and then to that, as if fearful that
there should not be time between sun and sun to see
them all. And the sun does not wait today–more than
in haying time.

   Amos Abner–Elnathan Ellridge–
      From steep pine bearing mountains to the plain.

   They may bring their fattest cattle–their fairest fruits
but they are all eclipsed by the show of men– These
are the yeomanry of the land.

   O these are stirring autumn days when the men
sweep by in crowds in the fall of the year, mid the
rustling of leaves, like migrating finches.

{*Two pages missing*}

and where is that quarry in the earth from which
these thousands were dug–   –Let us acknowledge the
propriety of the phrase "Who dug you up"? This
walking articulating earth.

   The day which usually combines all the prominent
features of the autumn everything reminding us of the
transition season–is ushered in by the low of–cattle
in the street, sounding as natural as if it were but
a hoarser trumpet of the wind, a low symphony or
running base to the hurry scurry of the leaves which
elf-like go rudely frolicking.

Sat 21st

O I have seen such a hollow glazed life as on a painted floor which some couples lead—with their basement parlor with folding doors—a few visitors cards and the latest annual. Such life only as is in the shell on the mantel piece— The very children cry with less inwardness and depth than in the cottage. There they do not live It is there they reside.

There is no hearth in the center of the house— The atmosphere of the apartments is not yet peopled with the spirits of its inhabitants, but the voices sound hollow and echo and he sees only the paint and the paper.

Sunday 22nd

Through all his vice and deformity the ineradicable health of man is seen.— The superabundant mirth that will be seen in any all fools day, though the mob be composed the lame and blind and infirm—the poor and vicious—yet the innocent mirth will put a new face on the matter.

Epitaph on an Engraver.
By Death's favor
Here lies th'engraver,
And now I think o't,
Where lies he not?
If the archangel look but where he lies,
He ne'er will get translated to the skies.

Epitaph on Pursy.
Traveller, this is no prison,
He is not dead, but risen.
Then is there need,
To fill his grave,
And truth to save,
That we should read,—
In Pursy's favor
Here lies the engraver.

Ep– on a good man

There rises one

Here lies an honest man,
   Rear Admiral Van.
Faith then ye have
Two in one grave,
For, by your favor,
Here lies the engraver.

Ep on the World.

Here lies the body of this world,
Whose soul alas to Hell is hurled.
Its golden youth long since was past,
Its silver manhood went as fast,
And iron age drew on at last;
'Tis vain its character to tell,
The several fates which it befell,
What year it died, when 't'will arise,
We only know know that here it lies.

Donne was not a poet–but a man of strong sense
–a sturdy English thinker– Full of conceits and
whimsicalities hammering away at his subject be it
eulogy or Epitaph–sonnet or Satire–with the patience
of a day laboror–without the least taste, but with
an occasional fine distinction and poetic utterance of a
high order. He was rather Doctor Donne than the
poet Donne. He gropes for the most part. His letters
are perhaps best.

Lovelace is what his name expresses–of slight
material to make a poets fame– His goings and comings
are of no great account. His taste is not so much love
of the good as fear of the bad–though in one or two
instances he has written fearlessly and memorably.

Tuesday 24

Though I am old enough to have discovered that the
dreams of youth are not to be realized in this state
of existence yet I think it would be the next greatest
happiness always to be allowed to look under the eyelids
of time and contemplate the perfect steadily with
the clear understanding that I do not not attain to it.

Wed. Nov 1st

Though music agitates only a few waves of air, yet
it affords an ample plain for the hero's imagination to
maneuvre on. It is a solid ground and palpitating heaven
itself. Even science distinguishes its base and its air.
There are few things so evanescent and intangible
as music—it is like light and heat in physics still mooted
themes—

In AEsthetics music occupies the same mysterious
place. It seems vain to ask ourselves what music
is—if we ponder this question it is soon changed to
—what are we? It is everything but itself. It adorns all
nature and morals and remains hidden itself— It is
as unsuspectedly the light which colors all the landscape
— It is as it were the most subtile ether—the most
volatile gass. It is a sovereign electuary which enables
us to see all things

{*Two pages missing*}

You must store up none of the life in your gift—it is
as fatal as to husband your breath. We must *live* all
our *life*.

What shall we make of the wonderful beauty of
nature—which enchants us all our youth—and is
remembered till our death— The love we bear to the
least woody fibre—or earthy particle or ray of light—. Is

not here the true anatomy—where we study our own
—element and composition.— Why should man love
the sun flower? and the color grey of the walls and trees—

Thursday Nov 2nd

I believe that there is an ideal or real nature, infinitely
more perfect than the actual as there is an ideal life
of man. Else where are the glorious summers which
in vision sometimes visit my brain

When nature ceases to be supernatural to a man
—what will he do then? Of what worth is human life—if
its actions are no longer to have this sublime and
unexplored scenery. Who will build a cottage and dwell
in it with enthusiasm if not in the elysian fields?

Sat 4th

We must look to the west for the growth of a new
literature—manners—architecture &c Already there is
more language there,—which is the growth of the soil,
—than here—good Greekish words there are in abundance
—good because necessary & expressive—"diggings" for
instance— If you anylyze a Greek word you will not
get anything simpler truer more poetical— And many
others also which now look so raw slang-like and
colloquial when printed another generation will cherish
and affect as genuine American and standard. Read
some western stump speech and though it be awkward
and rude enough—there will not fail to be some traits
of genuine eloquence or some original and forcible
statement which will remind you of the great orators of
antiquity. I am inclined to read the stump speeches
of the west already rather than the Beauties of our
atlantic orators.

Here is an extract from the speech of a man named
Strong, whom the reporter "understood to live
somewhere over near the Mississippi, in the mining

country"–"he had a pitcher of Whiskey brought into
the Court room, and set on the table before him, from
which he drank long and frequently–" It was a speech
in defence of a member of the Legislative Council of
the territory (Wisconsin) who had shot a fellow member
in a dispute in the Council Chamber– This is a part
of his address to the Jury. "Gentlemen of the Jury, I
dont know what your religion is, nor I dont care,
haint got much myself, though Jesus Christ was a
mighty good man. Now, gentlemen, I am one of those
kind of men who live pretty fast. I believe men generally
live over about the same surface: some live long and
narrow, and others live broad and short." Adverting to
an old gentleman, one of the witnesses, he says, "I
would not like to charge him with perjuring himself
because he and I were members of the Council together.
We were tolerable good friends, though always
quarrelling. He was always on one side; he was just
like the handle of this pitcher, (taking up the pitcher
and pointing to the handle,) here gentlemen, this was
him, and here (pointing to the nose of the pitcher)
this was the estimable Moses, and these were our
relative positions. I bilieve we never got so near as to
drink a glass of water together, but I'll drink his health
now any how" (catching up the pitcher and pouring
down a strangler of whiskey.)" As for the murdered
man he said he "is dead; there is no doubt of it, he
is dead! dead! dead as a smelt; in the language of
Tippecanoe and Tyler too, he is 'a gone coon'." And
before he concluded he reeled with intoxication. And
the speech of the secretary of the state which followed
is said to have been "dignified, able, and suited to
the occasion, as was also the closing argument for the
prosecution." Perhaps it is needless to add that the
defendent was acquitted

Sunday Nov 5th

It is remarkable how language, as well as all things
else, records only life and progress never death and
decay. We are obliged often to contradict ourselves to
express these as the tree requires the vital energy to
push off its dead leaves. We have to say for instance
"grows or waxes less"

So the poet only records the actions of the coward
as well as the hero and the unjust as well as the just.

Tuesday 7th

When Ossian personifies the sun and addresses him,
it is unnecessary to suppose, as his editor does that
he believed the sun to be an "animated being" like a deer
or lion. wherein are we more believers in a God than
the heathen with their mysterious and savage rites?
As if one name were not as good as another. It is time to
have done with these follies. I confess to more sympathy
with the druidical and scandinavian as handed down
to us—than with the actual creeds of any church in
christendom. We would fain reverence "the ghosts of
our fathers" if we could.

It is the characteristic of all religion and wisdom to
substitute being for seeming—and detect the *anima* or
soul in every thing. It is surely an evidence of truer faith
when good is practically believed to be omnipresent.
None of the heathen are too heathenish for me but
those who hold no intercourse with their god. I love the
vigorous faith of those heathen who sternly believed
something— I say to these modern believers dont
interrupt those men's prayers

How much more do the moderns know about God
than the ancients The English than the Chaldaeans or
than the Tartars? Does English Theology contain the
later discoveries?

Ossian feels and asserts the dignity of the bard. His province is to record the deeds of heroes.

> I straightway seize the unfutile tales
> And send them down in faithful verse.

A heroic deed is his star in the night The simple impressive majesty of human life as seen through his mists, is that Ossian we know and remember. Who has discovered any higher morality than this any truer philosophy?—a simple brave life adorned with heroic deeds.

The reserved strength of Ossian and moral superiority to most poets of what is is styled a barbarous era —appears in the willingness to pass over the details of the battle—leaving the heroism to be imagined from what has already been described of the character of the hero—while he hastens to hint at the result. Most heroic poets of a rude period delight mainly in the mere sound of blows and the flowing of blood—

But Ossian has already described the result of the battle when he has painted the character of the heroes. from "Callon & (colvala)"

> "When I heard who the damsel was,
> Frequent dropped the warrior's tears.
> I blessed the radiant beam of youth,
> And bade the band advance.
>
>> Dweller of the mountain cave,
> Why should Ossian speak of the dead?
> They are now forgot in their land,
> And their tombs are seen no more. &c

or in Ca-Lodin

> We engaged, and the enemy won.

or in Croma

> We fought along the narrow vale;
> The enemy fled; Romarr fell by my sword.

No poet has done such justice to the island of foggy fame.

What a contrast between the stern and desolate
poetry of Ossian and that of Chaucer and the early
English bards The bard indeed seems to have lost much
of his dignity and the sacredness of his profession
He has lost all his sternness and bardic furor–and but
conceives the deed which the other has prepared to
perform. It is a step from the forest and crag to the
fireside–from the hut of the Gael or stonehenge with its
circles of stones–to the house of the Englishman.
No hero stands at the door, prepared to break forth
into song or heroic actions–but a studious gentleman
who cultivates the art of song He possibly may not
receive us   there is not room for all mankind about his
hearth. He does not love all things, but a few

I see in them a yellow fireside-blaze and hear the
crackling fuel and expect such heroism as consists
with a comfortable life.

In the oldest poems only the most simple and
enduring features of humanity are seen, such essential
parts of a man–as stonehenge exhibits of a temple.
We see the circlles of stone–and the upright shafts
– – We cannot tell whether this was civilized or savage
–truly it was neither. For these simple necessary traits
are before and after civilization and are superior to it.
All the culture that had a beginning must in the
world's history have an end. It is like the fashions of
France. It is like the tricks taught to a few tame Bears
and monkeys.

How wise we are how ignorant the savage– we
with our penknife with a hundred blades, he with his
knotty club–

When we come to the pleasant English verse it seems as if the storms had all cleared away and it were never to thunder and lighten any more.

It is still (in the poetry of the obscurest eras) the forms of men—such as can be seen afar through the mist, no costume no dialect—but for language you have a tongue—as for costume the skins of beasts or bark of trees is always to be had—what if he is naked?

The figurative parts of Ossian are like Isaiah and the Psalms— The same use is made of gaunt nature.

He uses but few and simple images but they are drawn from such objects as are familiar to men in all ages. To the poet who can use them greatly in his song—and make them convey his thoughts the elements and stars—seem to be nearer and more friendly— And other men involuntarily relinquish to him somewhat of their claim on nature— The sun and the sea and the mists are his more than ours.

Let two stand on the highway, and it and it shall be known that the sun belongs to one rather the other— And one will be found to claim—while the other simply retains possession. The winds blow for one more than another—and on numerous occasions the uncertain or unworthy possessers silently relinquish their right in them. The most doubtful have paid money and taken a deed of their birthright—but the owner is forever known to all men wherever he goes, and no one disputes his claim. For he cannot help using and deriving the profit —while to the dishonest possessor an estate is as idle as his parchment deed of it—and that is all he has purchased.

Wherever the owner goes inanimate things will fly to him and adhere.

What a fame was it that those Ossianic bards and heroes sought
 to Fingal Swaran says
  "The hunter, coming from the hills
  As he rests on a tomb, will say:
   'Here the mighties, Fingal & Swaran,
   Joined battle, with their hundred bands.'
  Thus will the weary hunter speak,
  And our fame will abide for ever."

             Thursday Nov 9th
In Pindar the same importance is attached to fame. Next to the performance of noble deeds—is the renown which springs from them.

Ossian is like Homer & like the Indian. His Duans are like the seasons of the year in northern latitudes.

Who are the Inhabitants of London and New York —but savages who have built cities—and forsaken for a season hunting and war— Who are the Blackfeet and the Tartars but citizens roaming the plains and dwelling in wigwams and tents.

When it comes to poetry the most polished era finds nothing wanting or that offends its taste in the real poetry of the rudest.

I must confess I fear that the muse has stooped in her flight when I come to the literature of civilized nations and eras. We then first hear of different ages of poetry of Augustan and Elizabethan ages—but the poetry of runic monuments is for every age.

The whole difference seems to be that the poet has come within doors— The old bard stood without How different are Homer & Ossian from Dryden & Pope and Grey and even Milton and Shakespeare— Hosts of warriors earnest for battle could not mistake nor dispense with the ancient bards There was no danger

of their being overlooked by their generations. They
spoke but as they acted. Take one one of our modern well
arranged poems and expose it to the elements as
stonehenge has been exposed, let the rains beat on it
and the winds shake it and how will its timbers look at
the end of a few centuries. I like to hear when they
dig beneath some mysterious flat stone far under
the mould of the few huge bones they find and the
sword which modern men cannot wield.

When the stern old bard makes his heroes weep–they
seem to weep from excess of very strength and not from
weakness–it is as a sacrifice a libation of fertile natures.
We hardly know that tears have been shed. Truly only
babes and heroes may weep.

Their pleasure and their sorrow are made of the
same stuff as are the rain and the snow–the rainbow
and the mist.

Nov 19th

Pastoral poetry belongs to a highly civilized and
refined era. It is the pasture as seen from the hall
window The shepherd of the manor. Its sheep are never
actually shorn nor die of the rot. The towering misty
imagination of the poet has descended into the plain and
become a lowlander and keeps flocks and herds.

Between the hunting of men and boars and the
feeding of sheep is a long interval.

Really the Shepherds pipe is no wax-compacted
reed, but made of pipe clay–and nothing but smoke
issues it. Nowadays the sheep take care of themselves
for the most part–

The older and grander poems are characterized by
the few elements which characterize the life they

descrbe   Man stands on the moor between the stars
and the earth–shrunk to the mere bones and sinews. It
is the uncompounded everlasting life which does not
depart with the flesh.

The civilized and the uncivilized eras chronicle but
the fluctuating condition, the summer or winter lean or
fat estate of man

Our summer of English poetry which like the Greek
and Latin before it seems now well advanced toward
the autumn, is laden with the fruit and foliage of
the season, but the winter of ages–will scatter its myriad
clustering and shading leaves with their autumnal
tints; and leave only the desolate boughs to sustain the
snow and rhyme, and creak in the winter wind.

Man simply lives out his years by the vigor of his
constitution He survives storms and the spears of his
foes, and performs a few heroic deeds–and then the
carns answer questions of him.

The scandinavian is not encumbered with modern
fashions–but stands free and alert a naked warrior.

Civilization does not much more than dress men–it
puts rings on the fingers and watches in the side pockets

What do inventions invent for the naked feet and
hands   they often only mend the gloves and the shoes
which they wear They make cloth of a finer texture
but they do not toughen the skin.

So when they come to narrative and description they
describe character only–not costume–which may change.

They knew how to threaten– Their threats might
have deterred a man. Now there is no such things as
vengeance and terror.

When I remember the tumultuous popular joy of our cattle-show mobs—how they rushed hither and thither with licence and without license—with Appetite for the huge delights of the day—now hastening with boisterous speed after the inspired negro from whose larynx their issued a strain—which made the very street vibrate and curl like a banner—under the palpitating sky—as if the melodies of all Congo and Guinea coast had irrupted into our streets—

Now to see the procession of a hundred yoke of oxen all as august and grave as Osiris—now to gaze at the droves of neat cattle and milch cows all as unspotted and πότνια as Isis and Io.

I cannot help thinking of the Feast of adonis at Sestos and Abydos.—   Such as had no love at all
    'Went lovers home from this great festival.'

So enriched and reinforced did men go home from this our fair.

My life is far among those clouds yonder—as if they hung over the land where I would fain dwell. I see its atmosphere through the distant boughs of the elms.

The grandeur of the similes is another feature which characterizes great poetry. The poet seems to speak a gigantic and universal language. Its images and pictures even occupy much space in the landscape as if they could only be seen from mountains and plains with as wide horizon—or across arms of the sea— They are not slight and transient like the stains on a white washed wall

Oivana says to the spirit of her father—"Grey-haired Torkil of Torne," seen in the skies—
    "Thou glidest away like receeding ships."

So when the hosts of Fingal and Starne joined battle
–the bard thus describes the approach of the enemy–
>   With murmurs loud, like rivers far,
>   The race of Torne hither moved.

Ossian expresses his wonder simply. His wonder is as
simple and shortly said as his life is single and of
few elements.

When his hero dies he allows us a short misty glance
into futurity yet into as clear and unclouded a life as
his first. When in Ca-Lodin Mac-Roine is slain–
>   "The hero fell lifeless &c

There are but few objects to distract these heroes
sight– Their life is as uncluttered as the course of the
stars which they gaze after–
>   The wrathful kings on carns apart

Through the grim night and the cloudy days–with
stern hope the bard and warrior wait but for one heroic
deed– The earth is a vast arena–a round plain or heath
for heroic actions.

The bard is sufficiently great and true to himself to
make his thought take place of everything else. There is
for the time no other philosophy no other poetry. For
all men can afford to ask no other question now than this

>   Nov. 21st 1843.

The philosophy of Ossian is contained in the opening
of the 3d Duan of Ca-Lodin–"Whence have sprung &c"

The only vicious and immoral is an unsuccessful
and ignoble warrior. He dies and is forgotten–
>   "Strangers come to build a tower" &–

Again the philosophy of life–and the simple forcible
statement of the thought
>   why shouldst thou build a hall of pomp,
>   Son of many winged time? &c

The size and grandeur of the machinery is again
illustrated by
     "A thousand orators inclined" &c
Even Ossian, the hero-bard, seems to regret the
strength of his sire.
        How beauteous, mighty man, &c
The death of the sun combines many of the
peculiarities of Ossian.

Their tears remind us of a weeping sinew. Crodar
blind and old receives Ossian son of Fingal—who comes
to aid him in war.
        "My eyes have faild;" says he &c

Here are more of Ossians natural and vigorous
similes—Cudulin in fight
        "As rills that gush" &c
and again Cudulin retires from fight
        "Dragging his spear behind" &c

When a hero dies the bard utters a short biblical
sentence—which will serve for epitaph or biography—
        The weak will find &c
And so of Fillan's tears. he weeps like a hero—
        "Fillan was no veteran in war" &c

The aged blinded heroes passed the remnant of their
days listening to the lays of the bards, and feeling
the weapons which laid their enemies low.

The reward of the hero is to be remembered
        "A generation comes like a rapid flood" &c

They move by vast strides—
        "Islands dart out of our way,
        And hide them behind our fleet."

When the hero falls it is still in the midst of peaceful nature—

"Stretched across a purling rill;" &c

{*One-fifth page blank*}

I have heard a painter who complained of the difficulty of representing the reflection in still water truly, Adviced to make ripples where he did not want reflections!!

Sunday Jan 7th 1844

I believe that no law of mechanics—which is observed and obeyed from day to day—is better established in the experience of men, than this that love never fails to be repaid in its own coin.— That just as high as the waters rise in one vessel just so high they will rise in every other with which there is communication—either direct or under ground or from above the stars. Our Love is beside is some such independent fluid element in respect to our vessels, which still obeyes only its own and not our lawes by any means, without regard to the narrow limits to which we would confine it.

Nor is the least object to small for the greatest love to be bestowed on.—

{*Twenty pages missing*}

shores of some continent man.

If we traverse the earth we shall discover no institution which friendship has established. It has no temple nor pillar— It governs nowhere—it is worshipped no where. But is as a thing unheard of if you inquire of it you may not hear. It has no gallery—no school—no

church. It is not recognized by any creed—nor taught by
any religion. The wisest books of the ancient world
—The Scriptures—do not contain its code—or inculcate
its maxims.

Why will we always trading and never conclude a
bargain. There goes a rumor that the earth is inhabited
—but not yet have we seen a footprint on the shore— The
hunter sometimes discovers fragments of pottery and
the mounds of former inhabitants.

Can we imagine man more starkly solitary! What
if there should be borne on the wind—mingling with the
sounds of the groves—the voice of a fellow? How very
remotely allied to us are our brothers and sisters. Only
small accidents remind us of this. I can go out in
the morning—in deep thought travelling till evening till
I come round again to my door—   And no one shall
cross my path.

I do not wonder that men read history, for I am
as nearly related to the men of history as to any
contemporary. Farthest India is nearer to me than
Concord & Lexington.

Yesterday I skaited after a fox over the ice. It was
like a slight trait of Scythia—to vary our modern town
life. I am always cheered by the sight of any such
phenomenon—any piece of wild nature. He sat on his
haunches and barked at me like a young wolf. It made
Me think of the bear and her cubs on the ice as related
by Capt. Parry I think—especially when the perplexed
brute would turn in its retreat and stretching its neck
—bark anxiously at me. He carries methinks but a
duller sunlight in his tawny hide.

All brutes I should say have a genius for mystery—an
oriental aptitude for symbols and the language of
signs— The fox manifested an almost human suspicion

of mystery— While I skated directly after him he cantered
at the top of his speed but when I paused and stood
stock still though his fear was not abated some strange
but inflexible law of his nature caused him to stop
also and sit again on his haunches. While I still stood
motionless he would go slowly a rod to one side then
sit and bark then a rod to the other side and sit and
bark again—but did not retreat—as if spell bound. When
however I commenced the pursuit again he found
himself released from his durance.

Plainly the fox belongs to a different order of things
than that which reigns in the village— Our courts
though they offer a bounty on his hide—our pulpits
though they draw many a moral from his proverbial
cunning—are in few senses contemporary with his
free forest life.

Writing may be either the record of a deed or a deed.
It is nobler when it is a deed though it is noble and
rare when it is fine and clear memory impartial—distinct.
Its productions are then works of art. And stand like
monuments of history— To the poet as artist his
words must be as the relation of his remotest and
finest memory. And older and simpler antiquity
— Contemporary with the moon and grasshoppers.

How cheering is the spring to all creatures And the
steady revolutions of nature. It cannot but affect our
philosophy favorably—to know of the schools of Salmon
shad alewives and herring which penetrate up the
innumerable rivers of our coast— —and again the young
fry which in still greater numbers wend their way
downward to the sea. Nature never suggests to me such
antiquity as the works of human art. Methinks I see
the tide of migratory fishes flowing upward through

the broad streams to our interior lakes, their scales
gleaming in the sun. I have seen a pond alive with the
spat of alewive which had just come up to deposit
their spawn.

{*Eighty-three pages missing*}

of the race the generation itself may be divine may
be an inspired one. And the race of imperfect mortals
die out.

We have wonderfully little faith. It seems so rare
and dear—as if it were imported from very far.

The world has been constantly expecting a divine
man—it has never been backward to hail the least
worthiness in human shape—it is the great miracle
which all the ages expect. They have not so steadily
awaited for anything else. But this prophecy is no
truer than of a divine race of men. When the faith of
men is equal to this then will it be begotten.

Has man lived so long as to have learned the whole
order of nature. Is it only the comets whose periods we
have not wholly learned. What periods may love and
Justice have. What longer years revolve in the steady
order of nature (whose spring our race never saw—)
quite distancing the weak memory of mankind—whose
new spring may even now at hand. Can our fathers tell
us even our forefathers what we may expect in the
future? What young experimentalists we are! There is
not one here who lived ever a whole human life. and
can say what that is.

As I stand today over the insect crawling amid the
needles of the pine, and endeavoring to conceal himselff
from my sight—and think what startling information
I could possibly give him— Concerning his lesser
fate and environments—I am led to ask if there may not

be some infinite intelligence standing over me the
human insect—and prepared to impart to me knowledge
as startling.— Why will it cherish these humble thoughts
and hide its head under leaves to avoid his benefactor.
I would cheer his puny race with fair news of great
events which concern it. Might I not contribute
something to strengthen its faith out of my superior
intelligence and make it bless that afternoon that led
me to the wood.

But my beneficence and my

{*Remaining leaves of MS Volume 9 missing*}

Appendix

INDEXES OF MS VOLUMES 1-6;
  "TRANSCRIPTS, 1840-1842";
  9: 1837-1844

MS Volume 1

Least truth changes our whole life   38   {24}
Manhood, advanced spring   48   {30}
Spending Sunday   50-1   {31}
Homer—bright moonlight—night   87–97   {52, 57}
Crickets & grasshoppers   90   {54}
stars overhead by day   91   {54}
Compensation in a rain   95   {56}
Hear the waves in a dream   113   {66}
Reality   124   {72}
I am central   130   {75}
The rising gen. not enhanced by the phil. of the risen
   147   {85}
No apology for despondency in rain   148–v 2nd
   129   {86, 160}
Ever anon we make a fresh sortie.
p 149   102   78   {86}   {60}   {47}

MS Volume 2

language   3   {92}
shadow & light   4   {93}
soldier as good as the priest   7–110   {94, 149}
Plato on music   11   {97}
brave praying   12   {97}
Brave stand alone   13   {98}
Friendship   15-7   v 1st 128   {98-100, 74}
Easy to establish a reform   26   {105}
Likeness in opposition   32   {108}
Duty—consciousness   33   {109}
Folded blots   34   {109}
The good have their own sun   35   {110}
nations may reconsider their votes   54   {120}
Summer rain   56-7   {120}
Stars do not make but signify   59   {121}
Inspiration of body   91   {137}

not to be shocked   92   {138}
True poem not printed   106—121   {147, 155}
change in particulars not in generals   112   {150}
preserve a medium   115-6   {152-153}
What Pittacus said   122-3   {156-157}
Bravery   130   {160}

MS Volume 3

No courage but hope   11   {167}
The pathless regions of thought   18   {171}
Cannot wheedle genius   44   {183}
The bird of paradise flies against the wind   47
   {185}
Sincerity deep laid like stone wall   51   {187}
Etiquette for little men   55   {189}
Every maggot lives downtown   57   {190}
Mathematics   71   {196}
35-6-7   39   43   45   47   54   {179-180, 181, 183,
   184, 185, 188-189}
24—56—78   {174, 189-190, 199-200}

MS Volume 4

complaint like the leaves on a tree struck by
   lightening   12   {234}
apologies   12   {234}
Trust not in God *idly—*   16   {235}
We whet our virtue with our vice   74   {260}
Fame first now among the great above   83   {264}
Live to tell the dreams of our childhood   93   {269}
22 to 30 about snow   {238-240}
Spring   p. 6.   {231}

MS Volume 5

What next best to spending a day well   1   {295}
Reform before opening the door   9   {299}

men need know but little   28-9   {308}
Various aspects of the same thing   33   {310}
mountain in horizon   69   {316}
Art not equal to nature.   70   {320}
Spring of poetry gleaming on Mt side   99   {332}

MS Volume 6

character in a maiden   7—10   {339, 341}
I love wildness   17   {344}
wise enough to know cause of happiness   28   {350}
popping corn   43   {357}
music sad   54   {362}
music is to sound what color is to matter   {370}
no trumpet when the dead arise   78   {373}
stars   102   {382}
Do not hurry   108   {385}
Cant forget him who understand you   122   {391}
agree to act as if did'nt know each other   135
   {397}
Why do not hens let you touch them? cows do—   Is it
   because they are birds?
experience in the head—not heart   140 Fr—   {400}
objects in their eternal relations   141   {401}
V p 15   for winter woods   {343-344}
v p 34   " falling snow   {352}

"Transcripts, 1840-1842"

37—   It is now easy &c   {*missing*}
113   Every author be he &c   {428}
113   As for the tenets &c   {428}
7   How thrilling   {408}
65-6   Any Moral phil.   {424}
97   These sublime passages   {427}
69   Some of their old distinctions   {*missing*}
68   These fixed sentences   {*missing*}

99   English Sense has   {*missing*}
101   Why will he be imposed on &c &c &c &c
35   where is India   {418}
10-11—33—38—45—   {*missing*}   72   {425-426}
    86—100—107-108-109-110   {*missing*}

MS Volume 9

Vide 9th
Museums   5—14—15   {465, 472}
carew old Eng drama by   {*missing*}
Donne   29   {479}
Lovelace   29   {479}
listening to a tree sparrow after a shower   11
    {469}
Daniel   19   {473}
poet   20   {474}
Get sick & then reform the world   22   {475}
Epitaphs   28   {478}
Live long & narrow or broad & short   35   {482}
Jesus Christ good man   {482}
Let not the mind interfere too much with the life of
    the body which is natural   {*missing*}
skating after a fox   74   {494}
gifts of the gods never gratuitous   {*missing*}

Annotations

THE ANNOTATIONS provide the following kinds of information: the sources of direct quotations; translations of passages in foreign languages; topical references; identification of persons and places not included in *Webster's Biographical Dictionary* and *Webster's Geographical Dictionary*; identification of obscure or archaic terms not contained in *Webster's New Collegiate Dictionary*; completion of references to authors and books; important biographical facts that pertain to the Journal.

In general, information given in the text is not repeated in the annotation. Short-title references are expanded in the Bibliography, which follows the Annotations, and the edition Thoreau used is cited whenever possible. Where his edition is unknown, the Bibliography lists either his probable source (for example, the edition Emerson owned) or a currently available one. Translations are by the staff of the Thoreau Edition unless otherwise noted. Thoreau's errors or changes in the substantives of quotations are also indicated. Definitions of archaic words are taken from the *Oxford English Dictionary*. Contextual punctuation appears outside of quotation marks when ambiguity would result from using the standard form. The following abbreviations are used throughout this section:

AN	Annotations
Days	Walter Harding, *The Days of Henry Thoreau* (New York: Alfred A. Knopf, 1965)
EEM	Henry D. Thoreau, *Early Essays and Miscellanies*, ed. Joseph J. Moldenhauer et al.

(Princeton: Princeton University Press, 1975)

JMN | *The Journals and Miscellaneous Notebooks of Ralph Waldo Emerson*, ed. William H. Gilman et al. (Cambridge: The Belknap Press of Harvard University Press, 1960-)

(Loeb) | Translation from the Loeb Classical Library

(OED) | *Oxford English Dictionary*

RP | Henry D. Thoreau, *Reform Papers*, ed. Wendell Glick (Princeton: Princeton University Press, 1973)

(T) | Thoreau's translation

TN | Textual Notes

MS Volume 1

4.1-6 "By . . . mind.": "The Church Porch," in *The Temple*, stanza 25.

4.9-12 "Friends . . . *privacy*.": "The Author's Abstract of Melancholy," in *The Anatomy of Melancholy*, ll. 65-68.

4.14-15 "Two . . . alone.": "The Garden," ll. 63-64, reads " 'twere" not "are".

5.2-3 "What . . . journal?": Questioner was probably Emerson; see *JMN* V, 409.

5.7 Roman emperor's . . . mirrors?: Domitian, emperor from 81 to 96 A.D., described by Suetonius in *The Lives of the Caesars*, "Domitian," part XIV.

5.10-11 Es . . . wirst.: "Everything through which you are bettered is true"; see *JMN* V, 346-347.

6.8-15 "The . . . not.": *Torquato Tasso*, in *Werke*, IX, 107 (T).

6.19-32 "His . . . places.": *Torquato Tasso*, in *Werke*, IX, 107-108 (T).

7.2-13 "A . . . him.": *Torquato Tasso*, in *Werke*, IX, 113 (T).

7.15-24 "As . . . time": *Torquato Tasso*, in *Werke*, IX, 131 (T).

7.26-27 "That . . . honor.": *Torquato Tasso*, in *Werke*, IX, 144 (T).

8.31 John: John Thoreau, Jr. (1815-1842), T's brother.

9.19 Tahatawan: Indian sachem living near Concord when English settlers arrived in 1635.

10.22-23 "siluer . . . spring": "Another of the same Nature, Made Since" (anon.), in *England's Helicon* (anon.), ll. 11-12.

11.3-4 whole lesson of to-day: Miss Anna Jones, a Concord resident whose obituary T later wrote (*EEM*, p. 121), died on this day.

11.19-12.6 "And . . . nature.": *Die Italiänische Reise*, in *Werke*, XXVII, 36 (T).

12.9-10 "in . . . wandering": Milton, *Paradise Lost*, VII, 302, reads "with serpent-error wand'ring."

12.19 whig victory: Whigs gained a majority in the Massachusetts House of Representatives on November 13, 1837.

12.27-29 "that . . . walls": *Die Italiänische Reise*, in *Werke*, XXVII, 45-47 (T).

13.17 "Pulsae . . . valles—": *Eclogues*, VI, 84; "the re-echoing valleys fling them again to the stars" (Loeb).

13.19 "agrestem musam": *Eclogues*, VI, 8; "rustic Muse" (Loeb).

13.21-22 Cogere . . . Olympo.: *Eclogues*, VI, 85-86; "till Vesper gave the word to fold the flocks and tell their tale, as he set forth over an unwilling sky" (Loeb).

13.30 Battle of Prague: Musical piece, imitative of battle sounds, by Franz Kotzwara (d. 1791).

14.9 "jam . . . gemmae,": *Eclogues*, VII, 48; "now the buds swell on the joyful stem" (T).

14.10 "Strata . . . poma.": *Eclogues*, VII, 54; "The apples lie scattered every where, each under its tree." (T).

16.11 My friend: Emerson; see *JMN* V, 265.

16.23-24 His description . . . Marcusthurm: *Die Italiänische Reise*, in *Werke*, XXVII, 107-108. "Marcusthurm" is the bell tower of St. Mark's in Venice.

17.16-18 "O'er . . . flies;": Milton, *Paradise Lost*, II, 948-950, reads "his" not "*her*".

18.4-6 "which . . . fruit.": Unidentified.

18.27 "high . . . imbower": Milton, *Paradise Lost*, I, 304.

18.32 Sprengel: Kurt Polycarp Sprengel (1766-1833), German botanist; T's reference is probably to Candolle and Sprengel, *Elements of the Philosophy of Plants*, p. 203.

19.3-5 "before . . . close.": Milton, *Paradise Lost*, II, 535-537.

19.11 "long-levelled rules": Milton, *Comus*, l. 340, reads "rule".

19.21-22 "put . . . blossoms.": Unidentified.

19.29-30 "were . . . things.": Turner, *History of the Anglo-Saxons*, I, 22.

20.2-7 "The . . . theologians.": Turner, *History of the Anglo-Saxons*, I, 23.

20.9-12 Göthe . . . contemplated.: See Goethe, *Iphigenie auf Tauris* (1788).

20.15-18 The Athenians . . . moon—: See Turner, *History of the Anglo-Saxons*, I, 29.

20.28 Sakai-suna: See Turner, *History of the Anglo-Saxons*, I, 34, for the etymology of "Saxon."

21.4 Saxons of Ditmarsia: See Turner, *History of the Anglo-Saxons*, I, 44.

21.8-11 "They . . . base.": Turner, *History of the Anglo-Saxons*, I, 45.

21.13-16 "Francis . . . criminis.": Turner, *History of the Anglo-Saxons*, I, 51n, reads "ipsum" not "ipsam": "It is customary with the Franks to weaken faith with ridicule. . . . The nation of the Franks is treacherous. If a Frank swears falsely, what is strange in his action, since he thinks perjury a figure of speech, and not a crime?"

22.15-17 robin . . . requieted: In an old English ballad known variously as "The Children in the Wood" and "The Babes in the Wood," a robin buries the bodies of two murdered children by covering them with leaves. T's exact source is unknown; Percy's *Reliques*, III, 170-177 gives the ballad the first title above.

23.15 cyules: Plural of "cyule"—"boat, sailing vessel" (OED).

23.16-17 "Three . . . cnihten": Turner, *History of*

the Anglo-Saxons, I, 90, reads "threo . . . threo": "Three good ships came on that tide, three hundred knights."

23.23-24 "not . . . future": Turner, *History of the Anglo-Saxons*, I, 101.

23.26-28 "had . . . island": Turner, *History of the Anglo-Saxons*, I, 106.

23.28 Cymri: Ancestors of the Welsh.

23.33-24.3 "If . . . death.": Turner, *History of the Anglo-Saxons*, I, 113.

24.4-11 Homesickness . . . Atlantic.: See Turner, *History of the Anglo-Saxons*, I, 52-53.

24.17-21 "caused . . . experienced": Turner, *History of the Anglo-Saxons*, I, 141.

24.21-22 Arthur's twelve battles.: See Turner, *History of the Anglo-Saxons*, I, 103.

25.1 *disjecta membra*: Literally, "torn apart members"; normally untranslated.

25.10-11 years of the gods: Manu, *Institutes of Hindu Law*, II, 11.

26.3-5 "You . . . you!": T's probable source is Thomson, *Travels in Sweden*, p. 38: "You will find at Trollhaette excellent wine, meat, bread, and indeed every thing, *provided you bring it along with you.*"

26.25-27.18 Zeno . . . less.": T's facts and quotations derive from Lempriere's *Classical Dictionary* (s.v. "Zeno").

27.1 *lebens-tag*: "day's life" (T).

27.2 στοα: "stoa" or "portico" (see AN 28.29-31).

27.8 Palinurus: Helmsman for Aeneas in Virgil, *Aeneid*.

28.29-31 Pierian spring . . . Academus grove . . . sculptured portico!: Haunts of the Muses, Platonic philosophers, and Stoics.

29.28 "the . . . grass": Unidentified.

30.15-17 "Signor . . . eyes.": *Die Italiänische Reise*, in *Werke*, XXVII, 75; "Pardon me, sir! this is my homeland."

30.25 "drags . . . along": Pope, *Essay on Criticism*, l. 357.

31.13 ὁ . . . ἐοικώς.: *Iliad*, I, 47; "and his eyes were like a blazing fire" (Loeb).

31.19 ὄσσε . . . ἐίκτην.: *Iliad*, I, 104; "and his coming was like the night" (Loeb).

31.30-32.2 "But . . . people": Homer, *Iliad*, I, 259-263 (T).

32.18 "Germany by De Stael": Anne Louise Germaine, baronne de Staël-Holstein, *De L'Allemagne* (1810).

33.7-10 ἐπειὴ . . . between—: *Iliad*, I, 156-157 (T).

33.12-13 διάνδιχα μερμήριξεν: *Iliad*, I, 189; "his heart was divided in counsel" (Loeb).

33.15 θυμῳ . . . τε: *Iliad*, I, 196; "for in her heart she loved them both alike and had care of them" (Loeb).

33.22-24 "And . . . tongue": Homer, *Iliad*, I, 247-249 (T).

33.30 Phithian hero: Achilles, whose homeland was Phthia in Thessaly.

34.34 ran-tan: "A word expressive of a loud banging noise" (OED).

37.15 μεροψ ανθρωπος: See Homer, *Iliad*, I, 250; "man endowed with an articulate voice."

37.19-24 "has . . . blow.": Unidentified.

39.14-18 But . . . water: See Goethe, *Die Italiänische Reise*, in *Werke*, XXVII, 132.

40.3-13 "In . . . them.": *The Holy and Profane States*, p. 62.

44.16 Segraddo: Unidentified.

48.24 thrins: "Three children at a birth" (OED).

52.14 The Zendavesta: The main Zoroastrian scripture and prayerbook, composed in the ancient Ivanian language of Avestan during the Sasanian period (3rd-7th c. A.D.).

52.29-32 "As . . . heart.": Homer, *Iliad*, VIII, 555-559 (T).

53.31 Faustus and Amyntas: Conventional shepherds' names from pastoral poetry.

55.28-31 When . . . sea: See *Iliad*, IX, 182.

56.14 Alma Natura: "nourishing nature."

57.3-4 Hector . . . cloud—: See *Iliad*, XI, 62-65.

57.4-8 We . . . trees.: See *Iliad*, XI, 86-90.

57.10 Nestor's . . . Machaon: See *Iliad*, XI, 628-641.

57.16-21 "A . . . source": *Iliad*, XI, 722-726 (T).

57.31-58.3   "The . . . waves.":   *Iliad*, XII, 278-285
(T).

60.25   Selden's butcher: See *Table Talk of John
Selden*, in Young, *Library of Old English Prose Writers*,
II.

62.11-29   Anacreon's . . . gods.:   *Carminum Poetarum
Nouem*, p. 67 (T). This poem as well as "Return of
Spring" and "Cupid Wounded," on p. 65, are not by
Anacreon himself, but are part of a group of poems
known as the "Anacreontea," originally published in 1554
by Henricus Stephanus (Henri Estienne) from an otherwise unknown manuscript.

64.10-11   "When . . . itself,":   Thomas Gray, "Letter
to Mr. Stonhewer (29 June 1760)," in *Poems*, IV, 60.

65.3-17   Return . . . flourishes.:   *Carminum Poetarum
Nouem*, pp. 63-64 (T).

65.18-34   Cupid . . . smite?:   *Carminum Poetarum
Nouem*, p. 65 (T).

70.20   Tom-and-Jerry: Heavy overcoat.

71.22   Atlantides: Daughters of Atlas and Hesperis;
hence, also called Hesperides and sometimes associated
with the mythical western isles of the same name. See
Lempriere, *Classical Dictionary* (s.v. "Atlantides" and
"Hesperides").

72.16   illuminated pictures: Deacon Nehemiah Ball
frequently presented diorama shows at the Concord
Lyceum.

73.24-25   "by . . . resigned.":   Sir Walter Scott, *The
Lady of the Lake*, I, xxxv, 19-20.

74.11-12   I . . . spirit: Possibly Edmund Sewall,
brother of Ellen, whom T met on June 17, 1839; see
Days, p. 77.

74.25   The "Book of Gems":   *The Book of Gems*, ed.
S. C. Hall, 3 vols. (London: 1836-1838), is an anthology
of English poetry and prints.

82.32-85.25   Prom. . . . hand.:   T's translation of
passages from Aeschylus, *Prometheus Bound*; see his
translation of the complete text in *The Dial* 3 (January
1843): 363-386.

85.27-28   Πταίσας . . . δίχα: Aeschylus, *Prometheus
Bound*, ll. 924-925; "Stumbling upon this ill he'll learn /
How different to govern and to serve" (T).

86.21-27   Linnaeus . . . biped: See Linnaeus, *Lache-sis Lapponica*, I, 1-2.

87.11   he . . . Florida: During the Seminole Indian War (1836-1842), men drafted for military service could hire substitutes.

87.18-27   "The . . . evermore.":   See TN 87.16.

88.6-7   With . . . far: Chios and Lesbos, the Aegean islands, and Falernus in Italy were famous in classical times for their excellent wines.

MS Volume 2

91.23   χειρ . . . δρασιμον: Aeschylus, *Seven Against Thebes*, l. 554; "his hand sees what's to be done" (T's translation in Huntington Library manuscript HM 13193).

92.7-9   Samuel Johnson . . . country: See Boswell, *Life of Johnson*, p. 41.

92.14   *vir* and *virtus* . . . αγαθος and αριστος: "man" and "manliness"; "good" and "best."

93.28-31   "things . . . hand.":   Plutarch, *Morals*, II, 254 [282D], reads "stand directly."

94.21   Tyrian dye: Dark purple dye which in classical antiquity was manufactured chiefly in the Levantine seaport of Tyre.

97.1-7   "Take . . . rest.":   *Table Talk*, II, 23.

97.11-18   "Plato . . . agreement.":   Plutarch, *Morals*, I, 166 [167B-C], reads "disordered" not "discordant."

97.23-26   "Homer . . . armor.":   *Morals*, I, 172 [169C].

97.27-30   "Which . . . yard.":   Plutarch, *Morals*, I, 172 [169B].

97.31-33   "Homer . . . plowtail.":   Plutarch, *Morals*, I, 172 [169B], reads "Hesiod" not "Homer."

98.1   Ἀρχὴ . . . θαρρεῖν: Plutarch, *Lives*, VIII, 2.

98.3   "made . . . Fortitude,":   Plutarch, *Morals*, IV, 205 [318F].

98.6-7   *fortis* . . . *fors* . . . *vir summae fortis*:   "strong . . . fortune (or chance) . . . man of highest courage."

98.8   "carry . . . fortune":   Plutarch, *Morals*, IV, 206 [319D].

98.11   *meâ . . . involvo*:   Horace, *Odes*, III, 29, ll. 54-55.

98.13-14 Tumble . . . yet: Herrick, "To Fortune," ll. 1-2.

106.11-13 "An . . . prominent.: *Seven Against Thebes*, ll. 387-390 (T).

107.5 Criticism . . . Flaccus: T's first printed essay, on the Roman satirist Aulus Persius Flaccus, appeared in the first issue of *The Dial* (January 1840): 117-121; by the time T transcribed the Journal for this date, the essay was already in print.

107.9-12 "Truth . . . lights.": Bacon, "Of Truth," in *Essays*, p. 2.

107.29-108.3 "Sit . . . God.": Browne, "A Letter to a Friend," in *Miscellaneous Works*, p. 260.

108.29 *ce que devrait etre*: "that which ought to be."

110.4 *Sedes beatas*: "blissful groves"; see Virgil, *Aeneid*, VI, 639.

110.5-6 Largior . . . nōrunt.: Virgil, *Aeneid*, VI, 640-641; "Here an ampler ether clothes the meads with roseate light, and they know their own sun, and stars of their own" (Loeb).

115.11-12 Pythian priestess: Attendant at Apollo's oracle in Delphi.

119.4 periplus: "the action of sailing round, circumnavigation" (OED).

121.26-29 "Origen . . . events.": *True Intellectual System*, I, 74.

123.2-3 Thales . . . immortal: See Cudworth, *True Intellectual System*, I, 108.

123.10 Rance des Vaches: (*Ranz-des-vaches*) "One of the melodies peculiar to Swiss herdsmen, usually played on an Alpine horn, and consisting of irregular phrases made up of the harmonic notes of the horn" (OED).

124.8 Miltons' . . . camp.: See *Paradise Lost*, V, 648-655.

124.27-126.33 We . . . it: T describes the trip with his brother on the Concord and Merrimack Rivers, August to September 1839 (see also 134-137, 316, 466, 476).

127.2 Λόγος . . . 'ύλης.: Aristotle, *Parts of Animals*, in Cudworth, *True Intellectual System*, I, 336; "the reason of the thing without matter" (Cudworth).

127.4 Ὁ ... ἄνθει.: "Chaldaic Oracles," in Cudworth, *True Intellectual System*, II, 71; "that Intelligible . . . that cannot be apprehended otherwise than by the flower of the mind" (Cudworth).

127.6-7 Ἐγώ . . . ἀπεκάλυψεν.: Plutarch, *Isis and Osiris*, in Cudworth, *True Intellectual System*, II, 170; "I am all that hath been, is, and shall be, and my peplum or veil no mortal hath ever yet uncovered" (Cudworth).

127.10-12 "ἐπαφὴν . . . συνάπτειν.": Plotinus, *Ennead* VI, in Cudworth, *True Intellectual System*, III, 39; "a kind of tactual union, and a certain presence better than knowledge, and the joining of our own centre, as it were, with the centre of the universe" (Cudworth).

127.14 Μέλλει . . . φύσει.: Euripides, *Oresteia*, in Cudworth, *True Intellectual System*, IV, 172; "The Deity is slow or dilatory, and this is the nature of it" (Cudworth).

127.17-19 "The . . . first.": See Cudworth, *True Intellectual System*, I, 112.

127.23-24 "in . . . side": Wordsworth, "Resolution and Independence," ll. 45-46, reads "Following his plough, along the mountain-side."

128.27 Attic bee: According to Lempriere, Xenophon was "styled, from the sweetness and simplicity of his language, the 'Attic bee'" (*Classical Dictionary*, s.v. "Xenophon").

129.15 "Banquet" of Xenophon: See Xenophon, *The Banquet*, dialogues on friendship and love.

132.2-3 a . . . lady: Probably Ellen Sewall, who visited Concord in June; see *Days*, p. 99.

132.20 "When . . . night": Campbell, "Hohenlinden," in *Poetical Works*, p. 102, l. 6.

133.24 semper . . . cadit: "always falling, never fallen."

134.21 *terra incognita*: "unknown land."

136.17-18 Mr. Mitchels': Probably Joseph Mitchell, innkeeper in Hooksett.

136.27 "Stone Flume" and "Basin": Mountain chasm and granite depression in the White Mountains.

136.28 the "Notch": A two-mile defile between cliffs in the White Mountains.

136.28-29 "old man of the mountain": Cliff resembling a human profile on Mount Jackson near Franconia, New Hampshire.

137.15-16 Thomas J. Crawford's: Inn at Crawford's Notch in the White Mountains.

140.2-15 "What . . . it.: See TN 140.2-15.

140.18-19 atomists . . . Pythagoras: See Cudworth, *True Intellectual System*, I, Chapter 1, *passim*.

140.31-141.4 "of . . . blood.": *True Intellectual System*, I, 179.

141.4-5 This . . . "romantical": *True Intellectual System*, I, 180.

141.27-142.24 "Though . . . o'clock.: See TN 141.27-142.24.

142.18 "stepping westward": Title of a poem by Wordsworth.

142.30 Juggernaut: "A title of Krishna . . . ; *spec.*, the uncouth idol of this deity . . . annually dragged in procession on an enormous car, under the wheels of which many devotees are said to have formerly thrown themselves to be crushed" (OED).

147.26-27 When . . . him.: Unidentified.

148.1 Godfrey and Gonzalve: Heroes of Tasso, *Jerusalem Delivered*, and of Florian, *Gonsalve de Cardoue*.

149.10 The Townsend Light Infantry: Volunteer militia of Townsend, Massachusetts, called to muster periodically.

150.11 "Great Ball": Symbol of opposition to President Van Buren, rolled by Harrison and Tyler supporters from Concord battleground to Bunker Hill on July 4, 1840.

151.26 "Angler's Souvenir": William A. Chatto, *The Angler's Souvenir*.

151.27-28 "Can . . . cloud?: Shakespeare, *Macbeth*, III, iv, 109-110.

152.10-11 "it . . . things.": Fénelon, *Vie des Philosophes*, p. 13.

153.6-11 When . . . side.: See Fénelon, *Vie des Philosophes*, p. 18.

153.16-21 thread . . . asylum: See Fénelon, *Vie des Philosophes*, p. 19.

154.11 Encke's comet: Predicted to appear in 1822

by Johann Franz Encke (1791-1865), German astrono-
mer.

155.18 Guido's Aurora: Baroque painting (1614)
by Guido Reni (1575-1642).

156.11-13 "it . . . occasion": Fénelon, *Vie des Philosophes*, p. 45.

157.4-5 Pittacus . . . moment.: See Fénelon, *Vie
des Philosophes*, p. 51.

157.6-9 Go . . . wise.": Fénelon, *Vie des Philosophes*,
p. 57.

157.10-12 When . . . lost.": Fénelon, *Vie des Philosophes*, p. 62.

157.28-158.3 In . . . me.: See Fénelon, *Vie des Philosophes*, pp. 63-64.

158.5-6 *ex tempore . . . pro tempore*: "unpremeditated" and "temporary."

160.1 peace society: The American Peace Society,
organized by William Ladd in 1828, was still active in
1840.

MS Volume 3

163.14-16 valor . . . Aulis: See Homer, *Iliad*, II,
816; 645; 297.

164.18-20 "On . . . infinitely.": Fénelon, *Vie des
Philosophes*, p. 124.

165.6 *Spes sibi quisque*: *Aeneid*, XI, 309; T's translation, used as a motto for "The Service" (*RP*, p. 3), is
"Each one his own hope."

165.10 sixth champion: Amphiaraus in Aeschylus,
Seven Against Thebes.

165.12-15 "bearing . . . wish.": Aeschylus, *Seven
Against Thebes*, l. 588 (T).

165.16 "Discretion . . . soul": Donne, "To the Count-
ess of Bedford (Honour is so sublime perfection)," l. 34.

168.10-11 "Battle of Prague": See AN 13.30.

168.12 "Hero's Quickstep": Military march by Henry
Schmidt, first published in 1836.

169.14-15 "the far blue mountain.": Uncanoonuc
Mountain in New Hampshire.

171.10 "descry new lands": Milton, *Paradise Lost*,
I, 290.

171.20-26 Addison . . . motion.": *The Spectator*, no.

6 (March 7, 1710-1711); the author of this issue was Richard Steele, not Joseph Addison.

172.12 George Minot and Mr. Alcott: Concord farmer and philosopher, whom T associates respectively with Scythia, an agricultural region north of Greece, and Stoa, where Zeno founded a philosophical sect.

172.15-16 Britains . . . Rome: See Bosworth, *Elements*, pp. 265-267.

172.20-21 George Minot's barn: Minott's residence was on Lexington Road near Emerson's home.

173.16-22 "The Sepoys . . . themselves.": Anonymous article, "Review of *The Life of Robert Lord Clive*," in *Edinburgh Review* 70 (January 1840): 309-310.

173.24-30 ordinances . . . Culucca: See Manu, *Institutes of Hindu Law: or the Ordinances of Menu, according to the Gloss of Culúcca, Comprising the Indian System of Duties, Religious and Civil*, p. 1.

174.13-14 "with . . . condemned": Oldys, "Life," in Raleigh, *Works*, I, 382, reads "with admirable erection, yet in such sort as a condemned man should do."

175.5-6 "that . . . examination: Oldys, "Life," in Raleigh, *Works*, I, 489.

176.20 "He . . . terribly": *Eminent British Statesmen*, V, 16.

176.24-33 " 'His . . . comfortable.' ": Anonymous article, "Review of *The Art of Deer-Stalking*," in *Edinburgh Review* 71 (April 1840): 114.

176.31 *ventre à terre*: "at full speed"; literally, "belly to the ground."

177.24-26 "pine . . . strawberry": Murray, *British India*, I, 26-27.

177.31 "lilly . . . dandelion,": Murray, *British India*, I, 27.

178.11-17 In . . . instruction: Gérando, *Histoire Comparée*, I, 262 (T).

178.26-28 To Thales . . . nature.": Gérando, *Histoire Comparée*, I, 347 (T).

180.16-19 "Plato . . . end.": *Histoire Comparée*, I, 84 (T).

186.7-11 Alwákidi's . . . action.": Ockley, *History of the Saracens*, I, xxi-xxii, reads "*Jabalah Alchatgami*".

Alwákidi's history describes the Moslem conquest of Syria.

186.29-187.8 The traveller . . . him'.: Stephens, *Incidents of Travel*, I, 205.

187.21-23 "As . . . forever.": Lyell, *Principles of Geology*, I, 22.

187.24-28 "It . . . Geology.: Lyell, *Principles of Geology*, I, 26.

193.20-21 "attitude . . . prone.": Theophrastus, *The Characters of Theophrastus*, p. 167.

193.24-26 "The . . . exit.": Theophrastus, *The Characters of Theophrastus*, p. 178.

194.23 Dr. Ware Jr.: Henry Ware, Jr. (1794-1843), professor at Harvard Divinity School and predecessor of R. W. Emerson as minister of the Second Church in Boston.

195.5-10 "thin . . . excluded.": Lyell, *Principles of Geology*, III, 13.

196.11 Gibbon's memoirs: Edward Gibbon, *Memoirs* (1796), collected in *Miscellaneous Works*.

197.28 circumferentor: Surveyor's instrument used for determining angles.

198.1-22 *Height* . . . mark.: T probably used this survey as a field exercise for his students; see Edward Emerson, *Henry Thoreau As Remembered by a Young Friend* (Boston: Houghton Mifflin, 1917), p. 129.

206.28-207.24 I find . . . to read.: See Gibbon, *Memoirs*, *passim*, in *Miscellaneous Works*.

209.7-28 The character . . . dead.: See Guizot, *Essay on the Character and Influence of Washington*, *passim*.

210.19-20 Abu Musa . . . world.": Ockley, *History of the Saracens*, II, 34.

212.2 Dante and Virgil: See *Inferno*, Canto 1, and *Aeneid*, VI, 282-283.

212.23-28 "In . . . shine.: Virgil, *Georgics*, I, 43-46 (T).

212.32-213.2 "That . . . streams.": Virgil, *Georgics*, I, 109-110 (T).

213.5-10 "He . . . flint.: Virgil, *Georgics*, I, 131-135 (T).

214.9 Friendship . . . 1840: When T transcribed this entry, "Friendship" had been accepted for *The Dial* 1 (October 1841): 204-205, so he probably thought it unnecessary to copy the poem here.

215.26 "*Nosque . . . anhelis*": Virgil, *Georgics*, I, 250; "And when on us the rising sun first breathes with panting steeds" (Loeb).

215.29 "*Illic . . . Vesper*": Virgil, *Georgics*, I, 251; "There glowing Vesper is kindling his evening rays" (Loeb).

216.25 "winter of their discontent": See Shakespeare, *Richard III*, I, i, 1.

217.18-19 Virgil says as much.: See *Eclogues*, I, 57.

221.13 "Sic Vita" . . . Dial.: When T transcribed this entry, "Sic Vita" had already appeared in *The Dial* 1 (July 1840): 81-82, so he probably thought it unnecessary to copy the poem here.

222.28-29 "He . . . first.": *Aids to Reflection*, p. 39.

225.1-2 "through . . . Fesolé.": Milton, *Paradise Lost*, I, 288-289.

MS Volume 4

230.28-32 "*ideas . . . increase.*": *The Statesman's Manual*, p. 32.

231.7 Cornwallis: In *The Biglow Papers*, Lowell defines this New England custom as "a sort of muster in masquerade; supposed to have had its origin soon after the Revolution, and to commemorate the surrender of Lord Cornwallis" (p. 143).

234.13-14 When . . . valor: See Homer, *Iliad*, V, 311ff.

238.5-10 "As . . . pole—: Milton, *Paradise Lost*, II, 636-640; 642.

241.14 Elean youths: Eleans supervised the ancient Olympic games.

242.7 Heaven . . . infancy.: Wordsworth, "Ode: Intimations of Immortality," l. 66, reads "Heaven lies about us in our infancy!"

242.19-21 British . . . sun.: T's source for these statistics is an unsigned article, "Review of *A History of the Cotton Manufacture in Great Britain*," in *North American Review* 52 (January 1841): 36.

244.16-17 When . . . Revolution: Unidentified.

246.12 Tyrolese peasants: The Rainers, two sisters and two brothers, performed in Concord on February 3, 1841.

249.25 These Rainers: See AN 246.12.

251.27-30 He . . . picturesque: See Volney, *Travels through Syria and Egypt*, I, 133.

254.4 "All . . . torture": *Catiline*, in *Works*, III, 17.

254.22-23 "finds . . . there.": Herbert, "Man," in *The Temple*, ll. 23-24, reads "Find their".

255.27 the notch: See AN 136.28.

256.5-10 "They . . . hydra?": *Catiline*, in *Works*, III, 41.

257.19 "The . . . acts.": *Catiline*, in *Works*, III, 41.

261.8-9 "Good . . . gods.": *Catiline*, in *Works*, III, 96.

261.17-18 Whoe'er . . . prais'd: Jonson, "To My Muse," *Epigrams*, LXV, ll. 15-16.

261.27 mede: Reward or recompense.

262.27-28 *"Whils't . . . one."*: Jonson, "To Thomas Lord Chancelor," *Epigrams*, LXXIV, ll. 7-8.

263.15 I . . . land: Request was granted, but T later decided the responsibility would limit his freedom; see *Days*, p. 122.

265.9-10 My neighbor . . . together": Possibly on Fairhaven Hill; see *Days*, p. 122.

266.9-10 verse . . . horses: See Zechariah 14:20.

267.26 hydrostatic paradox: "the principle (depending on the uniform pressure of liquids) that any quantity of a perfect liquid, however small, may be made to balance any quantity (or any weight) however great" (OED).

268.31-32 Coleridge . . . wall": T's source in Coleridge is unknown. In an October 27, 1839, letter to Samuel Gray Ward (printed in *Letters from Ralph Waldo Emerson to a Friend, 1838-1853*, ed. Charles Eliot Norton [Boston: Houghton Mifflin, 1899], p. 14), Emerson employs a similar image, and Norton points out a relationship to Leonardo da Vinci's *Treatise on Painting*, which he translates: " 'If thou wilt look carefully at walls spotted with stains . . . thou mayst see in them similitudes of all sorts of landscapes . . .'" (p. 14). At 490.29-30, T repeats the image in a different context, without quoting.

275.10   thridded: Variant of "threaded."

277.30-31   As . . . heaven.:   Perhaps a reference to Brook Farm in West Roxbury, Massachusetts, established by George Ripley and other Transcendentalists in 1841; see *Days*, p. 125.

278.7-8   He . . . Vice.":   Jonson, "On Gut," *Epigrams*, CXVIII, l. 4.

278.29-30   "That . . . contrary.":   Jonson, "To Sir Ralph Shelton," *Epigrams*, CXIX, ll. 11-12.

279.13-286.23   "The Sphinx . . . herself.:   Emerson's poem "The Sphinx," which T explicates here, appeared in *The Dial* 1 (January 1841): 348-350.

280.6-7   "supreme . . . *slumbering*.":   *Institutes of Hindu Law*, II, 426.

283.7   Faustus and Amyntas: See AN 53.31.

287.24-288.6   "a . . . nature.":   Aubrey, *Letters Written by Eminent Persons*, II, pt. 2, 354 (287.24-30), 364 (287.33-288.1), 365-366 (288.1-3), 398-399 (288.3-6).

291.7-8   I . . . holder.:   See AN 263.15.

MS Volume 5

295.15-16   "grounded . . . learning.":   Jonson, "Hymenæi," in *Works*, III, 302.

304.16   At R.W.E.'s: T moved into the Emerson household on this date, and remained until May 1843.

306.29-32   "For . . . hue.":   Morton, *New England's Memorial*, p. 35.

310.10-11   *Erret . . . viae*.:   Claudian, "De Sene Veronensi," ll. 21-22; "Let who will be a wanderer and explore farthest Spain: such may have more of a journey; he of Verona has more of a life" (Loeb). T's source is unknown.

311.18-19   That title . . . Culucca: See AN 173.24-30.

311.28   years of the gods: See AN 25.10-11.

312.7   Mr. Wattles: Unidentified.

313.10-11   "Immemorial . . . law":   Manu, *Institutes of Hindu Law*, II, 17.

313.19-20   "years of the gods":   See AN 25.10-11.

315.22   *Natures Corn Law Rhymes*:   See Elliott, *Poetical Works*. Corn Laws were British tariffs on grain crops; they were repealed in 1846.

316.1   book of the Hindoos: I.e., Manu, *Institutes of Hindu Law*.

316.2-3   table land of the Gauhts: Plain between the Ghauts Mountains and Coromandel coast in India; see Murray, *British India*, I, 34.

316.13   Woloffs: Moslem tribe in Senegal, Africa.

316.32   Merrimack nights: See AN 124.27-126.33.

319.20   shadow . . . disk: Total inner eclipse was visible in Concord on August first and second 1841.

320.2   swamp by Charles Miles':   Miles Swamp was about two and a half miles southwest of Concord, at the head of Nut Meadow Brook. From 1727 to 1832, four men in the Miles family bore the name Charles; T may refer either to Captain Charles, b. 1757, d. 1827, or to his son Charles, b. 1791.

322.2   stent: Variant of "stint."

323.29   Johnson . . . Milton: See Johnson, *The Rambler*, essays 86, 88, 90, 94, 139, and 140 (in *Works*, V, 90-96, 103-109, 115-121, 143-151, 429-436, and 436-443), and "Life of Milton" (in *Works*, IX, 84-182).

324.18   "the divine male":   Manu, *Institutes of Hindu Law*, II, 3.

324.30-31   "From . . . out.":   Manu, *Institutes of Hindu Law*, II, 5.

326.20   Bristol spar: Lustrous nonmetallic mineral, colorful when exposed to light.

329.18-23   this half . . . Mr. Hosmer: First Parish meeting house in Concord added a Greek Revival portico in 1840, which Nathan S. Hosmer helped to build.

330.19   our annual fair: Exposition conducted by Society of Middlesex Husbandmen and Manufacturers, usually called the "cattle-show"; see text, 476.29-477.32 and 490.2-19.

333.15   Sampson Wilder of Bolton: Sampson Wilder (1780-1865) lived in Bolton, Mass., from 1814 to 1845, where he maintained extensive orchards and vineyards. See [Esther K. Whitcomb et al.], *History of Bolton 1738-1938* (Bolton, Mass., 1938), pp. 250-265.

334.3   capt. Bobadil: Character given to bombastic

accounts of his swordsmanship in Jonson, *Every Man in his Humour*, IV, vii.

MS Volume 6

337.2 Cambridge: T was in Cambridge from November 29 to December 10 reading and transcribing English poetry at the Harvard Library.

337.7-8 President . . . application: T addressed requests for Harvard Library borrowing privileges to President Josiah Quincy and Librarian Thaddeus William Harris.

337.22-24 Mickle . . . Bramins.": Chalmers, XXI, 713-733.

339.13-18 It . . . period.: See Bosworth, *Elements*; Conybeare, *Illustrations*; Percy, *Reliques*; Ritson, *Ancient English Metrical Romances*; Evans, *Old Ballads*; and Jamieson, *Popular Ballads*, which T used in Cambridge.

340.16-17 I . . . there: Neptune, the eighth planet, was discovered in 1840.

341.11-14 Now . . . distance: Possibly Mary Russell, who lived at the Emersons' in 1841 before returning to Plymouth, Massachusetts, in the fall; see *Days*, pp. 107-110.

343.14-15 Old Scotch Poet Douglas: See Gawin Douglas, prologue to Book XIII of his translation of the *Aeneid*.

343.23 thridded: See AN 275.10.

346.31-33 It . . . whetstones.": Ritson, "The Life of Robin Hood," in *Robin Hood*, I, xiii.

347.2 grove of Egeria: In Aricia, Italy; Egeria became a fountain as she wept for her dead husband, Numa. See Ovid, *Metamorphoses*, XV, 547-551.

347.4 "Barnsdale wood": Site in Nottinghamshire, England, associated with Robin Hood; see Ritson, "The Life of Robin Hood," in *Robin Hood*, I, iv.

347.13 the pond: Flint's (Sandy) Pond in Lincoln; see *Days*, p. 123.

351.15-16 O . . . mater: A hymn, "O sweet mother of the Redeemer."

353.3 Audubon: *Ornithological Biography, passim.*

356.4-8 "cannot . . . desire": "Life of Chaucer," in Chalmers, I, x.

357.3 King . . . Scotland: The probable source for T's comment is Warton, *The History of English Poetry*, II, 437n; III, 102-103.

362.32-33 Hindo . . . gods: Manu, *Institutes of Hindu Law*, II, Chapter XI, 361-405, *passim*.

364.12 Feb. 20th 1842: T's brother John died on January 11, and T himself was stricken with a sympathetic illness for several weeks afterward; see *Days*, pp. 134-137.

364.26-365.5 "Examine . . . Gratér.: T's source for this quotation was probably the edition published by Elizabeth Peabody in 1842, which she apparently translated as well (see *JMN* V, 60-61n); T's attribution of the translation to "Gratér" is difficult to explain, unless he had some knowledge of the publication of the manuscript.

371.4-5 Herbert . . . God": Herbert's "Bitter-sweet" begins "Ah my dear angry Lord."

373.16 child . . . man.": Wordsworth, "My Heart Leaps Up When I Behold," l. 7.

373.19-20 Testament of Love: An allegorical prose work by Thomas Usk (d. 1388), formerly ascribed to Chaucer; see Chalmers, I, 466-512.

376.34 Raleigh's Maxims: Raleigh, *The Maxims of State*, in *Works*, VIII.

377.32-378.1 "The . . . law;": Raleigh, "A Discourse on War in General," in *Works*, VIII, 254.

384.29 Charlemagne's egg account: See Gibbon, *Decline and Fall*, IX, 177-178.

386.8-11 "the . . . correspondence": Anonymous article, "Review of Botta's *Travels in Arabia*" in *Athenaeum* (January 1, 1842), p. 3.

386.30-34 "The . . . conversation.": Anonymous review of Botta's *Travels in Arabia*, p. 4 (see AN 386.8-11).

387.16-17 Sadi . . . Pilpay: See Sa'di, *The Gulistan; or, Rose Garden*; Scott, trans., *Arabian Nights Entertainments*; and the "Fables of Pilpay" in Wilkins, trans., *The Hëëtōpădēs of Vëëshnŏŏ-Sarmā*; all these books were in Emerson's library.

387.26 As . . . scribe: See Manu, *Institutes of Hindu Law*, II, xvi.

388.21 Veeshnoo Sarma: See AN 387.16-17.

389.10 old philosopher: I.e., Veeshnoo-Sarma.

397.9   "common sense and labor.":   Unidentified.

399.13   Lydgate's "Story of Thebes,":   An imitation (ca. 1420) of the *Canterbury Tales*; see Chalmers, I, 570-606.

400.20-21   The Daughters of Zion—the Last Sigh of the Moor: Unidentified.

"Transcripts, 1840-1842"

407.11-12   The Laws . . . Culluca: See AN 173.24-30.

407.25   years of the gods: See AN 25.10-11.

408.21   table land of the Gauhts: See AN 316.2-3.

409.1-3   "pine . . . strawberry":   See AN 177.24-26.

409.8-9   "lily . . . dandelion,":   See AN 177.31.

409.16-17   fowls . . . India: See Murray, *British India*, I, 27.

409.25-410.25   It . . . extremities":   See Plutarch, *Lives*, V, 275-276.

412.13-16   The . . . moon.:   See AN 20.15-18.

412.28-413.2   "Those . . . day.":   Manu, *Institutes of Hindu Law*, II, 12.

413.8-10   "the . . . Brama.":   Murray, *British India*, III, 290, reads "fancifully" not "fantastically."

413.11-21   "the . . . elapsed.":   Murray, *British India*, II, 209.

415.20-21   Charlemagne's egg account: See AN 384.29.

416.13-18   Alwákidis . . . action":   See AN 186.7-11.

417.1-6   history . . . experienced.":   See AN 24.17-21.

417.6   Arthur's twelve battles: See AN 24.21-22.

417.10   a painting of our village: Probably by Ralph Earle (1775); see frontispiece to Ruth Wheeler, *Concord: Climate for Freedom* (Concord, Mass.: Concord Antiquarian Society, 1967).

418.22   Britons . . . Rome.:   See AN 172.15-16.

419.16-420.7   "the Véda . . . Law.":   Sir William Jones, "Preface," in Manu, *Institutes of Hindu Law*, II, xvi (419.16-21), II, viii (419.24-25), II, xvi (419.26-29), II, xvii (419.31-420.2 and 420.3-7).

420.12-17   The . . . evening.:   See Manu, *Institutes of Hindu Law*, II, Chapter I, 1-19, *passim.*

420.19-421.12 "Menu . . . spirits.":   Manu, *Institutes of Hindu Law*, II, 1, 2.

421.14-18   He . . . animals.:   See Manu, *Institutes of Hindu Law*, II, 3-8.

421.19-422.7 "He . . . creatures.":   See Manu, *Institutes of Hindu Law*, II, 8-10.

422.8-9   Menu . . . sages.:   See Manu, *Institutes of Hindu Law*, II, 10.

423.17-425.21 "The . . . man.":   Manu, *Institutes of Hindu Law*, II, 27 (423.17-19), II, 40 (423.20-23), II, 41-42 (423.24-28: source reads "a priest just returned," and 423.29: source reads "all those"), II, 125 (425.15-21).

425.31   table land of the Gauhts: See AN 316.2-3.

426.13-20   The . . . Ouates.:   See Turner, *History of the Anglo-Saxons*, I, 23.

426.24 "the divine male.":   See AN 324.18.

428.8-10   atomists . . . Confucius: See AN 140.18-19.

MS Volume 7

433.2   north eastern angle: Concord town line near Ball's Hill.

434.26-29   As for . . . expressions.":   Sidney, *Works*, I, 9.

434.31-435.2 "he . . . virtue.":   Sidney, *Works*, I, 18, reads "virtues."

435.3-8 "It . . . Friend.":   Sidney, *Works*, I, 23-24.

435.16   the Churchyard: Thomas Gray, "Elegy Written in a Country Churchyard" (1750).

438.25   Godfrey of Boulogne: See AN 148.1.

443.18-444.27   And . . . "spent: See Tytler, *Life of Sir Walter Raleigh*, *passim*, and esp. pp. 284-285 (444.1-12), 300 (444.16-19), 301 (444.20-24), 312 (444.25-26), 313 (444.27: source continues "all the day in distillations.").

443.23   the Earl: Robert Devereux, second Earl of Essex (1567-1601).

446.6   Richter's single line: Probably an allusion to a remark by Richter that Emerson copied (*JMN* V, 346 and VI, 227) and used in the essay "Love": "Away! away!

thou speakest of things which throughout my endless life I have found not and shall not find"; Emerson's source was Chorley, *Memorials of Mrs. Hemans*, I, 282.

446.6-16 De Quincey . . . effects.": T's probable source for this passage from *Confessions of an English Opium Eater* is a footnote in Wilkin's edition of Browne's *Works*, II, 106.

446.11 Twelfth Night: Shakespeare, *Twelfth Night*, I, i, 1-15.

446.17-447.16 "It . . . rhythm.": Browne, *Works*, ed. Wilkin, II, 106-107.

448.25 "The . . . light,": *Emblems*, Book II, Emblem II, 1. 15, reads "night" not "light".

MS Volume 8

453.27 Kanskalkan: Kansk, city in southern Siberia.

455.29 hortus siccus: "An arranged collection of dried plants; a herbarium" (OED).

456.13 "the mower . . . scythe.": Milton, "L'Allegro," l. 66.

457.22 poetic madness: See Drayton, "To my Dearly Loved Friend," in Chalmers, IV, 399.

458.15 ultra plus ne: Cf. *ne plus ultra*, "the ultimate."

459.22-23 Channing's . . . poets: See [Emerson], "Mr. Channing's Poems," *Democratic Review* 13 (September 1843): 309-314.

461.11-12 Soc. Library: New York Society Library, from which T withdrew books during his stay on Staten Island, May to December 1843.

462.1 it . . . takes: See Shakespeare, *Merchant of Venice*, IV, i, 186.

MS Volume 9

466.1-2 Rollin and Ferguson: Charles Rollin, *Ancient History of the Egyptians*, and Adam Ferguson, *History of the Roman Republic*.

466.18-23 The . . . late.: See AN 124.27-126.33.

466.24-25 Carew . . . it: See Carew, "Notice," in *Works*, pp. vii-viii.

469.6-7 Scott . . . wreck: See Sir Walter Scott, "Thomas the Rhymer," in *Works*, III, 33-36.

474.1-4 He . . . say.: See "Life of Daniel," in Chalmers, III, 449.

476.5 Woloffs: See AN 316.13.

476.15-16 the . . . says: See Winthrop, *A Journal of Transactions*, pp. 247-248.

477.14 From . . . plain.: Marlowe, *Hero and Leander*, I, 116.

478.21-479.18 Epitaph . . . lies.: Poems by T; names are probably fictitious.

481.32-482.34 a man . . . prosecution.": Moses Strong (1810-1894), defense attorney in *The United States* v. *James R. Vineyard* (October 15, 1843); T quotes from the *New-York Daily Tribune* for November 4, 1843, p. 4.

483.11-14 When . . . lion.: See Macpherson, *Ossian*, p. 444n.

483.20-21 "the ghosts of our fathers": Malcolm Laing, "Dissertation on the Poems of Ossian," in Macpherson, *Ossian*, p. 80.

484.3-487.9 I . . . ever.": Macpherson, *Ossian*, pp. 182 (484.3-4), 208 (484.22-29), 139 (484.31), 197 (484.33-34), 296 (487.4-9).

487.14 Duans: Macpherson's term for divisions in an Ossianic poem.

489.18 carns: Variant of "cairns."

490.14 πoτνια: "revered."

490.15-17 I . . . festival.': See Marlowe, *Hero and Leander*, I, 91-96.

490.29-30 stains . . . wall: See AN 268.31-32.

490.31-493.3 Oivana . . . rill;": Macpherson, *Ossian*, pp. 124-125 (490.31-33), 132 (491.3-4), 134 (491.11), 138 (491.15), 137 (491.26), 167 (491.29), 175 (491.32-33), 176 (492.3 and 492.6), 181 (492.7), 195 (492.12), 237 (492.15), 252 (492.17), 280 (492.20), 343 (492.22), 194-195 (492.23-25), 391 (492.27), 520 (492.29-30), 415 (493.3); see T's essay, "Homer. Ossian. Chaucer." (*EEM*, pp. 154-173).

494.26-28 It . . . Parry: Sir William Edward Parry, *Three Voyages*, II, 49.

Indexes of Original Journal Volumes, 1837-1840

500.31 Falk: Johannes Daniel Falk (1768-1826), philanthropist and writer.

BIBLIOGRAPHY

Addison, Joseph, and Steele, Richard. *The Spectator*. In *The British Essayists. With Prefaces, Biographical, Historical, and Critical*. Ed. James Ferguson. 2d ed. 40 vols. London: J. Richardson, 1823.

Aeschylus. *Tragœdiae. Ad Exemplar Glasgvense Accurate Expressae*. Lipsiae: Tauchnitii, 1819.

Aubrey, John et al. *Letters Written by Eminent Persons in the Seventeenth and Eighteenth Centuries; . . . and Lives of Eminent Men, by John Aubrey. . . .* 2 vols. London: Longman, Hurst, Rees, Orme, & Brown, 1813.

Audubon, John James. *Ornithological Biography; or, An Account of the Habits of the Birds of the United States of America. . . .* 5 vols. Edinburgh: A. Black, 1831-1839.

Bacon, Francis. *Essays. Moral, Economical, and Political*. Boston: Joseph Greenleaf, 1807.

Boswell, James. *The Life of Samuel Johnson*. London: Jones, 1827.

Bosworth, Joseph. *The Elements of Anglo-Saxon Grammar, with Copious Notes, illustrating the Structure of the Saxon and the Formation of the English Language. . . .* London: Harding, Mavor, & Lepard, 1823.

Browne, Sir Thomas. *Miscellaneous Works*. Ed. Alexander Young. Cambridge, Mass.: Hilliard and Brown, 1831.

————. *Works, including His Life and Correspondence*. Ed. Simon Wilkin. 4 vols. London: W. Pickering, 1835-1836.

Burton, Robert. *The Anatomy of Melancholy. To which is now first prefixed, an Account of the Author*. 11th ed., cor. 3 vols. London: J. & E. Hodson, 1804.

Campbell, Thomas. *Poetical Works, including Theodoric, and many other pieces not contained in any former edition*. Philadelphia: J. Crissy and J. Grigg, 1826.

Candolle, Augustin Pyramus de, and Sprengel, Kurt Polycarp. *Elements of the Philosophy of Plants . . . Tr. from the German*. Edinburgh: W. Blackwood, 1821.

Carew, Thomas. *The Works of Thomas Carew*. Edinburgh: W. & C. Tait, 1824.

Carminum Poetarum Nouem. In Pindari. *Olympia, Pyth-*

ia, Nemea, Isthmia. Graece & Latine . . . and *Carminum Poetarum Nouem, Lyricae Poesas Principum, Fragmenta.* 2 vols. in 1. [Heidelbergae]: Apud Hieronymum Commelinum, Elect. Palat. typographum, 1598.

Chalmers, Alexander, ed. *The Works of the English Poets, from Chaucer to Cowper.* 21 vols. London: J. Johnson, 1810.

Chatto, William Andrew [P. Fisher]. *The Angler's Souvenir . . . With Illustrations by Beckwith & Topham.* London: C. Tilt, 1835.

Chorley, Henry F. *Memorials of Mrs. Hemans.* 2 vols. London: Saunders and Otley, 1835.

Coleridge, Samuel Taylor. *Aids to Reflection. First American, from the first London edition.* Ed. James Marsh. Burlington, Vt.: Chauncey Goodrich, 1829.

————. *Specimens of the Table-Talk of the Late Samuel Taylor Coleridge.* 2 vols. in 1. New York: Harper, 1835.

————. *The Statesman's Manual; or, The Bible the Best Guide to Political Skill and Foresight: A Lay Sermon, addressed to the Higher Classes of Society.* Burlington, Vt.: Chauncey Goodrich, 1832.

Conybeare, John Josias. *Illustrations of Anglo-Saxon Poetry, edited with additions by William Daniel Conybeare.* London: Harding and Lepard, 1826.

Cudworth, Ralph. *The True Intellectual System of the Universe: wherein all the Reason and Philosophy of Atheism is Confuted, and its Impossibility demonstrated . . . A New Edition; with References to the Several Quotations in the Intellectual System; and an Account of the Life and Writings of the Author, by Thomas Birch.* 4 vols. London: J. F. Dove, for Richard Priestley, 1820.

Dante Alighieri. *La Divina Commedia.* . . . 3 vols. Avignone: F. Seguin Ainé, 1816.

Donne, John. *Poems on Several Occasions . . . With Elegies on the Author's Death.* . . . London: Jacob Tonson, 1719.

Douglas, Gawin. *The Aeneid of Virgil translated into Scottish Verse by Gawin Douglas.* 2 vols. Edinburgh: [T. Constable, printer], 1839.

Elliott, Ebenezer. *The Poetical Works of Ebenezer Elliott, the Cornlaw Rhymer.* Edinburgh: W. Tait, 1840.

[Emerson, Ralph Waldo.] "Mr. Channing's Poems." *Democratic Review* 13 (September 1843): 309-314.

Eminent British Statesmen. Ed. Dionysius Lardner. 7 vols. London: Longman, Rees, Orme, Brown, and Green, 1831-1841.

England's Helicon. In *The Paradise of Dainty Devices, reprinted from a transcript of the first edition. . . .* and *England's Helicon. A Collection of Pastoral and Lyric Poems . . . To which is added a biographical and critical introduction.* 2 vols. in 1. London: T. Bensley, for Robert Triphook, 1812.

Evans, Thomas. *Old Ballads, Historical and Narrative, with Some of Modern Date, Collected from Rare Copies and Manuscripts. New ed., rev. and . . . enl. by R. H. Evans.* 4 vols. London: W. Bulmer, for R. H. Evans, 1810.

Fénelon, François de Salignac de la Mothe, Abp. de Cambrai. *Abrégé de la Vie des Plus Illustres Philosophes de l'Antiquité. . . .* Nouv. éd. Paris: Delalain, 1822.

Ferguson, Adam. *The History of the Progress and Termination of the Roman Republic.* New ed. 5 vols. Edinburgh, 1813.

Fuller, Thomas. *The Holy and Profane States. With Some Account of the Author and his Writings.* Cambridge, Mass.: Hilliard and Brown, 1831.

Gérando, Joseph Marie, Baron de. *Histoire Comparée des Systèmes de Philosophie, Considérés Relativement aux Principes des Connaissances Humaines.* 2d ed., rev., cor. et augm. 4 vols. Paris: A. Eymery, 1822-1823.

Gibbon, Edward. *The History of the Decline and Fall of the Roman Empire.* New ed. 12 vols. London: W. Allason, 1821.

————. *Miscellaneous Works. With Memoirs of his Life and Writings, composed by himself, illustrated from his letters. With occasional notes and narrative, by John, Lord Sheffield.* London: B. Blake, 1837.

Goethe, Johann Wolfgang von. *Werke: Vollstandige Ausgabe Letzter Hand.* 55 vols. Stuttgart und Tübingen: J. G. Cotta, 1828-1833.

Gray, Thomas. *Poems of Mr. Gray, to which are added Memoirs of His Life and Writings, by William Mason.* 4 vols. York: A. Ward, 1778.

Guizot, Francois Pierre Guillaume. *Essay on the Character and Influence of Washington in the Revolution of the United States of America.* Boston: Munroe, 1840.

Hall, S. C., ed. *The Book of Gems. The Poets and Artists of Great Britain.* 3 vols. London: Saunders and Otley, 1836-1838.

Herbert, George. *The Temple: Sacred Poems and Private Ejaculations.* 13th ed. London: John Wyat, 1709.

Herrick, Robert. *Poetical Works.* 2 vols. London: William Pickering, 1825.

Homer. *The Iliad of Homer, from the Text of Wolf, with English Notes and Flaxman's Designs.* Ed. C. C. Felton. Boston: Hilliard, Gray, and Company, 1833.

Horace. *Quinti Horatii Flacci Opera Omnia ex Editione J. C. Zeunii.* 2 vols. Londoni: Valpy, 1825.

Jamieson, Robert. *Popular Ballads and Songs. . . .* 2 vols. Edinburgh: A. Constable, 1806.

Johnson, Samuel. *Works. New Edition. With an Essay on his Life and Genius, by Arthur Murphy.* 12 vols. London: Luke Hanford, 1806.

Jonson, Ben. *Works.* 6 vols. London: J. Walthoe, M. Wotton, J. Nicholson, etc., 1716-1717.

Lempriere, John. *A Classical Dictionary; containing a copious Account of All the Proper Names Mentioned in Ancient Authors; with the Value of Coins, Weights, and Measures, Used among the Greeks & Romans: and a Chronological Table.* 6th ed., cor. London: T. Cadell and W. Davies, 1806.

[Linnaeus] Linne, Carl von. *Lachesis Lapponica; or, a Tour in Lapland. . . .* Ed. James Edward Smith. 2 vols. London: White & Cochran, 1811.

Lowell, James Russell. *The Biglow Papers.* Boston: Ticknor, Reed, and Fields, 1848.

Lyell, Charles. *Principles of Geology.* 5th ed. 4 vols. London: John Murray, 1837.

Macpherson, James. *The Genuine Remains of Ossian.* Ed. Patrick MacGregor. London: Smith, Elder, 1841.

Manu. *Institutes of Hindu Law; or, the Ordinances of*

Menu, according to the Gloss of Cullúca. Comprising the Indian System of Duties, Religious and Civil. Verbally Translated from the Original, with a Preface, by Sir William Jones. A New Edition, Collated with the Sanscrit Text, by Graves Chamney Haughton. . . . 2 vols. London: Rivingtons and Cochran, 1825.

Marlowe, Christopher. *Works*. 3 vols. London: W. Pickering, 1826.

Marvell, Andrew. *The Works of Andrew Marvell Esq*. 2 vols. in 1. London: E. Curll, 1726.

Milton, John. *Paradise Lost*. Philadelphia: Johnson & Werner, 1808.

————. *Poetical Works of John Milton, . . . with a Life by Henry John Todd*. 6 vols. London: J. Johnson, 1801.

Morton, Nathaniel. *New England's Memorial*. Ed. John Davis. 5th ed. Boston: Crocker & Brewster, 1826.

Murray, Hugh et al. *Historical and Descriptive Account of British India, from the most remote period to the present time*. . . . 3 vols. New York: Bradley, 1832.

Ockley, Simon. *The History of the Saracens*. . . . 2d ed. 2 vols. London: R. Knaplock, 1708, 1718.

Ovid. *Publii Ovidii Nasonis Metamorphoseon Libri XV ad usum serenissimi delphini*. Philadelphia: Long & DeSilver, 1823.

Parry, Sir William Edward. *Three Voyages for the Discovery of a Northwest Passage*. 2 vols. New York: Harper's Family Library, 1841.

Percy, Thomas, ed. *Reliques of Ancient English Poetry: consisting of Old Heroic Ballads, Songs, and Other Pieces of Our Earlier Poets*. . . . 3 vols. London: J. Dodsley, 1765.

Plutarch. *Lives. Tr. from the Original Greek, with Notes Critical and Historical and a Life of Plutarch by John Langhorne and William Langhorne. New ed., with Corrections and Additions by Francis Wrangham*. 8 vols. New York: Samuel Campbell, 1822.

————. *Morals: Translated from the Greek by Several Hands*. 5th ed., rev. and cor. 5 vols. London: W. Taylor, 1718.

Pope, Alexander. *Poetical Works*. 5 vols. Baltimore: Neals, Wills, & Cole, 1814.

Quarles, Francis. *Emblems*. London: [n.p.], 1766.

[Raleigh] Ralegh, Sir Walter. *The Works of Sir Walter Ralegh, Kt. Now First Collected: to which are prefixed the Lives of the Author by Oldys and Birch.* 8 vols. Oxford: The University Press, 1829.

"Review of Edward Baines's *A History of the Cotton Manufacture in Great Britain.*" *North American Review* 52 (January 1841): 31-56.

"Review of Paul Émile Botta's *Travels in Arabia* [*Relation d'un Voyage dans l'Yémen, entrepris en 1837, pour le Museum d'Histoire Naturelle de Paris*]." *Athenaeum*, January 1, 1842, pp. 3-5.

"Review of Sir John Malcolm's *The Life of Robert Lord Clive.*" *Edinburgh Review* 70 (January 1840): 295-362.

"Review of William Scrope's *The Art of Deer-Stalking.*" *Edinburgh Review* 71 (April 1840): 98-120.

Ritson, Joseph, comp. *Ancient English Metrical Romances.* 3 vols. London: W. Bulmer, for G. & W. Nicol, 1802.

————, comp. *Robin Hood: A Collection of All the Ancient Poems, Songs, and Ballads.* 2 vols. London: T. Egerton and J. Johnson, 1795.

Rollin, Charles. *The Ancient History of the Egyptians, Carthaginians, Assyrians, Babylonians, Medes & Persians, Macedonians, and Grecians.* 4 vols. New York: Long, 1837.

Sa'di. *The Gulistan; or, Rose Garden.* Tr. Francis Gladwin. London: W. Bulmer, 1808.

Scott, Jonathan, trans. *Arabian Nights Entertainments, Carefully Revised and Occasionally Corrected from the Arabic. To Which is Added, a Selection of New Tales, now First Translated from the Arabic Originals. . . .* 6 vols. Philadelphia: R. W. Pomeroy, 1826.

Scott, Sir Walter, Bart. *Complete Works.* 7 vols. New York: Conner & Cooke, 1833-1834.

Shakespeare, William. *The Dramatic Works.* 2 vols. Hartford, Conn.: Andrus & Judd, 1833.

Sidney, Sir Philip. *The Works of the Honourable Sir Philip Sidney, Kt., in Prose and Verse.* 14th ed. 3 vols. London: W. Innys, 1724-1725.

Stephens, John Lloyd. *Incidents of Travel in Egypt, Arabia Petrae, and the Holy Land.* 4th ed. 2 vols. New York: Harper & Brothers, 1838.

Suetonius Tranquillus, C. *The Lives of the First Twelve Caesars; tr. from the Latin: with Annotations, . . . By A. Thomson.* London: G. G. and T. Robinson, 1796.

Theophrastus. *The Characters of Theophrastus; Tr. from the Greek, and Illustrated by Physiognomical Sketches. To which are subjoined The Greek Text, with Notes, and Hints on the Individual Varieties of Human Nature. By Francis Howell.* London: Josiah Taylor, 1824.

Thomson, Thomas. *Travels in Sweden During the Autumn of 1812.* London: Robert Baldwin, 1813.

Turner, Sharon. *History of the Anglo-Saxons.* 2d ed. 2 vols. London: Longman, Hurst, Rees, & Orme, 1807.

Tytler, Patrick Fraser. *Life of Sir Walter Raleigh, . . . including a View of the Most Important Transactions in the Reigns of Elizabeth and James I, . . . with a Vindication of his Character from the Attacks of Hume etc.* Edinburgh: Oliver & Boyd, 1833.

Virgil. *Opera ad usum Serenissimi Delphini. Juxta Editionem Novissimam Londoniensem.* Philadelphia: M. Carey & Son, 1817.

Volney, Constantine Francois Chasseboeuf, comte de. *Travels through Syria and Egypt, in the years 1783-1785. . . . Trans. from the French.* 2 vols. in 1. Dublin: White, 1793.

Warton, Thomas. *The History of English Poetry from the Close of the Eleventh to the Commencement of the Eighteenth Century. . . . Ed. Richard Price.* 4 vols. London: T. Tegg, 1824.

Wilkins, Charles, trans. *The Hĕĕtōpădēs of Vĕĕshnŏŏ-Sarmā, in a Series of Connected Fables, interspersed with Moral, Prudential, and Political Maxims. Translated from an Ancient Manuscript in the Sanskreet Language. With Explanatory Notes.* Bath: R. Cruttwell, 1787.

Winthrop, John. *A Journal of the Transactions and Occurrences in the Settlement of Massachusetts and the Other New-England Colonies, from the year 1630 to 1644.* Hartford: Elisha Babcock, 1790.

"Wiskonsan—Trial of J. R. Vineyard: Correspondence of the New-York Tribune." *The New-York Daily Tribune,* November 4, 1843, p. 4.

Wordsworth, William. *Complete Poetical Works*. Philadelphia: Kay, 1837.

Xenophon. *Minor Works: viz., Memoirs of Socrates; The Banquet; Hiero, on the Condition of Royalty; and Economics, or the Science of Good Husbandry. Translated from the Greek, by Several Hands*. London: J. Walker, 1813.

[Young, Alexander, ed.] *Library of the Old English Prose Writers*. 9 vols. Cambridge, Mass., 1831-1834.

Index

Editorial Appendix

Notes on Illustrations

Title page of Thoreau's first transcribed Journal
volume   page 3

From 1837 to 1841, Thoreau kept his Journal in two
manuscript volumes that are now lost. Sometime in
1841, he began transcribing the contents of these
volumes into a series of new blank books. His title
for the first of these may indicate either that he
had excised many leaves of the original volumes or
that he was editing and selecting his early writing
and transcribing only passages he judged to have
stood the test of time.—Pierpont Morgan Library.

Journal manuscript volumes   following page 616

This photograph of manuscript volumes of Thoreau's
Journal was taken at the home of E. H. Russell on
February 26, 1901, by Herbert W. Gleason. Russell
had inherited the manuscripts from Thoreau's friend
H.G.O. Blake. A few years later, he sold the publication rights to the Journal to Houghton Mifflin
and the manuscripts themselves to George S. Hellman. Eventually they were acquired by J. Pierpont
Morgan; they are now at the Pierpont Morgan Library in New York.—The Herbert W. Gleason Collection, Conover & Mills, Prop. © 1981.

Page of MS Volume 6 (pp. 378-379)

The variation in handwriting and ink on this page is
typical of the volume, which appears to consist of
both transcribed and original entries. The pencil revision visible at the top of the page was eventually
incorporated in part in *A Week on the Concord and
Merrimack Rivers* (see p. 134 in the Princeton Edition) and is not printed in the Journal.—Pierpont
Morgan Library.

Fragmentary Journals of the 1840s

> This photograph of Journal manuscripts now at the Huntington Library includes material printed in MS volumes 7, 8, and 9 in *Journal 1: 1837-1844*. At this time in his career, Thoreau used his Journal for drafting literary works, and thus the surviving manuscripts are fragmentary and scattered.—The Herbert W. Gleason Collection, Conover & Mills, Prop. © 1981.

"Frost crystals in entrance to fox hole"

> One of the hundreds of photographs taken by Herbert W. Gleason to illustrate Thoreau's Journal. Thoreau made several entries on this phenomenon in the Journal during the winter of 1837 to 1838; see pages 15 to 26 of this volume.—The Herbert W. Gleason Collection, Conover & Mills, Prop. © 1981.

Facsimile of Journal text   page 628

> These lines from page 5 of MS volume 5 show Thoreau's pencilled revisions in a passage that he later used in *A Week on the Concord and Merrimack Rivers*; they help to illustrate the rationale for Princeton's copy-text policy.—Pierpont Morgan Library.

Acknowledgments

FOR permission to refer to, copy, and publish manuscript material, the editors are indebted to the Pierpont Morgan Library, New York; the Huntington Library, San Marino, California; Houghton Library, Harvard University; Humanities Research Center, University of Texas at Austin; Henry W. and Albert A. Berg Collection, The New York Public Library, Astor, Lenox and Tilden Foundations; Barrett Library, University of Virginia Library, University of Virginia; Abernethy Library of American Literature, Middlebury College; William K. Bixby Collection, Special Collections, Washington University Libraries, Washington University; and to Professor Raymond Adams and The Herbert W. Gleason Collection, Conover & Mills, Prop.

Contributions of time, expertise, and good will were made by Hans Aarsleff, Holly Bailey, John Beer, James F. Bellman, Jr., Mary Bertagni, Andrew R. Booth, Fredson Bowers, Matthew Bruccoli, Herbert Cahoon, W. R. Connor, Don L. Cook, Barbara Dentinger, Mary Fenn, Mary Gail Fenn, Edward G. M. Grant, Carolyn Jakeman, Mary Janzen, Verlyn Klinkenborg, Robert Lawson-Peebles, A. Walton Litz, Anne McGrath, Henry K. Miller, Janet Miller, Joseph J. Moldenhauer, Caroline Moseley, Marcia Moss, Joel Myerson, David J. Nordloh, Charles Passela, Jean Preston, Miguel A. Quirós-Lugo, Marilynne K. Roach, James R. Saucerman, Evelyn Semmler, Nancy Simmons, Eleanor M. Tilton, Michael Witherell, Theodore Ziolkowski, and the Advisory Board of the Center for Editions of American Authors of the Modern Language Association.

The following members of the Textual Center staff worked on this volume (in addition to those mentioned in Editorial Contributions): Mary Jane Wallace, Linda Laughlin, Lorna C. Mack, Lydia Ostenson, Mark Patterson, Celeste Schenck, Martha Strom, Elizabeth Von Bergen, Pamela White. Carolyn Kappes prepared typed printer's copy of the Appendix, Annotations, and Editorial Appendix.

Material assistance was generously provided by Princeton University, the University of Texas at Austin, the State University of New York, the University of Minnesota at Duluth, the University of Missouri-Columbia, Principia College, and the National Endowment for the Humanities through both the Editing and Publication Programs and the Center for Editions of American Authors of the Modern Language Association.

Editorial Contributions

THE editing of Thoreau's *Journal* for 1837 to 1844 has been a cooperative enterprise. Initial transcripts and preliminary textual tables were prepared by the following: Wendell Glick for MS volumes 1 and 2; Paul O. Williams for 3 and 4; William L. Howarth for 5 and 6; Linck C. Johnson for "Transcripts, 1840-1842"; Thomas Blanding for 7, 8, and 9; and Mr. Blanding and Mr. Johnson for the Appendix. The Index was prepared by John C. Broderick, with the assistance of Mr. Howarth, Veronica Makowsky, and Elizabeth Hall Witherell. Subsequent editing of the text and textual apparatus was the responsibility of Mr. Blanding, Mr. Broderick, Mr. Howarth, Robert Sattelmeyer, and Ms. Witherell. The General Introduction is the work of Mr. Howarth and Mr. Sattelmeyer; the Historical Introduction of Mr. Sattelmeyer; and the Textual Introduction of Mr. Blanding, Mr. Howarth, Mr. Sattelmeyer, and Ms. Witherell. Annotations were prepared by William Brennan, Verlyn Klinkenborg, Susan McCloskey, Ms. Makowsky, Nancy Simmons, and Kevin Van Anglen. The following shared the tasks of perfecting transcripts and proofreading galley and page proofs: Mr. Blanding, Mr. Broderick, Mr. Glick, Mr. Howarth, Mr. Johnson, Leonard Neufeldt, Mr. Sattelmeyer, Mr. Williams, and Ms. Witherell. Carolyn Kappes, Mr. Neufeldt, and Ms. Simmons reviewed the tables.

General Introduction

> I do not know but thoughts written down thus in a journal might be printed in the same form to greater advantage—than if the related ones were brought together into separate essays. They are now allied to life—& are seen by the reader not to be far fetched— It is more simple—less artful— I feel that in the other case I should have no proper frame for my sketches.
>
> MS Journal, January 27, 1852

WHEN Henry Thoreau died in 1862, he was known only to a relatively small audience for two books and a scattering of poems and essays. His Journal, which contained over two million words in forty-seven manuscript volumes, was known only to his family and close friends. During the next fifty years, as posthumously published works swelled the canon, public awareness of the richness and extent of the Journal grew; and, influenced by nineteenth-century estimations of Thoreau as a gifted literary naturalist, the text itself gradually emerged: first in four volumes of seasonal extracts edited by H.G.O. Blake from 1881 to 1892, and then in the fourteen-volume Walden Edition published by Houghton Mifflin in 1906. Edited by Francis H. Allen and Bradford Torrey, the Walden Edition has remained standard to the present. Torrey and Allen did not print all the material that was available to them nor did they attempt to preserve the original form and character of the Journal. Moreover, since 1906 a number of additional Journal manuscripts have come to light. Because Thoreau's literary stature has risen dramatically during the twentieth century and because the Journal is the central document of his imaginative life, the aim of the Princeton Edition is to print an accurate text of the complete Journal as Thoreau originally wrote it.

Although much of *A Week on the Concord and Merrimack Rivers*, *Walden*, and many of Thoreau's lectures and essays were built upon passages from the Journal, no clear evidence exists of any attempt to publish portions of it during his lifetime. In 1843, J. L. O'Sullivan, editor of the *Democratic Review*, asked Thoreau to send him "some of those extracts from your Journal, reporting some of your private interviews with nature, with which I have before been so much pleased." But O'Sullivan was probably seeking an essay like "Natural History of Massachusetts," which Thoreau had compiled in part from Journal extracts and published in *The Dial* the previous year; at any rate, no publication of extracts from the Journal ensued as a result of O'Sullivan's request. In 1853, R. W. Emerson urged Ellery Channing to prepare a book based on their walks around Concord, lending him his own journal for this purpose. According to F. B. Sanborn, Thoreau was involved in the enterprise as well and lent his Journal to Channing for copying also. But no contemporary document mentions Thoreau's participation, and Channing's manuscript, "Concord Walks," was not published at the time.[1] Channing did have access to

[1] Sanborn's account is in his edition of Ellery Channing's *Thoreau: The Poet-Naturalist* (Boston: Charles E. Goodspeed, 1902), pp. ix, 132. The contemporary accounts, however, imply that only Channing and Emerson were involved. See Walter Harding, "Two F. B. Sanborn Letters," *American Literature* 25 (May 1953): 230-234; Rollo G. Silver, "Ellery Channing's Collaboration with Emerson," *American Literature* 7 (March 1935): 84-86; and Bronson Alcott, *The Journals of Bronson Alcott*, ed. Odell Shepard (Boston: Little, Brown and Company, 1938), p. 269.

the Journal, however, apparently both during and after Thoreau's life, and his volume of extracts from it provided the basis of the first two posthumous publications of Journal text.

Emerson used Channing's extracts in preparing the eulogy he delivered at Thoreau's funeral in May 1862, and in June he copied many more pages from the Journal (probably from the original volumes in the possession of Thoreau's family) into his own journal while expanding the funeral oration for the August 1862 *Atlantic Monthly*. Emerson's biographical essay printed the first selection of Journal text, and its judgments of Thoreau acquired a wide authority: it was reprinted as the Introduction to the first posthumous collection of Thoreau's writings, *Excursions* (1863), in Emerson's *Lectures and Biographical Sketches* (1884), as the Introduction to the *Miscellanies* volume of Thoreau's *Writings* in the Riverside (or New Riverside) Edition (1894), and as the Introduction to the first volume of the Manuscript and Walden (1906) Editions.

The passages that Emerson selected in order to call attention to "their power of description and literary excellence" naturally emphasized Thoreau's ability to construct apothegms and make pithy observations of natural phenomena, such as "Some circumstantial evidence is very strong, as when you find a trout in the milk," or "The chub is a soft fish, and tastes like boiled brown paper salted." In addition to unavoidably distorting the contents of the Journal through this kind of selectivity, Emerson's essay originated the two most enduring shibboleths of Thoreau studies. First, he found in Thoreau's career a lamentable waste of talent and energy: "I cannot help counting it a fault in him that he had no ambition. Wanting this, instead of engineering for all America, he was the captain of a huckleberry party." The second claim, somewhat contradictory to the first, was that "The scale on which his studies proceeded was so large as to require longevity" and that "It seems an injury that he should leave in the midst his broken task."[2] These judgments bracket the selections from the Journal, and they foreshadow what was to become a major role for it: providing critics with evidence either that Thoreau's powers were misdirected or that he was at work on projects of so vast a scope that they would require many more years to complete.

Excerpts from the Journal appeared in an even more distorted form in the first biography of Thoreau, Ellery Channing's *Thoreau: The Poet-Naturalist* (1873). Drawn from twenty years of intimate acquaintance, Channing's quirky volume provides an invaluable picture of how Thoreau organized his walks and excursions, took careful field notes, and wrote his Journal entries on a daily basis (see Textual Introduction, pp. 615-616, n. 2). But when the publisher complained that the book would be too short, Channing retrieved his 1853 manuscript of "Concord Walks," added heavily revised passages from Thoreau's Journal, and inserted the resulting hodge-podge into the middle of his biography with no explanation other than that it would "furnish a more familiar idea of Thoreau's walks and talks with his friends." These "Walks and Talks" are imaginary conversations—in poetic diction—among unidentified speakers, interspersed with ponderous repartee and

[2] See Joel Myerson, "Emerson's 'Thoreau': A New Edition from Manuscript," in *Studies in the American Renaissance 1979* (Boston: Twayne, 1979), pp. 17-92.

quotations of verse. Channing's selection from the Journal represents Thoreau as a man whose absorption in natural history amounted to a kind of dandified pastoralism.

Nevertheless, because Sophia Thoreau, Henry's sister and literary executor, was for a long time unwilling to permit publication of the Journal, Emerson's and Channing's abridged and altered extracts constituted the only Journal material to see print for many years. Although she had worked with both Emerson and Channing to edit and publish several posthumous works by Thoreau between 1863 and 1867, Sophia regarded the Journal manuscripts as "sacred" and felt "inclined to defer giving them to the public." Eventually she named H.G.O. Blake, Thoreau's long-time friend and correspondent from Worcester, to succeed her as executor. She died in 1876, and Thoreau's manuscripts passed to Blake.

Blake had been devoted to Thoreau and was conscientious to a fault, but he had always played the role of a disciple seeking guidance and was unsure about what to do with the papers he had inherited. In 1877, he consulted Bronson Alcott, who had held the manuscripts in Concord while Sophia spent her declining years in Bangor, Maine, and who had read the Journal and wished it to be published. Alcott had compiled a book from his own journal, *Concord Days* (1872), in which he had arranged passages into seasonal chapters, and he advocated a similar arrangement for his friend's manuscripts: "A delightful volume might be compiled from Thoreau's *Journals* by selecting what he wrote at a certain date annually, thus giving a calendar of his thoughts on that day from year to year." Blake accepted this basic plan, and over the next fourteen years, working in a deliberate and leisurely fashion, he prepared four volumes of such Journal extracts for publication by Houghton Mifflin: *Early Spring in Massachusetts* (1881), *Summer* (1884), *Winter* (1888), and *Autumn* (1892). Although a few reviewers pointed out that Blake had imposed an artificial structure on the Journal, his volumes were in general favorably received and served to stimulate interest in Thoreau.[3] Despite Blake's estimable intentions, however, he did damage the manuscripts: he mislabeled and misdated several volumes, marked passages for selection with heavy blue or black pencil in the text, and at some point lost a volume of the Journal—Thoreau's third volume of transcribed entries for 1840-1841—which was not recovered for many years.

When Houghton Mifflin gathered Thoreau's writings for the first collected edition, the Riverside Edition of 1894, Blake's four volumes of seasonal extracts were included. Thus, by the end of the century, the Journal had finally achieved a place of some prominence in Thoreau's work. Still it appeared in a form chosen by Alcott and Blake rather than Thoreau, a form that reflected their belief that Thoreau had intended to use the Journal in a similar way, to compile a "Kalendar" or "Atlas" of Concord. Addi-

[3] An unsigned review in *The Nation* complained that *Summer* illustrated only "the narrow range of his [Thoreau's] misanthropic spirit" (39 [July 31, 1884], 98); and after *Autumn*, the last of Blake's volumes, appeared, *The Nation*'s critic thought it was "unfortunate for his reputation" that Thoreau should be known by the seasonal volumes (56 [January 26, 1893], 65). More characteristic was the tone of *The Critic*, which praised the "cool beauty and clarity" of *Winter* (9 [March 3, 1888], 100), and observed with satisfaction that "The circle of the year, as Thoreau knew it and noted it in his Journal, finds completion in the volume called 'Autumn'" (18 [November 26, 1892], 292).

tionally, the seasonal volumes suggested that the Journal contained the raw material of books but was not in itself an integral document—its contents could be selected and rearranged to make new books; this point of view has persisted ever since. The popularity of such natural history writers as John Burroughs, Wilson Flagg, Bradford Torrey, and John Muir—in some sense literary descendants of Thoreau—helped to create the climate in which Blake's volumes were welcomed. And despite Blake's desire to portray the philosophical side of Thoreau as well, the seasonal books maintained and advanced the popular estimation of Thoreau as a progenitor of American natural history writing, a Yankee version of Gilbert White whose Selborne was Concord, Massachusetts.

This image was strengthened by other appearances and treatments of Journal material generated by Blake's work. Blake himself published some of his selections serially in the *Atlantic Monthly* in 1878 and 1885 under the titles "April Days," "May Days," "Days in June," and "Winter Days." In 1878, writing for *Scribner's Monthly*, Ellery Channing edited extracts from the Journal, which he called "Days and Nights in Concord," and this collection, along with Blake's "May Days," was included in the Riverside Edition of *Excursions*. Just after the turn of the century, F. B. Sanborn published an enlarged edition of Channing's *Thoreau: The Poet-Naturalist* (1902) that contained additional Journal passages, and the children of Thoreau's friend Daniel Ricketson edited a memorial volume for their father, *Daniel Ricketson and His Friends* (1902), that contained passages from the Journal recounting the visits Thoreau made to Ricketson in New Bedford. Throughout the period of Blake's ownership, critics and biographers, including Sanborn, T. W. Higginson, H. S. Salt, Annie Russell Marble, and Horace Scudder, continued to allude to and quote from the unpublished manuscripts, and it was clear that the seasonal selections had not entirely satisfied the demand for publication of the Journal.

After Blake's death in 1898, the manuscripts passed to his friend E. H. Russell, a schoolteacher from Worcester who had known Thoreau only slightly. Whereas Blake had been concerned to put Thoreau before the world according to ideals he thought his mentor embodied, Russell's principal interest was to turn a profit from his inheritance. Ironically, his mercenary approach speeded the publication of the whole Journal and led eventually to the manuscript volumes being permanently housed in the Pierpont Morgan Library, where they remain today in the pine box Thoreau is supposed to have built for them. In 1903, after successful litigation to bar the Thoreau heirs from any share in his profits, Russell sold the publication rights to the Journal (along with bundles of loose manuscript for binding into deluxe sets of a new Thoreau edition) to Houghton Mifflin. Bliss Perry reported to the Houghton Mifflin editorial conference that the Journal manuscripts contained "materials of priceless value" and urged that they be "printed in full as they appear now." The firm agreed, and Perry secured Bradford Torrey, a well-known naturalist and regular contributor to the *Atlantic Monthly*, as general editor for the project, assigning Francis H. Allen from Houghton Mifflin to assist him. Allen was also interested in natural history and had recently compiled a book called *Nature's Diary* (1897) in which he had included passages from Blake's seasonal volumes along with excerpts from the journals of other New England writers, with blank facing pages for the owner's thoughts.

Most of the actual editorial labor fell to Allen, with Torrey annotating the transcribed text. Working at first alone and then with the aid of a transcriber, an indexer, and a proofreader, Allen took a little over three years to produce the fourteen-volume text of the Journal printed in the standard twenty-volume 1906 Walden Edition of Thoreau's *Writings*. Considering the pressures under which the editors worked —Houghton Mifflin was impatient to issue the set, and Russell was anxious for the return of the manuscripts, having in the meantime made a separate bargain to sell them—the 1906 Edition was an impressive achievement. A landmark in American literary publishing, it was also crucial to the establishment of Thoreau's reputation. It was the first large multivolume edition of an American author's journal to be included in his complete works, and the Journal, presented for the first time in the chronological order in which it was composed, had every appearance of being definitive. Henceforth it would have to be considered in any thoughtful evaluation of Thoreau's life and art or of his place in nineteenth-century American literature. The 1906 Edition has been reprinted twice (by Houghton Mifflin in 1949 and by Dover in 1962) and has served as the source of a great many volumes of selections from the Journal on themes varying from *Thoreau's Bird Lore* to *A Writer's Journal*.

The rise in Thoreau's stature in American letters in the twentieth century—doubtless due in part to the addition of the Journal to his canon—has moved him from the periphery to the center of American litera-

ture and made him a major figure in the first generation of writers to give mature articulation to a national literature. If Thoreau remains a controversial
figure it is not because he was, as Isaac Hecker once
grumbled, a "consecrated crank—rather be crank than
president," but because his contrariness is expressive
of one-half of a deep-seated antiphony in American
culture. The interest that has been generated in
Thoreau's thought, in the composition and genesis
of his literary works, and in the quality of his language and his metaphoric imagination demands a
level of textual accuracy, completeness, and fidelity
that the 1906 Edition of the Journal does not provide.

Some editorial liberties taken by Torrey and Allen
were no more than minor impositions of conventional
and genteel standards—a few proper names deleted
where living people or descendants might take offense,
for example, or the omission of Thoreau's explicit
drawing of a phalluslike fungus in an entry for
October 16, 1856. For the most part, however, Thoreau the man is faithfully represented in the 1906
Journal, despite the somewhat patronizing attitude
toward Thoreau's taxonomic abilities expressed by
Torrey, himself a naturalist of some skill. Unlike
Emerson's early editors, who sought to preserve the
genteel reputation of their subject, Torrey and Allen
did not attempt to make Thoreau into an Olympian,
or even a conventionally respectable figure.

The most serious limitation of the 1906 Edition is
its incompleteness. The so-called "Lost Journal" that
had disappeared from Blake's possession (manuscript
volume 3, pages 161-226 in the first volume of the
Princeton Edition) was not available to Torrey and
Allen: it was not published until 1958, when Perry
Miller edited it with elaborate and intrusive com-

mentary in *Consciousness in Concord.* The fragmentary Journal volumes of the 1840s, key documents in the genesis of both *A Week on the Concord and Merrimack Rivers* and *Walden,* were unknown to the editors; these manuscripts have been collected and assembled for the first time in the present edition. Other volumes of the Journal—titled by the present editors "Transcripts 1840-1842" in the first volume of Journal and "Long Book" in the second volume—were available to Torrey and Allen, but with the exception of a very few dated entries, the earlier editors did not consider these manuscripts to be significant enough for inclusion in their edition; they viewed Thoreau, unconsciously no doubt, from their own perspective as natural historians, deciding that volumes of transcriptions and original material used in the preparation of literary works were extrinsic to the Journal.

In addition, since the Journal was intended to accompany Thoreau's other works as part of a complete edition, Torrey and Allen omitted passages that duplicated material in the published writings whenever this could be done without damaging the context. Accordingly they deleted early versions of literary works in the Journal, including drafts for *A Week,* *Walden,* *Cape Cod,* and *The Maine Woods*—the very material that would be of most interest to students and scholars concerned not only with the genesis of Thoreau's works but with his methods of composition and revision as well. These omissions, probably in part the result of pressures for economy and haste by the publisher, have the effect of both misrepresenting by understatement Thoreau's concerns and activities as a writer and of magnifying the distance between his Journal and his works for publication.

Thoreau revised the Journal extensively, most

often interlining pencil corrections and additions within original ink composition, usually with a view toward using the revised passage in some literary work. Torrey and Allen solved the problem of which level of composition to print by treating each case individually, "using the original form where that seemed best, and the revised form where the corrections and improvements seemed to warrant it." Thus any judgments based on the 1906 text about Thoreau's adaptation of Journal material for the composition of other works are unreliable, since the reader cannot know whether the passage is original or has already been revised with the given work in mind. The present edition prints Thoreau's original stage of composition—the Journal as unmediated by any later intentions—reporting later revisions selectively in the Editorial Appendix.

Deciding that for a commercial venture readability was more desirable than strict fidelity to the text, Torrey and Allen freely corrected Thoreau's spelling, punctuation, capitalization, and even sentence structure to make the Journal read smoothly (see Textual Introduction, pp. 628-629). These changes convey an impression of the Journal as a more polished and final work than it actually is; in their original form, Thoreau's thoughts are frequently tentative, provisional, and hastily noted. His punctuation, for example, was not always careful, but his idiosyncrasies even in this regard are occasionally significant: for example, his use of the dash as an all-purpose mark of punctuation adds an energetic visual dimension to his prose that the 1906 Edition eliminates. Finally, certain design features and printing conventions observed in the 1906 Edition amplify the misleading representation of the Journal as a finished product:

running heads provide titles for the contents of every other page, the text is divided by months into chapterlike units, long paragraphs condense a number of separate units in the manuscript, and each volume is accompanied by a table of contents—all supplied by the editors.

Although the present edition is intended to supersede the 1906 Edition as a standard scholarly source, it is designed for the convenience of the general reader as well. Like other volumes in *The Writings of Henry D. Thoreau*, the Journal is printed in "clear text," with all editorial commentary and apparatus confined to the back of the volume. Thoreau's text is, on the whole, easily understood without drastic emendation; mistakes, anomalies, and inconsistencies in the manuscript have been allowed to stand unless sense is seriously threatened. Thoreau's own speculation that "thoughts written down thus in a journal might be printed in the same form" expresses the basic editorial policy for the Princeton Edition, in the belief that the entire original Journal clearly displays the contours of Thoreau's career—the cultivation of his ideals, his studies, and his craft—and provides the simple and sincere account of life that he most valued.

SOURCES

Information and direct quotations in the General Introduction not cited in footnotes may be verified in the following primary and secondary sources: Pierpont Morgan Library manuscripts MA 1302:15 (Journal), MA 609 (Ellery Channing's extracts from the Journal), and MA 1443 (letter of Sophia Thoreau to T. W. Higginson refusing his request to edit the Journal); *The Correspondence of Henry David Thor-*

eau, ed. Walter Harding and Carl Bode (New York: New York University Press, 1958); *The Journals of Ralph Waldo Emerson*, Vol. 9, 1856-1863, ed. Edward Waldo Emerson and Waldo Emerson Forbes (Boston: Houghton Mifflin, 1909-1914); "Introduction" to *The Journals and Miscellaneous Notebooks of Ralph Waldo Emerson*, Vol. 1, 1819-1822, ed. William H. Gilman et al. (Cambridge, Mass.: The Belknap Press of Harvard University Press, 1960); *The Letters of A. Bronson Alcott*, ed. Richard L. Herrnstadt (Ames, Iowa: The Iowa State University Press, 1969); Walter Harding, *The Days of Henry Thoreau* (New York: Alfred A. Knopf, 1965); Francis H. Allen, *A Bibliography of Henry David Thoreau* (Boston: Houghton Mifflin, 1908); and William L. Howarth, *The Literary Manuscripts of Henry David Thoreau* (Columbus: Ohio State University Press, 1974). Details of the publication of the 1906 Edition derive from William L. Howarth, "Editing Thoreau's Journal: A Brief History of the 1906 Text," a typescript based on a partial transcription of the Houghton Mifflin letter books for 1903 to 1906, which are presently housed in the Houghton Library, Harvard University.

Historical Introduction

> For a long time I was reporter to a journal, of no
> very wide circulation, whose editor has never yet
> seen fit to print the bulk of my contributions, and,
> as is too common with writers, I got only my
> labor for my pains. However, in this case my pains
> were their own reward.
>
> *Walden*, p. 18

In the pages of his Journal, Henry Thoreau
commented from time to time on the problems of his
craft, but this passage from *Walden* is his only public
acknowledgment of the crucial role the Journal
played in his development as a writer. Characteristi-
cally, the reference is doubly veiled: a contemporary
audience would have recognized in it an allusion to
The Dial, for which Thoreau wrote, without compensation, from 1840 to 1844; and its tone of nonchalance and casual self-deprecation masks the disappointment that it confesses. In a similar way, the
prevalent air of high aspiration in the Journal for
1837 to 1844 may obscure the struggle for vocation
that it records.

The Journal was eventually to become the major
written work of Thoreau's life, but it went through a
distinct evolution, and its relation to his literary career shifted over the years. From 1837 to 1844 it
changed (in its surviving form) most dramatically,
from a kind of display case for his reading, his poetry,
and his original thoughts and aphorisms to a writer's
workbook, fragmentary and almost irrecoverable because so many pages were excised for his compositions. The Journal rarely reveals Thoreau's personal
reactions in this period of extraordinary change and

growth as he moved slowly toward the themes of his maturity, but its development predicts what would be very difficult to discern from the uncertainty and frequent failure in the outward life. By 1844, Thoreau was on the verge of his literary independence, preparing to go to live by the pond, where in the next two years he would complete drafts of *A Week on the Concord and Merrimack Rivers* and *Walden*.

For a young intellectual with literary aspirations who had been converted to the "new views" of Transcendentalism by Emerson's *Nature* while in college, keeping a journal was an inevitable first step toward a career in letters. Culturally there was ample precedent and stimulus, for however enervated the old religious orthodoxy had become by Thoreau's day, the New England tradition of self-examination was still powerful. Members of his own family, classmates at Harvard, and fellow townsmen kept ledgers, "day books," diaries, and journals, testifying to a twin impulse to record the particulars of life and to inquire into the state of the soul, a tradition reaching back to the first generation of Puritan divines. Thoreau's sister Sophia and his brother John kept journals intermittently, and Henry anticipated his own Journal while in college by keeping both a commonplace book entitled "Miscellaneous Extracts" and an "Index rerum" that contained extracts from his reading (alphabetically arranged), book reviews for a Harvard literary society, and reading lists. (Later Thoreau used the "Index rerum" for indexes of his first two Journal volumes and a catalogue of his library.) As a sophomore, he wrote a required theme on "keeping a private journal," in which he argued that the practice of daily writing would assist one "in settling accounts with his mind" and help him "turn over a new leaf, having carefully perused the last one," embryonically foreshadowing what were to become his favorite metaphors for self-cultivation and growth in *Walden*.

If the practice of journal keeping was widespread, it was particularly highly developed and organized among the loose band of religious seekers and high thinkers who were gradually coming under Emerson's influence in Concord and with whom Thoreau soon became associated following his graduation from Harvard in 1837. Ostensibly a private genre, the journal became a favored channel of communication among the Transcendentalists, who exchanged journal passages as a sort of formal supplement to the meetings and "Conversations" through which they tried to promote the sharing of spontaneously generated insight. One version of the story of Emerson's first meeting with Thoreau, in fact, is that the older man was attracted to the younger on hearing that a passage in Thoreau's Journal had anticipated a remark he was to make in a lecture. The journal had a high place in the Transcendentalists' hierarchy of literary forms precisely because it captured the transitory moment of illumination (Emerson once criticized Margaret Fuller for writing too few aphorisms in her journal) and admitted the eclectic range of the sources of truth—reading, conversation, the correspondence of friends, nature, and solitary meditation. *The Dial* routinely printed selections from journals and other works in progress with such titles as "Notes from the Journal of a Scholar," "A Leaf from 'A Voyage to Porto Rico'," and "Days from a Diary."

The most important stimulus to and influence on Thoreau's Journal at its inception, however, was Emerson. After the publication of *Nature* in 1836 and the "American Scholar" address at Thoreau's Harvard commencement exercises in 1837, he was already the leading figure of New England religious and literary reform. As Thoreau himself acknowledged in a Journal entry in 1846, probably not without some ambivalence, Emerson's "personal influence upon younger persons [is] greater than any man's." Emerson was in all probability the questioner who prompted Thoreau's first Journal entry, and throughout the period covered in this volume, their relationship was close and complex. Emerson's direct influence was probably at its height from April 1841 to May 1843 when Thoreau lived at his house, receiving his room and board in return for labor as a general handyman. In addition to being Thoreau's employer during this time, Emerson was his friend and mentor, his editor, and his unofficial literary agent. Emerson by turns encouraged and discouraged his poetry, lent him his own commonplace book for copying, solicited and promoted his contributions to *The Dial*, guided his reading, first encouraged him to turn to use in his writing a talent for the observation of nature, interceded with the publishers who failed to pay him for his first essay printed outside *The Dial*, and even lent him money to undertake research for a literary project at the Harvard College Library. While the advantages of this arrangement were immeasurable to Thoreau, he found himself at the same time in the most awkward of positions: principal disciple of the apostle of self-reliance. Not for several years would Thoreau acknowledge the deep tensions that gradually grew up between them, and even during these early years of friendship Thoreau rarely mentioned the older man by name. Yet Emerson's presence and his influence on the early Journal are always to be inferred.

OCTOBER 1837 TO APRIL 1842

Although the Journal for these early years presents what appears to be a fairly complete chronological record, a great deal remains uncertain about its origins, how it was kept, and even its original contents. As Thoreau noted on December 27, 1855, when he made a brief chronology of the important dates in his life, he began his first Journal volume, which he called "the big Red Journal" or the "Journal of 546 ps," in October 1837. It ran to June 1840 and was followed by a second volume, the "Journal of 396 ps," which covered the period from June 1840 to January 31, 1841. Neither of these two volumes is extant, although a few scattered leaves from the first volume and Thoreau's partial indexes to both volumes survive (see Appendix). The Journal for these years is preserved in a transcription of the original volumes that Thoreau made some time after completing the second volume. A comparison of the indexes of the original volumes with the contents of the transcribed volumes does not indicate any significant change in the nature of the material, but it is impossible to determine the extent to which Thoreau may have rearranged, compressed, revised, or otherwise altered the original entries in the process of transcribing them. Thus, while the Journal is often the only source of information about Thoreau's literary activities during this time, the light it sheds on the beginnings of his career is not direct. The only Journal text available for these years is actually a redaction of the original, selected and edited to an unknown degree by Thoreau.

Thoreau headed the first of his transcript volumes "Gleanings—Or What Time Has Not Reaped Of My Journal" (p. 3), leaving some ambiguity about why he undertook the transcriptions: it may be that the leaves of the original volumes had literally been "reaped"—that is, cut out for inclusion in drafts of literary works; or it may be that his motive was chiefly editorial, and he chose to preserve only as much of his early work as seemed to him worthy or representative of his aspirations. In any case, a greater problem is posed by the dating of these "Gleanings," for as the editors of the 1906 Edition observed, it is impossible to determine just when Thoreau made these transcriptions or where the transcribed portion ends and original material begins. Since this problem bears upon the nature and purpose of the Journal during these years, its components must be described in some detail.

The volume headed "Gleanings . . ." is the first in a series of nine sequentially numbered MS notebooks in which Thoreau kept his Journal from the time he began transcribing until 1844 (see Textual Introduction, p. 620). Transcriptions from the first original Journal filled all of the first volume in this new series and ran to page "73" in the second, where Thoreau noted "End of my Journal of 546 ps" (p. 126). Transcriptions from the second original volume ran from page "74" of the second volume to page "33" of the fourth, where Thoreau again noted "End of my Journal of 396 ps" (p. 243). The next entry, dated "Tuesday Feb. 2nd 1841," begins "It is easy to repeat but hard to originate," suggesting at least the possibility that the Journal from this point on may be original— although the passage that begins with this observation is not concerned with composition but with repetition in nature. Supporting this possibility is the fact that there is no evidence of any additional original Journal volume beyond the "Journal of 396 ps."

Thoreau refers explicitly to the "Journal of 546 ps" and the "Journal of 396 ps" in three separate places: in the transcribed volumes, in his autobiographical chronology in 1855, and in his indexes to both volumes; nowhere does he refer to a third or subsequent original volume or volumes.

The appearance of the manuscript itself, however, suggests that the Journal continued as a transcription for some time. The pages of the rest of MS volume 4 and all of MS volume 5, covering the period from February 2 to September 30, 1841, are relatively clean, with few of the kinds of errors (false starts, cancellations, etc.) associated with original composition. Some errors, on the other hand, are characteristic of transcription, as in MS volume 5 (pp. 319, 322), where Thoreau noted in an entry made between August 18 and 20, 1841, that he had omitted a sentence in an earlier entry for August 9 and inserted it in the later entry.

MS volume 5 ends with an entry for September 30, 1841, and MS volume 6 does not begin until November 29—leaving a gap of two months in the Journal. Earlier in September, Thoreau had described in the Journal (p. 330) an idea for an ambitious long "poem to be called Concord." Since he mentioned in a September 8 letter to Lucy Jackson Brown that he was "in the mid-sea of verses," and since Emerson described him in a letter from the same period as being "full of noble madness lately," perhaps he was working on his long poem during his absence from journalizing. But he may also have been transcribing his early Journal during this time, copying the "Journal of 546 ps" and the "Journal of 396 ps," and transcribing from some other source his Journal from February to September. In the September 8 letter to

Lucy Jackson Brown, he also quotes a fragment of a Saxon poem that he had entered in his Journal on December 27, 1837. It seems quite likely that he had his early Journal before him as he composed the letter, for he misquotes the poem in the same way in both (see Annotation 23.16-17). Thus he may have filled MS volumes 1 to 5 at this time.

MS volume 6, which covers the period from November 29, 1841, to April 3, 1842, appears to contain a combination of transcribed and original material. On the one hand, in some places, the appearance of this manuscript suggests original composition, since it contains proportionately more cancellations and false starts than MS volumes 1 to 5 and since more variation in Thoreau's handwriting occurs from entry to entry. Near the end of the volume, Thoreau noted in the margin in two places that he had "Set the Red Hen Sunday March 21st" and "Set the grey hen Ap. 1st" (pp. 385, 399), information of current interest that would not be worth transcribing unless the transcription were made within a matter of days. On the other hand, some portions of MS volume 6 appear to have been transcribed. A series of incorrect dates in December 1841 can be plausibly explained only as errors due to a lapse of time between composition and transcription: an entry for December 12 was first headed "Sunday Nov. 15th 1841," after which Thoreau crossed out the "1" in "15" and wrote "5th" above the line. Then, some time later, he must have discovered that he was still off by a week, for he crossed out the "5th" and wrote "12th" above it. The twelfth and the fifth were both Sundays in December, but not in November, and the entry follows one for November 30, but Thoreau never changed the month to December. He made precisely the same sequence of errors in the following four consecutive entries, first changing the original to a day ten days earlier and then changing the second date to one a week later.

Another bit of physical evidence suggests even more strongly that the Journal was still being transcribed as late as the end of MS volume 6. The end of a sentence that closes MS volume 6 also appears at the top of the first surviving leaf in a commonplace book that Thoreau kept from 1840 to 1848, suggesting that he used the leaves preceding it, now lost, to compose material for volume 6. Thoreau entered material in the first surviving leaves of this commonplace book in March or April 1842; the entry in volume 6 is dated April 3, 1842. The surviving text in the commonplace book, at the top of the verso of a leaf whose recto contained new material on Sir Walter Raleigh that Thoreau wished to preserve, reads "desert, still keeps in advance of the immigrant, and fills the cavities of the forest for his repast." Volume 6 closes with the following sentence: "But the little economist which fed the evangelist in the desert—still keeps in advance of the immigrant, and fills the cavities of the forest for his repast" (p. 402).

The sum of the evidence suggests that Thoreau kept his Journal somewhat erratically at this time, occasionally making original entries in MS volume 6 and at other times transcribing entries from another source—other notebooks or loose sheets. During this period of just over four months, he led what was for him a quite transient and unsettled life, living with Charles Stearns Wheeler in Cambridge for two weeks in November and December while he worked at the Harvard College Library, and moving back and forth between Emerson's and his family's house during the turmoil of the winter of 1842. His brother

John and Emerson's son Waldo both died in January 1842, and Thoreau himself was so desolated by his brother's death that he suffered for several weeks afterward from a sympathetic illness.

To summarize, the editors' best judgment about the composition and keeping of the Journal from October 1837 to April 1842 is that (1) Thoreau transcribed the contents of his two large original volumes into MS volumes 1 to 4 some time after January 31, 1841 —perhaps during his two-month break from journalizing during October and November 1841; (2) the rest of MS volume 4 and all of MS volume 5, covering the period from February through September 1841, also appear to have been transcribed, probably during the fall of 1841, although there is no evidence of an original source volume; (3) MS volume 6, covering from November 29, 1841, to April 3, 1842, appears to contain both transcribed and original entries, as Thoreau moved gradually toward the practice of using his Journal volumes directly for whatever purpose was at hand, whether Journal entry or literary composition—his characteristic practice for the rest of the 1840s.

This early transcribed Journal is chiefly a repository rather than a source book, a record of the results of Thoreau's intellectual and literary labors, not of his efforts to compose. All of MS volume 1 and part of MS volume 2 resemble a commonplace book as much as a journal, since quotations from his reading bulk large—Goethe, Homer, Virgil, Aeschylus, and Plutarch appear prominently—and original entries have synoptic titles like "Small Talk," "Influence," "Fear," and "Old Books." Thoreau's familiarity with both the Bible and the tradition of English poetry is evident in his frequent quotations and allusions to these sources. He entered few descriptions of natural phenomena such as were to fill later volumes of the Journal, and a separate album of nature notes and bird sightings kept with John and Sophia from 1836 to 1842 suggests the possibility that he did not yet perceive regular observations of nature as germane to the purpose of the Journal.

Thoreau's literary compositions in the early Journal are neither numerous nor particularly successful, for he was chiefly employed running the Concord Academy with his brother (and was sometimes working in the family pencil factory) and still thinking of himself, in the hours he could devote to study, as a fairly conventional man of letters, albeit with an Emersonian tinge. From the beginning of the Journal in 1837 to the inception of *The Dial* in 1840, Thoreau published nothing in fact except an obituary he wrote for a Concord newspaper. During these two and a half years, however, he managed to distill into the Journal a good deal of poetry and portions of a lecture and three essays.

Thoreau's verse fills many pages in the early Journal, reflecting the primacy of poetry in his imagination at this time. The poems themselves are generally fair copies and are little revised. Since the manuscript leaves that have tentatively been identified as survivors of his original "Journal of 546 ps" contain mostly poetry, it is possible that in the original, his verse occupied an even larger place (see Textual Introduction, pp. 617-618, n. 4). From the spring of 1838 onward, his writing of poetry gradually increased, reaching a peak in the fall of 1841. It was then that he contemplated the long "poem to be called Concord" and described himself as "in the mid-sea of verses." At the same time, Rufus W. Griswold had inquired about including some of Thoreau's poems in an anthology of American verse he was planning, independently confirming the young man's promising future as a poet. Within a few weeks, however, he had received from Margaret Fuller a rather chilling critique of a long poem he had submitted to *The Dial*; her letter began "I do not find the poem on the mountains improved by mere compression, though it might be by fusion and glow," and she characterized the poet himself as "a somewhat bare hill which the warm gales of spring have not visited." None of his poems were printed in Griswold's anthology, and even Emerson, after an initial period of enthusiasm, grew decidedly tepid in his praise; in the fall of 1842, he noted in his journal that the chief virtue in Thoreau's poetry was that its "mass [was] a compensation for quality." Whether because of its poor reception or because Thoreau gradually found prose to be his proper metier, the proportion of verse in the Journal gradually decreases after this time.

Thoreau also composed his early prose elsewhere and copied selections from it into the Journal. His only public performance during these years was a lecture he read in April 1838, which he entered in the Journal as "Scraps from a Lecture on 'Society' written March 14th 1838. delivered before our Lyceum April 11th" (pp. 35-39). In a similar fashion, he copied into the Journal under the appropriate dates "Some scraps from an essay on 'Sound and Silence' written in the latter half of this month. Dec. 1838," part of an essay on "Friendship– Fall of 1839," and some passages "From A Chapter on Bravery–Script. Dec. 1839" (pp. 60-64, 98-100, 91-98). Later Thoreau would draw together separate passages from the Journal for the composition of his lectures, essays, and books; but it is impossible to determine from the transcribed Journal whether these "scraps" were more scattered or extensive, or even whether drafts of the essays were completed in the original.

"Sound and Silence" and "Friendship" were never printed separately, though both were revised for and included in *A Week on the Concord and Merrimack Rivers*. The "Chapter on Bravery," along with some passages on the same theme entered under "July & August, 1840" (pp. 165-168) were eventually used in "The Service," the essay on moral courage which Thoreau submitted to *The Dial* in 1840 and which Margaret Fuller sent back in December, complaining in an accompanying letter that she could hear "the grating of tools on the mosaic"—a criticism that went to the heart of Thoreau's difficulties in composition at this time. Whereas Emerson, with his associational and hortatory collections of aphorisms and insights, could achieve a satisfying finish in his essays—"a beautiful square *bag of duck-shot*," Carlyle called his style—Thoreau's early efforts in the same vein struck readers as forced and contrived. He seems to have sensed this difficulty himself, for two months after Margaret Fuller's rejection of "The Service" he confessed: "When I select one here and another there and strive to join sundered thoughts, I make but a partial heap after all" (p. 253). The only other prose project Thoreau completed before 1842 was an essay on the Roman satirist Aulus Persius Flaccus that appeared in the first issue of *The Dial* (July 1840); Thoreau may have composed this essay in the Journal of 546 pages. It had already been published by the time he began transcribing, and rather than copying the original Journal version, he noted only the date of its composition in the transcribed Journal: "Crit-

icism on Aulus Persius Flaccus. Feb. 10th 1840"
(p. 107; see also Annotations 214.9 and 221.13).

The germ of a much more important project, however, is preserved in the early Journal. In September
1839, Thoreau and his brother John took a two-week
boating and hiking excursion from the Concord and
Merrimack Rivers to Mt. Washington in the White
Mountains of New Hampshire. No record of the trip
appears in the Journal for 1839, but Thoreau kept
a log, and in June 1840 he began to draft in the
Journal some narrative and descriptive passages
about the trip, including a fairly detailed itinerary
"Copied from pencil" (pp. 134-137). He may have
had an essay in mind, but his plans for the material
were still indeterminate at the time, and there is no
evidence that he envisioned a book growing from it.
The full significance of this voyage would not begin
to occur to Thoreau until after John's death and
until after his own first attempts to write narrative
prose in 1842, at which time he found in it both a
structural framework for a book and an opportunity
to commemorate his brother. His thoughts about
boating in the summer of 1840, however, probably
centered on Ellen Sewall, whom he took rowing on
the river in June (and who later refused his proposal
of marriage). And, since John Thoreau was his rival
for her affection, it is doubtful that Henry was thinking fraternal thoughts about their journey together
the previous year.

After the brothers' school closed and Thoreau
moved into the Emerson household in the spring of
1841, he probably did desire to undertake a major
literary project. He may have hoped to gather a collection of his planned essays, such as the one Emerson had just published, and he almost certainly fore-

saw some kind of critical collection of English poetry growing out of his extensive research on the subject beginning in the fall of 1841. MS volume 6 begins with Thoreau's trip to Cambridge in November and December to read the English poets in the Harvard Library; over the next two years, Thoreau commented frequently in his Journal on the character and qualities of the major English poets while he was simultaneously filling his commonplace books with extensive extracts from their works. The completion of MS volume 6 in April 1842 marked the end of Thoreau's early Journal and a significant shift in his literary career as well. His move to Emerson's was a step toward acquiring the broad margin to his life that he needed for his studies and writing, and *The Dial* had given him the opportunity to begin to shape the results for publication. Margaret Fuller's editorial scruples still presented a judicious and, on the whole, beneficial obstacle to access to its pages, and Thoreau himself had still not discovered the particular bent of his own genius; but circumstances would soon offer him new opportunities that would lead to a different and expanded role for the Journal in his literary life.

SPRING 1842 TO SPRING 1844

During the two years following the completion of MS volume 6 in April 1842, Thoreau filled three more Journal volumes numbered 7, 8, and 9, along with an additional volume mostly of transcriptions from volumes 3 to 6. MS volumes 7 to 9 now exist in a fragmentary state, their leaves unbound and dispersed among various libraries (see Textual Introduction, pp. 625-627); they have been collected, ordered, and printed for the first time in this edition. The pagination of surviving leaves indicates that these volumes once contained over a thousand pages, but fewer than 10 percent are extant—most of the rest were presumably used in drafts of essays and other literary works during this period. Thoreau played an increasingly active role in writing for and editing *The Dial* in 1842 and 1843, and he was beginning to write for other periodicals as well. From May to November 1843, he lived with the William Emerson family on Staten Island, making a diligent but unsuccessful effort to establish himself in the New York literary market. Since he was beginning to use his Journal volumes more to compose drafts of literary works he later excised and less to record his thoughts and observations, the relatively small amount of Journal material that survives actually reflects an increase in his literary activities and output.

The most important factor prompting this change was Emerson's assumption of the editorship of *The Dial*. In March 1842, after contending for two years with unreliable contributors, insolvent printers, a shrinking subscription list, and scornful reviewers, Margaret Fuller resigned. Emerson was at first unwilling to take on such an irksome responsibility, but after returning to Concord later in the month from a lecture trip in New York, he changed his mind. He probably discussed the matter with Thoreau on his return: to overcome the problem of weak contributions, he proposed to rely on a backlog of selections "from old or from foreign books" that could fill space "whenever a dull article is offered and rejected," and Thoreau shared the task of making these selections for the "Ethnical Scriptures" column that became a regular feature of the magazine. In a letter of April 10, in fact, Emerson referred to Thoreau as "private secretary to the President of the Dial." In the same letter, he described another and ultimately more significant push he had given Thoreau's career: he had acquired four recently published volumes of surveys of the flora and fauna of Massachusetts and had immediately "set Henry Thoreau on the good track of giving an account of them in the Dial."

This account was published in the July 1842 *Dial* as "Natural History of Massachusetts," Thoreau's first natural history essay. He composed it rapidly during the spring—by May 9 Emerson informed Fuller that Thoreau had "fifty or sixty pages of MS in a state approaching completion"—drawing together passages from earlier Journal volumes and probably drafting the essay into the beginning of MS volume 7: the first ninety pages of that volume are missing, and the first dated entry is July 18. On the nineteenth of July, Thoreau began a hiking trip with Margaret Fuller's brother, Richard, that he described in "A Walk to Wachusett," an essay drafted in the fall and published in the *Boston Miscellany* in January 1843. Surviving portions of text in MS volume 7 indicate that he was also drafting in the Journal passages for "A Winter Walk" (*Dial*, October 1843) and "Sir Walter Raleigh," a lecture he delivered before the Concord Lyceum in February 1843. Not surprisingly, only 28 pages remain from a volume originally containing at least 356 pages. Many surviving pages not taken up with draft material for these works contain commentary on English poets—Gray, Tennyson, Sidney, Gower, and Quarles—thereby continuing the work begun in MS volume 6 during the winter of 1841 to 1842.

The additional volume of primarily transcribed material, titled by the editors "Transcripts, 1840-

1842," also dates from this period and is printed in the text preceding MS volume 7. It is included in the Journal because it contains original passages in addition to topically arranged transcribed entries, often combined and revised, from MS volumes 3 to 6. "Transcripts" was compiled in mid- or late 1842: the volume contains Journal passages from as late as March 1842 and a draft of the preface of "The Laws of Menu," which appeared in the January 1843 issue of *The Dial*. Emerson's plan to print selections from old or foreign books in *The Dial* may have occasioned this volume, for most of its contents reflect Thoreau's reading of and attitudes toward old books, especially the Oriental scriptures. He used some of this material for a brief essay called "Dark Ages," printed in the April 1843 issue of *The Dial* that he edited while Emerson was away, and eventually the "Dark Ages" passages as well as much of the other material in the volume appeared in the meditative interpolations in "Monday" of *A Week*.

Though its contents frequently duplicate other Journal entries, "Transcripts" is particularly significant for the light it sheds on Thoreau's growing awareness of his Journal as a source book for his writings. Probably influenced by Emerson's example if not his advice, Thoreau was finding that by collecting and arranging Journal entries thematically he could gradually build up the outlines of larger works. In fact, he began another such volume of copied and original entries at about the same time in 1842. He called this volume his "long book": it contained transcriptions and original entries relating to the 1839 voyage on the Concord and Merrimack Rivers that eventually became the basis for the first draft of *A Week*. Since Thoreau used that volume from 1842 to

1846, it will appear in the second volume of *Journal* in this edition, but both notebooks illustrate how the Journal provided the building blocks for *A Week* and *Walden*.

MS volume 8, covering only the spring and summer of 1843, has the briefest temporal span and is the most fragmentary of these Journal volumes: only 20 pages, plus two anomalous leaves continuing dated entries from this period, remain from an original total of at least 464 pages. Surviving text indicates that Thoreau was at work on "A Winter Walk" at the beginning of MS volume 8 in April; he finished the essay and sent it to Emerson on June 8, a month after he moved to Staten Island. The extensive gaps in the Journal for the summer of 1843 probably reflect Thoreau's work on several projects he began in New York: "The Landlord" and an essay-review entitled "Paradise (To Be) Regained," printed in the October and November 1843 issues of the *Democratic Review*; a translation of *The Seven Against Thebes*, which he had completed by August 7; and translations of Pindar, which appeared in the January and April 1844 issues of *The Dial*. Journal text that does survive continues Thoreau's commentaries on English poets, whom he was now reading in New York libraries; otherwise it gives few clues to his activities, though his correspondence reveals that he met a good many people (including the elder Henry James), that he was ill a good deal of the time, and that he missed Concord. The anomalous leaves, which contain entries for August 26 and 28 and September 1, indicate that he was still occasionally making Journal entries on loose sheets, perhaps intending to transfer them later to a bound volume.

Most of MS volume 9 covers Thoreau's last two

months on Staten Island, before his general unhappiness and lack of success in finding regular literary employment brought him back to Concord permanently around Thanksgiving. He continued to read Greek and English poetry and to write up his impressions of the latter and became particularly enthusiastic about James Macpherson's spurious *Genuine Remains of Ossian*. He shared the contemporary interest in rude and primitive poetic utterance, adapting many of the extracts and comments in the Journal for a lecture on "Ancient Poets" that he read before the Concord Lyceum in late November and published in *The Dial* in January 1844 as "Homer. Ossian. Chaucer."

Although he was back in Concord, Thoreau had no prospective employment (even *The Dial* was about to cease publication), and the Journal that survives provides only a meager record of his activities. In fact, the next dated Journal entry after that headed "Sunday Jan 7th 1844" (p. 493) appears in a volume Thoreau began eighteen months later on July 5, 1845, the day after moving to Walden. He published a review of the antislavery newspaper *Herald of Freedom* in the last issue of *The Dial* (April 1844), and beyond that almost no records of his literary activities during the year survive. He seems to have devoted most of his time to manual labor, working in the pencil factory and helping his father build a new house; perhaps he kept no Journal, or kept one so unsystematically that it has not been preserved. At any rate, these eighteen months between dated entries are a puzzling interlude, for the numerous projects and abundant if fragmentary Journal of the preceding year are amply matched and continued by his literary and Journal output after his move to Walden.

The "long book" of transcriptions and original passages dealing with the brothers' river trip in 1839 is the only Journal volume to span this gap. Its contents suggest that whatever disappointment Thoreau felt about his work to date, he was nevertheless gathering material in preparation for going to the pond-side to transact that private business which would result in his first two books.

SOURCES

Manuscript materials cited in the Historical Introduction are: Henry E. Huntington Library manuscript HM 945 (Thoreau's "Index rerum"), Pierpont Morgan Library manuscript MA 594 (Thoreau's "Miscellaneous Extracts"), and Thoreau's 1840-1848 commonplace book in the Library of Congress, published in a facsimile edition by Kenneth W. Cameron as *Thoreau's Literary Notebook in the Library of Congress* (Hartford: Transcendental Books, 1964).

The following published sources are chronological in nature and may be consulted by reference to dates provided in the Historical Introduction: *The Correspondence of Henry David Thoreau*, ed. Walter Harding and Carl Bode (New York: New York University Press, 1958); *The Letters of Ralph Waldo Emerson*, ed. Ralph L. Rusk, 6 vols. (New York: Columbia University Press, 1939); *The Correspondence of Emerson and Carlyle*, ed. Joseph Slater (New York: Columbia University Press, 1964); the *Journal* of Henry D. Thoreau, ed. Bradford Torrey and Francis H. Allen, 14 vols., in *The Writings of Henry David Thoreau*, Walden Edition, 20 vols. (Boston: Houghton Mifflin, 1906); *The Journals and Miscellaneous Notebooks of Ralph Waldo Emerson*, ed. William H. Gilman et al., 14 vols. to date (Cambridge, Mass.:

The Belknap Press of Harvard University Press, 1960-).

Other details of Thoreau's life and literary activities from 1837 to 1844 were provided by Walter Harding, *The Days of Henry Thoreau* (New York: Alfred A. Knopf, 1965); Linck C. Johnson, Historical Introduction to Henry D. Thoreau, *A Week on the Concord and Merrimack Rivers*, ed. Carl F. Hovde, William L. Howarth, and Elizabeth Hall Witherell (Princeton: Princeton University Press, 1980); Robert Sattelmeyer, "Thoreau's Projected Work on the English Poets," in *Studies in the American Renaissance 1980* (Boston: Twayne, 1980); pp. 239-257; Henry D. Thoreau, *Reform Papers*, ed. Wendell Glick (Princeton: Princeton University Press, 1973); and Henry D. Thoreau, *Early Essays and Miscellanies*, ed. Joseph J. Moldenhauer and Edwin Moser, with Alexander Kern (Princeton: Princeton University Press, 1975).

Textual Introduction

THE PRINCETON EDITION of Thoreau's Journal, 1837 to 1844, is printed in clear text from his surviving holograph manuscript and is accompanied by Annotations, an Index, and an Editorial Appendix detailing significant textual information. The sections that follow describe the relevant versions of the text, the copy-text manuscripts, the choice of copy-text, and editorial procedures and decisions. Contextual punctuation appears outside of quotation marks when ambiguity would result from using the standard form.

RELEVANT VERSIONS OF TEXT

A genealogy of the Journal text, 1837 to 1844, includes four stages of textual descent: preliminary, original, transcribed, and later versions of entries. More than half of the extant Journal for these years consists of Thoreau's transcriptions of manuscript volumes now lost; the rest is original composition. Thus, the copy-text for *Journal 1* is based on both transcribed and original materials. Preliminary and later versions are also relevant to a critical text; for convenience, these are described in the following sections.

Preliminary

During this period, and indeed throughout his literary career, Thoreau kept commonplace books of extracts from his reading, infrequently commenting on these extracts. In a few instances, he developed these comments in Journal entries. For example, an observation on Marlowe that appears in an 1843 commonplace book is the basis for a Journal entry of June 9, 1843.[1] The relevant portions of these commonplace books are preliminary versions of the Journal. After 1850, Thoreau kept pocket notebooks in which he entered observations that he later expanded in his Journal.[2] After transcribing from two original manuscript volumes, Thoreau may have copied his entries for parts of the Journal for 1837 to 1844

[1] The observation appears on p. 258 in Kenneth Cameron's facsimile edition of the commonplace book, *Thoreau's Literary Notebook in the Library of Congress* (Hartford: Transcendental Books, 1964): "I read with pleasure *Dr Faustus Dido Queen of Carthage* and *Hero and Leander*." The Journal entry on p. 475 includes this observation in a paragraph about Marlowe.

[2] F. B. Sanborn's edition of W. E. Channing's *Thoreau: The Poet-Naturalist* (Boston: Charles E. Goodspeed, 1902) contains a description of these notebooks and Thoreau's use of them:

In these walks, two things [Thoreau] must have from his tailor: his clothes must fit, and the pockets, especially, must be made with reference to his out-door pursuits. They must accommodate his note-book and spy-glass; and so their width and depth was regulated by the size of the note-book. It was a cover for some folded papers, on which he took his out-of-door notes; and this was never omitted, rain or shine. It was his invariable companion, and he acquired great skill in conveying by a few lines or strokes a long story, which in his written Journal might occupy pages. Abroad, he used the pencil, writing but a few moments at a time, during the walk; but into the note-book must go all measurements with the foot-rule which he always carried, or the surveyor's tape that he often had with him. Also all observations with his spy-glass (another invariable companion for years), all conditions of plants, spring, summer, and fall, the depth of snows, the strangeness of the skies,—all went down in this note-book. To his memory he never trusted for a fact, but to the page and the pencil, and the abstract in the pocket, not the Journal. I have seen bits of this note-book, but never recognized any word in it; and I have read its expansion in the Journal, in many pages, of that which occupied him but five minutes to write in the field. (Pp. 65-66)

from preliminary drafts written elsewhere (see Historical Introduction).

Later

Thoreau used his Journal entries in drafting texts of later compositions, either by revising the entries and transcribing them or by removing pages and incorporating them into the drafts. Thus these "later versions" of the Journal constitute preliminary versions of Thoreau's lectures and works intended for publication.

Original and Transcribed

From 1837 to 1841, Thoreau used two manuscript volumes for his Journal. He called the first both the "Journal of 546 ps" and the "Red Journal," and the second the "Journal of 396 ps."[3] Of what must have been more than nine hundred manuscript pages in these two volumes, nothing survives of the second and only a few leaves have tentatively been identified

---

In a Journal entry for November 9, 1851, Thoreau described Channing's unsuccessful attempt to keep such a notebook: "In our walks C. takes out his note-book sometimes and tries to write as I do, but all in vain. He soon puts it up again, or contents himself with scrawling some sketch of the landscape. Observing me still scribbling, he will say that he confines himself to the ideal, purely ideal remarks; he leaves the facts to me."

[3] The first title for this earliest Journal volume—"Journal of 546 ps"—follows the June 11, 1840, entry in MS volume 2 (p. 126); the second is in an autobiographical Journal passage written December 27, 1855: "Began the big Red Journal, October, 1837." Thoreau's title for the second of the original Journal volumes—"Journal of 396 ps"—follows the January 31, 1841, entry in MS volume 4 (p. 243). Partial indexes for both of these volumes appear in the "Index rerum" at the Huntington Library (HM 945); see Appendix, pp. 499-505.

Journal manuscript volumes

Expediencies differ — they may clash —
English law may go slow with
American law — that is English
interest with American interest —
but what is expedient for the whole
world will be absolute right — and
synonymous with the law of
God — So the law is only partial
right — it is selfish, and cruel to for
the interest of others.
Somehow strangely the view of men
gets & well represented and protected
but their intere has none to plead
its cause — nor any charter of immunities and rights. The Magna
Charta is not chartered rights but
chartered wrongs.

Thursday March 18th
I have been making pencils all day — and
then at evening walked to see an old
schoolmate who is going to help to
make the Welland canal navigable
for ships round Niagara. —

Page of MS Volume 6 (pp. 378-379)

Fragmentary Journals of the 1840s

"Frost crystals in entrance to fox hole"

as belonging to the first.[4] As it now exists, the Journal for 1837 to 1841 consists of five manuscript volumes. The first three volumes and the fourth volume through the entry for January 31, 1841, on p. "73" contain Thoreau's transcription of these original versions, made some time in 1841. Thoreau called the first of these transcribed volumes "Gleanings—Or What Time Has Not Reaped Of My Journal," perhaps to indicate that he had excised many leaves of the original volumes for other compositions, perhaps to denote that he was editing and selecting his early

[4] Eleven leaves of white wove paper, 25 x 20 cm., unlined and unpaged, have been tentatively assigned to the Journal of 546 pages. These leaves contain chiefly poetry, rather than continuous dated Journal text. Repositories, dates, number of leaves, and contents are as follows:

Professor Raymond Adams, Chapel Hill, North Carolina, October 22, 1837: one leaf. Title page and motto; poems added later in pencil.

Huntington Library (HM 13201): six leaves. Original text (on three leaves): complete essay, "Gratitude," February 24, 1838; three lines followed by "The Cliffs," July 8, 1838; three stanzas of "Friendship (I think awhile of Love, and while I think,)" beginning "That Love of which I purposed to sing," April 8, 1838 (see Henry D. Thoreau, *Collected Poems of Henry Thoreau*, ed. Carl Bode, enl. ed. [Baltimore: The Johns Hopkins Press, 1964], pp. 89-91). Possible original Red Journal text: one stanza from "The Bluebirds" (April 26, 1838) beginning "Meanwhile old earth jogged steadily on" (see *Collected Poems*, pp. 93-96). Poetry, prose, and diagrams in pencil and ink on two leaves with no Red Journal text.

New York Public Library (Berg Collection), April 25, 1836: one leaf. Poem: "The Cliffs & Springs" (see *Collected Poems*, p. 92); other verse added later in pencil.

Huntington Library (HM 13186), before July 18, 1839: one leaf. Poem: "Independence" (see *Collected Poems*, pp. 132-133); other verse added later in pencil.

Huntington Library (HM 13207), between fall 1839 and June 11, 1840: one leaf. Copy of poem: "A Poet's Love," attributed by Thoreau to "The Unknown" and later, in pencil, to "William Ellery Channing." (Emerson received a

writing and transcribing only passages that he judged had stood the test of time. Thoreau's method of keeping his Journal from February 2, 1841, until April 3, 1842, the end of MS volume 6, is uncertain.[5] Though the remainder of MS volume 4 and all of MS volume 5 display the physical characteristics of transcription rather than original composition, no evidence of additional volumes from which they could have been copied exists. More frequent cancellation and revision in MS volume 6 suggest that it may be original composition, but errors in several series of dates indicate that all entries were not composed in the volume.

In summary, it seems likely that Thoreau wrote the first versions of at least some entries for the end of MS volume 4, as well as MS volumes 5 and 6, elsewhere, copying them into the manuscript volumes at relatively short intervals. The last three volumes, 7 to 9, appear to consist of original composition. As he worked on his Journal, Thoreau continued to revise passages and excise leaves from all his manuscript volumes, often for use in his literary projects. Today, about 90 percent of the leaves from MS volumes 1 to 6 survive, while only unbound leaves remain of MS volumes 7 to 9. In 1842, Thoreau made an additional volume of transcriptions, mostly copied from

---

copy of this poem in a packet from Samuel Gray Ward in the fall of 1839 and later included it in "New Poetry," *The Dial* 1 [October 1840]: 227-228. Thoreau and Channing did not meet until December of 1840; hence Thoreau's earlier attribution of the poem to "The Unknown.")

Olin Library, Washington University, St. Louis, Missouri, before June 11, 1840: one leaf. Poem: "Tell me why should I live" (for another version, see *Collected Poems*, p. 137).

[5] For a fuller discussion of the editors' conclusions, see Historical Introduction, pp. 597-601.

volumes 3 to 6 but also containing material—either transcribed or original—not found elsewhere. This volume is designated "Transcripts, 1840-1842" in this edition.

The following diagram portrays the relationship among the four stages of textual descent; titles of manuscript volumes on which copy-text is based are italicized in the diagram, and descriptions appear in the next section.

PHYSICAL DESCRIPTIONS OF COPY-TEXT MANUSCRIPTS[6]

MS Volume 1

Plum boards, embossed with 45° diagonal bands; dark blue spine embossed with horizontal gold rules. Mark, possibly "1," scratched on spine. Originally eighty-four leaves, bound [A-G¹²], with four flyleaves; now seventy-five leaves, pages [1-150], with four fly-leaves, paged "1-150, 152-153" (first two flyleaves, pages 151 and 154 unnumbered). Leaf paged "37-38" attached by wax to stub of original leaf; leaves paged "35-36" and "45-46" repaired. Leaves are white wove paper, 20.2 x 16.8 cm., lined; edges originally

---

[6] Measurements of the manuscript volume leaves vary by approximately 0.2 cm., depending on positions in gatherings. Single leaves have greater variations because of torn or cut edges. Several boards and spines of volumes have minor repairs by the Morgan Library. In these descriptions, pastedown endpapers are unnumbered unless otherwise noted. The following abbreviations are used in the physical descriptions:

CSmH Henry E. Huntington Library, San Marino, California
MA Manuscripts at the Pierpont Morgan Library
MH Houghton Library, Harvard University
NNPM Pierpont Morgan Library, New York
TxU Miriam Lutcher Stark Library, University of Texas, Austin, Texas

Preliminary	Original	Transcribed	Later
	"Journal of 546 ps" ("Red Journal") 1837-1840 (lost)	"Gleanings" MS vol. 1 to MS vol. 4, p. "33" (copied 1841)	
	"Journal of 396 ps" 1840-1841 (lost)	MS vol. 4, p. "34" through MS vol. 5 (1841)	"Transcripts, 1840-1842"
Commonplace books, [notes] drafts, (1836-1844)	MS vol. 6 (1841-1842)		Drafts & revisions for literary works (1837-1862)
	MS vol. 7 (1842-1843)		
	MS vol. 8 (1843)		
	MS vol. 9 (1843-1844)		

green, now mostly faded to white. Only one of the nine missing leaves has been identified; it is mounted in MA 920 (see Textual Note 68.3). Nonauthorial contents are: H.G.O. Blake's label on front board, with ink, pencil, and blue pencil; Blake's vertical blue-pencil use-marks indicating passages he had transcribed on forty-nine MS pages; NNPM accession number "MA 1302 (38V.)" in pencil on front paste-down endpaper; erased pencil "62 1/2," probably by stationer, on first front flyleaf; NNPM pagination, "1-79," in pencil on rectos. An impression of a paper clip appears on leaf paged "23-24." Repository: NNPM (MA 1302:1).

MS Volume 2

Green boards, embossed with 45° and 135° diagonal bands; dark blue spine embossed with horizontal gold rules. Orange "2," probably by Thoreau, on spine. Thoreau excised the first fourteen leaves, inverted the volume, and wrote the Journal text from back to front. The following description observes the order of the text. Originally eighty-two leaves, bound [A-E^{12}F^{10}G^{12}], with free endpapers and flyleaves; now sixty leaves, pages [1-120], with free endpapers and flyleaves, paged "1-56, 59-62, 67-126, 128-130" (front free endpaper, front flyleaf, page 127 unnumbered; pages 57-58, 63-66 missing). Leaves paged "23-24" and "27-28" repaired. Leaves are white wove paper, 20.2 x 16.8 cm., lined; green edges. Nonauthorial contents are: Blake's label on front board, with ink, pencil, and blue pencil; Blake's blue-pencil use-marks on fifty-seven MS pages; pencil "2," possibly by Thoreau, on front paste-down endpaper; pencil "2" on front free endpaper; inverted "62 1/2," probably by stationer, on back free endpaper. Repository: NNPM (MA 1302:2).

MS Volume 3

Marbled red/olive/black boards; brown spine embossed with horizontal gold rules. Black-ink "3" and red-ink "3," probably by Thoreau, on spine. Originally seventy-two leaves, bound [A-F¹²], with free endpapers and flyleaves; now sixty-five leaves, pages [1-130], with free endpapers and flyleaves, paged "1-136" (front free endpaper unnumbered). Leaves are white wove paper, 18.8 x 15.6 cm., lined. Nonauthorial contents are:[7] bookplate of Stephen H. Wakeman on front paste-down endpaper; pencil "3," probably not Thoreau's, and NNPM accession number "MA 1718" on front free endpaper; inverted pencil "97," probably by stationer, on back free endpaper; "WHC" (Warren H. Colson) stamped on MS page "49" and back paste-down endpaper; heavy black-pencil use-marks, possibly Blake's, but often indistinguishable from Thoreau's. Repository: NNPM (MA 1718).

MS Volume 4

Marbled green / blue / yellow / red boards; brown

---

[7] The absence of Blake's usual front label from this so-called "Lost Journal," not included in the 1906 Edition and not printed until it was edited in *Consciousness in Concord* by Perry Miller (Boston: Houghton Mifflin, 1958), suggests that it left his possession before he began labelling the manuscript volumes. Since he included entries from this volume in his last book of seasonal selections from the Journal, *Autumn* (Boston: Houghton Mifflin, 1892), Blake probably lost this manuscript volume and labelled the others between 1892 and his death in 1898. Blake marked the passages he had selected for these seasonal books with the blue- and black-pencil use-marks noted in the descriptions of nonauthorial contents of MS volumes 1 to 6.

spine embossed with horizontal gold rules. Orange
"4," probably by Thoreau, on spine. Originally seventy-two leaves, bound [A-F¹²], with free endpapers and
flyleaves; now seventy-one leaves, pages [1-142], with
front free endpaper, front flyleaf, and back free endpaper, paged "1-142, 145-147" ("147" on back paste-
down endpaper cancelled; front free endpaper and
front flyleaf unnumbered, pages 143-144 [back fly-
leaf] missing). Leaves are white wove paper, 18.4 x
15.4 cm., lined. Nonauthorial contents are: Blake's
label on front board, with ink, pencil, and blue pencil; Blake's blue-pencil use-marks on 104 MS pages;
"H D Thoreau Vol 4" and "4" in pencil on front free
endpaper; NNPM accession number "MA 1302-4" on
page "2"; inverted pencil "37," probably by stationer,
on back free endpaper. Repository: NNPM (MA
1302:4).

MS Volume 5

Marbled green/red/yellow boards; tan spine. Undecipherable ink markings on spine. Originally nine-
ty-two leaves, bound [A-F¹²G⁸H¹²], with free endpapers and flyleaves; now seventy-two leaves, pages
[1-144], paged "1-43, 59-101, 114-115" in ink, "44-
58, 102-111" in pencil, and "112-113" in ink written
over pencil (pages 116-144 unnumbered). Leaves
are white wove paper, 21.6 x 16.5 cm., unlined;
edges green. Nonauthorial contents are: Blake's label
on front board, with ink and pencil; pencil "34,"
probably by stationer, on front paste-down endpaper; pencil "5" on page "1"; NNPM accession number
"MA 1302-5" on page "2"; crushed spider on pages
[140-141]; heavy black-pencil use-marks, possibly
Blake's, but often indistinguishable from Thoreau's.
Repository: NNPM (MA 1302:5).

MS Volume 6

Marbled yellow/red/blue/brown boards; tan spine. Black-ink "6./Nov/29'41/—/Ap./3./'42," probably by Thoreau, on spine. Originally seventy-two leaves, bound [A-F¹²], with free endpapers and flyleaves; now sixty-six leaves, pages [1-132], with free endpapers and flyleaves, paged irregularly in pencil from "4" to "141" on forty-two MS pages, page "69" paged in ink. Text continues on back paste-down endpaper. Leaves are white wove paper, 20.7 x 17.3 cm., lined. Nonauthorial contents are: Blake's label on front board in ink; NNPM accession number "MA 1302-6" on page [2]; Blake's blue-pencil use-marks on forty-six MS pages; black-pencil use-marks after page "50," possibly Blake's, often indistinguishable from Thoreau's; pencil "6" on front flyleaf; note by Blake in ink on page [43] (see Textual Note 357.8); paper clasp on pages "51-52"; pencil "37 1/2" inverted in lower left corner of back free endpaper. Repository: NNPM (MA 1302:6).

"Transcripts, 1840-1842"

Marbled orange/red/brown boards; brown spine. Thoreau excised the first fifteen leaves (possibly including the free endpaper and flyleaf) on which John Thoreau, Jr., kept records for the brothers' Concord Academy, and then inverted this volume and wrote the Journal text from back to front. The following description observes the order of text. Originally eighty-four leaves, bound [A-G¹²], with free endpapers and flyleaves; now twenty-six leaves, pages [1-52], paged "1-8, 13-32, 35-36, 39-44, 47-48, 65-66, 71-72, 79-80, 101-102, 113-114, 125-126" (endpapers, flyleaves, pages 9-12, 33-34, 37-38, 45-46, 49-50, top of 51-52, 53-64, 67-70, 73-78, 81-100, 103-112, 115-

124 missing). Leaves paged "47-48, 65-66, 71-72, 113-114" have been repaired; leaf numbered "101-102" is at CSmH (HM 926; see "These sublime passages . . . his scribe.", text pages 427.14-428.3). Also hinged in on back board is a fragment from a draft of "Natural History of Massachusetts." Leaves are white wove paper, 20.2 x 16.7 cm., lined, with marginal vertical rules. Nonauthorial contents are: label by Blake on front board in ink; label, probably by George Hellman, on spine; title and NNPM accession and call numbers, "MA 608," "V-2/11/A," on front paste-down endpaper; NNPM pagination, "1-25," in pencil on rectos; Concord Academy records by John Thoreau, Jr., inverted on page "126." Repositories: NNPM (MA 608) and CSmH (HM 926).

MS Volume 7

Boards and binders' leaves are missing. Originally at least 356 pages; fourteen leaves, pages [1-28], survive. Repositories, number of leaves, pagination, and position in the present text are as follows:[8]

MH (bMS Am 278.5)	1 leaf "91-92"
	2 leaves "103-106"
	1 leaf "119-120"
	1 leaf "151-152"
	1 leaf "161-162"
CSmH (HM 13182)	3 leaves "193-198"
(HM 935)	1 leaf "215-216"
MH (bMS Am 278.5)	1 leaf "239-240"
	2 leaves "257-260"
CSmH (HM 13182)	1 leaf "355-356"

[8] The sequence of fragmentary leaves in MS volumes 7, 8, and 9 has been established from (1) calendar dates and page numbers on the leaves; (2) text continuous with paged or dated leaves; and (3) the order of transcribed entries in a later Journal volume (MA 1303). Other evidence bearing on the order of text appears in the Textual Notes.

Leaves are white wove paper, 24 x 19.7 cm., unlined. Four leaves (paged "193-198, 355-356") have
matching pinholes in the left margin; one leaf, re-
versed ("216-215"), is inserted in the draft of "Sir
Walter Raleigh," CSmH (HM 935). Nonauthorial
contents are: folder numbers in pencil on MH leaves;
F. B. Sanborn's circled "C" ("copied") in pencil on
MS page "197."

MS Volume 8

Boards and binders' leaves are missing. Originally
at least 464 pages; nine leaves plus two anomalous
leaves, pages [1-22], survive. Repositories, number of
leaves, pagination, and position in the present text
are as follows:

MH (bMS Am 278.5)	1 leaf "143-144"
	1 leaf "179-180"
	2 leaves "191-194"
	1 leaf "197-198"
	1 leaf "451-452"
	1 leaf "463-464"
TxU	1 folio (2 leaves), after "464"

MH leaves are white wove paper, 24 x 19.7 cm., unlined. TxU folio is white wove paper, 24.8 x 19.9
cm., unlined. Nonauthorial contents are: folder numbers in pencil on MH leaves, pencil "18" on recto of
first leaf of TxU folio.

MS Volume 9

Boards and binders' leaves are missing. A partial
index appears on the front paste-down endpaper of
MS volume 5 (see Appendix, p. 509). Originally

exceeded 161 pages; twenty-four leaves survive, pages [1-48]. Repositories, number of leaves, pagination, and position in the present text are as follows:

CSmH (HM 13182)	1 leaf "5-6"
MH (bMS Am 278.5)	1 leaf "7-8"
CSmH (HM 13182)	4 leaves "9-16"
	3 leaves "19-24"
	2 leaves "27-30"
	10 leaves "33-52"
	2 leaves "73-76"
	1 leaf "160-161"

Leaves are white wove paper, 25 x 19.7 cm., unlined. The leaves paged "5-6, 9-16, 19-24, 27-30, 33-52" are sewn together with heavy binding thread; pinholes appear in the upper right margin of the leaf paged "160-161." Pages [20-21, 33, 36-37, 39, 43, 52] are unnumbered. The conjugate fold on the leaf paged "160-161" indicates it came from the first half of a gathering. Nonauthorial contents are: Sanborn's ink notes on MS pages "5, 75" and his pencil notes on MS pages "73-74, 160"; MH folder number in pencil on MS page "7."

The Textual Notes describe additional details of the Journal manuscripts, including text on boards and binders' leaves, possible contents of missing leaves, remnant text on page stubs, unusual pagination sequences, and blank pages.

The text is followed by an Appendix containing Thoreau's indexes to both his original Journal volumes of 546 and 396 pages of 1837 to 1841 and to his MS volumes 1 to 6, "Transcripts, 1840-1842," and MS volume 9.

CHOICE OF COPY-TEXT

Although the prevailing rule of modern textual theory generally requires that editors determine an author's final intentions for his work as the basis of a critical edition, copy-text for the Princeton Edition of Thoreau's Journal is his earliest stage of composition.[9] Since he worked on the Journal at various times for various purposes and never prepared its text for printing, Thoreau's final intentions are often indeterminate. In addition, his revisions were in many cases made for preliminary or intermediate stages of other, separate literary works. Thus, the only level of the Journal text that represents Thoreau's consistent intention for the Journal itself as a discrete work is his first stage of composition. The following versions of a Journal entry for April 7, 1841 (including the text as printed in 1906) illustrate the rationale for the Princeton Edition copy-text policy:

(1) Facsimile of Journal text (MS vol. 5, p. 5, ll. 19-26; all revisions in pencil)

[9] "Almost necessarily it is the finally revised form of the text that must be transcribed" (Fredson Bowers, "Transcription of Manuscripts: The Record of Variants," *Studies in Bibliography* 29 [1976]: 213). But last intentions are not the only possible basis of copy-text; variations are described in a manual issued by The Center for Editions of American Au-

(2) Princeton Edition, p. 297

What have I to do with plows— I cut another furrow than you see— Where the off ox treads, there is it not—it is nigher—where the nigh ox walks will it not be—it is nigher still. If corn fails, so do not all crops fail. What of drought—what of rain—

(3) 1906 text (Vol. I, p. 245)

What have I to do with plows? I cut another furrow than you see. Where the off ox treads, there is it not, it is farther off; where the nigh ox walks, it will not be, it is nigher still. If corn fails, my crop fails not. What of drought? What of rain?

(4) *A Week on the Concord and Merrimack Rivers* (p. 54)

What have I to do with plows? I cut another furrow than you see. Where the off ox treads, there is it not, it is further off; where the nigh ox walks, it will not be, it is nigher still. If corn fails, my crop fails not, and what are drought and rain to me?

The interlineations and cancellations in pencil made sometime after Thoreau composed the Journal entry in ink (1) were destined for inclusion, still further revised, in *A Week* (4). In addition to incorporating these later revisions, the editors of the 1906 text (3) emended the passage heavily for the sake of smoothness. The Princeton Edition (2) prints the passage as Thoreau first wrote it, before he revised it for another literary project.

---

thors, *Statement of Editorial Principles and Procedures* (New York: Modern Language Association, 1972). See also William Gilman, "How Should Journals Be Edited?" *Early American Literature* 6 (1971): 73-83.

Except for this significant but necessary departure from customary procedures, Thoreau's Journal has been edited according to the established principles of textual scholarship. The copy-text becomes the foundation of a critical edition, and other authorial versions of the text, prior and subsequent, become possible sources for necessary emendations to the copy-text. Differences or "variants" between the copy-text and other versions are of two types: "substantives" are differences in meaning, usually changes in words or word order; "accidentals" are changes in appearance, usually punctuation, spacing, and other formal conventions that do not affect meaning. Sometimes a variant in accidentals has a substantive effect, as for example in *god's* / *gods* or *God* / *god*. Thoreau's Journal is edited from the holograph manuscripts and is emended from other sources only when the manuscript is mutilated or undecipherable. Since no printed version of the Journal was prepared or authorized by Thoreau during his lifetime, variants introduced through the process and conventions of printing, such as compositor's errors, house styling, and unauthorized editorial changes have no textual significance in the present edition.[10]

Copy-text policy for the Princeton Edition allows for one major exception to basing the text on the first stage of composition. In the present volume, *Journal 1: 1837-1844*, Thoreau's first intentions for the original two manuscript volumes of his Journal are irrecoverable; these volumes do not survive, and in transcribing their contents into volumes 1 to 4 he apparently revised them, indicating abridgement, for example, with special marks of ellipsis (see pp. 641-642,

---

[10] See the General Introduction for a discussion of other printed versions of the Journal.

Series of dashes in MS). These transcripts, therefore, do not represent Thoreau's first intentions but rather the earliest surviving state of his intentions. For the years 1837 to 1844, the editors have included as Journal all of Thoreau's original and transcribed manuscript volumes with the exception of the material on the eleven leaves conjectured to have been part of the first of the original three volumes, the Journal of 546 pages. This text survives in too fragmentary a state to supplant the transcribed text of MS volumes 1 and 2.

The copy-text policy is also designed to be flexible enough to accommodate Thoreau's minor corrections and revisions made during the first stage of composition. These revisions to the on-line text may be interlined, inserted on line, or written in the margin. When they merely correct or complete the text, and when they are in the same hand and ink as the on-line text, they are accepted as current revisions and reported in the Editorial Appendix as Alterations.

Other revisions are not related to Thoreau's first intentions for the Journal. Although these revisions also appear as cancellations, interlinings, and marks for inserting or transposing (see pp. 628-629), they were clearly made later for post-Journal compositions. They are usually in pencil or in ink differing from that of the copy-text. These later revisions usually do not correct or complete the copy-text; instead, they expand, compress, or otherwise refine entries for the first stage of composition of Thoreau's lectures, essays, and books. While the Princeton Edition does not adopt these later revisions as copy-text for the Journal, the editors recognize an obligation to readers who may be interested in the revisions in the Journal manuscripts. A selective reporting of later revisions appears in the Editorial Appendix as a separate table. This table includes later revisions of three types: (1) substantives that never reached later versions; (2) substantives that differ markedly from later versions; (3) substantives not positively identified as current or later revisions. Scholars interested in the genesis of Thoreau's texts may also consult the printer's copy for the Princeton Edition, which consists of literal typed transcripts of all legible text on Journal pages, including all stages of revision. The printer's copy is on file at Firestone Library, Princeton University.

EDITORIAL PROCEDURES AND DECISIONS

The Princeton Edition of Thoreau's Journal, 1837 to 1844, is based upon a literal transcript or typed facsimile of photocopies of the original manuscript. The editors prepared preliminary tables of Alterations, Emendations, and End-of-Line Hyphenation. After initial editorial proofreadings, the transcripts and preliminary tables received four close readings against photocopies of the manuscript by staff members and editors. The Textual Center staff perfected transcripts and tables, reading against the original manuscripts. The perfected transcripts and tables were copy-edited for publication, and this printer's copy was read word for word against photocopies of the manuscript by the general editor for the Journal. During production of the printed volume, galley and page proofs were read five times against printer's copy: twice by readers for Princeton University Press, and once each by editors, Textual Center staff, and the general editor. The Princeton Edition text of Thoreau's Journal, 1837 to 1844, has thus received multiple readings at every stage of its transmission, from original manuscripts to revised page proofs. In accordance with guidelines established by the Center for Editions of American Authors and carried out by the Committee on Scholarly Editions, this volume has been examined by an independent textual expert, Douglas Emory Wilson, LTC, AUS-Retired.

As with all volumes in *The Writings of Henry D. Thoreau, Journal 1: 1837-1844* is printed in clear text with a minimum of editorial intrusion and with all discussion of the text confined to a separate Editorial Appendix. The only interpolations not by Thoreau that appear in this text are references to physical gaps in the copy-text, which are printed in braces { }. The text is printed with a ragged right-hand margin to avoid hyphenating compound words at the ends of lines and to represent the informal character of the Journal. Annotations, an Index, and the Editorial Appendix follow the text.

Table of Alterations

The Table of Alterations lists Thoreau's current revisions, as defined in the previous section. Only substantives are reported, and the form of reporting usually describes the effect of these changes rather than their cause. For example, "come] comes" means that Thoreau first wrote "comes" and altered it to "come", but the report does not explain whether he altered by cancelling or erasing the "s". Small changes of this sort form a large percentage of Thoreau's alterations. However, some complex alterations are of necessity reported descriptively, allowing readers to reconstruct multiple revisions.

Normalized elements in the manuscripts, those alterations *not* reported, include all accidentals, or changes in the appearance of words that do not affect meaning. These include:

(1) Thoreau's corrections of meaningless misspellings, like "peope" altered to "people". Substantive changes, such as "Why" altered to "When", are reported, even if the first reading makes no sense in context.

(2) Thoreau's corrections of false starts, like a cancelled "cl" preceding "core". This is a change in accidentals because the cancelled letters never became a word. In this instance, Thoreau may have corrected a misspelling or he may have considered another word. Yet the possibility of a substantive change is only hypothetical, since neither the alteration nor the context can suggest a word.

(3) Thoreau's corrections of handwriting where he merely reformed, repeated, or retraced the same words and letters for greater clarity.

(4) Thoreau's corrections of handwriting where the original letters are now impossible to read, like the "st" of "breast" written over illegible letters or "pond" written over a completely erased word. If an erased word is still legible, it is reported in the Table of Alterations.

Any item marked with an asterisk in the Table of Alterations is discussed in the Textual Notes.

Table of Emendations

The Princeton Edition of Thoreau's Journal, 1837-1844, is conservatively emended, thus preserving many anomalies of the copy-text, a manuscript Thoreau never prepared for printing. Some physical features of the copy-text are normalized and not listed in the Table of Emendations. The table is a sequential list of all substantive corrections to the copy-text. The general policy has been to emend only when the meaning of copy-text is obscure and to report all emendations, including editorial interpretation of manuscript features difficult to decipher.

Unemended anomalies of the copy-text include Thoreau's errors of fact, spelling, and grammar, his inconsistent spelling, capitalization, punctuation, and word-division, and his occasional *lacunae* in words, sentences, or entries. If these anomalies do not seriously affect meaning, they are printed as Thoreau wrote them, without editorial correction. Textual Notes comment on these features, either by explaining how they occurred or by referring to Thoreau's treatment of them in later versions. In addition to the features just mentioned, the Princeton Edition also preserves the following anomalies:

(1) Incorrect dates and sequences of entries, as from December 1841 to March 1842 (341.9 ff.), or as on August 9, 1841, when Thoreau noted that a transcribed entry was continued later in the manuscript volume (319.14). These anomalies are not emended because they are not especially confusing and also because running heads throughout the Princeton Edition text provide correct, uniformly styled dates. When Thoreau did not date entries, the running heads give conjectured dates keyed to the nearest dated entry. When Thoreau gives an incorrect day or date, a Textual Note corrects the error (see Textual Note 331.12). Entries are not rearranged in calendar order; instead, the actual order of copy-text is preserved.

(2) Incorrect or missing diacritical marks in foreign words, as when Thoreau omits breathing or accent marks (20.17). These anomalies are understandable without emendation, and sometimes Thoreau's "incorrect" treatment of a foreign word is deliberate, as in his word play on *non chalance* at 167.18.

(3) Abbreviations of common words, which usually appear in datelines, such as "Sat. Oct. 27 —42." A less common form, like "Soc." in "Soc. Library" at 461.11-12 is initially explained in an annotation; the Index lists all appearances of that abbreviation under an expanded heading.

Normalized features of the copy-text include certain aspects of Thoreau's handwriting and spacing in the manuscript that are not meaningful or susceptible to typographic reproduction. The following features are normalized and not reported in the Table of Emendations:

(1) Imperfectly formed handwriting in short words of frequent occurrence (*a, after, an, and, as, at, by, for, from, in, into, of, or, our, over, the, their, to, upon, was, with*); in suffixes (*-ed, -ing*); in certain letters formed with loop or flourish strokes (*a, e, m, n, r, s, w*) and in "run-on" letters formed with linked strokes (*th, to, is, ey, ry*). If a possible ambiguity results from imperfectly formed handwriting (*sing/ ring, even/ever*, or *they/thy*), the forms selected and rejected by editors are reported in the Table of Emendations.

(2) Irregular spacing of dashes, hyphens, quotation marks, and apostrophes, owing to the slant of Thoreau's handwriting or his habits of punctuation. He used dashes for several purposes, which the editors have normalized as follows:

(a) Dashes used as internal punctuation (comma, semi-colon, colon, or parenthesis) are printed as a closed one-en dash: *word—word.*

(b) Dashes used as end punctuation (period, question or exclamation mark) are printed as a half-closed one-en dash: *word— Word.*

(c) Dashes used as a transition or to introduce a quotation are printed as a closed two-en dash: *word—word.*

(d) Dashes used to separate entries are printed as a centered two-en dash with space above and below.

(e) Dashes used as a paragraph sign are printed as an indented and half-closed one-en dash: *—Word.*

(f) Dashes used as an ellipsis indicating abridgement of a source text are printed as two open one-en dashes: *word — — word.*[11]

Thoreau irregularly hyphenated *today*, *tonight*, and *tomorrow*, often writing a long, unbroken stroke between syllables. Unless a manuscript hyphen is clearly present, the two syllables are joined in print. His placement of quotation marks and apostrophes often slanted far right (*word. "* or *word   's*); this spacing is normalized by closing up the space. His inconsistent positioning of text and punctuation (*word"*. or *whats'*) is respected, unless an ambiguity exists.

(3) Unusual features of the handwriting that elude exact reproduction in typography. All words and letters Thoreau underlined are normalized to italic type (see Emendations 27.2 and 441.16 for exceptions). His superscript letters (*th*, *d*, *nd*, *rd*, *st*) in dates, numbers, and abbreviations are often imperfectly formed and underlined; they are normalized to on-line, roman type, with consistent spellings. His pen strokes often run together separate words (*theboy*) or break within a word (*bro ken*); these features are normalized. In cases affecting possible com-

---

[11] The last form of dash is treated as an emendation of copy-text; see Series of dashes in MS, pp. 641-642.

pounds (*rail road*), the decision to read as one word or two (*rail road* or *railroad*) is either resolved according to the orthographic characteristics of the surrounding text or emended according to later versions.

(4) Elements in the manuscript that are not meaningful or relate only to Thoreau's later revisions for post-Journal works. The following elements are normalized by omission: blots, flourishes, and stray marks that cannot be construed as letters or marks of punctuation; use-marks drawn vertically across passages after Thoreau had revised or copied them; cross references (*v*, *V*, *vide*, with manuscript pagination) that key revised passages in Journal volumes to other Journal passages or separate manuscript drafts. Textual Notes describe these references only if they account for missing pages (see Textual Note 427.12) or errors in paging and indexing (see Textual Note 509.2).

(5) Irregular spacing of text on manuscript pages or in paragraphs and sentences. Blank space measuring one-fifth or more of a page is reported; anything less is normalized to a single line space. Thoreau's variable indentations for paragraphs, datelines, margins, and inset quotations are normalized to uniform indentations at page left, right, and center. In the manuscript, his paragraphs begin variably with an indentation from the margin, with a dash flush to the margin or flush to the margin but preceded by a line space or by a sentence that ends short of the right margin. In all these cases, the printed paragraphs are normalized by indentation. His irregular spacing of sentence endings is normalized as follows: a single word space for the norm (*go. Now*); a double word space if the sentence ends with a dash (*go— Now; go— now*), if the sentence has another end

mark but the first word of the next sentence is not capitalized (*go? now*), or if the sentence has no end mark but the next sentence begins with a capital (*go Now*); a quadruple word space if the sentence has no end mark and the first word of the next sentence is uncapitalized (*go now*). His combined period-dash is printed as —. or .— if the elements are separate, but it is normalized to a dash if they touch.

Emendations of the copy-text are listed in a sequential Table of Emendations. The general emendation policy is conservative; editors have emended only when they judge the copy-text to be confusing or misleading, and they have reported all emendations. Emended readings are derived from one or more levels of authority: identical or analogous forms in the copy-text itself; earlier or later versions of the copy-text passage, in manuscript and print;[12] Thoreau's sources or reference works; the editors' judgment.

The following situations call for emendation:

(1) Possible readings in MS. Thoreau's handwriting often suggests two or more possible readings, usually because certain letters (*r/s, j/y, s/z, u/w, A/a, C/c, M/m, S/s*) are indistinguishable or because his punctuation is doubtful. When the possible readings are substantives, the editors report them in the Table of Emendations.

(2) Emended errors in MS. Occasionally the copy-text is unclear because of Thoreau's errors. Thoreau's

[12] Usually only later authorial versions are considered as a source of emendation. The possibility exists, however, that on rare occasions an emendation might be derived from an earlier printed version of the Journal if it seems likely that a text element now illegible was readable seventy-five or a hundred years ago when the manuscript was in better condition (see General Introduction).

incorrect spelling is emended if the context does not clarify a word's exact meaning (e.g., at 469.6, from *scot* to *Scott*) or if the spelling strongly affects pronunciation (e.g., at 133.22, from *Tt* to *It*). Occasionally his punctuation—or lack of it—is misleading (e.g., at 240.4), and the same is true of his highly variable practices of hyphenation and word division. In all these cases, copy-text readings are emended when they are judged to be misleading or confusing.

(3) Alternate readings in MS. At many points in his Journal, Thoreau wrote a word on-line and interlined a word above, without making a final choice. The Princeton Edition adopts the on-line word, since it was written first, but reports the "alternate reading" in both the Table of Alterations and the Table of Emendations because a current revision has been omitted that Thoreau did not cancel.

(4) Blotted words, letters, or punctuation in MS. Blots are reported only if they obscure more than half of a word, letter, or mark of punctuation, or if the reading conjectured from them suggests an ambiguity of meaning or spelling. In all cases, the original manuscript was studied in an effort to decipher the blotted element.

(5) Undeciphered words or letters in MS. Some undeciphered words or letters cannot be normalized as "imperfectly formed." Wherever possible, these are emended from other sources—usually Thoreau's later version of the passage. Undeciphered words that cannot be emended are printed in the text as { }; an approximate count of undeciphered letters is reported in the table.

(6) Ambiguous placement of text in MS. Unusual placement of text is emended if it cannot be normalized or if it is seriously misleading, for example, mar-

ginalia not marked for insertion in the text (see Emendation *385.16). In three instances, spacing of the copy-text has been emended to permit more convenient arrangements of mottoes and index entries (see Textual Note 3.2-4.16; Emendations 506.16 and 507.17).

(7) Mutilations in MS. Physical gaps are reported in the text in the following manner: {*Four leaves missing*}. Some partially surviving words have been emended, for example, *habitual* (408.27) and *Penobscots* (418.22); for those words that cannot be reconstructed, an approximate count of missing letters is reported in the table. Plausible readings in other versions appear in the Textual Notes.

(8) Thoreau's pagination in MS. Thoreau's references to his manuscript page numbers are emended to those of the Princeton Edition text, except in his indexes (see Appendix, pp. 499-509), where manuscript page numbers are retained because they identify the length of lost entries. For convenience, bracketed Princeton Edition page numbers also appear in the indexes.

(9) Accepted later revisions in MS. In rare instances, later revisions are accepted as emendations because copy-text is incomplete (see Emendation 185.22) or misleading (e.g., Thoreau's pencilled correction of *human* to *humane* at 241.11).

(10) Incomplete letters in MS. Handwriting that cannot be normalized as "imperfectly formed" is emended only when the letters are less than half-formed and when those letters are not ones that Thoreau often wrote imperfectly.

(11) Series of dashes in MS. In his transcribed "Gleanings," mostly MS volumes 1 to 4, Thoreau often used a series of dashes to indicate his abridge-

ment of original entries or sources (e.g., 288.1). Similar dashes appear in his commonplace books when he copied partial extracts from sources. Any series of three or more dashes, whether used to indicate ellipsis or not, is emended to two open one-en dashes (− −), and an actual count of copy-text dashes is reported in the table. Two dashes in a series are also printed in this form, without emending.

(12) Uncancelled false starts in MS. Although Thoreau's cancelled false starts are not reproduced in the text or reported in the Table of Alterations, his uncancelled false starts, which are part of the copy-text, are removed by emending.

(13) Unhyphenated end-of-line syllables in MS. Words Thoreau neglected to hyphenate at ends of lines, for example, *com / pleted* (329.26), are emended by closing up the space. For compounds or possible compounds, see End-of-Line Hyphenation, following.

(14) Ambiguous flourishes in MS. Flourishes that in context may represent letters, marks of punctuation, or meaningful symbols are emended.

(15) Ambiguous stray marks in MS. Stray marks that in context may represent letters, marks of punctuation, or meaningful symbols must also be emended.

In addition, unusual aspects of Thoreau's handwriting or peculiar features of the copy-text are emended. Any item marked with an asterisk in the Table of Emendations is discussed in the Textual Notes.

End-of-Line Hyphenation

When Thoreau's end-of-line hyphens in the copy-text divide compound words (*heart- / break*), the words must be emended to one of two possibly intended forms: closed (*heartbreak*) or hyphenated (*heart-break*). If the evidence from the first three levels of authority described on p. 639 is inconsistent or insufficient, the hyphens are retained (e.g., *spyglass* at 243.12). All line-end hyphenated compounds have been resolved to the forms that appear in the table. The Princeton Edition typesetting has a ragged right-hand margin and introduces no new end-of-line hyphens. Any item marked with an asterisk in the End-of-Line Hyphenation Table is discussed in the Textual Notes.

Textual Notes

These notes report both significant features of the copy-text and editorial decisions requiring more explanation than is provided by the Textual Introduction.

Design

Certain nontextual design features in this edition are not dependent upon editorial judgment: they include front matter, including title page, copyright notice, and Table of Contents; chapter titles and half-titles; running heads, page numbers, and signature numbers; the size and style of typography, indentations, or margins; and back matter, including the Annotations, Index, and Editorial Appendix. Page and line numbers of the text were determined by the series format adopted for *The Writings of Henry D. Thoreau*. The line-scale printed on the dust jacket and endpapers of this volume provides an accurate count for those pages with ordinary typography and no extra spacing between lines; for any pages with smaller type or extra spacing, a literal line-count applies. In the tables that follow, literal page and line numbers appear.

Textual Notes

THE TEXTUAL NOTES report significant features of the manuscripts and sources for editorial emendations. They also rectify Thoreau's incorrect dates in the text. Contextual punctuation appears outside of quotation marks when ambiguity would result from using the standard form. Abbreviations in the Textual Notes refer to the following works:

A Week	Henry D. Thoreau, *A Week on the Concord and Merrimack Rivers*, ed. Carl F. Hovde, William L. Howarth, and Elizabeth Hall Witherell (Princeton: Princeton University Press, 1980)
bMS Am	Manuscript at the Houghton Library, Harvard University; followed by catalogue number
Collected Poems	Henry D. Thoreau, *Collected Poems of Henry Thoreau*, ed. Carl Bode, enl. ed. (Baltimore: The Johns Hopkins Press, 1964)
EEM	Henry D. Thoreau, *Early Essays and Miscellanies*, ed. Joseph J. Moldenhauer et al. (Princeton: Princeton University Press, 1975)
Excursions	Henry D. Thoreau, *Excursions* (Boston: Ticknor and Fields, 1863)
HM	Manuscript at the Henry E. Huntington Library, San Marino, California; followed by catalogue number
MA	Manuscript at the Pierpont Morgan

Library, New York; followed by catalogue number

RP   Henry D. Thoreau, *Reform Papers*,
ed. Wendell Glick (Princeton: Princeton University Press, 1973)

Thoreau's   MS commonplace book in the Library
Literary   of Congress; published in a facsimile
Notebook   edition by Kenneth W. Cameron as
*Thoreau's Literary Notebook in the
Library of Congress* (Hartford: Tran-
scendental Books, 1964)

TN   Textual Note

ViU   Alderman Library, University of Virginia, Charlottesville, Virginia

VtMiM   The Julian W. Abernethy Collection
of American Literature, Starr Library, Middlebury College, Middlebury, Vermont

Walden   Henry D. Thoreau, *Walden*, ed. J.
Lyndon Shanley (Princeton: Prince-
ton University Press, 1971)

MS Volume 1

3.1 *endpaper*}: Pencil "1" in upper left corner of
paste-down endpaper; written three times in upper right
corner of recto of first front flyleaf.

3.2-4.16 Henry . . . Marvell's "Garden": Autograph,
descriptive title, and mottoes appear centered on recto
and verso of first and second front flyleaves; first dated
entry is on recto of first leaf.

12.28 ears"—: Possibly a period after "ears" in MS;
no period and a longer dash in a later version (*A Week*,
p. 326).

23.30-24.7, 24.14-25 Bretagne . . . Euxine *and* fluctuating . . . all: Leaf cut along inner edge and repaired
beside these lines on recto and verso of MS leaf paged
"35-36."

24.26 *blank*}:   Leaf paged "37-38" attached by wax to stub.

24.27-25.3 Dec. . . . basket.:   Written in different ink on verso of attached leaf (see TN 24.26).

29.32 *missing*}:   MS paging continuous.

30.1-20 Feb. 27th . . . round.:   T cut out two preceding leaves and copied the February 19 entry in pencil below entry for February 27, later tracing over it in ink. See 87.29-31 for a copy of February 19 entry.

34.24 —Carlyleish—:   Written vertically in margin beside text at 34.14-24.

45.31 Hollowwell: "Hollow- / well" in MS; "Hallowell" in John Hayward, *The New England Gazetteer* (Concord, N.H.: Israel S. Boyd and William White, 1839), s.v.

45.31 May 6th — — May 7th: T originally wrote four dashes after "May 6th" but later wrote "May 7th" over last two dashes and drew a line from left to right margins, separating the two dates and probably indicating a new paragraph.

47.27 May Morning: Title set off by flourishes in MS. Flourishes also emended at 98.15, 98.25, 100.17, 107.4, and 127.21.

58.24 *missing*}:   Text and MS paging continuous.

68.3 Since the volume was set in type, the leaf missing at this point has been located at the Pierpont Morgan Library (MA 920); it contains another copy of the last four stanzas of "The Peal of the Bells," as follows:

And the metal goes round 't a single bound,
A-lulling the fields with its measured sound—
Till the tired tongue falls with a lengthened boom,
As solemn and loud as the crack of doom.

Then changed is their measure to tone upon tone,
And seldom it is that one sound comes alone,
For they ring out their peals in a mingled throng,
And the breezes waft the loud ding-dong along.

—

When the echo has reached me in this lone vale,
I am straightway a hero in coat of mail,

I tug at my belt and I march on my post,
And feel myself more than a match for a host.

I am on the alert for some wonderful thing,
Which somewhere's a taking place,
'Tis perchance the salute which our planet doth ring
When it meeteth another in space.

68.5   with its: "with is" in MS; "with its" in version on excised leaf (see TN 68.3).

69.11   *missing*}:   MS paging continuous.

69.21   he . . . all: Originally "he may after all come up with us." Marked for transposition.

72.24   the artist . . . it?:   This line, added at the bottom of the page in a different ink, may have been copied from the first of the three missing leaves that followed, beginning at 72.25.

72.25   *missing*}:   MS paging continuous; ink remnants on the third stub are illegible except for "ing" on verso.

87.18-27   "The farmer . . . Phe-be.:   Text appears on verso of first back flyleaf; recto blank. Though placed in quotation marks, the material is original; for 87.23-27, cf. "Natural History of Massachusetts" (*Dial* 3 [July 1842]:26). See also 134.14-136.29, 137.15-25, 140.2-15, and 141.27-142.24.

88.19-28   Stretched . . . noon.:   On verso of second back flyleaf, written over erased pencil text or index.

88.30   *endpaper*}:   Back paste-down endpaper contains a partial index of MS volume 1 in pencil (see Appendix, pp. 505-506), written over an erased pencil text or index.

MS Volume 2

91.1   *flyleaf*}:   Pencil "2" in upper left corner of front paste-down endpaper. Front free endpaper and flyleaf contain pencil draft for "The Service."

103.10   *missing*}:   MS paging continuous; following leaf partially cut and repaired.

105.18   *missing*}:   MS paging continuous; following leaf partially cut and repaired.

107.26   *missing*}:   MS text and paging continuous.

121.13   *missing*}:   MS paging discontinuous: "56

[57-58] 59"; stub has a torn rather than cut edge. See Appendix, p. 506 for T's index entry for p. "[57]."

123.16 *missing*}: MS paging discontinuous: "62 [63-66] 67"; illegible ink remnants on stub of "[64]."

127.2 —Λόγος . . . Art.: Double horizontal lines below 127.2, 127.4, 127.8, 127.12, and 127.15 emended to dashes.

128.18 science: Underlining in MS is possibly a cross-stroke for "tt" in "attempted", directly below.

140.2-15 "What . . . it.: Though placed in quotation marks, the material is probably original.

141.27-142.24 "Though . . . o'clock.: Though placed in quotation marks, the material is probably original.

159.9 *missing*}: MS paging continuous; ink remnants on several stubs.

159.10-160.19 The drapery . . . vines.: On back flyleaf and free endpaper.

160.20 *blank*}: Ink "Henry D. Thoreau" and pencil "62 1/2" (not in T's hand) inverted at bottom edge.

160.21 *endpaper*}: Paste-down endpaper contains partial index of MS volume 2 (see Appendix, pp. 506-507).

MS Volume 3

163.1 *endpapers*}: Pencil "3" in upper left and upper right corners of front paste-down and free endpapers; ink "Henry D. Thoreau." on recto of free endpaper; endpapers contain pencil and ink draft, some of which was later used in *A Week*.

163.2-9 I've . . . sprite.: Text on front flyleaf, paged "1" in pencil.

163.11 *missing*}: MS paging continuous.

166.14 a man must: "a must" in MS; "a man must" in a later version (MA 607).

172.2 or: "of" in MS; "or" in a later version (*A Week*, p. 304).

201.28 *blank*}: Although no Journal entry for December 13, 1840, survives, a text titled "The Best Criticism Dec. 13th 1840" is now at the Lilly Library, Indiana University. See T's first index entry (Appendix, p. 499).

225.9 *missing*}: MS text and paging continuous.

225.10-226.21 countenances. . . . reader.: On back flyleaf and endpaper.

226.23 *endpaper*}: Pencil and ink text, similar to pencil text reported in Selected Later Revision 220.16, on verso of back free and paste-down endpapers: partial index in pencil on back paste-down endpaper (see Appendix, p. 507).

MS Volume 4

229.1 *endpapers*}: Pencil "4" in upper left corner of front paste-down endpaper; pencil text on front paste-down endpaper and recto of free endpaper. Top eighth of front free endpaper cut out, possibly to remove T's signature. "H D Thoreau Vol 4," in another hand, in upper right corner of free endpaper.

235.17-19 If . . . all.: Cancelled and partially erased.

240.4 take: Comma following in MS, resulting from incomplete erasure of original text, "forests,".

242.31 *missing*}: MS text and paging continuous.

253.11 surely: "ur" undeciphered in MS; "surely" in later version (*Dial* 4 [January 1844]:303).

260.23 thee: "the" in MS; "thee" in a later version (ViU, 6345-e).

285.22 13: MS reads "sym- / 13 phonies. Let . . . finite"; in a later version (bMS Am 1280.214.1), "13" introduces a new paragraph beginning "Let us expect no finite satisfaction."

285.28 concludes: "cucludes" in MS; "concludes" in a later version (bMS Am 1280.214.1).

286.12 cunning: "cumning" in MS; "cunning" in a later version (bMS Am 1280.214.1).

291.3 *missing*}: Text and MS paging discontinuous: "142 [143-144] 145."

291.4-22 Under . . . beside.: On recto and verso of back free endpaper. Pencil "37," probably not in T's hand, inverted on verso of free endpaper.

291.24 *endpaper*}: Paste-down endpaper contains partial index in pencil of MS volume 4 (see Appendix, p. 507). Cancelled pencil "147" in upper right corner.

MS Volume 5

295.1 *endpaper*}: Pencil "5" in upper left and right corners of front paste-down endpaper; pencil "34" in lower left corner.

295.2 *missing*}: Text begins on first surviving leaf, paged "1."

309.13 Westward-ho!: Centered horizontal line below title is represented here and at 309.18 as centered dash.

314.34 *blank*}: Blank leaves paged "43" in ink, "44-58" in pencil.

326.9 sleep: "steep" in MS, but the "t" is probably a crossed "1"; "sleep" in a later version (*A Week*, p. 150).

327.12 private and: "private: and" in MS; no colon in later version ("Transcripts, 1840-1842," 424.22).

331.12 Sat.: September 5, 1841, was a Sunday.

333.15 Bolton: "Boton" in MS (see Annotation 333.15).

334.21 *endpaper*}: Contains partial index in pencil of MS volume 5 (see Appendix, pp. 507-508) and several pencil versions of entries from the volume.

MS Volume 6

337.1 *flyleaf*}: Front paste-down endpaper contains pencil "6" in upper left corner and partial index of MS volume 6 and MS volume 9 (see Appendix, pp. 508, 509). Top eighth of front free endpaper cut out, possibly to remove T's signature. Verso of front flyleaf contains pencil text.

341.9 Sunday Nov. 12th 1841: The correct date is Sunday, December 12, 1841. For a discussion of this and other incorrect dates in MS volume 6, see Historical Introduction, pp. 599-600.

348.25-26 Experience . . . Wisdom: T originally wrote "Wisdom bereaves us of our ignorance / Experieence [emended to "Experience"] bereaves us of our innocence", then marked these sentences for transposition by underlining the first word of each and numbering "Experience . . . innocence" "1" and "Wisdom . . . ignorance" "2." Another "1" also written in margin next to "Experience".

349.22 it is: "ist" in MS; "it is" in a later version (*A Week*, p. 264).

352.13 cold light of the moon: MS reads "cold loght of the noon," with "loght" altered from "low"; a later version reads "still light of the cheerful moon" (*Dial* 3 [July 1842]:19).

352.14 twig: "twgis" in MS; "twig" in a later version (*Dial* 3 [July 1842]:20).

352.29-30 field fare: "re" undeciphered in MS; "fieldfare" in a later version (*Dial* 3 [July 1842]:20).

357.8 Monday . . . 1841: Ink correction of year to "1842" by H.G.O. Blake in margin.

362.9 I feel very when: As in MS; later revised in pencil to "I feel a sad cheer when".

364.12 Saturday: The correct date for this entry is February 19.

365.10 see p. 368: "see p 69" in MS, referring to continuation of text at 368.20.

365.11 *missing*}: MS paging continuous.

365.13 Feb. 21st: Written vertically in margin of page "[61]."

365.26-366.10 I . . . firmament—: Cancelled in ink; the passage is probably a response to the death of John Thoreau, Jr., on January 11, 1842.

370.24 *missing*}: MS paging discontinuous: "72 [73-78] 79."

372.21 Sunday: March 14, 1842, was a Monday.

383.21 do not wish: "do wish" in MS; "do not wish" in a later version (*A Week*, p. 266).

385.16 Set . . . 21st: Written vertically in margin with no insertion mark; T originally wrote "Sunday March 21st" at 383.8 and later corrected the date to "20." The marginal text probably belongs to the March 20 entry and thus is included with it.

389.26 look below 3 ps: "look below 6 ps" in MS, referring to a parallel text at 392.28-30.

399.28 Set . . . 1st: Written vertically in margin beside entry for April 2, with no insertion mark.

399.29-402.7 Saturday . . . repast.: Text appears on the back flyleaf, free endpaper, and paste-down endpaper. Pencil "48 49-57-58 92-3-4" at bottom of paste-down endpaper refer to pages 359-360, 363-364, 376-378.

"Transcripts, 1840-1842"

408.27 habitual: "ha-" in MS; "habitual" in a previous version (316.22).

408.28 *missing*}: MS paging discontinuous: "8 [9-

12] 13." See 177.17-22 for an earlier version of the incomplete text at 408.29-30.

415.10-11 but . . . fence: Cancelled in ink; "p17" and caret in left margin refer to text at 410.27-30. At 410.30, T wrote "for p. 26".

418.21 *missing*}: MS text and paging discontinuous: "32 [33-34] 35." See 172.14-16 for an earlier version of the incomplete text at 418.22.

418.22 Penobscots: "scots" in MS; "Penobscots" in an earlier version (172.15).

419.15 *missing*}: MS text and paging discontinuous: "36 [37-38] 39." See Appendix, pp. 508-509 for T's index of contents of missing pages.

419.16-21 "the . . . human.": T later supplied beginning of sentence in pencil at top of page:
> We learn from the preface of the
> translation that "Vyása, the son
> of Parásava, has decided, that '

422.10 *missing*}: MS text and paging discontinuous: "44 [45-46] 47"; leaf paged "47-48" laid in.

423.30 *missing*}: A previous version (MA 594) completes the text at 423.29 as follows: "time, the priest just returned home and the prince are most to be honored; and of those two, the priest just returned home should be treated with more respect than the prince."

424.15 *missing*}: MS text and paging discontinuous: "[52] [53-64] 65."

425.14 *missing*}: MS text and paging discontinuous: "66 [67-70] 71"; leaves paged "65-66" and "71-72" laid in. See Appendix, p. 508 for T's index of contents of missing pages.

426.9 *missing*}: MS text and paging discontinuous: "72 [73-78] 79." See 316.19-29 for an earlier version of the incomplete text at 426.8.

427.12 art—: "v p 83" below these words; page 83 is missing from the volume.

427.13 *missing*}: MS text and paging discontinuous: "80 [81-100] 101"; leaf paged "101-102" is at the Huntington Library (HM 926). See Appendix, pp. 508-509 for T's index of contents of missing pages.

427.14 These sublime passages: Text is on MS page "101," but T's index (see Appendix, p. 508) lists it for page "97." Another entry, which does not survive, is listed for page "101." Thus the present text may be a redrafting, composed after T indexed the volume.

428.4 *blank . . . missing*}: MS paging discontinuous: "102 [103-112] 113." T later inverted leaf and wrote ink text for his translation of *Prometheus Bound* in blank space.

428.31 *blank . . . missing*}: MS text and paging discontinuous: "114 [115-124] 125"; "or an i" written vertically on stub of fifth missing leaf.

429.11 *blank . . . missing*}: T later used blank space for pencil text: "Veda sentences / Kapila / How Hindoo calculates / Mod. civilization of." and partial index of "Transcripts" (see Appendix, pp. 508-509). Ledger entry by John Thoreau, Jr., inverted below index (see Textual Introduction, p. 624).

MS Volume 7

433.1 *missing*}: MS volume 6 ends April 3, 1842; first extant date in MS volume 7 is July 18, 1842. Missing pages "[1-90]" probably included drafts for "Natural History of Massachusetts" (*Dial* 3 [July 1842]:19-40).

434.3 *missing*}: Missing pages "[93-102]" probably included text for "A Walk to Wachusett" (*Boston Miscellany* 3 [January 1843]:31-36). See *Collected Poems*, p. 211, for complete text of "One more is gone" incomplete at 433.31. T indexed page "98" of missing sequence under heading "Style—Carlyle—&c" in a later MS volume (MA 1303).

435.23 dank: Possibly "dark"; also "dank" in a later draft version (New York Public Library); "dark" and "dank" in two later printed versions of "A Walk to Wachusett": *Boston Miscellany* 3 (January 1843):31 and *Excursions*, p. 77 respectively.

436.3 *missing*}: Missing pages "[107-118]" probably included text for "A Walk to Wachusett." Draft version of essay (New York Public Library) refers to pages "107" and "118"; printed version (*Boston Miscellany* 3 [January 1843]:34, 36) completes text incomplete at 436.2 and 436.4.

437.7 *missing*}: Missing pages "[121-150]" probably included text for "A Walk to Wachusett" (*Boston*

Miscellany 3 [January 1843]:31-36). Draft version of essay (New York Public Library) refers to pages "121" and "124." See *Collected Poems*, p. 212, for complete text of "In some withdrawn untraversed mead" incomplete at 437.8. T indexed page "129" of missing sequence under heading "Style—Carlyle—&c" in a later MS volume (MA 1303).

437.15   had undertaken . . . rather than high: "had unterken . . . rather high" in MS; "has undertaken . . . rather than high" in a later version (MA 1303).

438.22   The herdsman: "Therdsman" in MS; "The herdsman" in a later version (HM 13197).

438.31   whispered: Undeciphered in MS; "whispered" in a later version (*Collected Poems*, p. 324).

439.16   *missing*}:   Missing pages "[163-192]" possibly included text for "A Winter Walk" (*Dial* 4 [October 1843]:211-226). See *Collected Poems*, pp. 192-193, for complete text of "Oh ye proud days of Europes middle age" incomplete at 439.15.

440.7   kine: "dogs" in MS; "kine" in a later version (*Dial* 4 [October 1843]:212).

442.27-28   In . . . behind: Written in pencil and traced in ink, possibly later.

443.11   which: "why" in MS; corrected to "which" in pencil.

443.17   *missing*}:   Missing pages "[199-214]" probably included text for lecture on "Sir Walter Raleigh," which T delivered in Concord on February 8, 1843.

444.7   times: "tim{*MS torn*}" in MS; "times" in a later version (HM 943) and in T's source (see Annotation 443.18-444.27).

444.28   *missing*}:   Missing pages "[217-238]" included text for "Sir Walter Raleigh." See *EEM*, p. 195, for later version of text incomplete at 444.27.

445.34   *missing*}:   A later version (*A Week*, p. 315) completes the text incomplete at 445.33.

446.30   (Catholic)*:   Asterisk supplied by editors to key T's footnote.

447.11   heaven.)*:   Asterisk supplied by editors to key T's footnote.

MS Volume 8

453.1   *missing*}:   Missing pages "[1-142]" included

text for "A Winter Walk" (*Dial* 4 [October 1843]:211-226). T indexed page "39" of MS volume 8 under heading "red bird" in a later MS volume (MA 1303).

454.4   *missing*}:   Missing pages included text for "A Winter Walk" (*Dial* 4 [October 1843]:211-226).

455.10   *missing*}:   Missing pages "[181-190]" probably included text for an unfinished prose composition titled "Conversation" (VtMiM). A later version (MA 1303) contains beginning of sentence incomplete at 455.11:   "Men sometimes do as if they could eject themselves like bits of pack thread from the . . ."

457.10   *missing*}:   Missing pages "[195-196]" included text for "A Winter Walk." See *Dial* 4 (October 1843):215 for later version of text incomplete at 457.9.

457.11   Thursday: May 19, 1843, was a Friday.

458.4   *missing*}:   T indexed pages "239," "296-7," and "397 & 413," missing in this section of MS volume 8, under the respective headings, "Spring in Virgil," "Style —Carlyle–&c," and "Marlowe" (MA 1303).

460.12   8:   Last dated entry in MS volume 8 is August 25, 1843. Entries for August 26, 28, and September 1, 1843, are on different paper, three pages of a folio sheet.

MS Volume 9

467.18   shakspeare: "shaksp" written at inner edge of detached leaf (bMS Am 278.5); "eare" written on surviving stub (HM 13182).

467.27   (Shakspeare):   "(Shakspea" written at inner edge of detached leaf (bMS Am 278.5); "re)" written on surviving stub (HM 13182).

469.6   Scott: "scot" in MS; "Scott" in an earlier commonplace book (*Thoreau's Literary Notebook*, p. 53).

473.18   *missing*}:   Missing pages "[17-18]" probably included text used in *Walden*:   after "winter." at 471.5, T later wrote "Forward 18" in pencil, apparently referring to text on the missing page "18." In the first MS version of *Walden* (HM 924: A; see J. Lyndon Shanley, *The Making of Walden* [Chicago: University of Chicago Press, 1957], pp. 203-204), two paragraphs ("I never tire . . . tresses of summer.") complete the description of winter vegetation ending at 471.5. See also *Walden*, pp. 309-310.

475.1   Saturday: October 13, 1843, was a Friday.

475.17   Monday: October 15, 1843, was a Sunday.

475.27-28   he learned . . . hitherto . . . what: T apparently changed his mind about the order of these clauses as he composed. After writing "If he has faild in all undertakings hitherto—learned that life is short—errare est humanum and what does he do—", T parenthesized "has . . . hitherto" and "learned . . . and" and wrote a large "X" over the dash between "hitherto" and "learned" to indicate transposition.

476.11   wests: As in MS; "wersts" and "versts" in later MS versions (bMS Am 278.5, folders 18A, 18B); "versts" in *RP*, p. 183. A verst is a Russian measure of distance equal to about two-thirds of a mile.

476.15   Field: "iel" undeciphered; "One Darby Field an irishman" in T's source, Winthrop, *A Journal of Transactions*, p. 247 (see Annotations, p. 540); and "John Field, an Irishman" in a later version (*Walden*, p. 204).

477.21   *missing*}:   Missing pages "[25-26]" probably included text used in *A Week*, pp. 337-338. A later MS volume (MA 1303) provides text missing between 477.20 and 477.22.

479.1   good man: "god man" in MS; "goodman" in a later version (MA 1303).

479.3-8   Here . . . engraver.:   Written vertically in margin of MS page next to text printed from 478.31 to 479.2, with no mark for inserting.

481.20   a Greek: "a" possibly not in T's hand.

492.17   spear: "pear" in MS; "spear" in T's source (Macpherson, *Ossian*, p. 252 [see Annotations, p. 537]) and two later versions (*Dial* 4 [January 1844]:295; *A Week*, p. 347).

493.23   *missing*}:   A later version contains beginning of sentence incomplete at 493.24: "Who would not sail through mutiny and storm farther than Columbus—to reach the fabulous retreating . . ." (MA 1303).

495.11   different: "differ{*MS torn*}" in MS; "different" in a later version (MA 1303).

APPENDIX

All of Thoreau's indexes are in pencil. The indexes for his original journal volumes are in HM 945, interspersed with other text. The editors have put the entries into sequential order and provided Princeton Edition page numbers in braces.

Indexes of Original Journal Volumes, 1837-1840

502.3   Tent life 568:   Followed by horizontal pencil line across page, indicating end of Red Journal index.

Indexes of MS Volumes 1-6; "Transcripts, 1840-1842";
9:1837-1844

505.23-506.16   First . . . 78:   On back paste-down endpaper of MS volume 1, in pencil.

506.31   56-7:   Page "57" missing from MS volume 2.

507.2   106 . . . {147:   Refers to pencil addition at 147.7-9 not printed. Text appears in substantively same form in *A Week*, p. 343.1-4.

507.28-29   22 . . . p. 6.:   On front free endpaper; rest of index of MS volume 4 on back paste-down endpaper.

508.21   140 Fr—:   "Fr" possibly not in T's hand.

508.23-24   V . . . snow: On front flyleaf; rest of index of MS volume 6 on front paste-down endpaper.

509.2   101 . . . &c: Page "101" does not contain this entry; see TN 427.14.

509.7-23   Vide 9th . . . gratuitous: On front paste-down endpaper of MS volume 6. The "9" in "Vide 9th" appears to be written over an "8" and a "7"; the index is clearly to volume 9, though T may have had other numbering sequences for these volumes at one time.

Table of Emendations

THIS table lists all changes made from copy-text other than normalized features described in the Textual Introduction (pp. 636-639), and it reports editorial resolutions of ambiguous manuscript features. Numbers at the left margin key the emendation to page and line, and if the number is marked with an asterisk, the emendation is discussed in the Textual Notes. The emended reading appears to the left of the bracket, and the original copy-text reading appears to the right; editorial descriptions are italicized. A wavy dash (~) to the right of the bracket replaces the word to the left of the bracket in cases where only punctuation is emended. A virgule (/) indicates line-end division.

MS Volume 1

*	3.2-4.16	Henry . . . Marvell's "Garden"] *autograph and subtitle, 3 mottoes centered on 4 successive pages*
	5.9	arranged.] *followed by 3 dashes*
	5.10	The] *preceded by 3 dashes*
	5.19	forest] *followed by 3 dashes*
	5.20	mould.] *followed by 3 dashes*
	5.25	growth.] *followed by 17 dashes*
	6.11	Tasso.] *followed by 3 dashes*
	8.2	Fog.] *followed by 16 dashes*
	8.11	hills.] *followed by 7 dashes*
	9.18	shades!] *followed by 6 dashes*
*	12.28	ears"–] *possibly ~."–*
	14.9	laeto] *possibly* Caeto
	18.32	Sprengel,] *possibly ~,–*
	19.12	sector-wise,] *possibly ~;*
	19.13	Lord.] *period blotted*
	19.17	season] *possibly* reason
	21.12	same] sam *in MS*
	23.18	British] Bitish *in MS*

23.32	claim] clain *in MS*
27.2	στοα] *underlined*
28.26	wherever] *final* r *incomplete at outer edge*
32.7	explore] ex / plore *in MS*
32.11	school] *possibly* schools
32.16	rights] *possibly* right
32.21	chance] *line of 4 dashes below*
32.27	suna-day] *followed by 7 dashes*
33.34	to?] *followed by 3 dashes*
34.6	path.] *followed by 5 dashes*
* 34.24	—Carlyleish—] Carlyleish *written in margin between flourishes*
34.26	How] *preceded by 5 dashes*
35.11	them] *followed by 4 dashes*
35.13	convincing.] *followed by 8 dashes*
35.22	Man] *possibly* man
36.13	mob.] *followed by 4 dashes*
37.6	mile.] *followed by 7 dashes*
37.8	gods.] *followed by 8 dashes*
37.16	voice.] *followed by 6 dashes*
38.18	lump.] *line of 12 dashes below*
39.19	chanting our] chant— / our *in MS*
41.25	Resistlessly.] *line of 4 dashes below*
42.6	generation] *followed by 3 dashes*
42.10	business.] *followed by 3 dashes*
43.22	smocks] *possibly* mocks
43.24	old] *possibly* Old
44.23	unroll] uroll *in MS*
44.35	it.] *followed by 3 dashes*
45.2	creation] *followed by 9 dashes*
45.4	sea-sick] *possibly* sea sick
45.11	here.] *followed by 1 dash; line of 9 dashes below*
45.12	4th] *followed by 3 dashes*
45.14	neither] nither *in MS*
45.15	bustle.] *followed by 5 dashes*
45.21	5th.] *followed by 3 dashes*
45.23	ground.] *followed by 3 dashes*
* 45.31	6th —] *followed by transverse line (see Alterations)*
* 45.31	— May 7th] *possibly* ¶
45.34	ourselves.] *followed by 3 dashes*

72.32	degree.] *followed by 4 dashes*
74.16	even] *possibly* ever
74.26	decked] *final* d *incomplete at inner edge*
75.2	way-side] *possibly* way side
75.3	teeming] *second* e *blotted*
79.17	Breeze's] *apostrophe written as flourish*
81.32	plain] *followed by 3 dashes*
82.36	unapproached] unapprached *in MS*
84.6	memory] menory *in MS*
84.13	sailors] *followed by 4 dashes; line of 9 dashes below*
85.8	nature.] *followed by 9 dashes*
87.7	she.] *followed by 3 dashes*
88.21	soul] *possibly* Soul
88.22	tiniest] tinniest *in MS*
88.22	cloud.] *line of 3 dashes below*

MS Volume 2

91.22	eye] *possibly* aye
94.5	peace.] *followed by 3 dashes*
95.27	brass] *possibly* brave
96.10	anywhere] *possibly* any-where
98.1	γὰρ] *possibly* γὰς
100.5	piecemeal] picemeal *in MS*
104.29	unexplored] uexplored *in MS*
106.22	desired] *possibly* devised
106.23	round] *possibly* sound
108.3	offerings] s *incomplete at outer edge*
110.27	sort] sot *in MS*
111.13	four or] four of *in MS*
112.8	sand.] *lines of 4 and 5 dashes below*
116.29	day.] *line of 3 dashes below*
117.16	peck] *possibly* pick *or* peek
117.21	approached] approach / ed *in MS*
119.18	Susquehannah] *preceded by question mark in margin*
120.14	quiet] quit *or* quet *in MS*
122.16	—40] *dash written with dry pen stroke*
122.25	that] *possibly* than
125.10	launched] lauched *or* lanched *in MS*
126.17	teem] *second* e *blotted*
126.30	and in] an in *in MS*

*127.2   Art.] *double horizontal line below*
127.11   ἑαυτῶν] *possibly* ἑαυτὸν
128.8   background] *possibly* back-ground
*128.18   science] *possibly underlined*
129.14   those] *possibly* these
130.3   smoothness] n *blotted*
130.14   lenses] *followed by 3 dashes*
132.2   lovely] *possibly* lonely
132.23   dark] *followed by 4 dashes*
133.22   It] Tt *in MS*
135.11   and foxes] an foxes *in MS*
137.2   Cascade] *followed by 3 dashes*
137.5   rock] *followed by 5 dashes*
138.22   fresh water] *possibly* fresh-water
139.11   for] fore *in MS*
140.4   words] *possibly* woods
142.5   waiteth] *possibly* waileth
142.8   and evening] an evening *in MS*
142.12   hurry-skurry] *possibly* hurry skurry
142.20   "With] *quotation mark in margin;* With
           indented
143.22   27th] *followed by stray mark, possibly* o
144.19   as] *possibly* As
145.12   sail] *possibly* sails
147.12   constellations.] *possibly* ∼ :
148.2   them, and] them, an *in MS*
148.2   reenact] *possibly* re-enact
148.12   midday] *possibly* mid-day
149.2   lips] s *incomplete*
149.11   enclosure.] *followed by 3 dashes*
149.18   dawn,] *possibly* ∼ ;
151.27   be,] *possibly* ∼ ,–
152.6   roundly] *possibly* soundly
156.14   accommodate] accommotate *in MS*
156.27   necessity] es *blotted*
159.10   altogether] atogether *in MS*
160.1   worsted] *possibly* wasted

MS Volume 3

*166.14   a man must] a must *in MS*
168.14   arm chair] *possibly* armchair
*172.2   or] of *in MS*

MS Volume 4

275.27	ships] *final* s *incomplete*
276.2	diversion] diverion *or* divesion *in MS*
276.15	trick] *possibly* tricks
277.14	cow-bells] *possibly* cowbells
277.26	Here] *possibly* there
279.30	1] *written in margin*
281.1	3] *written in margin*
282.18	7] *written in margin*
283.26	pursues] pusues *in MS*
284.1	8] *written in margin*
284.5	disease] dis / ease *in MS*
284.16	9] *written in margin*
*285.22	13] *written in margin*
285.24	else] elsle *in MS*
285.28	14] *written in margin*
285.28	14] 4 *blotted*
*285.28	concludes] cucludes *in MS*
285.35	eyebeam] *possibly* eye-beam
286.12	16] *written in margin*
*286.12	cunning] cumning *in MS*
286.16	17] *written in margin*
287.8	though he] thoughe *in MS*
288.1	marble] *followed by 3 dashes*
290.25	independence] in / dependence *in MS*

MS Volume 5

295.18	On] *possibly added later*
295.26	men's] *possibly* man's
297.2	Even] *possibly* Ever
297.24	sanded] *possibly* ~ :
300.8	men] *interlined in pencil*
300.18	That's] *possibly* That's
302.25	cursing] *possibly* cussing
303.10	ring] *possibly* sing
303.15	tree-sparrow] *possibly* tree sparrow
303.28	eye lids] *possibly* eyelids
303.30	when] *possibly* where
305.8	Even] *possibly* Ever
305.25	man.] *possibly* ~ :
306.6	shed] *possibly* shod
306.16	with] widh *in MS* (*see Alterations*)
306.28	occasionally.] *followed by 3 dashes*

*309.13	Westward-ho!] *underlined*
309.17	heard . . . Woods.] *underlined*
311.19	Culucca] *possibly* Calucca
312.23	mountain] moun / tain *in MS*
312.33	there] *possibly* then
313.21	these] *possibly* those
313.32	we] *possibly* We *or* me
314.11	societies] scieties *in MS*
314.11	remembered] remenbered *in MS*
314.24	to] *possibly* &
314.27-28	and makes] amd makes *in MS*
314.28	serene] *possibly* severe
315.5	even] *possibly* ever
315.8	imported] *possibly* imparted
315.22	Far] Fare *in MS*
315.22	*Natures*] *possibly natures*
316.25	unnecessary] unncessary *in MS*
317.26	All] *possibly* all
318.21	Societies] *possibly* societies
319.14	322] 77 *in MS*
319.30	harmonizes] *possibly* harmonises
320.26	invades] v *blotted*
320.27	sounding] *possibly* rounding
321.12	sing] *possibly* ring
321.18	Eastern] Easten *in MS*
322.30	319] 68 *in MS*
323.1	that so] *possibly* thus so
323.4	that.] *double horizontal line below*
323.8	wider] wder *in MS*
323.19	plain.] *added in pencil*
324.12	heart strings] *possibly* heart-strings
325.2	learned] learnd *in MS*
325.32	unexpensively] *first* n *incomplete*
326.8	conventicle] v *incomplete*
*326.9	sleep] steep *in MS*
326.14	pleasure] *possibly* ∼—
326.29	her] he *in MS*
*327.12	private] *followed by stray mark, possibly* colon
327.24	derive] *possibly* desire *or* devise
327.32-33	And would] *possibly* and would
328.11	purification] *possibly* purefication

328.14	also—] *possibly* ~.
329.26	completed] com / pleted *in MS*
329.30	unnecessary] umecessary *in MS*
330.7	called] *followed by stray mark, possibly dash*
330.19	annual] anmual *in MS*
332.1	sing] *possibly* ring
333.4	Ye] *possibly* We
333.13	season] *possibly* reason
*333.15	Bolton] Boton *in MS*
333.20	thickness] *followed by stray mark, possibly dash*
334.2	bricks] *possibly* brick

MS Volume 6

338.3	atmosphere.] *possibly* ~,
338.6	You] *possibly* ~—
338.11	complete] complte *in MS*
338.25	that when] *possibly* than when
338.31	than] thany *in MS*
339.7	lies . . . to them.] l, *first* t, them. *incomplete at torn top edge*
339.7	them.] them. {*MS torn, approximately* 15 *letters missing*}
339.12	has] *possibly* was
339.29	own] *undeciphered*
340.12	your] ur *undeciphered*
340.15	all] ~. *in MS*
341.6	From] Frm *in MS*
341.10	character.] *possibly* ~:
341.12	had] haed *or* hadl *in MS*
341.37	small] snall *in MS*
342.1	eastern] easter *in MS*
342.8	broad] brud *in MS*
342.17	roaring] *possibly* soaring
343.22	thank] than *in MS*
344.6	more] nore *in MS*
344.13	Is] *possibly* In
344.17	come] *possibly* cane *or* cone
344.32	on to] *possibly* onto
345.14	feather] er *incomplete at inner edge*
345.14	rod] *possibly* sod

388.26	younger] yunger *in MS*
388.29	be] *undeciphered*
388.33	the easiness] the *preceded by uncancelled false start*
389.8-9	It . . . labyrinth.] *written in margin, marked for inserting (see Alterations)*
389.14	invented] *possibly* inserted
389.14	story] stoy *in MS*
389.22	so] o *undeciphered*
*389.26	3] 6 *in MS*
389.32	nor] *possibly* and
390.7	When] *possibly* Where
390.8	quarry] *second* r *undeciphered*
390.30	Our] *possibly* One
391.5	Terni] e *blotted*
391.13	such] suech *in MS*
391.17	our] *possibly* an
391.29	dream] *possibly* dreams
391.32	cannot] camnot *in MS*
392.15	make] *possibly* makes
392.28-29	But . . . that] *vertical mark opposite in margin*
392.30	hills] *possibly* hill,
393.33	Two] *possibly* The
394.6	more] mor *in MS*
394.29	nominally] in *undeciphered*
395.33	How] Hur *in MS*
396.4	an] *possibly* and
396.6	even] *possibly* ever
396.23	her] *undeciphered*
396.23	are] *undeciphered*
396.33	licenses] *possibly* licences
397.7	blancness] *possibly* blanckess
397.8	return] returrn *in MS*
397.16	imbedded] inbedded *in MS*
397.25	meet] *second* e *blotted*
397.25	ground] n *undeciphered*
397.29	each] ach *in MS*
398.5	what] *written in margin in pencil*
398.20	an] *possibly* our
399.5	true] *possibly* the
399.19	there] ere *undeciphered*

*399.28	Set . . . 1st] *written in margin, not marked for inserting* (*see Alterations*)
400.27	hill side] *possibly* hill-side
400.29	mortals] *or undeciphered*
401.24	The] T *preceded by uncancelled false start*

"Transcripts, 1840-1842"

406.11	it, It] *possibly* ~. ~
406.18	lonely] *possibly* lovely
408.12	consider] *possibly* Consider
408.27	an] *possibly* as
*408.27	habitual] ha- *in MS; 2 leaves missing*
409.7	stateliness] statelines *in MS*
409.11	era] r *blotted*
409.28	philosophy] *interlined with a caret in pencil*
410.2	forward] *possibly* ~.
410.3	gymnosophists] gynosophists *in MS*
410.30	415] 26 *in MS* (*see Textual Note 415.10-11*)
411.11	during] durings *in MS*
412.19	reaching] *possibly* searching
413.8	says] a *blotted*
413.9	period] r *blotted*
413.16	years] *possibly* ~.
413.17	Yug,] *followed by 11 dashes*
413.18	Yug,] *followed by 5 dashes*
414.12	to] *blotted*
414.28	trees] *possibly* ~,
*415.10-12	soul . . . the] p17 *and caret in margin*
415.13	these] he *blotted*
415.16	The] Thhe *in MS*
415.29	works] ks *blotted*
416.4	to] *blotted*
416.10	remembered—] *possibly* ~!
416.23	universal] univeral *in MS*
*416.32	modernize] *possibly* modernise
417.26	present] nt *undeciphered*
417.29-30	the Parthenon] the *possibly underlined*
417.32	sultriness] sutriness *in MS*
417.32	sultriness] ri *undeciphered*

418.5	ourselves] ouselves *in MS*
*418.22	Penobscots] {*MS torn*} scots
418.23	west—who] *possibly* ~ ~
422.18	footing] *possibly* fooling
423.5	realize] *possibly* realise
*423.30	*missing*}] *undeciphered letters at cut edge*
425.8	unfold] *possibly* unfolds
425.27	demands] de / mands *in MS*
425.31	Gauhts] h *blotted*
426.3	on] *possibly* in
427.4	these] ese *undeciphered*
427.7	themselves] them / selves *in MS*
*427.12	art—] art–v p 83 *in MS*
429.2	oversee] *possibly* over see
429.3	again.] *possibly* ~—
429.7	If there] *possibly* It then

MS Volume 7

433.6	White,] ~ *in MS*
433.11	contracted] *possibly* contrasted
433.23	stem] *possibly* ~—
434.13	failures] es *undeciphered*
434.15	prospect] prosprect *in MS*
434.22	have] ve *blotted*
434.23	men] been *in MS*
434.29	conceits] conceifts *in MS*
434.31	over] e *blotted*
435.23	and] *preceded by uncancelled false start*
*435.23	dank] *possibly* dark
435.28	There] T *incomplete*
435.28	then] *possibly* thus
436.9	not for] nt for *in MS*
436.30	barefoot] barefootte *in MS*
*437.15	undertaken] unterken *in MS*
*437.15	rather than high] rather high *in MS*
437.23	approach] apprach *in MS*
438.16	was] *undeciphered*
*438.22	The herdsman] Therdsman *in MS*
*438.31	whispered] *undeciphered*
439.3	beacons] n *incomplete*
439.12	Godfrey] Godsfrey *in MS*
439.20	farmers] *possibly* farmer

439.20	emitting a] a *undeciphered*
439.34	green] gren *in MS*
440.5	sound] n *incomplete*
*440.7	kine] dogs *in MS*
440.22	nuthatch] nuthach *in MS, second* h *crossed*
441.12	bark] *possibly* bank
441.16	fuming] *underlined*
441.16	fuming run] *uncancelled* purling—rippling? *written in margin*
441.34	clear] *possibly* clean
442.9	horn] or *undeciphered*
442.13	tinkling] *uncancelled* rattling *interlined above*
442.33	not] n *incomplete*
*443.11	which] *interlined in pencil above cancelled* why
443.15	through] *uncancelled* into *interlined above*
443.15	scar] *uncancelled* wound *interlined above*
444.4	ever] *possibly* even
*444.7	times] tim {*MS torn*}
444.14	said] d *blotted*
444.31	with] wth *in MS*
444.33	describes] descrcribes *in MS*
445.24	surrounding] surroinding *in MS*
445.26	fringe] n *incomplete*
445.27	are] aree *in MS*
445.27	wanting] *first* n *incomplete*
446.3	ever] *possibly* even
446.26	note] noote *in MS*
*446.30	(Catholic)*] *asterisk supplied*; not in most editions *interlined below*
*447.11	heaven.)*] *asterisk supplied*; 'omitted in most editions' *interlined between* heaven. *and*)
447.23	miserable] s *blotted*
448.2	water] *possibly* "~
448.12	Tuesday] *possibly cancelled*
448.30	then] *possibly* them

MS Volume 8

453.3	summer] sunmer *in MS*
453.9	rabbit] rabebit *in MS*

453.10	watch] wathch *in MS*
453.14	every] evey *in MS*
453.17	shall] shaell *in MS*
453.20	These] *possibly* There
453.21	recognise] recorgnise *in MS*
453.26	even] *possibly* ever
453.28	or] *undeciphered*
454.2	time] im *undeciphered*
454.7	steam] *uncancelled* vapor *interlined above*
454.10	lurked] *possibly* lurkest
454.15	pleasure be read] pleasure read *in MS*
454.30	base] *possibly* bare
455.13	of any] f any *in MS*
455.24	there] r *undeciphered*
456.13	whet] *underlining of* t *possibly stray mark*
456.19	villages] v *blotted*
456.34	books] *possibly* works
457.6	Round] un *undeciphered*
457.7	gathered] ed *undeciphered*
457.7	the robin] tthe robin *in MS*
457.9	A healthy] *possibly* ¶ A healthy
457.13	parallelled] *second* le *blotted*
457.14	luxuriant] t *incomplete at outer edge*
457.16	tenderness] tendlerness *in MS*
457.17	which way] whiich way *in MS*
457.30	unquestionable] unquestionalble *in MS*
458.15	plus] *undeciphered*
458.31	embosomed] embossmed *in MS*
460.1	Eremite] Eermite *in MS*
460.17	stands] stonds *in MS*
460.30	the] thre *in MS*
461.12	yielded] yeelded *in MS*
461.13	taste] tatste *in MS*
461.20	more] *possibly* mere
462.2	stock] stwck *in MS*

MS Volume 9

465.26	stuffed] sturffed *in MS*
465.27	sawdust] *possibly* saw-dust
466.25	show] *possibly* shew
467.8	Its] Itc *in MS*
467.12	enough] enoug {*MS torn*}

467.13	literature] *possibly* literatures
467.19	mystics] msytics *in MS*
467.26	name] n *undeciphered*
467.26	than] thean *in MS*
467.26	were] r *undeciphered*
468.17	influences] influcences *in MS*
468.30	but] *possibly* But
*469.6	Scott] scot *in MS*
469.31	earth] *uncancelled* fields *interlined above*
470.15	withered] re *incomplete*
472.19	bears] *possibly* wears
472.32	Sometimes] *second* e *blotted*
473.20	serenity] *first* e *blotted*
473.20	us] u *blotted*
473.24	Syria] a *blotted*
473.30	too] *possibly* to
474.12	and] nd *blotted*
474.15	multitudes] mulitudes *in MS*
474.28	an age] and age *in MS*
475.24	functions] fimctions *in MS*
476.11	chinese] chinesse *in MS*
*476.15	Field] iel *undeciphered*
476.23	who] whoy *in MS*
476.27	over] o *undeciphered*
476.30	dry] *possibly* every
477.15	their fattest] h *blotted*
477.23	—Let] *possibly* ¶ —Let
478.2	have] hae *in MS*
478.5	latest] lastest *in MS*
478.12	he] *possibly* we
478.31	Then] *preceded by uncancelled false start*
479.1	good] god *in MS*
*479.3-8	Here . . . engraver.] *written in margin, not marked for inserting*
480.7	understanding] understand / ing *in MS*
481.2	element] *possibly* elements
481.3	sun flower] *possibly* sun-flower
481.8	sometimes] eti *blotted*
481.20	anylyze] z *incomplete*
481.20	a Greek] and Greek *in MS*
*481.20	a Greek] a *interlined above* and *in pencil*
481.22	raw] *possibly* ram

482.16	I] *blotted*
483.12	suppose] sup / pose *in MS*
484.25	band] *possibly* bard
485.5	has] *possibly* was
486.2	storms] m *incomplete*
486.10	Psalms] Psalams *in MS*
486.27	all] *possibly* ~.
487.24	muse] *possibly* Muse
488.9	men] *followed by flourish*
488.31	characterized] characterizeed *or* charac-teriseed *in MS*
488.32	characterize] charactaerize *in MS*
489.3	everlasting] *possibly* ever-lasting
489.8	summer] mer *undeciphered*
489.8	poetry] poery *in MS*
489.11	scatter] scatteres *in MS*
489.14	winter] *preceded by uncancelled caret*
489.20	fashions] fahions *in MS*
489.22	pockets] ets *blotted*
489.24	shoes] ashoes *in MS*
490.24	to] *blotted*
491.9	yet] "~ *in MS*
491.17	wait] waifo *in MS*
491.23	now] *possibly* ~.
491.27	unsuccessful] n *incomplete*
491.31	of the] *possibly* of their
*492.17	his spear] his pear *in MS*
492.17	&c] cc *in MS*
493.13	its] *possibly* its'
494.5	we] *possibly* be
495.1	skated] skalted *in MS*
*495.11	different] differ {*MS torn*}
495.29	and] *preceded by flourish*
496.3	to] tto *in MS*
496.27	ever] *possibly* even
496.31	startling] strartling *in MS*
496.31	startling] *uncancelled* cheering *interlined above*

Indexes of Original Journal Volumes, 1837-1840

500.14	Homer] *preceded by* x *in margin, probably added later*

500.22	Seeds] *preceded by* x *in margin, probably added later*
*502.3	Tent life 568] *horizontal line below*
503.32	events 119] *interlined above* confidence in the *and marked for inclusion*
504.26	Night] *possibly* Might

Indexes of MS Volumes 1-6; "Transcripts, 1840-1842"; 9: 1837-1844

506.4	moonlight—night] *possibly* ∼-∼
506.16	p 149 . . . 78] *written in a column*
507.17	35 . . . 54] *written in a column*
507.24	Trust] *possibly* trust
508.5	poetry] petry *in MS*
508.32	their] *possibly* these
509.3	35 . . . India] *cancelled*
*509.7	9] *possibly* 8
509.9	by] *possibly* 7
509.16	sick] *possibly* rich
509.16	world] *possibly* word

Table of Alterations

THIS table reports Thoreau's substantive current alterations to the copy-text. Several types of changes, discussed in the Textual Introduction (pp. 633-634), are not reported. Numbers at the left margin key the alteration to page and line, and if the number is marked with an asterisk the alteration is discussed in the Textual Notes. The revised reading appears to the left of the bracket, and the original reading appears to the right; editorial descriptions are italicized. A wavy dash (~) to the right of the bracket replaces the word to the left of the bracket in cases where only punctuation is altered.

MS Volume 1

8.12	Pond] pond
15.30	angles] *interlined with a caret*
18.9	of the fact] *interlined with a caret*
21.4	their] this
24.12	Facts] facts
* 34.24	—Carlyleish—] *in margin*
34.36	otherwise] other
36.5	show] *interlined with a caret*
40.5	come] comes
40.8	valleys] valley's
41.11	Where under] *below erased* Where under
* 45.31	May 6th — — May 7th] May 6th — *separated from* — May 7th *by line from left to right margin*
* 45.31	May 7th] *written over two dashes*
47.9	what] *interlined with a caret*
48.24	Goodness] goodness
49.19	Seeds, . . . enough] *interlined with a caret*
52.14	The] *written over dash*
69.19	distance] distant
* 69.21	he may after all] *marked for inserting*
70.20	Tom-and-Jerry] tom-and-Jerry

70.30-31	and . . . pin-heads] *written in margin and marked for inserting*
74.16	unconscious] hardly conscious
74.31	pastures] pages
79.6	flow,] *followed by erased* springing
79.7	Springing] Spring
79.30	dale,] *followed by erased* riding on
82.5	was a seer] *interlined with a caret*
86.31	Fortune] fortune

MS Volume 2

91.3	as in] in *inserted*
98.8	fortune] *partly erased*
100.7	her] his
106.18	of his youth] *written after* manhood. *and marked for inserting*
109.7	unconsciousness] consciousness
115.16	itself] himself
116.13	— 1840] *preceded by erased* March
117.26	rise] rising
119.8	here] New England
121.28	Divine] divine
126.21	some] *interlined with a caret*
132.6	and] or
132.11	note] sound
138.31	edge] *interlined with a caret*
141.23	love] l *written over* of
146.7	A man's] A *in margin*
146.7	man's] *written over* Our
149.23	to tent,] *interlined with a caret*
150.11	Great Ball] great ball
160.8-9	She . . . it.] *written as new paragraph after* cheek. *and marked for inserting*

MS Volume 3

170.21	men,] *followed by erased* who dreaded
173.5	flowed] floated noiselessly
173.6	in] *interlined above cancelled* through
178.5	ere] are
178.16	God's] *preceded by cancelled* Out of mans
181.8	case] *interlined with a caret*

182.12	site] *in margin, preceded by cancelled* sight
182.27	carries] carry
183.24	loneliness] loveliness
184.16	that] *interlined with a caret*
184.21	No] Nor
186.5	it] *preceded by cancelled* she
188.2	walking] waking
189.20	lid] *interlined above cancelled* wind
189.25	beach] shore
198.1	*Hill*] *hill*
207.17	Rise] rise
209.20	President] president
211.25	where] *interlined with a caret*
215.12	lie] lay
216.30	if] I
217.14	did] dig
218.15	But if . . . will forget] But a man may forget
218.19	ears] eyes
218.28	fretful] *interlined above cancelled* selfish
220.19	*perfect*] *uncancelled* τελεία *interlined above*
222.4	cost begins] cost *interlined with a caret*
222.7	capital] *followed by erased* is
223.24	never] *interlined with a caret*
224.9	Happiness] happiness
224.9	Is] is
224.10	floating] *interlined with a caret*

MS Volume 4

229.22	ground] wall
230.7	inexpressible] inexpressibly
230.29	Old . . . New] old . . . new
234.6	sere] *interlined with a caret*
236.4	who] which
236.11	God] god
237.22	on] of
238.17	fantastic] fantastical
239.24	me] my
239.26	trail] track
*240.4	take] forests,

274.6   none—]   ~,
276.2   It]   We
276.26   observe]   *followed by cancelled* us
277.7   the rattling . . . team]   *originally* some
            team the rattling of *marked for transposing*
277.8   Days']   days'
277.23   God]   god
277.27   drudge]   drug
278.21   conscience]   conscious
282.2   precedence]   *interlined above cancelled*
            place
282.7   his departure]   *interlined with a caret*
282.22   but]   *interlined with a caret*
283.6   meadow]   meadows
285.8   world]   worldly
285.14   her]   him
285.22   13]   14
287.12   Most]   *followed by cancelled* men
287.19   brim]   prim
289.18   diseased,]   *comma added*
289.18-19   and as . . . reformers]   *originally* as the
            reformers and as much possessed with a
            devil *marked for transposing*
290.8   finishing]   *followed by erased* of
290.23   any]   and
291.10   muscles]   *followed by erased apostrophe*

MS Volume 5

297.4   God]   god
306.16   with]   wide
307.22   there?]   ~,
311.18   Gloss]   gloss
311.20   unobstructed]   unobstructedly
312.30   its outside]   *interlined with a caret*
313.29   That . . . world,]   *written in margin and*
            marked for inserting
314.13   Laws]   laws
316.1   cannot]   can
318.2   more]   *interlined with a caret*
319.29   its]   is
320.8   us]   *inserted*

320.32	rock to] *preceded by cancelled* stone to stone
324.1	surface—] superficial
324.8	and splits] and *inserted*
325.8	supreme] *interlined with a caret*
325.15	him] them
329.18	of Greece] *interlined with a caret*
330.4	of evening] *interlined with a caret*

MS Volume 6

337.13	when . . . paw.] *inserted*
337.23	Tenets] tenets
338.10	collating] collecting
339.11	that] than
340.35	Wher'eer] *preceded by cancelled* And
341.4	hum] human
*341.9	12th] *interlined above cancelled* 5th *and* 15th
341.13	has] *followed by cancelled* since
341.27	gay] day
342.18	13th] *interlined above cancelled* 6th *and* 16th
343.13	14th] *interlined above cancelled* 7th *and* 17th
343.25	word] world
343.28	15th] *interlined above cancelled* 8th *and* 18th
344.32	have to] *interlined with a caret*
344.32	on to] to *inserted*
345.13	as a] a *interlined above cancelled* the
345.23	descries] discovery
345.27	18th] *interlined above cancelled* 11th *and* 21st
348.16	29] *interlined above cancelled* 30
*348.25-26	Experience . . . ignorance] *sentences marked for transposing*
349.8	my] may
349.27	God] good
349.29	sings] sing
350.1	a season] *interlined above* for, as
350.14	health] heath
350.25	demigod] demigood

350.31	he] *preceded by cancelled* we
351.3	Pro. to the] *interlined with a caret*
351.10	of character] *interlined with a caret*
351.10-11	every where] *uncancelled* constantly *interlined above*
351.34	By] by
352.7	heard] *followed by cancelled* with
*352.13	light] low
352.27	of] oft
352.28	reality] *interlined above cancelled* real life of nature
353.18	do] does
353.27	Hill] hill
354.32	Atlantic] atlantic
355.8	toll] too *or* tool
355.16	men's souls] men soul
355.16	reflection] *preceded by cancelled* men
355.32	extravagance] *interlined above cancelled* enjoyment
356.2	to some] so some
356.4	works] *interlined with a caret*
356.5	base] *followed by cancelled* of
356.19	grossness] *followed by cancelled* is
357.11	may be] may see
357.19	more] my
357.28	I] It
357.30	these] *followed by cancelled* so
358.14	find] *followed by cancelled* the
358.32	sentences] *preceded by cancelled* pages
359.3	shows] *preceded by cancelled* should
359.26	Stonehenge] stonehenge
360.5	If] if
361.6	cheered] cheering
362.10	be] me
362.32	Hindo] hindo
363.10	much] my
364.9	The] *inserted*
364.25	20] 21st
365.3	Examined] examined
367.27	circle] *preceded by cancelled* course
369.19	Hence] hence
370.21	but] by

370.27	11th] 12th
371.8	sees] seen
371.10	church] *interlined with a caret*
372.7	thou] you
372.12	12th] 13th
372.17	of continuance] *interlined with a caret*
372.28	seem] seems
373.5	as] a
373.8	rise] *uncancelled* blow *interlined above*
373.10	14th] 15th
373.17	an] and
373.33	you] *followed by cancelled* my
374.11	faint hearted] fainted heated
374.21	Future] future
374.30	15th] 16th
375.23	Cold] cold
375.33	some] *interlined with a caret*
376.20	of recognition . . . body] *interlined with a caret*
376.33	16th] 17th
376.34	Raleigh's] Ralegh's
377.11	Luther,] *followed by cancelled* or
377.34	kind of] *interlined with a caret*
378.21	without] within
379.9	17th] 18th
379.12	help] *followed by cancelled* him
379.20	good] *followed by cancelled* for
379.31	if] I
379.33	18th] 19th
380.8	made] make
380.16	meekly] *interlined above cancelled* unconsciusly
380.24	blood] bloody
380.26	19th] 20th
381.29	wood] *interlined with a caret*
382.2	that] *interlined with a caret*
382.2	that] the *or* their
382.7	Indian] indian
382.27	date] *uncancelled* year *interlined above*
383.8	20] 21st (*see Textual Note 385.16*)
383.18	I dont] It dont
383.22	our bodies] *interlined above cancelled* us

383.33	met] meet
384.29	egg] *preceded by cancelled* butter an
384.30	Palestine] palestine
384.33	window] *interlined with a caret*
*385.16	Set . . . 21st] *written in margin*
385.17	21st] 22nd
385.19	22d] 23d
386.1	23] 24th
386.7	Hussein] *preceded by cancelled* The
386.7	Hussein] *uncancelled* Hussein *interlined above*
386.9	it:] ~:"
386.30	tree] *interlined with a caret*
387.16	Nights] nights
387.24	Vedas] Vegas
388.7	sentences] *interlined above cancelled words*
388.9	24th] 25th
388.18	my] *interlined with a caret*
389.8-9	It . . . labyrinth.] *written vertically in margin and marked for inserting*
389.23	dividing] divining
*389.26	look . . . ps] *written vertically in margin and marked for inserting*
390.1	mutually] *interlined with a caret*
390.1-2	of their] *interlined above cancelled* that they stand upon a
390.11	goes] *followed by cancelled* way
390.15	25th] 26th
390.22	marshes] marches
391.19	Charity] charity
392.1	26th] 27th
393.21	principal] principle
394.2	swung] *preceded by cancelled* they
395.10	stringy] *preceded by cancelled* stringy
395.28	over] *preceded by cancelled* of
395.29-30	But . . . all.] *inserted*
396.7	man] mans
397.1	it] is
397.23	bald] *interlined with a caret*
398.4	said] *interlined with a caret*
398.4	to me] *interlined with a caret*

398.27   does]   doest
399.3   most]   *interlined above cancelled* first
399.12   verses]   *preceded by cancelled* poetry
399.21   tell]   *followed by cancelled* or
*399.28   Set . . . 1st]   *written vertically in margin*
400.16   bees]   bays
401.12-13   God . . . ethics]   *written vertically in mar-*
                gin and marked for inserting

"Transcripts, 1840-1842"

406.21-26   Let . . . But]   *written at bottom of preced-*
                ing page and marked for inserting
406.27   How]   how
406.28   there]   *interlined with a caret*
407.11   Gloss]   gloss
407.24-25   eastward and backward]   backward and
                eastward
409.8   In]   *followed by cancelled* the
409.11   earth]   *interlined above cancelled* world
409.18   Menu]   menu
410.2   forward]   *followed by cancelled* certain
410.6   strip]   *followed by cancelled* himself
410.9   interested]   interesting
410.13   saying]   *preceded by cancelled* with
410.18   afterward]   *interlined with a caret*
414.26   researcher]   *preceded by cancelled* crowd
416.17   Alchâtquarmi]   alchâtquarmi
416.28   The]   *preceded by cancelled* But
418.8   creatures]   *interlined above cancelled* eyes
418.29   Scythia]   *interlined above cancelled* India
424.1   practical]   *followed by cancelled* wisdom
424.1   Genius]   genius
424.4   I observe]   *preceded by cancelled* The mind
                which
426.14   Druids]   druids
426.19   Druidical]   druidical
426.20   Bards—Druids]   Druids—Bards
426.26   Brahmá]   Bráhma

MS Volume 7

433.16   faint]   *interlined above cancelled* sweat
434.1   flowerbells]   flowers

434.25	in] *inserted*
434.31	over] on
435.5	Lord] lord
435.20	they] their
436.28	Great] great
437.26	fair] far
437.28	of the original] *interlined with a caret*
438.10	he speaks] *preceded by cancelled* or a
438.23	Far] far
439.1	Night hung upon] *interlined above cancelled* Along
439.1	stream] *preceded by cancelled* dusky
439.6	Harem] harem
439.9	The lightning . . . gleam] *followed by cancelled* Succeede by a thunder tone *interlined below*
439.19	Still] still
439.25	heaven] *preceded by cancelled* the
439.33	fewer] few
440.4	is] as
440.20-21	The winter . . . frost] *written in margin and marked for inserting*
440.24	peeps] *interlined above cancelled* creeps
440.25	The rabbit leaps] *written in margin and marked for inserting*
440.27	The mouse out-creeps] *followed by cancelled* From his snug nook
441.16	fuming] *underlined; uncancelled* purling —rippling? *written in margin*
442.13	tinkling] *uncancelled* rattling *interlined above*
442.22	upon the hill] *written in margin and marked for inserting*
*442.27-28	In treacherous . . . behind] *written in pencil and traced in ink*
442.31	Thursday] *inserted*
443.10	at evening . . . looks] how his horizon looks at evening
443.15	through] *uncancelled* into *interlined above*
443.15	scar] *uncancelled* wound *interlined above*
443.27	any] and
443.28	feigning] *preceded by cancelled* former

444.4   spent—]   spent"—"
444.13   it should]   It should
444.31   fields]   *preceded by cancelled* lane *and*
           followed by cancelled the farm
444.33   old-fashioned]   *interlined with a caret*
445.18   least]   *interlined above cancelled* most
446.2   so]   *preceded by cancelled* so much has
           been said and yet
446.3   has been said]   *interlined with a caret*
446.3   few]   *preceded by cancelled* But
446.4   inadequacy]   *followed by cancelled* of what
           has been said,
446.4   I am]   *followed by cancelled* even
446.6   DeQuincey]   DeQuincy
446.13   it is]   It is
446.15   it]   if
446.17   whole of the]   *interlined with a caret*
446.29   church-music]   church-musick
446.31   I do]   do I
447.1   deep]   *interlined with a caret*
447.12   hath]   *preceded by cancelled* it
447.26   trailing]   trailed
448.7   rivers—]   *interlined with a caret*
448.21   her,]   *inserted*
448.23   lips are not]   *interlined with a caret*

MS Volume 8

453.5   are]   as
453.16   Perhaps]   perhaps
453.21   in my]   *preceded by cancelled* at
453.30   Ural]   ural
454.7   steam]   *uncancelled* vapor *interlined above*
455.13   unless it be nonsense]   *interlined with a*
           caret
455.30   stand]   stands
455.31   air]   *interlined with a caret*
456.15   now]   *interlined with a caret*
456.15   have]   *interlined with a caret*
456.17   edge]   *interlined with a caret*
456.24   they]   thy
456.26   by the world]   *preceded by cancelled* they
458.7   and]   in

458.7	hemlocks] *preceded by cancelled* my
458.14	her] he
458.18	moments] *interlined above cancelled* hours
458.25	night] *preceded by cancelled* day
459.2	apt] *inserted*
459.21	deep] *interlined with a caret*
459.23	vein] vain
462.4	strong] *interlined with a caret above cancelled* flight
462.5	fastidious wing of] *interlined with a caret*

MS Volume 9

466.12	system] *followed by cancelled* and the
466.13	is] *preceded by cancelled* was
467.8	strain of] *interlined with a caret*
467.26	thing] thought
467.26	and a name] *interlined with a caret*
467.26	than] the
468.1	not] *inserted*
468.19	at once] *interlined with a caret*
468.34	relapsed] lapsed
469.31	earth] *uncancelled* fields *interlined above*
471.10	than] *written over dash*
472.23	elements] *preceded by cancelled* matter
472.26	myself] self *interlined with a caret and followed by cancelled* a place
473.2	God] god
474.3	himself] *written in margin*
474.21	ever] *preceded by cancelled* as
474.25	our breaths] of breaths
474.30	think] *followed by cancelled* not
475.13	naked] *interlined with a caret*
475.17	15] 14
*475.27-28	he . . . hitherto—] he has failed in all undertakings hitherto—learned that life is short—errare est humanum and *marked for transposing*
476.1	ye] you
476.5	it] is
476.5	ye Tartars] ye—
476.11	Indian and] *interlined with a caret*
476.31	from out the fields] *interlined with a caret*

476.33   of duck or kersymere]   *interlined with a caret*

477.13   Ellridge—]   *followed by cancelled* from
478.5   latest]   last
478.7   than]   *followed by cancelled* else
478.22-25   By . . . not?]   *written vertically in margin and marked for inserting*
478.27   ne'er will]   never'll
*479.3-8   Here . . . engraver.]   *written vertically in margin*
479.14   at last]   *interlined above cancelled* as fast
479.16   several]   *interlined above cancelled* various
479.17   What year it died,]   *interlined above cancelled* Its birth, its death,
480.26   none]   not
481.15   look]   *preceded by cancelled* to
481.19   & expressive]   *interlined with a caret*
482.2   Court]   court
482.4   Legislative]   legislative
482.4   Council]   council
482.16   Council]   council
482.25   any how]   anyhow
482.26   As]   "~
482.27   "is dead]   is dead
482.33   occasion,]   occasion."
482.35   defendent]   *followed by cancelled* got the case a
483.5   requires]   *followed by cancelled* some
483.19   of]   *followed by cancelled* of
483.27   those]   *followed by cancelled* fastidious
483.33   English]   *preceded by cancelled* their
484.8   any]   *followed by cancelled* pure
484.9   brave]   *written in margin*
484.13   details]   *preceded by cancelled* deeds of the
484.15   been]   here
484.19   already]   *interlined with a caret*
484.21   from]   *inserted*
485.8   Gael]   *followed by cancelled* to the
485.24   are superior to]   *interlined above cancelled* supersede
485.26   an]   *preceded by cancelled* and
485.27   tame]   *interlined with a caret*
485.30   a]   our

486.6   language]   *interlined above cancelled*
             tongues
486.25   money]   *followed by cancelled* for
487.3   to]   In
488.2   one of]   one *written in margin*
488.11   excess of]   *interlined above* from
488.12   sacrifice]   *preceded by cancelled* sacrificial
488.16   are]   ice
489.12-13   with their autumnal tints; and]   *inter-*
             lined with a caret
489.24   hands]   *preceded by cancelled* the
489.25   finer]   finger
490.9   if]   *followed by cancelled* all
490.19   this]   these
490.19   our]   *inserted*
490.19   fair]   fairs
490.25   and universal]   *interlined with a caret*
490.32   skies—]   *followed by cancelled* the
491.1   joined]   *interlined above cancelled*
             approached to
491.2   thus . . . enemy—]   *interlined above can-*
             celled says
491.32   pomp,]   ~,"
492.3   inclined"]   *followed by cancelled* to hear
492.10   old]   *interlined above cancelled* infirm
493.18   only]   *written in margin*
493.28-29   if you . . . hear]   *interlined with a caret*
496.6-7   may . . . one]   *interlined with a caret*
496.21   Justice]   *preceded by cancelled* truth
496.24   Can]   can
496.27   and]   *inserted*
496.28   can]   or
496.28   what]   *followed by cancelled* it
496.31   startling]   *uncancelled* cheering *interlined*
             above
497.3   will]   *followed by cancelled* he
497.4   avoid]   *followed by cancelled* me

Indexes of Original Journal Volumes, 1837-1840

499.29   Crystalization . . . 6]   *added after* 83
499.29   (139-142]   *interlined above* Crystalization
             . . . 114-5-6
499.32   96 thought]   *inserted with a caret*

500.15   (539] *interlined above* 284-6-7
501.6   Simple . . . 7] *added after* 391—
501.11   (30)] *interlined above* 463
502.12   Sphericity 19] *written over erased* We lay
            the chief
504.15   Menu] menu

Indexes of MS Volumes 1-6; "Transcripts, 1840-1842"; 9: 1837-1844

505.26   eve . . . 13] *written in margin and marked
            for inserting*
506.11   risen] *interlined above cancelled* present
507.23   apologies 12] *interlined and marked for
            inserting*
*509.7   9] *written over* 8 *and* 7

End-of-Line Hyphenation

THIS table lists all compound or possibly compound words that are hyphenated at end-line in manuscript and must therefore be resolved as hyphenated or closed. The table derives from a master list of *all* end-line hyphens in manuscript. The editors identified as "compounds" any word containing two or more words of standard English: *keystone, highways, childlike*. They excluded prefixes and suffixes, such as *unguarded* or *forward*, and words inadvertently resembling compounds, such as *seasons* or *handsome*. For a discussion of the rationale affecting resolution of compound words as hyphenated or closed, see Textual Introduction, pp. 642-643.

Numbers at the left margin key the entry to page and line numbers, and if the number is marked with an asterisk the item is discussed in the Textual Notes.

Because this text is printed with a ragged right margin, it introduces no unauthorized end-of-line hyphens. Subsequent reprintings or quotations of the Princeton Edition text should therefore honor its hyphenation as authorial.

MS Volume 1

8.27	darn-it-how-he-nicks-'em	20.28	Sakai-suna
10.3	light-armed	23.7	keystone
10.25	sunlight	24.5	homesickness
11.6	henceforth	24.18	highways
12.5	henceforth	26.12	superincumbent
15.3	overflowing	29.15	woodland
17.20	dewdrop	31.9	childlike
18.5	notwithstanding	34.10	Dolittle
18.26	hedge-rows	34.18	meanwhile
19.9	hilltops	36.25	himself
19.20	master-workmen	37.28	clap-boarded
		45.27	nevertheless
		* 45.31	Hollowwell

46.13	steamboat
46.23	deer-skin
49.34	itself
53.31	haymakers
54.4	woodland
57.29	thitherward
58.9	network
58.16	chop-fallen
60.20	midnight
61.7	spokesman
62.1	undercurrent
63.2	however
72.22	without
73.13	cannot
74.5	sunrise
75.30	forget
85.16	rank-growing

MS Volume 2

94.19	pinchback
99.26	themselves
105.4	straightway
114.13	henceforth
118.4	go-between
118.5	each-other
119.16	Yellowstone
121.17	withdrawing
123.14	myself
129.31	whip-poor-wills
130.3	lawn-like
135.8	nose-wise
141.2	*quasi-carnem*
142.5	overtake
152.2	cannot
152.28	without
157.18	gentleman
158.12	starlight

MS Volume 3

163.26	forelock
166.26	warfare
168.12	Quick-step
171.20	somewhat

171.25	instead
171.27	grasshopper
177.3	westward
177.11	footsteps
184.10	withdraws
184.23	supple-jointed
184.27	road-side
185.12	white-wash
189.7	Gentlemen
192.14	nevertheless
194.8	withheld
194.14	faithfully
200.2	sometimes
200.28	watercourses
200.30	crosswise
201.30	gracefully
203.17	ourselves
209.4	somewhere
209.27	withdraw
210.27	household
217.9	sunshine
217.14	sunshine
217.17	wood-chopper
223.12	thigh-bones
225.25	themselves
226.19	burr-millstones

MS Volume 4

237.13	whatever
237.22	hill-side
239.5	outlines
242.6	youthfullest
242.17	himself
243.8	herself
243.12	spy-glass
247.29	manhood
253.7	upland
253.24	commonweal
258.12	anything
259.2	forever
266.13	withdrawn
266.25	self-sustained
267.28	yourself

268.24	sometimes
269.1	manhood
273.24	without
273.26	almshouse
275.32	without
276.32	something
278.11	thorough-fares
282.5	at-one-ment
282.21	without
283.5	haymakers
286.23	herself
289.15	understood
290.1	withdraw
290.6	something
290.30	overflowing
291.15	without

MS Volume 5

297.18	clam-shell
300.8	overlook
306.26	gentlemanly
309.6	cannot
309.7	weather-cock
311.12	Sometimes
312.2	overlook
318.7	sunset
318.19	itself
322.14	afternoon
322.14	forenoon
323.27	overlook
327.3	themselves
331.3	themselves

MS Volume 6

345.12	housewife
346.28	highwayman
360.1	somewhat
360.14	poke-weed
367.29	themselves
367.32	without
368.2	without
374.11	short-lived
374.26	meanwhile

377.13	something
385.6	himself
393.4	mankind
394.33	something
397.15	sunshine
397.30	one-another
398.6	each-other
399.26	no-where
400.1	fault-finding

"Transcripts, 1840-1842"

407.19	old-times
412.24	cannot
417.17	cannot
417.28	daylight
427.30	noontide

MS Volume 7

437.27	sometimes
437.34	cannot
443.28	himself
444.34	red-mavis
446.25	understanding
446.29	church-music
446.32	tavern-music
448.29	gentlemen

MS Volume 8

456.14	Maryland

MS Volume 9

470.30	withstood
474.21	himself
481.22	slang-like
481.34	somewhere
485.15	fireside-blaze
488.1	overlooked
488.16	rainbow
488.24	lowlander
491.10	Mac-Roine
491.26	Ca-Lodin
496.6	itself
496.30	himself

Selected Later Revisions

THIS table is a selective list of Thoreau's revisions and additions to his Journal. It does not include revisions of passages that appear in later printed works. When the reading of pencil text is uncertain, alternate readings follow in braces { }.

MS Volume 1

11.7 Nov. 13th 1837.: It is a sure evidence of the health & innocence of the beholder if the senses are alive to the beauty of nature *added in pencil at top of page*

53.23-25 If . . . resolutely.: *revised in pencil to read* But let him who has lost a tooth open his mouth wide and gabble lisp & sputter never so resolutely.

71.25 society.: I sometimes see them & sail for them but alas, alas, I man {moor} my tow boats & fire my stern chasers in vain. *added in pencil*

85.13-19 I . . . soils.: To remember children that they exist upsets all our theories—which confound & dispense with so much It is a fact—the growing man or woman that we do not allow for— *interlined in pencil;* We are not commonly aware that there is a rising as well as a risen generation. It is a fact the growing man or woman which we do not allow for—to remember which would disturb many a fair theory Speak for yourself old man. *added in pencil*

MS Volume 2

107.19 sun shines.: It is not the sun that shines any more than the mote in its beams The sun does not shine with its own light. *interlined in pencil*

119.7 chances.: and how many more things may I do with which there are none to be compared. *added in pencil*

133.27 partially.: we begin to praise when we begin to see that a thing needs our assistance{.} *interlined in pencil*

MS Volume 3

172.9 immigrants: *underlined in pencil*; squatters *added in pencil after* interests

182.5-6 Surely . . . experience.: of the dumb members. *added in pencil*

189.5 To study: Our etiquette is for little men— *added above in pencil*

197.2 and have . . . humanity.—: It is Math—applied to humanity *interlined in pencil*

205.11-13 Nothing . . . sometime.: The forest is full of attitudes, and every character in history is here represented. *interlined in pencil*

211.11 fire.: The oaks have more heat than the pines. green is a cold color. *written vertically in margin in pencil and marked for inserting*

217.22-32 I stand . . . his.: *revised in pencil to read* when I stand under her cope, instantly all pretension drops off—& I am swept by her influence as by a wind and rain, which remove all taint. I am fortunate that I can pass and repass before her each day—and prove my strength in her glances. She is far truer to me than to herself. Her eyes are like the windows of nature, through which I catch glimpses of the native land of the soul. and from them come a light which is not of the sun

220.16 London.: My friends know me pretty well— that is they have got a correct total impression—but yet they do not know my right side from my left— If I should stand on my head they would perceive the difference but if my right side should be exchanged for my left they would not. *added in pencil*

MS Volume 4

229.1 *flyleaf*}: What means this trust in God which is so solemnly preached in extremities. There is more of God & of divine help in a man's little finger than in idle prayer & trust. It is my arm alone that must rout the devil & his angels as much as bend aside the willow in my path. I cannot afford to relax discipline because God is on my side—for he is on the side where discipline is.

V. no 2. instances of bravery *added in pencil to front flyleaf*

231.21-23   To-day . . . winter: *revised in pencil to read* In the spring when the wild geese go over I too feel the migratory instinct strong in me, and the breaking up of winter.

268.28-30   exhibit . . . ague.:   The states have leisure to laugh from Maine to Louisiana at some Newspaper joke. The nonchalance of nature & of society tell of the lapse of infinite periods & N.E. shakes at the double entendres of Australian asides while the poor Reformer cant get a hearing. The nonchalance & dolce far niente airs of Nature & Society hint at infinite periods in the progress of mankind—*interlined and written vertically in margin in pencil*

MS Volume 5

297.4   will do.:   wont they Dea. Spaulding? *added in pencil*

301.18   respectable.:   He is to be envied by his neighbors *added in pencil*

305.26-29   taking . . . pasture.:   *revised in pencil to read* I approach a great nature with infinite expectation & uncertainty not knowing what I may meet   It lies as broad and unexplored before me as a scraggy hill side or pasture.

311.7   the ribbed bottom: *revised in pencil to read* the bottom which is strewn with the wrecks of the forest

315.6-8   The moral . . . her—:   *revised in pencil to read* The moral aspect of nature is a jaundice reflected from men

322.29   *blank*}:   How much will some officious meddlesome men give to preserve an old book of which perchance only a single exists while a wise God is already giving & will still give infinitely more to get it destroyed. *added in pencil*

332.26   {*Four-fifths page blank*:   One {Our} revolution is then taking root or hold on the earth—as seeds first send a shoot downward into the earth to feed on their own albumen ere they send one upward to the light. *added in pencil*

333.8 ear.: Perhaps we are not acquainted yet. *added in pencil*

MS Volume 6

337.7-10 The President . . . thief.: *revised in pencil to read* The officers of respectable institutions turn the cold shoulder to you—though they are known for genial & well disposed benevolent persons— They cannot imagine you to be other than a rogue.

369.22 March 8th 1842.: What has music to do with the lives of the Great Composers— It is the great Composer who is not yet dead, whose life should be written— Shall we presume to write such a history as the former while the winds blow. *added in pencil at top of page*

372.5 material—: Not that there not some artless & sincere communications from our country friends. *added in pencil*

383.33-34 The field . . . friendship: Comparatively speaking—I care not for the man or his designs who would make the very highest use of me short of an all adventuring friendship. *interlined in pencil*

398.5-8 Not only . . . met—: *revised in pencil and ink to read* we know each-other better than we are {ere} aware can tell to ourselves,—we are admitted to startling privacies with every person we meet

398.10 the reformer—: To my solitary & distant thought my neighbor is shorn of his halo and is seen as privately & barely as a star through a glass. *added in ink*

401.3 Pyramids.: And we wonder who set them up & what for *added in pencil*

"Transcripts, 1840-1842"

407.4 *blank*}: This then is the arena into which every book enters—and it must indeed be a healthy word and well spoken to be heard at all. *added in pencil*

412.11 *blank*}: We may suspect that these silent and reposing ages did something more than perfect the luxury of idleness. *added in pencil*

413.8 4.320,000,000 . . . form: *revised in pencil to read* for the satisfaction of the chronologist we might quote a few facts from Murray's History of India 4.320,-000,000 years form

419.4   east.:   So his audience got a clearer notion of the difference than they ever had before or you would believe possible *added in pencil*

428.31   *blank . . . missing*}:   The inhabitants of those eastern plains seem to possess a natural and hereditary right to be conservative and magnify forms and traditions—"Immemorial custom is transcendent law," says Menu. But their *added in pencil*

MS Volume 9

475.9   leaves—:   It is her symbol her standard emblem device *interlined in pencil*

485.4   profession.:   He does not impose upon us *interlined in pencil*

485.31   club—:   Ask his senses if they are not well fed—if his life is not well earned. *added in pencil*

486.3   more.:   These stern events are traditionary. *added in pencil*

Library of Congress Cataloging in Publication Data

Thoreau, Henry David, 1817-1862.
  Journal.

  (The writings of Henry D. Thoreau)
  "The complete Journal as Thoreau originally wrote it."
  Includes index.
  1. Thoreau, Henry David, 1817-1862—Diaries.
2. Authors, American—19th century—Biography.
I. Broderick, John C.
PS3053.A25   1981   818'.303 [B]   78-70325
ISBN 0-691-06361-3 (v. 1)